ECONOMY AND SOCIETY
IN BAROQUE PORTUGAL

Economy and Society in Baroque Portugal, 1668 - 1703

Carl A. Hanson

UNIVERSITY OF MINNESOTA PRESS □ MINNEAPOLIS

Financial assistance for this book
was provided by the
Andrew W. Mellon Foundation.

Copyright © 1981 by the University of Minneota.
All rights reserved.
Published by the University of Minnesota Press.
2037 University Avenue Southeast,
Minneapolis, Minnesota 55414
Printed in the United States.

Library of Congress Cataloging in Publication Data

Hanson, Carl A
  Economy and society in baroque Portugal, 1668–1703.
  Bibliography: p.
  Includes index.
  1. Portugal—Economic conditions. 2. Social classes—Portugal–History. 3. Portugal–Social conditions. I. Title
  HC 392.H3   330.9469'03   80–17588
  ISBN 0-8166-0969-1

The University of Minnesota
is an equal-opportunity
educator and employer.

To my parents,
Fredrick and Alice
Hanson

ACKNOWLEDGMENTS

This study could not have been completed without the aid and encouragement of numerous people. Prof. Manoel Cardozo of Catholic University gave numerous helpful suggestions during the initial stages of research. In Lisbon, Father António da Silva Rêgo provided valuable information on the Portuguese archives and helpful commentary on various aspects of the study. Work in the archives was further facilitated by the knowledgable staff who frequently brought little-known but useful documentation to my attention. Transcription of an important pamphlet in the British Library, which appears herein as appendix 2, was kindly provided by S. George West. Thanks are also due to Ronald Bishop Smith, and his wife Gina, Douglas Porch, and John Vincent-Smith, whose friendship made my stay in Portugal all the more enjoyable. I am very grateful to the Calouste Gulbenkian Foundation, which provided the funding for my research in Portugal.

My mentor during the years involved in bringing this study to completion, Prof. Robert W. Kern, has given me invaluable help and criticism. His vital contribution has been complemented by the efforts of three other scholars, Peter Bakewell, Donald Sullivan, and Alicia V. Tjarks, whose reading of chapter drafts yielded significant insights and suggestions. Conversations with Prof. Stuart Schwartz concerning his *A Governor and His Image In Baroque Brazil* furnished additional information and understanding. I am also grateful to Prof. Dauril Alden, who read the manuscript and offered numerous useful comments.

The Circulation and Inter-Library Loan Department personnel at the University of New Mexico's Zimmerman Library are owed a great deal of thanks for their resourceful pursuit of obscure and often difficult to locate material. The final typescript of the study was skillfully rendered by Judy Buckley and Mary Wicker. My greatest debt is owed to my wife Mary Ellen, who has been a constant source of encouragement and inspiration.

C. A. H.

CONTENTS

CHAPTERS
  I. INTRODUCTION . . . 3
  II. PRIVILEGE AND PROPERTY . . . 10
   Pedro the Pacific . . . 12
   The Land: Stronghold of the Privileged Estates . . . 17
   The Nobility . . . 21
   The Clergy . . . 27
  III. THE THIRD ESTATE . . . 39
   The Professional Classes . . . 42
   The Mercantile Class . . . 44
   The "Mechanical" Professions . . . 50
   The Popular Classes . . . 55
   The Lowest Strata . . . 61
   The Individual's Place and Social Equilibrium . . . 67
  IV. THE NEW CHRISTIAN CHALLENGE TO THE ESTABLISHED ORDER . . . 70
   New Christians and the Holy Office . . . 75
   Father António Vieira and Jesuit
    Support of the Mercantile Class . . . 85
   The Climactic Decade, 1671–1681 . . . 89
   The Triumph of the Established Order . . . 103
  V. THE MERCANTILIST MIND IN SEVENTEENTH-CENTURY PORTUGAL . . . 108
   Precursors of Colbertism . . . 112
   Mercantilism and Internal Development:
    The French Example . . . 122
   Portuguese Advocates of Colbertism . . . 126
  VI. PUBLIC FINANCE DURING AN ERA OF ECONOMIC DECLINE . . . 141
   Raising Taxes and Reforming
    Collection Procedures . . . 143

  Devaluation and Protectionist Legislation:
   The First Steps . . . 149
  Mounting Expenses and
   Monetary Reform, 1680–1688 . . . 152

VII. ERICEIRA AND THE ECONOMY . . . 160
  The Portuguese Colbert . . . 161
  Expansion of Textile Production . . . 163
  Mining, Metalworking, and Construction . . . 176
  The Impact of the Manufacturing Program . . . 182

VIII. ECONOMIC EXPANSION AND FOODSTUFF SHORTAGES . . . 185
  Portugal and the World Economy . . . 185
  The Growing Trade in Metropolitan Products . . . 188
  Food Imports and the Trade Deficit . . . 201
  The Foodstuff Problem: Neglect and Dependence . . . 205

IX. RECESSION AND RECOVERY IN THE COLONIES (Part 1) . . . 207
  Promoting Prosperity in the Eastern Empire . . . 209
  The Decline of the Brazilian Sugar Economy . . . 215
  Royal Efforts to Revitalize the Periphery . . . 222

X. RECESSION AND RECOVERY IN THE COLONIES (Part 2) . . . 238
  The Resurgence of Colonial Prosperity . . . 239
  Controlling the Periphery . . . 248

XI. CONCLUSIONS AND CONSEQUENCES . . . 260
  Defense and Commerce: The Treaties of 1703 . . . 262
  The Collapse of Colbertism . . . 265
  Portugal, England, and the Roots of Modern
   Dependency . . . 270

APPENDIXES

1. Persons Tried and Sentenced to Autos-da-fé
 by the Portuguese Inquisition, 1682–1691 . . . 279
2. "Whereas the Portugal Trade is
 very advantageous to this Nation" . . . 280
3. Vessel Arrivals in Oporto, 1657–1698 . . . 282

   4. Ships of the *Carreira da Índia*
       Reaching Bahia, 1663–1703 . . . 284
   5. The Bahian *Frota* of 1668 . . . 285
   6. Prices and Estimated Annual Production of the
       Best White Bahian Sugar, 1655–1710 . . . 287
   7. A Note on Currency, Weights, and Measures . . . 288

NOTES . . . 291

BIBLIOGRAPHY . . . 333

INDEX . . . 351

FIGURES

   1. Selected Commodity Prices
       in Portugal, 1667–1705 . . . 145
   2. Some Data on the Number of Foreign Vessels
       Arriving at Portuguese Ports, 1670–1705 . . . 189
   3. The Rise and Fall in the Value
       of Brazilian Sugar Exports, 1610–1690 . . . 216

TABLES

   1. The Leading Noble Families of Portugal, 1684 . . . 22
   2. Monasteries and Convents in Portugal, 1628 . . . 31
   3. Two Computations of Royal Revenues in 1681 . . . 155
   4. Salt Exported from Setúbal, 1680–1705 . . . 191
   5. English Imports of Portuguese Wines and Duties
       Imposed on Their Export by
       the Oporto Alfândega, 1675–1705 . . . 195
   6. Trade between England and Portugal, 1697–1715 . . . 200
   7. Income and Expenditure of Various African
       and Eastern Enclaves, 1684–1687 . . . 212
   8. Rolls of Brazilian Tobacco Shipped to
       Portugal, 1680–1704 . . . 240
   9. Bahian Vessels Carrying Tobacco to Angola and the
       Mina Coast, 1681–1710 . . . 242
 10. Slaves Delivered to Cartagena de Indias by
       the Cacheu Company, 1698–1701 . . . 243

11. Shipments of Brazilian Gold to Lisbon, 1699–1705 . . . 245
12. Brazilian Commodity Exports to Portugal and
    Their Estimated Value, circa 1700 . . . 248
13. Tobacco Shipments from Bahia to the Mina
    Coast, 1698–1704 . . . 257

MAPS

1. Portugal in the Late Seventeenth Century . . . xiv
2. The Portuguese Empire . . . After 209

PLATES
(Following page 146)
1. Lisbon's Terreiro do Paço in the seventeenth century.
2. D. Pedro II, king of Portugal.
3. A Portuguese noble couple of the seventeenth century.
4. Frei António das Chagas.
5. Padre António Vieira.
6. Fish vendors in Lisbon's Praça da Ribeira.
7. An auto-da-fé procession wending its way through Lisbon's Rossio.
8. D. Nuno Álvares Pereira de Melo, first duke of Cadaval.
9. D. Luís de Meneses, third count of Ericeira.
10. Salvador da Bahia de Todos os Santos (circa 1671), foremost entrepôt of the Portuguese empire.
11. Manifest of the tobacco cargo borne by the Bahian *frota* of 1703.
12. Lisbon harbor (circa 1700).

A CAVEAT ON ORTHOGRAPHY

Portuguese orthography has undergone numerous changes and revisions during the last four centuries. Thus, when one draws from sources dating from the seventeenth century onward, differences in usage unavoidably crop up. In most instances, I have followed modern Portuguese usage in the text, but quotations from early sources are left in their original form. Citations for publications are taken from title pages. This invests the footnotes and bibliography with considerable variation in spelling and the use of accent marks (for example, Bahia and Baía, *história* and *historia*), for which the reader should be prepared. As to other othographic inconsistencies that may have escaped detection or resolution, I can only, to borrow a line from Stuart Schwartz, "point to the hallowed precedent of centuries of confusion in these matters."

Map 1
Portugal in the Late Seventeenth Century

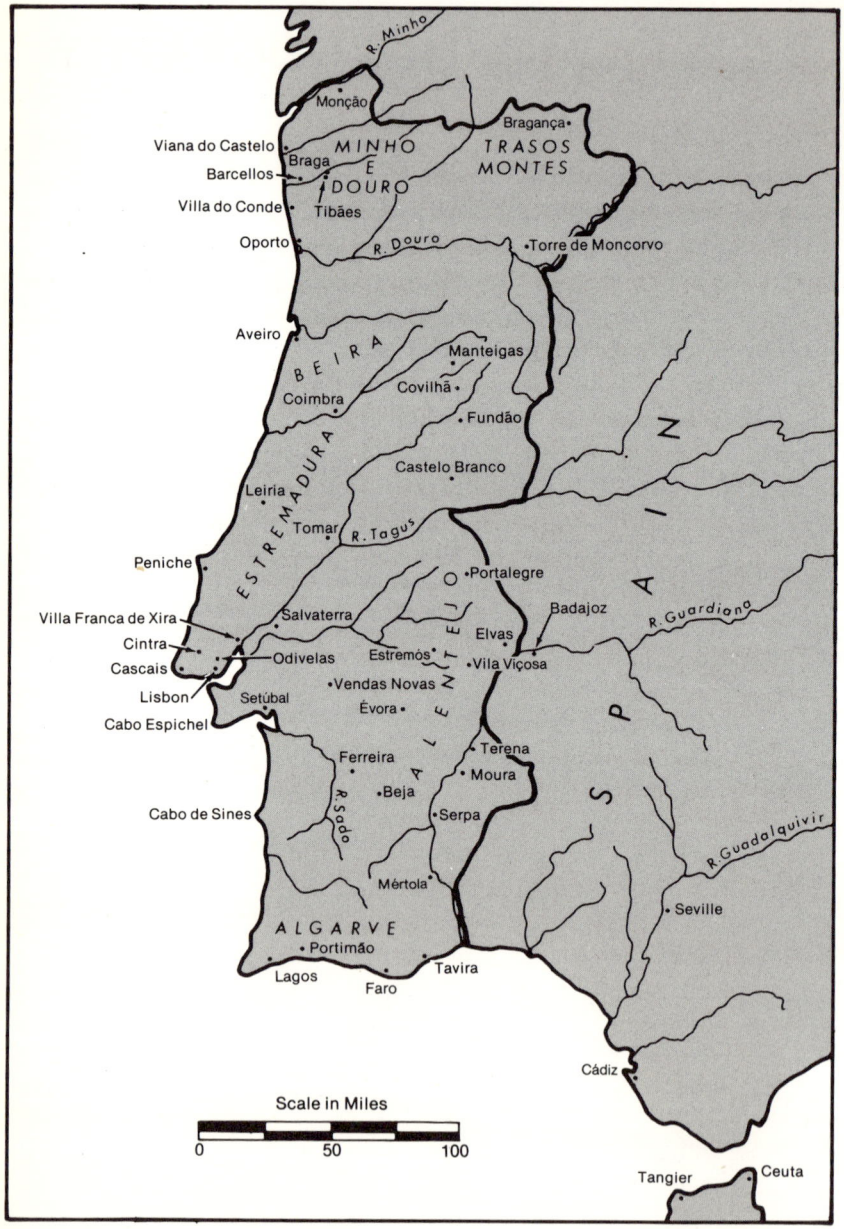

ECONOMY AND SOCIETY IN BAROQUE PORTUGAL

CHAPTER I

INTRODUCTION

Não são diferentes as idades porque as alterem os tempos; são diferentes as idades porque as desiquala a fortuna.

> Friar Alexandre da Paixão (1662)

Portugal tem sido sempre escandalosamente protegido pela Divina Providência.

> José António de Freitas (circa 1907)

Portugal is a small nation with a great history. Mariners and missionaries from this little country were in the forefront of European expansion from the fifteenth century onwards and helped establish a colonial enterprise that in its extent and longevity has few rivals in history. Many of the monumental voyages of discovery that thrust European power and influence into exotic and unknown lands were led by courageous Portuguese sailors like Vasco da Gama and Fernão de Magalhães (Magellan), whose attempted circumnavigation of the earth ranks him "as the first navigator of ancient or modern times, and his voyage the greatest single human achievement on the sea."[1] Under the banner of Portugal, great ecclesiastical figures such as Saint Francis Xavier (a Spaniard) and Father Manuel da Nóbrega carried European beliefs and culture to the farthest reaches of the globe. During the sixteenth century, Lisbon became one of the world's greatest commercial centers, sharing with Seville the role of principal entrepôt for products brought from the Far East and the recently discovered American continents. Although this splendid era of expansion and commerce lasted less than a century before larger, more advanced European economies surpassed that of Portugal, the country eventually regained a measure of its past glories during the eighteenth century, an age that was certainly gilded, if not golden. Before the dawning of the latter age, however, Portugal endured a series of setbacks that gravely challenged the limited human and material resources of the small nation.

Metropolitan Portugal, which includes the mainland territory as well as eleven inhabited islands in the Azores and Madeira archipelagoes, comprises an area of only 35,408 square miles.[2] During the early modern era (1500–1800), human and material resources within the country were usually inadequate to meet domestic needs, much less those required to support properly a far-flung imperial enterprise. Though estimates vary, Portugal's population at the midpoint of the early modern era (circa 1650) was probably no more than 1.5 million inhabitants.[3] After 1500, Portuguese expansion into the Atlantic and Indian oceans diverted thousands of men from careers as fishermen and agriculturalists and from other occupations in which their labor was sorely needed. Like Magellan, many seamen never returned to their native soil, perishing in battles and shipwrecks or as a result of other dangers arising from the imperial enterprise. This constant drain of manpower, which first flowed mostly to the Far East and later to Brazil, further depleted an already shallow labor pool.[4]

This chronic shortage of labor, which led to importation of African slaves into Portugal during much of the early modern era, was but one of the problems confronting an economy based primarily on agrarian production.[5] The soil in many regions of Portugal was too poor to support anything but subsistence agriculture, and numerous hills and mountain ranges in the northern half of the country inhibited farming. Indeed, much of the country was (and is) better suited for forestry and pastoral activity than for growing crops. Perhaps the greatest impediment to extending agricultural production arose from the nature of the agrarian regime itself. Large tracts of fertile, well-watered land were held by privileged noble and clerical elites, who frequently raised crops primarily for export or allowed potentially productive properties to lie fallow. This occurred even as peasants and tenant farmers struggled to eke out livings on small plots of land. Undoubtedly, landholding patterns had an important role in fostering the constant outflow of common people to the colonies. As a result of these and other problems, wheat and other essential grains were usually in short supply.[6]

During the seventeenth century, structural problems such as insufficient population, emigration, and an inadequately productive agricultural base were compounded by war, economic depression, and political instability. One source of such difficulties was the death of childless King Sebastião in 1578 and the subsequent passing of sovereignty to the Spanish Hapsburgs. But Portugal's so-called Babylonian Captivity (1580–1640) by Castile was by no means an era of unrelieved oppression and subservience to a succession of foreign monarchs. In fact, the years between 1580 and 1630 were generally characterized by economic stability and minimal political interference by the Castilians. Great profits were then being made from Portugal's near monopoly on the sale of sugar, production of which was largely confined to its Brazilian colony.

After 1630, disaffection with the Spanish overlords increased rapidly. Loss of Recife, capital of Brazil's sugar-rich captaincy of Pernambuco, to the Dutch in 1630, together with a series of defeats by the Hollanders in the Far East, gave clear evidence of Hapsburg inability (or unwillingness) to protect Portugal's far-flung empire. In its efforts to protect both Spanish and Portuguese possessions, the Castilian government had sown the seeds of revolt. During the reign of Philip IV of Spain (Philip III of Portugal), that king's chief minister, the duke of Olivares, had attempted to invigorate Iberia's imperial fortunes by exacting greater financial contributions from the provinces. Taxes in Portugal were raised to finance increasing defense costs, a policy that incensed the already disaffected Portuguese. Falling prices and food shortages added to an expanding reign of misery in Portugal, precipitating repeated rebellions by hungry peasants and townspeople.[7]

When, in 1640, Olivares sought to defuse suspected disloyalty in the ranks of the Portuguese nobility by ordering many of their number to Catalonia to help put down an anti-Castilian rebellion there, he triggered widespread revolt in Portugal. On December 1, 1640, pro-Spanish officials were ousted and the duke of Bragança, whose family was related to the defunct Avis line of King Sebastião, assumed power as João IV. Justifying the Restoration, as it came to be called, João Pinto Ribeiro, one of the principal conspirators against the

Hapsburg domination of Portugal, later wrote that the Spanish had "drained the realm of men and money."[8]

During the next twenty-eight years, the War of the Restoration further depleted Portugal's human and financial resources. In addition to fighting the Spanish, Portugal also struggled to regain colonial possessions lost to the Dutch and even confronted England in an ill-considered affray with Cromwell's protectorate (1652–1654). This conflict, however, led to the Anglo-Portuguese Treaty of 1654, a pact that reconfirmed a long-standing alliance between the two nations and acted as the touchstone for subsequent agreements. Though beleaguered on many fronts, the Portuguese managed to defeat the Spanish in a series of important battles during the early 1660s, making the dream of a permanently united Iberia much less attractive to a war-weary Madrid.[9]

The Portuguese were also weary after so many years of conflict and still uncertain as to the ultimate success of their cause. This latter concern became especially pronounced after D. João IV's death in 1656. Doubt was soon cast on the viability of the young Bragança dynasty. D. João IV's wife, D. Luisa de Gusmão (Guzmán), reigned briefly as regent but was deposed by an irresponsible and physically deformed son, who took the throne as D. Afonso VI in 1662. This coup d'etat took place largely at the instigation of the count of Castelo Melhor (D. Luis Vasconcelos e Sousa), a talented and ambitious aristocrat, who eventually oversaw the defeat of Spanish forces while dominating the feckless D. Afonso VI. Castelo Melhor was himself dismissed in 1667 after D. Afonso VI fell under the influence of his new bride, Marie Françoise of Nemours (D. Maria Francisca de Sabóia), who married the king in 1666 as part of an agreement with France, which led to formation of a Franco-Portuguese league against Castile. Though Castelo Melhor had played a crucial role in procuring the French league, he did not anticipate that the new queen, upon seeing his hold over D. Afonso VI, would turn the weak monarch against him.

With Castelo Melhor gone, D. Afonso VI became the pawn of Queen Maria and a pro-French faction within the nobility. This group's support of French interests stemmed in part from the fact that many aristocrats had lost influence during Castelo Melhor's strong ministry and were eager to regain their former power. Moreover, many of these same aristocrats had opposed D. Afonso VI's deposition of Queen Luisa, regarding him as unfit to rule. Members of the pro-French faction then pressured him to abdicate in favor of his brother, Prince Pedro. A major justification for this pressure was the alleged impotence of D. Afonso VI. Finally, in November 1667, D. Afonso VI, apparently convinced of his own lack of potency (which was confirmed by a scandalous inquiry), capitulated and let his brother take the throne so that the dynasty could be perpetuated.[10] A few months later, a peace agreement was signed with Spain and worries about the viability of the Bragança dynasty abated.

While Portugal advanced haltingly toward victory over Spain, the struggle to retain its far-flung colonies was also moving toward resolution. Angola, the principal source of the black slaves needed to work on Brazilian sugar plantations, was retaken from the Dutch in 1648 having been lost seven years earlier. In 1654, the Hollanders were ousted from Brazil, and, though several key possessions in the Far East were lost, the Portuguese were fortunate to hold on to as much of their empire as they did. Although the Eastern enterprise was little more than a shrunken collection of moribund trading posts in 1668, Portugal had won its freedom and regained most of its Atlantic possessions. (The most vital Atlantic holding lost to the Dutch was the great slaving fortress of São Jorge da Mina, which fell in 1637.)

The mother country and its Atlantic possessions (which, taken together, will be called the Luso-Atlantic world) comprised, at least in a mercantilist sense, complementary economies. West African holdings supplied Brazilian sugar plantations with slaves, Brazil forwarded sugar to Portugal, and the mother country exported finished goods of local and European manufacture to its Atlantic colonies.[11] After the 1668 treaty with Spain was signed, the Luso-Atlantic world appeared to be on the threshold of an era of peace and even prosperity. Despite the discontent and privations caused by Spanish domination and the struggle required to end it, Portugal was more fortunate than many European nations of the mid-seventeenth century, and the country enjoyed a modicum of prosperity even while embroiled in warfare with its Iberian neighbor.[12]

The reign of Prince Pedro (1668–1706), who assumed the title of D. Pedro II after D. Afonso VI died in 1683, was indeed peaceful;

but, during most of the new monarch's years on the throne, Portugal was confronted with numerous economic difficulties. Toward the end of his reign, conditions improved and Portugal's gilded age, the first half of the eighteenth century, dawned.

The period extending from D. Pedro's assumption of power in 1668 until the signing of the Methuen commercial treaty in late 1703 is the subject of the present study. In terms of diplomatic and political history, this was a rather tranquil era, especially when compared with the turbulent years of the struggle for the Restoration. Portuguese diplomats led genteel, if sometimes underfinanced, existences in the courts of Europe. Typically, their time was devoted to a round of innocuous ceremonial activities since Lisbon generally sought to minimize entanglements that might draw the country into war. In Portugal, meetings of the Cortes, the representative body in which clerics, nobles, and commoners occasionally gathered, were suspended in 1680 and were not reconvened again until 1697.[13] With the exception of weddings, funerals, and festive holidays, life at court was rather uneventful and D. Pedro II spent a good deal of time away from the capital, hunting and relaxing at the royal preserve at Salvaterra.

Portuguese culture was immersed in the conventions of the baroque era (1550–1750), and literature and the plastic arts experienced little significant change during D. Pedro II's reign. The outstanding literary figure of the day was Father António Vieira (1608–1697), a Jesuit priest whose letters and sermons contain some of the greatest prose ever written in Portuguese.[14] Vieira, as we will see in subsequent chapters, also influenced Portuguese economic policies, sedulously promoting the establishment of the famous Brazil Company in 1649. Painting in the baroque style found its clearest expression in the work of Bento Coelho da Silveira (circa 1620–1708), who produced great decorative canvases depicting religious themes. The leading architect of the period, João Nunes Tinoco (circa 1610–1690), designed a number of churches and monasteries and also collaborated on various other religious edifices, including the great seminary at Santarem.[15]

In typically baroque fashion, these figures, as well as numerous others, relied heavily on metaphorical expression to communicate their views of the world and, in the process, left an artistic legacy that reflects certain aspects of life in late seventeenth-century Portugal.

However, beneath the facade of baroque calm, which, at first glance, seems to characterize the age of D. Pedro II, Portugal's socioeconomic foundations were subtly shifting. Irving Leonard, an outstanding student of colonial Mexico, once observed that "times of quiescence may effect powerful, if subtle, transformations that shape the character of a people and condition subsequent events."[16]

Perhaps because of the relative quiescence of D. Pedro II's reign, it has attracted little scholarly attention. Indeed, the period remains one of the least-studied eras in Portuguese history.[17] When D. Pedro II died in 1706, conditions in Portugal had changed markedly since his assumption of power. Economic difficulties had burdened most of his reign, but, during the 1690s, conditions began to improve, thanks primarily to expanding wine exports, a burgeoning tobacco trade, and an influx of vast quantities of gold that had been recently discovered in Brazil. The crown's efforts to cope with economic problems had been favorably rewarded. Meanwhile, the stability of Portuguese society, as we will see, had been momentarily shaken. Largely because of renewed prosperity, the baroque facade of the Old Regime took on added embellishment, but its foundations had undergone significant stress since 1668 and perhaps had even crumbled slightly.

CHAPTER II

PRIVILEGE AND PROPERTY

> ... sendo o principal fundamento do Estado e obediencia dos vasallos, o alicerce e eminencia da virtude do Principe ... pois assim como os elementos e os corpos que delles se compoem, obedessem sem resistencia aos movimentos das spheras celestiaes, pela nobreza de sua natureza, e em os movimentos dos supperiores.
>
> Friar Miguel Soares, *Portugal Libertado* (1658)

The structure of Portuguese society during the seventeenth century conformed with that found throughout most of western Europe during the early modern era. Organized into orders, or "estates," European society was divided into three basic juridical categories: the nobility, the clergy, and the common people. Theoretically, the leadership of such societies was vested in national monarchies that, after centuries of combating papal pretensions to supremacy as well as fractious nobilities, had largely established their authority. Toward the end of the seventeenth century, an equilibrium was achieved by which absolutist regimes began to emerge, being based on alliances between monarchies and privileged classes.

This equilibrium was, to a large extent, the outgrowth of the social and political setbacks experienced by the noble estate that rendered it more amenable to cooperation with national sovereigns. Once the holder of a virtual monopoly on the fighting forces in Europe, the landed aristocracy during the seventeenth century faced the growing military power of the state. Moreover, many nobles simply failed to take advantage of their numerous opportunities for education and economic gain and lost family fortunes through mismanagement, conspicuous consumption, and overweening disdain for commercial activity. The latter was particularly true in sixteenth-century Spain, where no self-respecting noble would demean himself by engaging in commerce. By the seventeenth century, tales of impoverished noblemen, most notably Cervantes's *Don Quixote*, had become a recurring theme in Spanish literature. Declining economic independence thus gave the nobility further incentive to cooperate with the crown, from which pensions, grants, and appointments to office were secured.

Aristocratic fractiousness and violence, which accompanied the nobility's former control over armed force, were also undercut by the rising influence of the middle classes. (*Class* is used here in a purely generic sense and does not necessarily imply the existence of the common interests or the cohesion of a true "class.") Though ultimately dependent on the privileged estates for its own power and legitimacy, the crown periodically reached accommodations with the mercantile classes. Chronic financial need—which could often be traced to pensions, grants, and other expenditures supporting the swollen, nonproductive ranks of the privileged—and a desire to keep nobles and clerics on notice that it had other sources of support were major reasons for the crown's collaboration with the mercantile community. Although absolutist regimes acted to constrain the increasing strength of the mercantile classes, the merchants posed an everpresent threat to the established order.[1]

The growing military power of the state, endemic financial difficulties, and the challenge posed to its social position by the aspiring middle classes did much to foster the nobility's backing of absolutist regimes. Indeed, absolutism can be viewed as a realignment of power within the established order, which served to perpetuate the dominance of the privileged estates. Like the nobility, the clergy also found that absolutism served its interests. In Portugal, Spain, and France especially, the Church took an abiding interest in preserving the status quo. As with the aristocracy, clerical wealth derived primarily from the land, a fact that gave both the Church and the nobility little reason to countenance favorably the expansion of merchant-dominated commercial capitalism. Moreover, the ecclesiastical establishment in Iberia was especially suspicious of the mercantile classes, who were widely believed to be tainted by Judaism or Protestantism. The Church saw in absolutism a vehicle for the furtherance of its temporal and spiritual power. It could hardly have been otherwise, since the divine right by which absolute monarchs ruled was granted by God, for whom, after all, the clerical estate acted as earthly intermediaries.[2]

In Portugal, absolutism found favorable conditions in which to expand. With but occasional exceptions, both the Church and the nobility aligned themselves closely with the crown after 1667, joining forces to secure the continuance of the status quo. It was under D. Pedro II, who had usurped his brother D. Afonso VI's throne with the help of a powerful faction in the nobility, that an absolutist regime rooted in privilege and landed property flowered.

Pedro the Pacific

On Saturday afternoon, June 9, 1668, the three estates gathered together in the great room of the Paço da Ribeira, the Lisbon palace of the Portuguese monarchy, to pay homage to D. Pedro de Bragança and witness the baroque pageantry of his formal oath-taking ceremony. The great hall was sumptuously decorated with rich fabrics and gold and silver ornamentation. The fourteen windows of the hall, seven to a side, were hung with curtains of expensive damask. At the head of the grand hall, the royal throne, upholstered with crimson velvet and fringed with gold, was positioned on a podium reached by seven steps. These stairs were covered with luxuriantly patterned silk rugs, possibly brought from Goa. Before the throne rested a cushion, also of red velvet, and behind it stood a dossal of the same material that bore the famous *quinas*, the coat of arms of imperial Portugal.

Seating for the assembled dignitaries was assigned according to estate and rank. In the case of ecclesiastics, however, the papal refusal to appoint bishops after the 1640 Restoration (a sanction that ended in 1671 with Rome's initialing a new accord with Lisbon) left the clerical estate underrepresented. The only bishopric then occupied in Portugal was held by the aging and irascible bishop of Targa, Francisco de Sotomaior. By a decree of 1649, D. João IV had assigned officers of the military orders of Santiago and Avis to occupy the vacant seats. This arrangement did not please the old bishop, but the ceremony went forward.

The royal procession solemnly entered the great hall to the accompaniment of trumpets, drums, and oboelike shawms. Before D. Pedro came the powerful duke of Cadaval (D. Nuno Álvares Pereira de Melo), who by virtue of his recent appointment as constable (Condestavel do Reino) carried the ceremonial sword (*estoque*). Colorfully garbed in their finest costumes, other officials of the royal entourage followed D. Pedro. The prince regent himself approached the throne dressed in black silk and lace. After taking the throne and listening to an address in which the reasons for D. Afonso VI's removal from office were given, D. Pedro rose, took off his black hat, placed his right hand on missal and cross, and, reportedly in a strong voice, swore the following oath:

I swear and promise, by the grace of God, to reign and govern well and directly, to administer justice as completely as human frailty permits, to preserve the valued customs, privileges, favors and liberties which were given, declared and confirmed by my predecessors.

After this, the duke of Cadaval, passing the *estoque* from right to left hand, swore fealty to D. Pedro with his right hand on the same missal and cross, kissed the new monarch's hand, and then returned the sword to his right hand. The prince regent returned to his throne to listen to the reading of declarations of obeisance by the three estates. The oaths were thereafter published and deposited in the national archive, the Torre do Tombo.[3]

More than seven months had passed since D. Pedro and his noble cohorts had deposed D. Alfonso VI, but this delay was probably necessary, given certain delicate problems confronting the new regime. The question of what title D. Pedro should assume had greatly concerned his supporters. In sessions of the Cortes, which had been convened in January 1668, the three estates disagreed as to how best to resolve the matter. Representatives of the general population urged that Prince Pedro move boldly and take the title of king. They believed that such a step would make it easier for him to reach peace with Spain and deal with the myriad problems of war-torn Portugal. The noble and clerical estates took a more cautious and legalistic approach, recognizing that as long as D. Afonso VI lived the legitimacy of D. Pedro as king could be questioned. The clergy proposed that he take the title of prince governor. D. Pedro expeditiously solved the problem by declaring himself prince regent, a title he would hold until D. Afonso VI's death in 1683.

Meanwhile, two of Portugal's most influential noblemen, the duke of Cadaval and the marquis of Marialva (D. António Luís de Meneses) had acted as proxies for an unusual marriage, that between Prince Pedro and his brother's former bride, D. Maria Francisca of Savoy. The ceremony took place on March 28, 1668. This curious dynastic reshuffle was accomplished by means of some fast legal footwork, including the hasty annulment of D. Maria's marriage to D. Afonso VI by a French cardinal, who happened to be one of her relatives. It was claimed that, because of D. Afonso VI's physical shortcomings, the union had never been consummated and therefore could be legitimately dissolved. Because of the Vatican's continuing unwillingness to recognize Portuguese sovereignty, reliance on the French relative was necessary since the ecclesiastical dignitaries who could have granted the needed dispensation had not yet been appointed. Unlike many other parties to dynastic unions, Prince Pedro and D. Maria appear to have been truly taken by each other, their marriage being marked by enduring affection and romantic attachment.[4]

While the delicate matters of D. Pedro's title and marriage were being resolved, the new leadership also had to deal with the widespread desire for an end to the war with Spain. The prince regent had come to power largely at the instigation of the pro-French lobby at court, the most visible member of which was his Savoyard bride. France, however, did not have Portugal's best interests at heart. Louis XIV wished to prolong the Luso-Spanish conflict in order to keep Madrid off balance until he saw fit to himself renew hostilities with rival Spain. In March 1667, the Sun King finally granted the Portuguese the alliance that they had long sought, but this ten-year pact obligated Portugal to carry the fight to Spain, a condition that went beyond Lisbon's more modest desire for Spanish recognition of its sovereignty.

Louis XIV's scheme stimulated both Spain and England, the latter of which was allied with Portugal against the Spanish, to hasten the pace toward peace negotiations. After the ascent of the feeble Carlos II to the Spanish throne in 1665, the queen mother of Spain, Mariana of Austria, decided that the time had come to negotiate an end to the lengthy conflict. As might be expected, England saw no reason to prolong a conflict whose chief beneficiary was its French rival. Furthermore, Portugal had done much to persuade Madrid of the folly of continued warfare by inflicting a series of major defeats on its adversary, which culminated with the battle of Montes Claros (1665), the last great engagement of the War of Restoration.

Shortly after D. Afonso VI's capitulation in November 1667, Prince Pedro had faced a choice between adherence to the recently signed alliance with Louis XIV and thus to the wishes of the pro-French forces that had helped him to power or to the popular mass sentiment that strongly favored peace. There was, in fact, growing concern at this time that further delay in attaining peace might cause rioting by the war-weary population.[5] By December, D. Pedro had decided on a pacific course. Hence, on February 13, 1668, a peace treaty between Portugal and Spain was signed, ending twenty-eight years of sporadic but devastating conflict. The Bragança dynasty was recognized by its Hapsburg counterpart; Portuguese sovereignty over its colonial possessions was reconfirmed (except for the North African enclave of Ceuta, which had opted for Spanish rule); and agreements for the exchange of prisoners, the granting of reparations, and the restoration of commercial relations were reached.[6]

What sort of man was Prince Regent Pedro, a twenty-year-old who had just assumed titular leadership of the Portuguese world? Unfortunately, biographical studies of D. Pedro II, who reigned for the lengthy span of thirty-eight years (all but three of which found Portugal at peace), are virtually nonexistent.[7] The question cannot be adequately answered as of yet, but a few observations about Pedro the Pacific, as he came to be known, might shed some light on his character and on his impact on Portuguese society.

D. Pedro II was a complex and contradictory man whose moods ranged from deep and persistent depression to bawdy euphoria. His behavior suggests that of a manic-depressive. To some extent, he shared his deposed brother's irresolution and dependence on advisers; but, unlike D. Afonso VI, he also possessed a strong, if somewhat erratic, personality and a keen intellect. As a youth, he demonstrated talent as a student of history and the science of building fortifications. He also became dextrous in swordplay and developed skill as a horseman.[8] His personal habits were casual and even ascetic. He disliked the pomp of office and the pretensions of ever-present courtiers, was himself a teetotaler and expected others to be sober in his presence, and preferred to take his meals alone. D. Pedro II conducted affairs of state in an informal manner, granting audiences on Tuesday and Thursday to anyone seeking his ear and on Saturdays to officers of state and nobles. Unlike his counterparts in Spain and France, the king greeted dignitaries with a minimum of ceremony and had few palace guards about, a fact remarked upon by foreign envoys accustomed to less casual audiences.[9] D. Pedro's usual dress was black clothing, a mode of attire he would seek to impose on ostentatious nobles, clerics, and others by means of sumptuary legislation. His principal forms of recreation seem to have been hunting and bullfighting. The king had a passion for young women, an indulgence somewhat out of keeping with his usually sober demeanor.

Although this last diversion could not have pleased his wife, D. Pedro apparently maintained liaisons in which he displayed a preference for black women. According to an exaggerated but nonetheless revealing account made by an anonymous contemporary, the young ruler's nocturnal forays might include visits to the domiciles of two or three young women before sunrise.[10] As a result of these sallies into the night, the prince regent probably contracted venereal disease sometime during the early 1670s.[11] Our unknown informant also claimed that D. Pedro had fathered several mulattos, whom he later shipped off to the colonies. For male companionship, D. Pedro enjoyed gossiping with the junior officers of his household and also liked to associate with a number of fun-loving mulattos who acted as his incognito agents in the capital and as combatants in brawls that he would provoke and then join. Our anonymous source added the following comments about D. Pedro II's behavior.

In spite of his debauched life he is very pious and charitable and an easy victim of hard luck stories. He hates the bad in others and does what he can to correct it. He fasts on bread and water on Saturdays. He is scrupulous about rendering justice and always consults his Jesuit confessor. . . . He has reformed the grilles of the convents [in order to curtail scandalous liaisons between nuns and their lovers, yet] is always very pleased, if one attaches oneself to a nun. He is very serious and rarely laughs, but every month is in ill humor for some days, during which he is apt to strike his servants, although at other times he treats them well. During these fits his servants try to keep out of sight; if he is several months without an attack, he feels some very bad effects and makes some excuse not to show himself.[12]

Despite the peculiar combination of the ascetic and the promiscuous in his behavior, as well as long bouts with melancholia, D. Pedro II proved himself to be a generally stable and conscientious ruler. After 1683, the year his wife D. Maria and the hapless D. Afonso VI died, the king grew less rambunctious and began to put on weight. The loss of his spirited wife was the first and probably most traumatic of a succession of personal tragedies that occurred during the king's long reign. The subsequent loss of two daughters and his second wife undoubtedly had a further sobering effect. Tragedy and perhaps disease induced longer and darker sieges of depression during his later years. The peace and relative stability of his reign, however, suggest that D. Pedro II overcame quirks of personality, the loss of loved ones, and a possible venereal infection. Because of his not inconsiderable contribution to Portuguese history during nearly forty years in power, more remains to be said about the actions of D. Pedro II, but for now we will turn our attention to the economic foundation of his regime, that of landed property.

The Land: Stronghold of the Privileged Estates

The structure of Portuguese society during the reign of D. Pedro II was little different than that of one, two, or even three centuries earlier. The strength of the monarchy was growing, and changes had also come in the wake of imperial expansion and increasing commercial and cultural intercourse with western Europe. The emergence of a noble class of colonial administrators and the growing presence of foreign merchants, for example, represented new and even potentially disruptive forces within Portuguese society. Portugal's small mercantile class, the ranks of which had been swollen by an influx of Sephardic Jews after their expulsion from Spain in 1492, exerted considerable influence. Nevertheless, Portuguese society remained firmly in a corporatist mold, in which a social order based on landed property and privilege prevailed.[13]

Although presently available data on Iberian societies give only approximate percentages, nobles and clerics appear to have comprised a large and nonproductive portion of the population of Spain and Portugal.[14] In seventeenth-century Spain, the noble estate numbered about ten percent of the population,[15] while clerics comprised about three percent of the Spanish population.[16] Their Portuguese counterparts numbered around 55,000 nuns and priests[17] (about four percent of the population). If, as it seems plausible, the ratio of noble to cleric in Spain also applied in Portugal, it follows that the noble estate in Portugal numbered about 150,000 members. Given our previously suggested figure of 1.5 million for the total population in mid-seventeenth-century Portugal, the number of people within the privileged estates (around 205,000) would have comprised roughly fourteen percent of the country's inhabitants.[18]

A profusion of privileges set this favored fraction apart from the commoners. Among the special considerations enjoyed by the noble and clerical estates were exemption from most taxation, near monopolization of prestigious governmental and clerical posts as recognition of their elevated status, receipt of pensions and other income paid out of the royal treasury, exclusive rights to certain modes of dress and transportation and (if one of their number commited a capital crime) the right to a dignified form of execution. Moreover, clerical offenders were tried before ecclesiastical courts, not secular magistrates.

The dominance of the privileged estates, however, had its most tangible expression in landed property. One cautious estimate has put about two-thirds of the land in Portugal in the hands of nobles and clerics, a portion that no doubt included the most fertile and productive land in the country.[19] Ownership of what amounted to the vast bulk of the most productive property in Portugal allowed the nobility and clergy to maintain their positions in the social order. Thanks to their privileges, properties, and the labor of generally obedient rural masses, the noble and clerical estates possessed great economic resources with which to counter the pretensions of the urban bourgeoisie and threats by the crown.

The form and extent of landed wealth owned or controlled by the privileged estates varied considerably, resembling a crazy quilt made up of diverse and scattered pieces of property held by means of various legal titles. Monastic properties and noble estates bordered on one another in a pattern whose origins, in some instances, could be traced back at least to the Roman era. Most of the pieces of this pattern, however, were of later acquisition and typically had their origins during the period of national unification.

A great proportion of Portugal, perhaps three-fourths, lay unused. Noble or clerical owners simply held much more property than they used for agricultural and pastoral production. A good deal of land was of marginal productivity, but fertile properties also lay fallow, being used, for example, as hunting preserves for the nobility.

Exploitation of the land by the nobility was based upon primogeniture, commandery, and the captaincy-donatary. During the seventeenth century, primogeniture became increasingly important as a form of land transfer and forced greater numbers of younger sons to leave for the colonies or to join religious orders. This latter trend undoubtedly played a part in the expansion of the ecclesiastical estate and its landholdings. As for commanderies, the king, as grand master of Portugal's three most important military-religious orders (Christ, Santiago, and Avis), granted jurisdiction over these properties only to noblemen, usually for a period lasting two generations. Revenues obtained from commanderies usually came from tithes paid by landed peasants and tenants, but they also derived from clear and perpetual titles to various properties. The Order of Christ, for example, "owned the lands of Tomar, and Soura, the Order of Santiago the ports of Setúbal and Alcacer, the Order of Avis the lands of Benavente."[20] Finally, the captaincy-donatary was similar to the crown's granting of territory in colonies such as Brazil to *donatários*. In Portugal, however, *donatários* were seldom allowed to act as independently as did their colonial counterparts and were ceded the privilege of levying dues.[21]

Noble and ecclesiastical ownership of the land was often interlocked. The noble owners of private estates, or chattels, for example, frequently found their property burdened by the presence of chantries (*capelas*), which soaked up a goodly portion of the income obtained from the land. This left possessors in the position of being de facto trustees who received only one-sixth to one-third of the income produced by their properties.[22]

Like the clergy and nobility, the crown held extensive properties. Tenants on royal estates (called *reguengos*) paid the crown "a quarter or fifth or some other fraction of the produce of the soil as well as the *laudêmio* (fines on transfer)." But the most important properties were usually those on which the king levied dues in accord with a variety of accrued rights. These rights were the same as those ceded to *donatários* with the granting of captaincies-donatary.[23]

While the exploitation of private property in both the countryside and the city was outwardly a confusing tangle of legal forms in which the rights of the three estates often overlapped, "two basic categories are distinguishable: exempted properties, belonging to the Church (and subject to mortmain) or to the nobility, and taxed properties, belonging to commoners." Both exempted and taxed properties, according to V. M. Godinho, were holdings that

> could be directly exploited by the owner or leased—on tenancy, emphyteusis, or quitrent (*censo*). The first and last paid no *laudêmio* and carried no improvement obligations. The annuities payable as a rent-charge on emphyteutic leases were generally one-sixth below the rack-rent. Under such leases, juridically speaking, a 20-year annuity was supposed, in the aggregate, to equate with the capital value of the real estate, without the annual payment exceeding half the annual production (exclusive of what was needed for sowing); in practice, this consisted either of a portion of the produce (grains, wine, flax, etc.) varying from one-fifth to a tenth (after deduction for tithe) and payable in kind or cash, or of fixed quantities of produce—in which no commutation into money was permitted. While there were emphyteutic leases in perpetuity as well as leases for periods of ten years or more, contracts covering a period of three generations predominated.

Another landholding device, that of quitrent, provided the property owner with further flexibility in the exploitation of his holdings and was especially useful to landholders in a financial pinch. Godinho explained that

> the *censo*, introduced into Portugal before the sixteenth century, usually represented the sale, perpetual or redeemable, of an annuity on the produce of a property itself retained by the owner (though sometimes leased or even alienated to a third party); the *censo* would be offered for sale at a certain price, normally by a proprietor in need of ready cash, and the buyer would have first claim on the produce of the land so secured for payment of his annuity, but with no right to possession of the land. The converse form of contract, under which the seller reserved for himself an annual rent on a property

for sale, was almost invariably transformed into an emphyteutic lease.[24]

The multiplicity of legal forms of ownership or control of property in no way disguised the fact that the nobility and clergy were solidly ensconced as the chief powers in the countryside. Although the peasant class of seventeenth-century Portugal enjoyed some common rights, the usual state of affairs was one in which so many tithes, dues, tolls, and rents were paid that they were left with

only a minor fraction of the fruits of the soil, which went to fatten a swollen class of ecclesiastics and nobles. Yet it was not penetrated by the spirit of revolt. No doubt the possibility of emigrating overseas and the income which came back from there, as also the [post–1690] boom in agricultural exports, kept it quiet.[25]

The Nobility

Up to this point, discussion of the social groups has been confined to mention of the nobility, the clergy, and the common people. None of these three groups was homogeneous, and each contained numerous subdivisions. These subsidiary groups appeared and even disappeared at different times and often struggled more fiercely with their own brethren for position and privilege than they did with members of different estates. One need only review the incessant and often bitter squabbles between members of the secular and regular clergy to dispel any thoughts of group harmony. Both the clergy and the nobility enjoyed similar rights, exemptions, and privileges, which represented a common line of demarcation between themselves and the rest of Portuguese society.

By the end of the sixteenth century, the nobility had become differentiated into four functional categories: nobles of the robe, the provincial nobility, court and administrative nobility, and nobles of the sword.[26] These groupings were not hard and fast. Nobles of the robe, for example, also acted as court bureaucrats. Moving from one functional category to another was not a difficult process. If, for instance, a provincial nobleman aspired to an important post in the royal bureaucracy, his provincial background did not in itself present a significant obstacle. A far more crucial requirement for such aspirations was possession of sufficient rank within the noble estate.

There were six basic grades, or ranks, within the noble estate. The first of these were the *titulares* (or grandees), who held the highest ranks and included among their numbers dukes, marquises, and counts, many of whom could claim lineal ties to the royal family. The second rank was comprised of the *fidalgos* (or *fidalgos de solar*), who owned their own castles or fortified houses or lands from which they took their titles. Next were the *fidalgos dos Livros de El Rey*, whose coats of arms were registered with the crown. Below this rank were the *fidalgos simples*, a grade that included individuals whose families had engaged in no manual labor for at least four generations. *Fidalgos de espada*, holders of higher rank in the military, occupied the fifth level, and the bottom echelon was comprised of the *fidalgos togados*, the

TABLE 1
The Leading Noble Families of Portugal, 1684

Albuquerque	Freire de Andrada
Alencastro	Furtado de Mendonça
Almada Abranches	Gama
Almeida	Jacques
Ataíde	Malafaia
Atouguia	Manoel
Azevedo	Mascarenhas
Barreto	Melo
Botelho	Miranda
Brito	Moura
Câmara	Noronha
Carneiro	Portugal
Castelo Branco	Sá
Castro	Saldanha
César	Silva
Correia da Silva	Silveira
Costa	Sousa
Coutinho	Tavora
Crastro do Rio	Teles de Meneses
Cunha	Torres
Forjaz Pereira	Vasconcelos

SOURCE: J. V. Serrão, "Uma Relação," p. 146. For a list of noble participants in the 1668 Cortes, as well as important new titles granted during D. Pedro II's reign, see Caetano de Souza, *Historia Genealogica*, 7:394–99. A list of the thirty noblemen elected to officially represent the noble estate in the 1668 Cortes is in BA 44–XIII–43, fls. 2–2v.

chief civil ministers of the realm. This last grade included the rare individuals who had risen to important offices without already holding some higher title.[27]

Though most titles technically were not hereditary, renewal of enrolled status had become largely automatic by 1700. As might be expected, the few truly hereditary titles belonged to *titulares*. Thus, for example, the marquesate of Ferreira, a title inherited by the duke of Cadaval before his elevation to duke, was a hereditary title. Membership in any of the six grades carried with it theoretical exemption from the death penalty, but nobles convicted of treason were executed. Noble status also entitled its holders to pensions or grants of land, which were particularly important to lower-ranking nobles since these were frequently their only source of income.[28]

A further privilege available to *fidalgos simples* and holders of higher rank was membership in one of the military orders. Avis, Santiago, and Christ were founded in Portugal during the twelfth and thirteenth centuries as an outgrowth of the Crusades against Islam. A fourth, Saint John of Jerusalem, was introduced by Portugal's first king, Afonso Henriques (1109(?)–1185). These orders—which had begun as small aristocratic brotherhoods noted for charitable works, chivalrous behavior, and bravery in battle—rapidly evolved into influential organizations possessed of extensive properties, which, as noted above, were called commanderies. By the early eighteenth century, the Order of Christ had 454 such commanderies and those of Santiago, Avis, and Saint John had 150, 43, and 23, respectively. Membership in these brotherhoods provided an additional source of prestige and economic leverage for higher-ranking nobles.[29]

Higher-ranking nobles of the four functional categories, especially aristocrats from the provinces and nobles of the robe, had played crucial roles in launching the Restoration effort. During the six decades of Spanish domination, the position of the court nobility had been considerably downgraded while the influence of provincial nobles had increased. This trend reflected a general effort on the part of the Spanish rulers to erode centralized authority in Lisbon, which was perceived as a continuing threat to Hapsburg domination, and to encourage regionalism within Portugal itself. However, the nobility of the robe, schooled in the intricacies of modern legal theory at the University of Coimbra by such great teachers as Padre Francisco Suárez, preserved the principle of rule by a Portuguese king. An ongoing adherence to political integrity and dynastic legitimacy by this segment of the nobility was thus of fundamental importance for the recuperation of Portugal's independence in 1640.[30]

Indeed, the most important alliance of social groups making independence possible was that between the provincial nobility and nobles of the robe. The court and administrative nobility, which by 1640 lacked any real influence and owed to Madrid what standing it still had, played a relatively small part in the breakaway from Spain.[31] The most powerful of the provincial nobles, the duke of Bragança, assumed leadership of the independence movement, styling himself as D. João IV and basing his claim to succession on hereditary ties to the defunct Avis dynasty and on the legal doctrines preserved and refined at Coimbra.

After 1640, however, the critical role of the court and administrative nobility, without which the new dynasty could not have functioned effectively, was soon revived. This revival was nurtured above all with recruits from the provincial nobility.[32] One such recruit, the previously mentioned D. Nuno Alvares Pereira de Melo (1638–1727), first duke of Cadaval, would emerge as one of the most important members of the post–1640 court nobility. Born in Évora in 1638, D. Nuno was taken to Lisbon by his parents following D. João IV's acclamation. According to the Italian traveler Magalotti, who visited Portugal in 1669, most of the noble families of Évora had hastily left their frontline position after the acclamation and made their way to court.[33] While wealthier and higher born than most of his counterparts, the young nobleman's father, Francisco de Melo, marquis of Ferreira, probably typified the provincial nobles who embraced the Restoration cause.

Being the eldest son, D. Nuno assumed his father's titles and properties upon his death in 1645. The inheritance included the titles of marquis of Ferreira and count of Tentugal, as well as *seigneur* of the *vilas* of Paul de Muge, Cadaval, Ferreira de Aves, Tentúgal, Agua de Peixes, Buarcos, Póvoa, Vila Nova de Anços, Santa Cristina, Rabaçal, Alvaiázere, Abegaria, Vilalva, Vila Ruiva, Cercal, and Peras. He also became chief constable (*alcaide-mor*) of Alvor and Olivença. In 1648, D. Nuno, then ten years old, was elevated to the rank of duke by D. João IV in celebration of the birth of the future D. Pedro II.[34]

More than simple euphoria over the birth of a second son underlaid such largesse. The king quite clearly meant to reinforce the position (and loyalty) of the noble families that had come from the provinces to serve his regime in Lisbon. The choice of the productive region surrounding Cadaval (which had its seat at Muge) for the ducal title was appropriate. The property was an especially valuable possession of the Melo family and constituted one of the most important bases of its exceptional wealth. D. Nuno's extensive properties enabled him later to become one of the great wine producers of Portugal.

It is probably safe to say that the political upheaval caused by the Restoration did little to change the nature of the agrarian regime in Portugal. Agrarian exploitation as practiced at Muge, for example, continued to follow the traditional patterns of leasing and renting described above by V. M. Godinho. In 1733, the Melo family (as well as other great landholders), while engaging in some agricultural production on their own account, "did not promote large-scale agrarian exploitation but . . . ran great administrative set-ups centralizing the accountancy and revenue from the leases and rents received from their lands and controlling the distribution and investment of their revenue in produce and capital."[35] In the case of the first duke of Cadaval, limiting himself to collection of revenues from leased and rented property had definite advantages for a man who would spend most of his long life in Lisbon preoccupied with matters of state.[36] While Cadaval's career in the capital was hardly that of the idle courtier, he is representative of a nobility that by that time was "largely an urban *rentier* class divorced from its estates."[37]

The wealth that came to the nobility from its control of much of the land in Portugal was supplemented by income from the colonies, especially Brazil. Despite property and privileges, noble families often could not derive sufficient wealth from their metropolitan holdings to maintain themselves in comfortable fashion. The colonies gave the nobility further opportunity in its quest to maintain and expand its economic and social dominance. Thanks to the overseas possessions, some families amassed enormous fortunes. "For the first century-and-a-half of Portuguese-American history, few families, if any, could match the Albuquerque Coelho's of Pernambuco in prestige, power and wealth."[38] One family whose wealth could be compared with that of the Albuquerque Coelho's was the Correia de Sá's of Rio de Janeiro. In 1637, Salvador de Sá "had about seven hundred slaves employed on his various sugar-plantations and cattle ranches, and he was almost certainly the largest landed proprietor in the captaincy, possibly, indeed, the largest individual landowner in the whole of Brazil."[39] While most noble families did not acquire wealth from the colonies on a scale comparable to that of the Albuquerques and the Sás, many still managed to accumulate substantial sums.

Because of primogeniture, the younger sons of noble families were usually faced with the prospect of pursuing a career in the clergy or seeking their fortunes overseas. While neither option may have been to the liking of younger offspring, the emigration frequently benefited the noble class when scions who went to the colonies could use their positions as administrators to gain a share of the commerce between possession and mother country and thereby obtain wealth with which family coffers could be enriched.

António Teles da Silva (who died in 1651), a younger son born to one of the greatest noble families of Portugal, served as governor of Brazil during the 1640s. During his tenure, which, incidentally, was marked by a feud with the powerful Salvador de Sá,[40] he was able to augment an initially modest personal fortune by selling sugar, hides, tobacco, and jacaranda wood in Lisbon. The actual commercial transactions in the capital were handled by an agent the governor had hired. In the course of his dealings on behalf of the governor, the agent was not reluctant to consort with New Christian merchants, despite the animus felt toward them by much of the nobility. Noble ties to New Christians merchants (some of whom later ran afoul of the Holy Inquisition) were not limited to the astute D. António.[41] By entering the commercial arena dominated by New Christians, Teles da Silva, like many nobles who had gone to the colonies, found an almost surefire means of introducing additional wealth into his native land. This allowed him to live his last years in style on properties in Portugal and, in the process, reinforced the economic strength of the noble estate.[42]

Because of the general disdain in which mercantile pursuits were (in and of themselves) held by the nobility of Iberia, infusions of wealth such as that acquired by Governor Teles da Silva seldom found their way into further commercial activity.[43] Instead, they were usually invested in land, the traditional source of the nobility's wealth and prestige. Rare was the *fidalgo* who engaged in commerce for its own sake. Despite their aversion to commerce, Portuguese noblemen did become involved in commercial transactions, especially when a quick profit could be made. Funds thus obtained were certainly not tainted when used to begin, expand, or maintain a landed estate.[44]

Even with income derived from landed property, royal largesse, and colonial commerce, many noble families still sank into a state of chronic indebtedness, often as a result of trying to outdo one another in lavish displays of wealth. Upon the occasion of D. Pedro II's marriage to D. Mariana de Neuborg in 1687, for example, the count of Vila Flor expended vast sums while participating in the festivities that accompanied the arrival of the king's second wife. Vila Flor, who had received the honor of being chosen as chief bullfighter on one of the days of formal celebration, entered the ring strewing silver coins before him as if he were sowing corn. This spectacle, together with other episodes of ostentatious display, mired the count in debt for many years. According to a contemporary account of Vila Flor's profligacy, he was still paying for his moment of glory in 1696.[45]

Aristocratic indebtedness in Portugal is a subject that awaits more scholarly exploration. It is likely that mounting indebtedness fostered greater noble dependence on the crown, thus facilitating the imposition of an absolutist regime, which, as recent research has suggested, may have been the case in neighboring Spain.[46] Whatever the reason, the rise of absolutism in Portugal (as in Spain) basically hinged on an alliance between the crown and the nobility, which became increasingly obvious after 1667. The pretensions of the middle classes, many of whom pushed for greater socioeconomic freedom during the early years of D. Pedro II's reign, was still to be dealt with by the emerging absolutist order. That task was to be made easier by the collaboration of the largest single landholder in Portugal, the Church.

The Clergy

In many respects, the clerical estate existed as a state within a state since its first allegiance was usually to Rome. The crown's success in overcoming the power of the Roman Catholic Church during the centuries-long process leading to monarchical absolutism was by no means complete. Instead, as was true throughout most of western Europe, accommodation and compromise among the crown, the nobility, the clergy, and the commoner had fostered systems of countervailing power within national boundaries. Like the Portuguese nobility, the clergy of seventeenth-century Portugal maintained its preeminent position by exercising various privileges and controlling a great deal of landed property.

Clerical privileges included a variety of exemptions from obligations imposed upon commoners and even upon nobles. In most instances, clerics did not confront the legal machinery of the state when accused of illegal acts and instead were answerable to canon law in separate tribunals. Except under special conditions, the clergy, unlike the nobility, bore no obligation to serve in the military. Churches were places where neither civil nor military authority had the right to enter except, for example, in pursuit of a slave. Income from properties, gifts, and other sources of wealth was exempt from taxation except in special cases, and no tax could be imposed on the clerical estate unless a papal bull permitting payments to the state was promulgated.[47] Even then, the clergy did not always make contributions authorized by Rome.

According to V. M. Godinho, the Church owned between one-fourth and one-third of the land in Portugal.[48] Although income derived from lands under Church control was undoubtedly the principal source of ecclesiastical wealth, a number of other sources also swelled clerical coffers. Since 1218, the Portuguese Church had received the *decima de Deus*, a tenth share of royal revenues. The Church also secured funds through a variety of pious donations, which, though initially voluntary, had in many instances become practically obligatory over a long period of time and in some cases even owed by law. The clergy's constant demand for payment for all manner of religious services, ranging from baptisms to burials, further augmented the Church's wealth while increasing the common churchgoer's burden of debt.[49] Infusions of wealth also came to the clerical estate through mortmain when pious believers willed their worldly goods to the Church, often after being pressed to do so by priests or other ecclesiastics.

Like the nobility, the clerical estate had found additional resources in the colonies with which to support itself. The Jesuit order, for example, was the primary clerical exploiter of colonial land, and some of its Brazilian mission-villages (*aldeias*) were veritable plantations on which "tame" Indians (*Indios mansos*) labored. In Amazonia, the surplus produced by Jesuit *aldeias* was marketed in the commercial centers of Belem and São Luis and the proceeds were used for the building and upkeep of churches and hospitals.[50] Moreover, Jesuit mission-villages played a vital role in the development of the forest extractive economy of Pará and also acted as stations for the growth of plants brought to Brazil from Portugal's colonies in the Far East.

The Jesuits, as well as members of other orders, in Brazil also derived profit from the land as growers of sugarcane. In 1670, for example, Benedictine friars in Sergipe do Conde (a great sugar plantation largely under Jesuit control after 1659), whose predecessors had begun a cane-grinding operation there at least sixty years earlier, acquired additional cane fields for their order. It is not clear what was done with the proceeds from this enterprise, but it is probable that they were used to defray the operating costs of the local friary. Whatever the case, the Benedictines of Sergipe do Conde and other clerical sugar growers appear to have been small-scale producers working on the margins of the sugar economy.[51] In addition to outright purchases of property, colonial lands also came under the Church's control through mortmain, grants, and other forms of transfer.

As might be expected, a share of the wealth accumulated by the clerics in the colonies was forwarded to Portugal, where it further enriched an ecclesiastical establishment already possessed of great wealth. Though figures giving the Church's annual income during the reign of D. Pedro II have not been found, estimates made for the rule of his son, D. João V, provide some idea of the magnitude of clerical wealth in Portugal. In 1747, it was reported that revenues from properties, gold sent from Brazil, and other sources of income exceeded 1,017,500 cruzados.[52] Available data on the late seventeenth and early eighteenth century further suggest the scale of the Church's wealth. In 1691, the archbishopric of Évora yielded around 70,000 cruzados while the bishopric of Elvas, the poorest such jurisdiction in the country, produced about 10,000 cruzados. When D. João de Sousa, archbishop of Lisbon, died in 1710, his annual salary was more than 100,000 cruzados.[53]

The growth of the Church's wealth—whether it came from its

properties, the royal treasury, bequests, or the colonies—clearly reflected the expansion of the clerical estate itself. By 1750, the number of clerics in Portugal may have reached 200,000, a nearly fourfold increase over the 55,000 priests, nuns, and friars in the country a century earlier.[54]

During the reign of D. Pedro II, the top level of the Church's hierarchy comprised three archbishoprics (which had seats at Lisbon, Évora, and Braga) and eleven bishoprics (one of which was in Funchal, the capital of Madeira). Most of these positions were filled by the younger sons of noble families and even by the illegitimate offspring of highborn noblemen. An illegitimate son of the duke of Cadaval, for example, became bishop of Lamego.[55]

Below the noble and wealthy hierarchs holding archbishoprics and bishoprics, the ecclesiastical estate divided into two principal groups, the secular clergy and the regular clergy. The secular clergy comprised the Church hierarchy, which ranged from archbishops to uneducated parish priests. Many positions within the bureaucracy of the Holy Inquisition also were filled by secular clergy. The regular clergy was made up of at least twelve monastic orders (table 2) and included about 25,000 of the 55,000 clerics in Portugal around 1650.[56] The most obvious division within the regular clergy was that between orders whose members were either male or female. Orders ranged in size from the Carthusians, who had only 2 monasteries (*conventos*) in Portugal in 1628, to the Franciscans, who operated 197 during that year. In the archbishopric of Lisbon alone, the Franciscans could lay claim to 64 *conventos* in 1666.[57] By 1750, the number of monastic establishments had swollen to 538, of which 409 were monasteries and 129 convents.[58] This total represented an increase of 90 monastic communities since 1652, when 337 monasteries and 111 convents were counted in Portugal.[59]

The proliferation of both the secular and regular clergy during the seventeenth and eighteenth centuries undoubtedly played a role in fomenting incessant wrangling between the crown and its clerical allies over territorial jurisdiction, property rights, and revenues. In 1670, for example, revenues owed to the crown from lands near the *vila* of Coruche were being lost to clerical exemption as properties in the area were leased to ecclesiastics. By means of an *alvará*, a promulgation that theoretically remained in force for a minimum of one year, Prince Regent Pedro ordered that no one was to let lands to any cleric when doing so threatened royal revenues.[60]

Although the crown appears to have had no firm policy on the extension or maintenance of clerical properties, it does seem to have judged each case according to its merits and potential impact on the treasury. In 1685, for example, D. Pedro II ordered the abbot of the monastery at Bouro to stop using the title of captain-major (*capitão-mor*), which he had assumed on his own. In addition to arrogating himself to this position, the abbot, along with his brethren, had been preventing the local population from exercising its rightful use of the land and from fishing in local streams. This attempted land grab, which was hardly pleasing to the king since royal revenues were jeopardized, was stopped.[61]

Four years later, a request by members of the Augustinian order for a license to extend their term of possession of an urban property was turned down. Ostensibly, the friars wished to establish an infir-

TABLE 2
Monasteries and Convents in Portugal, 1628

Order	Number*
Franciscan	197
Bernardine	50
Augustinian	38
Dominican	38
Jesuit	31
Benedictine	26
Carmelite	23
Paulist	19
Hieronimite	10
Loios (Order of Saint John the Evangelist)†	9
Trinitarian	7
Carthusian	2
TOTAL	450

SOURCE: Almeida, *Historia da Igreja*, 3 (pt. 1):521–22.
*Figures include both monasteries and nunneries. Though no breakdown according to gender is given, the ratio, as shown above, was approximately three monasteries to one convent. Various other orders (for example the Oratorians) entered Portugal after 1628.
†For discussion of this small order, which was founded in Portugal in the fifteenth century, see Serrão, ed., *DHP*, 2:798–800.

mary in a Lisbon estate (*quinta*) willed to them by a doctor. They asserted that the *quinta* was a more comfortable and salutary place than their present domicile. But, in the document refusing the request, it was argued that the property would inevitably be absorbed as a tax-exempt, inalienable possession of the petitioners and that "this *quinta*, which today they want for convalescence . . . will tomorrow be a great monastery and will require yet another *quinta* for convalescence, as experience has shown."[62]

While the Augustinians' 1689 attempt to utilize the Lisbon *quinta* was rebuffed, their brethren in Coimbra had better luck that year. The purveyor (*provedor*) for the territory (*comarca*) surrounding the city of Oporto, apparently seeking new sources of revenue, had challenged the legitimacy of the Augustinian claim to the Couto de Vila Boa. After considering the friars' petition to retain control of the property, the crown found in their favor.[63] In 1670, two Spanish *conventos*, those of Santiago of Galicia and São Bento of Valladolid, asked for and received a continuation of small contributions from the spicery of the India House (Casa da India).[64] Apparently, this aid had originally been granted during the years of Hapsburg hegemony over Portugal.

In 1698, the Benedictine monastery of Santa Maria of Miranda requested and received confirmation of royal protection of its ancient holdings, which dated from the thirteenth century.[65] Though such requests were usually routine, it appears that during the last decades of the seventeenth century, the Benedictines (and perhaps other orders as well) may have feared a general encroachment by municipalities or other secular jurisdictions and therefore sought reconfirmation of their property rights. A decade before the 1698 request from the *convento* at Miranda was submitted, two other Benedictine monasteries, those at Travanca and Tibães, also had obtained royal confirmation of their jurisdiction.[66] The experience of the Benedictine *convento* of São Martinho of the Couto de Cucujães, which became embroiled in a lengthy jurisdictional dispute with the city council of the *vila* of Feira in 1691, suggested that there was reason for worry about secular encroachment.[67] The crown itself, as we will shortly see, also encroached on the privileges enjoyed by clerical landholders.

Thanks to a recently published study by Aurélio de Oliveira, historians now have detailed information on the economic operation of one of the monasteries mentioned above.[68] The great complex at Tibães was in the heart of the Benedictine monastic establishment, which had grown up in the populous regions of northern Portugal.[69] The abbey at Tibães controlled extensive properties, including its original *couto*, a land grant dating from the twelfth century. The Benedictine friars of Tibães exercised privileges of jurisdiction and exploitation typical of those granted by Portuguese rulers from the ninth through the thirteenth centuries, the great era of *couto* concessions.[70]

In addition to the *couto* at Tibães, the abbey controlled three other major properties. These were the *coutos* at Estela (or Mendo), São Salvador de Donim, and Vimeiro.[71] The *couto* of Estela was especially valuable to the abbey as a producer of wheat and barley. It grew quantities of these grains sufficient to provide for itself and Tibães when it was necessary and still have a surplus that could be sold. In 1667, the abbey was substantially enriched when it gained control of the monastery of São Cláudio, near the port city of Viana do Castelo, and its extensive wheat lands.[72] The abbey's large landholdings were complemented by its exclusive control of stretches of the Rio Tinto and a bank of the Rio Cávado.

Most of the lands controlled by the Benedictines of Tibães were fruitful and produced a variety of crops and livestock. Perhaps seventy percent, and possibly more, of the abbey's landholdings were of good quality and irrigable.[73] Agricultural products included wheat, corn, rye, barley, olives, chestnuts, cork, and wine. Livestock included cattle, pigs, and goats. The quantity and variety of plant and animal production at Tibães suggests that it was a well-provisioned, almost idyllic agrarian regime, which was virtually self-supporting except for the iron needed by blacksmiths and certain other commodities that could usually be acquired in the nearby city of Braga.

Although the Benedictines of Tibães labored on the abbey's *couto*, the bulk of their properties were let to contractors. The abbey most commonly ceded usufruct of these lands for three generations. This so-called *prazo* system of land exploitation[74] accompanied one of short-term contracts, which ranged from one to three years in length. Such contracts were let when, for example, the holder of the usufruct wished to use the land for some type of manufacturing. These contracts could be renewed periodically.

During the half-century examined in Aurélio de Oliveira's monograph, the pattern of tenancy on the abbey's land shifted toward larger holdings as the number of small- and medium-sized tenants declined. But this trend, while augmenting the numbers of a salaried rural proletariat, did not foreshadow any weakening of the abbey's resolve to maintain control over its properties. Apparently in concert with its larger tenants, the abbey actually promoted an enclosure system, usually with stone walls, to establish further its control over the land.[75]

Besides their ownership of land and water rights, the Benedictines at Tibães enjoyed a substantial measure of administrative autonomy. Unlike his counterpart at Bouro, the abbot of Tibães had the uncommon distinction of holding the military title of *capitão-mor*, a status that quite possibly played a role in frustrating the designs of secular officials who, as in the case of the *provedor* of Oporto versus the Augustinians of Coimbra, tried to extend their jurisdiction at the clergy's expense. In 1677, for example, the *provedor* of the *comarca* of Viana do Castelo, perhaps in response to the friars' recent acquisition of control over the neighboring monastery of São Cláudio, was similarly rebuffed when he sought to enlarge his jurisdiction at the expense of the abbey. The failure of occasional challenges such as these demonstrated the abbey's imperviousness to, if not independence from, outside authority.

When not acting to repel attempted encroachment, an elected general and two councils carried out the day-to-day administration of the abbey and its lands. A council of visitors (*conselho dos visitadores*) made annual inspections of the abbey to monitor the quality and effectiveness of its operation. The council of the abbey (*conselho da abadia*), over which the general presided, held monthly meetings for discussion of how best to administer the abbey and its properties. This council was especially important in the local economy since it set the prices for the cereals purchased from tenants and even controlled the prices at which they were sold in nearby markets. The abbey's self-contained council system was complemented by the Benedictines' right to name their own justices and notary.[76]

Thanks to the letting of contracts to a wide range of artisans, numerous useful items were produced within the confines of the abbey's property. By 1668, textile production had become so extensive as to necessitate the appointment of a justice to adjudicate disputes relating to cloth manufacture. Two years later, and probably as a result of the fact that textile workers were usually females, a woman was appointed as justice. The *couto* of Tibães contained two mills for linen production where, in 1671, twenty-four female weavers were at work. Perhaps all the clothing, bed covers, toweling, and other similar items used in the *couto* was produced in the linen mills. Even fishnets were fashioned out of the material. In addition to the weavers, numerous other artisans—including carpenters, potters, tilers, blacksmiths, cobblers, millers, masons, and tailors—worked for the abbey. Like the weavers, the members of each of these occupations had a justice to whom they could turn for settlement of disputes.[77] The presence of innkeepers, cattle dealers, butchers, and fishermen constituted further evidence of the diversification of the local economy.

Agricultural production on the abbey's properties, with the possible exception of wine, increased gradually over the fifty years examined by Professor Oliveira. Production grew considerably in the decade between 1670 and 1680, an especially prosperous period at Tibães. During the previous decade, Tibães, like other great agrarian establishments in the north, exported grain to Lisbon, a city hit hard by shortages of foodstuffs. Although it is not clear how much grain was sent to the capital from Tibães and when, it is known that wheat from the abbey's properties was sold in Lisbon in 1667.[78] The steady growth of agricultural production in areas such as Tibães certainly must have had a role in the success of the Restoration, particularly since much of Portugal's agrarian economy was devastated by the lengthy struggle with Spain.

Privileged self-sufficiency such as that enjoyed at Tibães inevitably came into conflict with the crown's efforts to impose an absolutist regime on Portugal. Even as early as the thirteenth century, when the granting of *coutos* was still at its height, measures were taken by the monarchy to curtail abuses of the virtual autonomy that monastic establishments were receiving. During the following centuries, Portuguese rulers thought better of continuing certain privileges granted to monasteries and gradually extended the crown's influence into the clerical sanctuaries. Finally, in 1692, the privileged status of all *coutos* was extinguished, but this revocation met with strong resistance. In 1703, D. Pedro II relented somewhat, promulgating a law that limited the application of the 1692 edict. The remaining *couto* privileges were not revoked until 1790.[79]

Despite their bickering over properties and privileges, the Church and the crown generally supported one another, especially when confronting the pretensions of commoners. Though the Jesuits, as will be seen in chapter IV, sometimes advocated policies countering those held by the established social order, they usually lent their considerable influence and talent to the service of the Old Regime. During the reign of D. Pedro II and D. João V, members of that order held a near monopoly on the position of spiritual adviser to the king. In 1704, the Jesuits even diverted revenues coming from properties in Portugal and merchandise shipped from the Far East to help finance expenses brought on by the War of the Spanish Succession (1701–1713).[80] The continuity of Jesuit influence at the highest levels was largely assured by their control of the universities at Coimbra and Évora, which gave them a virtual monopoly on higher education in Portugal. Whether students chose to study theology, philosophy, law, or medicine, Jesuits usually oversaw their instruction. The increasingly outmoded scholastic curricula offered at these (and other) Jesuit institutions was not to be revamped until the enlightened administration of Pombal, late in the eighteenth century.

While the Jesuits concentrated on directly influencing and supporting the monarchy, other orders cultivated associations with various social groups. For example, the Dominicans, who were the principal monastic supporters of the Holy Inquisition, aligned themselves closely with the *haute bourgeoisie* and the nobility. The popular Franciscans had great influence with the petty bourgeoisie. Like the Jesuits and the Dominicans, the Oratorians focused their attention on the highest levels of Portuguese society. Though relatively few in number, these three orders were probably the most erudite and intellectually capable groups among the regular clergy, with qualities that allowed them to exert great influence over elites in Portugal and its colonies.[81]

At the other end of the clerical spectrum was a large mass of secular clerics, perhaps 30,000 in number, who, unlike the wealthy noblemen who made up the Church hierarchy, received relatively little benefit from their privileged status. Although exempted from levies imposed on commoners, these clerics, most of whom had small ministries in rural areas, depended heavily on donations from their superiors within the Church hierarchy, wealthy patrons, and local parishioners. This large but relatively uninfluential group of clerics, which has been described as an "ecclesiastical proletariat," ministered chiefly to their less-advantaged counterparts among the peasantry.[82]

Poverty may have induced a measure of corruption and vice among the lower ranks of the secular clergy, but they seem, on the whole, to have been more moral in their behavior than members of most monastic orders. With the exception of the Jesuits and a few other orders, the regular clergy engaged in a wide variety of immoral and even illegal activities, ranging from fornication to tobacco smuggling. During the late seventeenth century, for example, the nuns of the Santa Ana convent in Viana do Castelo were rendezvousing with lovers in small buildings on the grounds of the nunnery. Although these little structures ostensibly had been erected to provide the nuns with places to practice their cooking on days when sisters were permitted to leave the convent, they really served as cozy hideaways for nuns and their lovers. When, in 1700, D. Pedro II heard of the scandalous goings-on at Santa Ana, he ordered the little "kitchens" torn down in 1700.[83] The sisters of Santa Ana, as we will see in a later chapter, were also selling large quantities of contraband tobacco even as their little love nests were being razed.

Though the immoral and illicit doings at Santa Ana may have taken place on a grander scale than those at other convents and monasteries, they exemplify the sort of moral torpor that characterized the Portuguese church during the late seventeenth century. Sexual scandals involving clerics were far from uncommon during the reign of D. Pedro II, who, despite his own peccadillos, frowned on the immorality of monastic communities. His son, however, was of a different mind, taking many nuns as lovers and doing little to curb the excesses of the regular clergy.

The decadence of Portuguese Catholicism during this era, which conformed to the generalized moral decline of the Roman Catholic Church, was symptomatic of the underlying contradictions within the Old Regime. Diversion of substantial numbers of potentially productive subjects into clerical life placed an inordinate burden on the rest of society, both as producers and procreators. Though celibacy may not have been the hallmark of Portuguese ecclesiastics, clerical abstinence undoubtedly depressed the population's growth. The Benedictines at Tibães, as well as many other monastic establishments, were largely self-supporting. Still, in exchange for exemption from taxes, control over vast tracts of land (much of which lay fallow), and absorption of great quantities of public and private funds, they produced relatively little. Instead, vast amounts of capital were channeled into ostentatious display and the building of great churches and monasteries. The impressive baroque church at Tibães, which has drawn scholarly attention, is fair evidence of the surplus wealth that the Benedictines and other clerical groups were able to accumulate.[84]

Together with the crown and the nobility, the clergy exploited its privileged and propertied position to the benefit of its own, even as the mass of Portugal's population remained immersed in poverty and ignorance. While absolutism prolonged the rule of the privileged estates, it also augmented and perpetuated a plethora of nonproductive groups within Portuguese society. But, given the general perception that noble or clerical status brought with it greater prestige and material well-being, there is little wonder that many members of the third estate entertained hopes that they or their offspring might one day be numbered among the privileged and propertied.

CHAPTER III

THE THIRD ESTATE

> Essa e a valentia desta arte—como a doz alquimistas, que se gabam que sabem fazer oiro de enxofre—de gente vil faz fidalgos, porque onde luz o oiro nao ha vileza.
>
> Anonymous, *Arte de Furtar* (1652)

The third estate in Portugal consisted of a broad spectrum of people, ranging from the lowliest slaves to commoners whose forebears, or even they themselves, had risen to such a high station that they stood at the threshold of ennoblement or appointment to important ecclesiastical offices. Such great diversity is perhaps not surprising, given the overwhelming number of people (at least eighty-six percent of the population) belonging to the third estate.[1] This great majority can be conveniently divided into two categories, the people of the town and the people of the country.

Of those groups living in the Portuguese countryside, by far the largest and most important were the peasant classes. The land on which they labored, as was true most everywhere in Europe before the advent of industrial capitalism, constituted the most essential asset of the national economy. "Agriculture," according to Henry Kamen, was "the mainstay of economy, society and state. The peasant classes were correspondingly, the mainstay of all three."[2] However, their great importance to the functioning of the Old Regime in Portugal went largely unrewarded. Peasants usually received little in return for their labor and, instead, were caught in a web of legal, social, religious, and economic obligations that virtually assured that much of their production would go into the hands of the privileged classes or wealthier members of the third estate.

Rents, tithes, tolls, and taxes—not to mention the often depressed prices paid for their produce and the low wages usually paid those who took seasonal jobs—dogged the lives of most peasants and made social advancement all the more difficult. Yet, over a period of generations, a peasant family could climb the social ladder by accumulating and holding property or moving to urban centers to pursue careers as artisans or traders. Undoubtedly, however, most rural migrants to urban areas found work as laborers or servants, exchanging agricultural pursuits for menial tasks.

Cities and towns were also home to merchants, lawyers, government officials, university professors, guildsmen, and others who secured their livelihood in an urban setting. Like the nobility, this middle class of townspeople, which is most typically called a bourgeoisie, was not a homogeneous class. According to Henry Kamen, such classes consisted, at the lowest level,

> of petty traders, minor officials, prosperous craftsmen and others who tended to have independent means and were not in the employ of another. At a higher level they were made up of bureaucrats, lawyers and others in the public service. At this level, too, the bourgeoisie were the capitalist class, makers of fortunes in wholesale trade, long-distance commerce, and moneylending.[3]

Above the bourgeoisie stood the privileged classes and below it the rest of the population: "The bourgeoisie were conceived to be sandwiched between two other classes, those at the bottom who had to toil for their living, and those who lived off unearned income at the top." These three categories "cannot be taken literally, however, since there were an infinite number of levels leading from one category to the next."[4]

The permeability of the noble classes to entry by commoners, though limited, was sufficient to permit many of the industrious and well connected to attain patents of nobility. Membership in the clergy was also open to the bourgeoisie and other commoners, but it undoubtedly held considerably less attraction for the material minded. Many of those who aspired to noble status for their families would seek to have their children admitted into universities as students of law or medicine. Those individuals who obtained a university education as lawyers or doctors and then entered the bureaucracy were well positioned for further social advancement. As functionaries of the crown or of municipal bureaucracies, especially that of Lisbon,[5] such individuals had the opportunity to rub shoulders with the nobility and perhaps find a patron who would help open doors not budged by talent and ambition alone.

The more fortunate (or more likely, their descendants) made their way into the lower ranks of the noble estate, receiving the rights and privileges of nobility (*fidalguía*) or at least those of cavaliers (*cavaleiros*). Upwardly mobile functionaries of this sort necessarily held a rather ambiguous status in Portuguese society since many of them were in transit from one estate to another or at least identified themselves most closely with the nobility.[6]

Prominent merchants, shipbuilders, and even ship's captains were also candidates for noble status, as were their descendants. The crown, itself deeply involved in commerce, could reinforce its commercial position by granting patents of nobility to members of the merchant class. An additional factor that helped remove some of the stigma from commercial enterprise was the nobility's own interest in commerce. As we have seen, the nobility was not always averse to commercial activity since the rewards of trade could be converted into landed property. By the same token, merchants who were eager to join the ranks of the nobility, and thereby enter the inner circle of the privileged, invested portions of their wealth in property. Both groups shared the belief that landownership was crucial to enhancing and preserving an elevated social position.

Although the subject awaits systematic study, it is probable that the Portuguese bourgeoisie, like the Castilian, transformed itself, in part at least, into a *rentier* class by buying up *censos* from financially pinched nobles and the peasants. "To the constant untiring pursuit of *censos*," wrote one authority,

all sections of the [Castilian] bourgeoisie—lawyers, office-holders, clergy, merchants—diverted their capital. Money was diverted from productive enterprises because they were too risky and put into *censos* and *juros* because they brought a steady return. These investments consequently became a highly prized article of property. What other way was there of obtaining an income without working for it?[7]

The esteem in which landed property was held by nobles and the middle classes and their common involvement in commerce made difficult "the existence of an autonomous bourgeoisie, with its own values."[8]

The buying of, and profiting from, offices was also an area of common involvement between the noble and the bourgeois. This practice, which had disastrous effects on administrative efficiency, was in fact generalized throughout western Europe during the seventeenth century.[9] It had become such a problem in Portugal that in 1681 Prince Regent Pedro had to order that no one was to hold two positions simultaneously.[10] Nevertheless, some six years later, D. Pedro permitted the city administration of Lisbon to defray the cost of a road-widening project by selling vacant municipal offices.[11] Obviously, the practice of selling offices was itself not under review. Nobles were among the purchasers of office, and, as in the interest in commerce they often shared with merchants, they joined the professional classes in the pursuit of office.

The Professional Classes

In discussions of class gradations within the framework of the three estates, the members of the so-called noble professions are difficult to categorize since, at any given time, some enjoyed some form of noble status while others were still working toward such recognition. Thus, in effect, the so-called noble professions (for example, law and medicine) were antechambers to the noble estate, which many individuals entered before attaining a coat of arms. A university degree was usually the ticket required of individuals seeking entry into the professions. Once having obtained a diploma, graduates in the various professions enjoyed varying degrees of privilege, even when they were not actually employed in their chosen fields.[12]

University graduates (*letrados*)[13] had played an important role in the process of national unification, lending their expertise to the drive to expand royal power. In Portugal, and later in the colonies, the *letrados* served as skillful representatives of the crown's interests in countering particularist tendencies. The prominence of lawyers had become clearly manifest after the Cortes of Coimbra of 1385. By the latter half of the next century,

their position was one of approximate equality with the knights and the *fidalgo* class, although the latter were unwilling to recognize this fact. By the middle of the next century the *letrados* began to assume some of the aspects of a caste in that by marriage and family relationships they became a self-perpetuating group occupying most of the judicial and many of the administrative positions of government. The sons of *letrados* followed in their fathers' footsteps, going from a course in canon or civil law (usually at the University of Coimbra but sometimes at Salamanca) into the royal service.[14]

Probably the most influential professional groups were men educated as physicians (*médicos*) and lawyers, the lawyers, of course, being far more important in furthering the crown's interests. Because of their revival of Roman law as set forth in the Justinian Code, lawyers throughout western Europe had helped considerably in legitimatizing the sovereignty of national states. In Portugal, the magisterial bureaucracy had become a bastion of royal authority whose power increased as the seventeenth century progressed.[15]

Besides serving in the judiciary, lawyers could also be found working as scribes, secretaries, and notaries in the crown's ministries and in municipal administrations. Mendo Foios de Pereira (1643–1708), for example, went to work for the city of Lisbon after receiving his bachelor's degree in jurisprudence from the University of Coimbra. In addition to being talented, Foios de Pereira, then in his twenties, enjoyed the extra advantage of having a father who had held the prestigious position of *desembargador* of the Casa da Supplicação, Portugal's preeminent High Court of Appeals. Prior to D. Pedro's 1681 ban on holding more than one office, the young lawyer had simultaneously held two positions, those of civil judge (*juiz de civil*) and scribe (*escrivão*) for the city council (*câmara*).[16]

While serving as *escrivão*, Foios de Pereira had occasion to communicate the *câmara*'s views on a number of issues to the prince regent. In 1674, for example, he wrote a letter asking the prince regent to reject a New Christian request for a general pardon.[17] D. Pedro's reaction to this particular letter is not certain, but he was sufficiently impressed by the talented *letrado's* abilities to appoint him ambassador to Castile in late 1679.[18] Seven years later, Foios de Pereira's star rose even higher when D. Pedro II appointed him secretary of state.

Though talented and well-connected individuals like Mendo Foios de Pereira stood out as honored members of the noble professions whose families had long since joined the nobility, many professionals enjoyed a status only slightly superior to that of the merchant class. One valuable index of such status was the order of march for groups participating in religious processions. In Lisbon's procession celebrating the Body of Christ (*Corpo de Deus*), for example, notaries (*tabeliães*) marched immediately before the merchants, who brought up the rear. Surgeons (*cirurgeâos*), whose status in seventeenth-century Portugal was below that of physicians, were situated above guildsmen in the social hierarchy, but they were not actually within the nobility. Thanks to certain exemptions, however, they did enjoy a quasi-noble status, and the surgical profession was itself regarded as being "noble" ("*nobre*").[19] Indeed, as a contemporary writer, Antonio das Villas Boas e Sampaio, put it, professionals such as goldsmiths, silversmiths, sculptors, painters, printers, booksellers, surgeons, apothecaries, as well as prosperous merchants, "belong to an estate distinct from the common people, which we call intermediate, and they enjoy a semi-nobility, by virtue of certain exemptions."[20]

Besides the possession of specialized bodies of knowledge, an important attribute of the noble professions, especially the legal fraternity, was their close identification with the crown's interests. Physicians, like lawyers and others, quite often were on the royal payroll and quite naturally felt some measure of allegiance to the crown. Such allegiance probably was also felt toward those local administrative units that had lawyers, practitioners of medicine, and other professionals in their employ. The two *médicos* and one surgeon employed by the Lisbon city council in 1661, for example, probably felt at least some identification with the interests of the municipality.[21]

As it has been already been indicated, however, the legal profession felt an especially close identification with the aims of the monarchy. Like many of their contemporaries in the nobility, they adopted "the attitudes and attributes of the military aristocracy. But whereas the magnates and lesser nobility struggled against the infringement of their traditional immunities and privileges inherent in royal centralization, the *letrados* owed their very existence to the expansion of royal power."[22] After 1668, the *letrados* and the nobility found common ground in supporting, or at least in acquiescing to, the increasingly absolutist regime of D. Pedro II.

The Mercantile Class

Like the *letrados* and other classes, the mercantile class of seventeenth-century Portugal was not a homogeneous group. The Portuguese merchant community has been described in terms of three basic categories: the "medium" merchant, the great merchant, and the merchant-banker.[23] These classifications are by no means exact, nor do they include the traders of modest means who carried on small transactions in Lisbon and other commercial centers, who marketed products of their own manufacture or commodities within a small radius of their home communities, or who sold their wares at the many local fairs. "Medium" merchants engaged in trading and lending, usually specialized in one commodity (for example, cloth, grain, spices), held some real estate, and sometimes invested in enterprises such as the Brazil Company. Unlike shopkeepers and nomadic traders who were usually involved only in domestic retail trade, "medium" merchants acted as importers and exporters while also engaged in retailing.[24]

Great merchants dealt in considerably larger volumes than did "medium" merchants, were less prone to specialization, and were deeply involved in international and maritime affairs. They owned considerable amounts of real estate, as well as luxurious personal possessions, and probably held full or part ownership in at least one merchant ship. The proportion of their business activity devoted to borrowing and lending at interest was undoubtedly larger than that of the typical "medium" merchant.

Merchant-bankers devoted an even greater portion of their enterprise to the extension of credit, the state being their principal customer. Their role as lender to the state was facilitated by a global network of business contacts. Trading in a wide variety of products, including sugar, tobacco, wine, oriental rugs, and diamonds, was not neglected, however. The buying and selling of such items could take place on a grand scale because of the merchant-banker's access to large amounts of credit. As was the case throughout Europe, individuals engaged solely in banking were not yet on the scene in Portugal.[25]

An important division common to the three categories is that between Old and New Christian merchants. However, the standard historical treatment of the Portuguese merchant classes has been to identify them as being nearly synonymous with New Christians. Since the seventeenth century, terms such as *homens de negócio* and *tratantes* commonly have been interchanged with designations used for New Christians (for example, *cristãos novos* and *homens da nação*).[26] Thanks to the recent work of Dr. David Grant Smith on the merchant community of Lisbon, historians now know that the number of Old Christian merchants was larger than was previously suspected.[27] Using a sample of 364 merchants, Dr. Smith has calculated that between one-third and one-fourth of the members of the mercantile class were Old Christians.[28]

The regional origins of the Old and New Christian merchants of Lisbon were generally different. Although New Christian members of the mercantile class were usually born in the capital, their male forebears typically were merchants from the provinces of Alentejo and Beira.[29] These provinces bordered on Spain, from which possibly as many as 120,000 Jews had come after their expulsion by Ferdinand and Isabela in 1492.[30]

Old Christian merchants were usually of more recent arrival in the capital, having themselves often come to Lisbon from the populous northern province of Entre-Douro-e-Minho. Villages near Lisbon, the district of Lamego, and even the island of Madeira also contributed a significant share of the young men who sought their fourtunes in the capital. Unlike his New Christian counterpart, the Old Christian merchant usually did not have forebears who were merchants. Instead, his father and grandfather were probably artisans or farmers. Thus, his business experience and associations were relatively limited when he arrived in Lisbon.[31]

Because of a ready mingling of the Old and New Christian merchant families of Lisbon, a pluralistic mercantile class was formed and was in a constant state of flux since "new blood" was continually entering the ranks and intermarriage was common. For the New Christian, however, attempts to forge matrimonial links with the nobility were blocked by the latter's passion for purity of blood (*limpeza da sangre*). Despite the advantages of being born in Lisbon and having relatives experienced in commerce, the typical New Christian merchant's climb up the capital's social ladder was almost invariably blocked by his Jewish ancestry. While wealthy Old Christian merchants could usually arrange matches between their daughters and young noblemen by offering handsome dowries, the ranks of the nobility were seldom breached by the female offspring of New Christian *homens de negócio*.[32] Instead, marriages were mostly limited to unions within the mercantile class, thereby precluding the assimilation of

New Christians for which Father António Vieira had once argued.[33] Intermarriage among the New Christian merchant families of Lisbon, according to Dr. Smith, created vast extended kinship groups, a very few of which incorporated nearly all of the important New Christian merchant-bankers of the city.[34]

On rare occasions, the stigma of "impure" blood were overlooked and exceptional individuals of New Christian parentage were granted noble status. One such figure was Francisco Carlos, a merchant-banker who, according to Dr. Smith, may be regarded as the archtypical New Christian businessman. Born around 1609, the financier's rise to prominence coincided with the Restoration era. He gained renown for his business expertise while serving, for example, as a consultant to the Brazil Company. Carlos himself became extensively involved in the Brazil trade, having a brother-in-law in Recife who acted as his chief correspondent. By 1667, he had risen to the office of treasurer of the Brazil Company and had received a patent of nobility, which allowed him to bear the title of *fidalgo da casa real*.

During his years as businessman and servant of the crown, Francisco Carlos acquired a substantial personal fortune. Besides a large, sumptuously furnished house in the Rossio, a major square in Lisbon, he owned a number of black slaves. The house was kept by a female slave, and two male slaves had the task of carrying him about the capital in a litter. Carlos also owned property in the Alentejo, from which he drew quitrents, and he held shares in three vessels that traded with Brazil. The lion's share of his capital, however, was loaned at interest to fellow merchants and to a variety of individuals ranging from D. Luís de Meneses, the count of Ericeira, to a chicken vendor. Still, even with all of his personal wealth and business connections and despite the esteem in which he was held by many Old Christians, Francisco Carlos was picked up by the Inquisition in 1672.[35] As we will see in the next chapter, he and many others fell victim to an upwelling of the anti–New Christian sentiment that suffused seventeenth-century Portuguese society.

Despite the constant threat posed by the Inquisition, New Christian merchants did not conduct their affairs as an isolated minority. They often entered into partnerships with Old Christians, who, for their part, felt little reluctance about associating with their New Christian colleagues and (as happened in the case of Francisco Carlos after he was imprisoned by the Holy Office) even appeared as witnesses for their defense during the Inquisition. In another instance, Francisco Malheiro, a wealthy Old Christian merchant-banker and himself a *familiar* of the Holy Office since 1638, testified to the good character of an unfortunate associate who had been brought before the Inquisition tribunal. (*Familiares* were auxiliary members of the Inquisition who acted as watchdogs for the Catholic faith as practiced in Portugal. They received certain privileges in return for their participation. More will be said about this group in chapter IV.) The close business and personal ties between Old and New Christian merchants were undoubtedly reinforced by shared aspirations. Both groups aimed at gaining patents of nobility and leaving entailed estates (*morgados*) to their descendants.[36] Such aspirations, as Virginia Rau has suggested, probably did much to immobilize the capital of the bourgeoisie in landholdings and other manifestations of noble status.[37]

Francisco Carlos and Francisco Malheiro, together with the rest of the Old and New Christian merchant-bankers of seventeenth-century Lisbon, comprised a group that functioned as an imperfect oligopoly. The commodity controlled most completely by this group was large-scale credit, especially that extended to the state. Merchant-banker participation in the trading of oriental and tropical products, while also extensive, never approached the sort of monopoly achieved in the lending of money.[38]

Though the distinction between merchant-banker and great merchant is most clearly shown by the former's emphasis on lending, the line between great merchant and "medium" merchant is less clear. Frédéric Mauro has observed that "medium" merchants tended to specialize in one commodity and had fewer business contacts or dealings outside of Portugal. The research of Dr. Smith revealed that the willingness of great merchants to accept royal contracts and tax farms was also an important distinction between the two categories. Participation in the crown's financial activities, often a chancy business, could further a great merchant's climb up the social ladder.[39]

Another important distinction between great and "medium" merchants appears to have lain in the greater willingness (or ability) of the great merchants to extend credit. One individual who exemplified this propensity was João Duarte de Resende. Born the son of a prominent New Christian merchant in 1613, Resende was active in the tobacco trade and, in partnership with other merchants, sent Bahian tobacco to India, where it was exchanged for textiles. Resende's lending activities appear to have been substantial. In one instance, it was found that a wealthy but unfortunate merchant held captive by the Inquisition owed him 11,500 cruzados at 6.25 percent interest, the maximum rate.[40] By way of comparison, it can be noted that the debt owed Resende was itself probably larger than the total assets of a typical "medium" merchant.[41]

As was the case of the nobility and the clergy, the acquisition of colonial possessions provided further economic opportunities for the Portuguese mercantile class and led to the establishment of powerful merchant communities in great ports such as Goa, Bahia, Recife, and, to a lesser extent, in Luanda. The triangular trade between the Portuguese, west African, and Brazilian coasts (not to mention all the intersecting links with Europe, the Spanish Indies, and the Far East), was of fundamental importance in the rise to prominence of great merchants such as João Duarte Resende and merchant-bankers such as Francisco Carlos. "Medium" merchants also profited from seaborne trade, typically importing goods in caravelles or other small ships, the use of which they could afford.[42]

Unfortunately, historians know relatively little about the metropolitan merchant communities outside of Lisbon. During the last half of the seventeenth century, however, it is clear that merchants in other Portuguese cities and *vilas* made their presence felt. The merchants of Oporto, Viana do Castelo, Vila do Conde, Aveiro, and the Atlantic islands, as well as the burgeoning mercantile communities of Brazil, successfully opposed monopolization of shipping by the Lisbon-based Brazil Company. Furthermore, the upswing in foreign demand for Portuguese wines was to be of even greater importance to the rising mercantile class in Oporto.

Inland cities such as Évora and Coimbra were home to merchants who most typically conformed to Mauro's category of "medium" merchant, specializing in the buying and selling of local products such as wine, grain, and textiles, or importing commodities from the colonies or finished goods from Europe. No doubt, these same merchants also engaged in rudimentary lending activities. Early in the seventeenth century, the number of individuals identified as merchants in Coimbra (twenty-two in 1617) was quite small, perhaps only ten percent of that in Lisbon. But, like their counterparts in the capital, the merchants of Coimbra aspired to noble status and privilege.[43]

Great merchants and merchant-bankers on the order of those in Lisbon were seldom found in places other than that city, Oporto, or Viana do Castelo. The great ports were the usual domain of such individuals, while "medium" merchants and smaller traders made up the commercial classes of other urban centers, where they probably enjoyed a local status similar to that of the great financiers of Lisbon and Oporto.

Smaller traders, together with the artisan classes and certain other groups, formed an energetic petty bourgeoisie. Many of the traders within this group traveled throughout the Portuguese countryside, going to local fairs and markets with an inventory of goods strapped to the backs of pack animals. Trade was often by barter since hard currency was in chronically short supply.[44] The functioning of internal trade was often dependent on muleteers (*almocreves*) and boatmen (*barqueiros*) who were not truly merchants or traders but, like ship's captains, were essential figures in moving the goods of the mercantile class from one place to another.[45]

Like the nobility, many individuals within the petty bourgeoisie felt threatened by the economic strength of the mercantile class. Great royal monopolies such as the Brazil Company, in which the major investors were New Christian merchants, were regarded with considerable suspicion. Both the nobleman and the small businessman resisted the disruption of the socioeconomic status quo that the continued success of the company (or other such enterprises) and its stigmatized backers would surely bring. The upshot of this shared concern was a tacit alliance between the *fidalgos* and the petty bourgeoisie.[46] Of the myriad groups that made up the petty bourgeoisie, the best organized and most influential were the crown-sanctioned guilds.

The "Mechanical" Professions

In addition to *letrados* and the merchants of varying wealth and standing, the third estate was also populated by men engaged in the so-called "mechanical" professions (*ofícios mecânicos*), which found their most vocal expression in privileged urban guilds. And, as was suggested earlier, certain artisans (for example, goldsmiths) enjoyed a status that, to a considerable extent, exempted them from the stigma usually attached to those who worked with their hands. The larger the city, of course, the greater the number and specialization of the artisan class. In Lisbon and other cities, the more prosperous guildsmen were often grouped together on a single street. Today, one can still visit the downtown shopping area of Lisbon to find the Rua Aurea and the Rua de Prata, streets where goldsmiths and silversmiths worked. By joining together on the same streets, the masters (*mesteres*) of the various "mechanical" professions felt themselves more secure from abuse and violence and better able to regulate the quantity and quality of their production. Moreover, customers could be more easily attracted and the collection of dues and imposts facilitated.[47]

During the late middle ages, guilds in various Portuguese cities and towns had gained royal sanction, especially after their loyal support of the crown in its struggle with the nobility during the late fourteenth century. In 1384, the *mesteres* of Lisbon were accorded representation on the city council, until then the province of rural property owners, the minor nobility, and the wealthier members of the bourgeoisie.[48] Thereafter, the fortunes of the guilds varied according to local conditions, but generally their influence increased in the larger population centers.

The principal artisan organizations in these centers were the famous Houses of the Twenty-four (Casas dos Vinte e Quatro).[49] This name, actually a misnomer, was a holdover from 1384, when twelve professions were called upon to designate two representatives each for the Lisbon city council. It is not clear, however, whether only twelve organized professions existed at that time.[50] During the following decades, more and more professions were recognized through royal orders (*regimentos*), which also laid down standards for workmanship, salaries, prices, et cetera. Proportional representation in the casa was reached by periodic elections, which usually ensured that the expanding professions gained greater influence and that those in decline were not overrepresented after their importance in the economy had waned.

In 1620, the chief official of the Lisbon Casa was granted the title of people's judge (*juiz do povo*) and became, in fact, the chief spokesman for the popular classes. After the Restoration of 1640, the casa was more frequently consulted by the crown about the levying of taxes on the general population.[51] The casa, in turn, more regularly communicated its views to the king. In 1642, for example, the *juiz do povo* asked that D. João IV act to prevent his ministry of finance from constricting the supply of goods and foodstuffs, a measure designed to bolster the war effort, since doing so would have caused undue hardship for everybody, especially the poor.[52]

Although the *juiz do povo* and his fellows exerted their greatest influence on municipal governments, usually in their own behalf, they also voiced concern for the interests of less fortunate commoners.[53] Such efforts on behalf of the people elevated the *juiz do povo* to a position of great prestige among the popular classes.[54]

In 1661, it was suspected that the Casa dos Vinte e Quatro of Oporto had gone beyond the simple vocalization of popular sentiment. In reaction to a royal decree of that year that imposed a tax on paper, riots broke out in the port city. A group of young men seized and burned the detested stamped paper and then threatened to set fire to the house of the notorious enforcers of the tax. Fortunately for those officials, a contingent of Dominicans bearing a cross dissuaded the rioters from such pyrotechnic reprisals. But other buildings were attacked, some looting took place, and the outbreak lasted through the night. Clerics who circulated throughout the city urging people to go home were instrumental in ending the disturbance.[55]

Subsequently, the crown accused the Oporto Casa of being the principal force behind the violent outbreak. The casa was disbanded for its alleged culpability, but two of its representatives were allowed to attend meetings of the city council. Later investigation revealed that the culprits were unidentified commoners and not guild members. Ulitmately, the only individuals punished were a sailor who was exiled to Brazil for five years and a mulatto who was flogged. In the Lisbon Cortes of 1668, representatives from Oporto successfully petitioned for the reestablishment of the casa, and shortly thereafter a new *juiz do povo* was elected.[56]

The fact that the Oporto *mesteres* were initially implicated is noteworthy. Very little is known about the 1661 riot beyond what was sketched above, but it seems likely that the artisan class was more directly affected by the paper tax than the average sailor or mulatto. Evidence of its unpopularity with influential elements in the taxpaying third estate is manifest in the fact that the despised tax did not survive the ill-fated rule of D. Afonso VI.

The seventeenth century has been called the "golden age" of the Casa dos Vinte e Quatro.[57] During that century, the efforts of guildsmen to maintain and increase their status and privileges often met with success. Individual corporations sought and received favorable alterations and additions to their *regimentos*. Those *regimentos* that were rewritten or altered during the reign of D. Pedro II were modified for a variety of reasons. Quite often, changes were made simply to conform with greater specialization, changes in production techniques, or oversights in the original *regimento* that necessitated revision of examinations for *mestere* status. In 1703, for example, the method for examination of shoemakers (*sapateiros*) was rewritten, stipulating how many pairs and what types of footwear were to be made by candidates for *mestere* status.[58]

Standard privileges such as freedom from military service, exemption from certain imposts, and provisions to benefit relatives or discourage free-lance competition were set down or reaffirmed in the *regimentos* of guilds or the municipalities in which guildsmen were represented. In a new *regimento* promulgated for the Lisbon city council in 1671, provision was made for the welfare of the wives and children of artisans who had served in the casa or any other city office.[59] In a letter published in 1685, D. Pedro II supported the sheet-metal workers (*batefolhas*) of Oporto in their complaints against unexamined individuals infringing on their craft.[60] The locksmiths (*serralheiros*) of that city, not certain as to the validity of their *compromisso*, one of the documents of incorporation, asked for and received royal confirmation of their status and privileges in 1695.[61] Five years later, the coopers (*tanoeiros*) of Oporto received royal agreement to a request that no guild member be allowed to buy wood for barrel making without the permission of the guild's officials. The crown took this action in order to prevent prosperous coopers from monopolizing barrel production by buying up wood supplies.[62] The then burgeoning wine and olive oil trade of Portugal may have strained the available stocks of wood and iron.[63]

A continuing preoccupation of the *mesteres* was to make certain that their sons inherited their positions and whatever privileges that went with them.[64] The maintenance and furtherance of family wealth and status were the primary reasons artisans frequently took only their sons as apprentices. Like the merchant class, the *mesteres* hoped that their offspring would one day attain noble status. In pursuit of this goal, the Casa dos Vinte e Quatro lobbied for the crown's assurance that the sons of guild members would gain admission into Portuguese universities.[65] A university degree, of course, provided access to the *letrado* class.

Not all offspring remained in the guilds of their fathers or moved up to the professional class by way of the universities. Some data, for example, show that about thirty-seven percent of the members of the Lisbon merchant class had grandfathers who were artisans and over seventeen percent of their fathers-in-law were also artisans.[66] Although virtually no research has been published on the kinship patterns or social mobility of the artisan class of seventeenth-century Portugal, it seems clear that their aspirations to higher standing were not always misplaced.

In some cases, however, individual guilds proclaimed rather unrealistically that the very nature of their professions bestowed noble status on guild members. Since they produced objects consumed, for the most part, by the privileged estates, it was argued that they deserved recognition as men of noble status. Goldsmiths and silversmiths were probably the most insistent on the nobility of their professions. During the late sixteenth century, the goldsmiths of Oporto managed to get themselves exempted from the onerous task of guarding the city's gates. This duty was necessary in order to deny entrance to people coming from places afflicted by bubonic plague. These same goldsmiths, while organized as a guild, stood aloof from the Casa dos Vinte e Quatro, regarding full association as a blemish on their noble pretensions.[67]

In Lisbon and Évora, workers of the noble metals also sought to enhance their status. In 1657, the goldsmiths of Lisbon began a squabble over what position they should take in the *Corpo de Deus* procession, a debate that was still unresolved in 1717.[68] They also attempted by petition in 1690 to freeze out competition by gaining a *regimento* modification that would limit all gold- and silversmithing done in Portugal to the *mesteres* of Lisbon, Évora, and Oporto. Furthermore, they wanted foreign goldsmiths to be banned from entering Portugal.⁶⁹ These and other self-aggrandizing proposals were summarily turned down by the king.

The argument for ennoblement used by the metalsmiths was also used by other guildsmen. In 1687, for example, the handful of sculptors working in Oporto petitioned for noble status, asserting that their creations went almost invariably to the clergy and the nobility.⁷⁰ Eight years later, the ribbon makers of Lisbon unsuccessfully employed the same argument, claiming that their production (which included ribbons made of silk, a fiber restricted to use by the privileged classes) warranted exemption from tasks carried out by the city council.⁷¹ Though such pretensions to full noble status were rejected, these artisan groups, as well as others, still enjoyed quasinoble status.

The organized guilds of the cities and *vilas* of Portugal constituted one of the most influential elements within the third estate. If the merchant-bankers are to be regarded as the chief figures of the *haute bourgeoisie*, then the *mesteres* may likewise be seen as the dominant group within the *petite bourgeoisie*. And, unlike the mercantile class, members of organized guilds were formally and directly represented in such bodies as the Cortes and the city councils.

Despite their strong identification with the nobility and their sharing of its concern over the economic strength of the mercantile class, the guilds sometimes stood in opposition to the wishes of the privileged classes, especially when championing their own interests or those of the lower classes. This was clearly evident in 1678 when agents (*procuradores*) of the *mesteres* of Lisbon were chastised for not signing documents (in this case, *consultas*) in which they took various policies of the crown to task. One nobleman who sat on the city council felt compelled to condemn the unruliness of the guilds, declaring that, since "His Majesty [is] a sovereign prince, there should not be created within this body a parliament which impedes the execution of his commands."⁷²

The Popular Classes

In the Old Regime, the people (*o povo*), or popular classes, were broadly, if somewhat misleadingly, described as being all groups within the third estate except rich merchants and the lowest members of society.⁷³ Though normally part of *o povo* the organized guilds had sufficient influence and privilege, not to mention their pretensions to noble status, to distinguish them from the mass of Portuguese society. That mass, which ranged from humble rural tenants to prosperous vendors and growers, was comprised of the gainfully, if modestly and often sporadically, employed.

As with the organized guilds, numerous other occupational groups had gained, in varying degrees, privileges and exemptions as recognition of their importance to the functioning of the economy. The already mentioned *almocreves*, whose work constituted a vital link in the infrastructure of the economy, had received a *regimento*, gave competency examinations, and functioned under other regulatory and organizational strictures even though they never achieved admittance into the Casa dos Vinte e Quatro.⁷⁴ Other groups less formally organized than the *mesteres* (for example, fishermen and farmers) also received special consideration from the crown in order that their important role in the economy continue unimpeded. When, for example, a military commander attempted to impress sons of the fishermen of the port of Setúbal into his *terço* (an old-style regiment that theoretically contained four companies of 250 men each) in 1684, D. Pedro II promulgated an *alvará* reaffirming the seafaring community's exemption from all but naval service.⁷⁵

Besides granting or reconfirming military exemptions, the crown sometimes extended new privileges to valuable workers. In one instance, this time in 1700, the cart drivers of Moita, a village across the Tagus from Lisbon, petitioned the king to grant pasturage privileges to their oxen. The drivers, who transported wine and other commodities to market, soon obtained the right to graze their animals in certain suitable areas.⁷⁶

Not unexpectedly, however, the crown was seldom predisposed toward furthering the interests of humble but productive subjects when those of the privileged classes were threatened. After receipt of a petition from the nunnery at Odivelas that complained of falling revenues, for example, Pedro II ordered in 1698 that all landed farmers and tenants increase their payments to the convent. This exaction was patterned after a similar measure taken on behalf of the All Saints Hospital in Lisbon some years earlier.⁷⁷

THE THIRD ESTATE 57

These examples confirm the fact that groups within *o povo* did receive recognition and support from the crown when the prerogatives of the privileged estates were not adversely affected, but they tell us little else about the lower classes. Unfortunately, as Joel Serrão has pointed out, information about the various strata of Portuguese society below the Casas dos Vinte e Quatro is scanty.[78] Further archival research, especially in notarial and Inquisition records, will undoubtedly reveal much detail about the social and economic lives of commoners, but at present only the general outlines of their place and activity in the Old Regime are visible.

The Portuguese economy depended on the labor power of commoners (and slaves), for from it sprang the surplus production that the privileged claimed for themselves and the remainder that sustained the peasants and the workers. The productive but usually exploited masses of society fell into two basic categories: the agrarian masses, which was by far the largest, and commoners living in cities and *vilas*. Many commoners in rural areas worked land that they rented from the privileged classes or that they sometimes owned. Though serfdom had long since ended, free tenants inherited many of the traditional obligations associated with that institution.[79] Furthermore, according to one estimate, over half the agrarian population was composed of day laborers (*jornaleiros*).[80]

Predictably, those farmers who owned their own land enjoyed greater social standing than the unpropertied agrarian masses and sometimes received special consideration in recognition of their contribution to the economy. Such was the case with the small winegrowers within the city limits (*termo*) of Lisbon. During the struggle for the Restoration these farmers (*lavradores*) were briefly exempted from a tax on wine. Evidently, the winegrowers made too much of a good thing during this hiatus, acting as their own contractors and sending their wine outside the *termo*, where prices were better.[81] This incensed the city council, which used its influence to have the levy reimposed on the growers in 1674. In response, the *lavradores* petitioned the crown to restore their exemption, decrying the *câmara's* heavy handed action and claiming that among their numbers were "many poor and miserable, many widows and maidens" who would be further impoverished by the tax. A year later, the prince regent rejected the petition. In its *consulta* to D. Pedro, the *câmara* successfully argued that, since the clergy had agreed to pay the tax, the growers were certainly in no position to claim an exemption.[82]

Although the special exemption enjoyed by the winegrowers did not last long, their example should serve to illustrate two characteristics that the popular classes shared with the privileged and well-to-do. First, of course, the aspiration to (or defense of) privilege or exemption was hardly limited to the upper classes, as the growers' petition makes clear. Secondly, the winegrowers—like nobles, merchants, and guildsmen—had definite gradations within their own group, ranging from enterprising *lavradores* who sough to expand their share of the wine market to impoverished widows subsisting on small vineyards. Thus, it is obvious that *o povo* should not be viewed as a monolithic homogeneous mass, but as an agglomeration of groups that, when possible, sought and even obtained small increments of privilege and status.

Another example, this time taken from the second category, the common people of cities and *vilas*, should reinforce the point just made. Although a numerically smaller group than that found in the countryside, urban commoners undoubtedly were characterized by greater occupational diversity. Lisbon, of course, required workers of all sorts to meet the needs of a major European port and population center.[83] Moreover, urban centers, as well as rural areas, received periodic infusions of labor as a large transient work force moved from countryside to city and back again to sell their labor power as harvesters, woodcutters, charcoal makers, et cetera. Within the cities themselves, a multitude of laborers lived and worked, employed in jobs ranging from stevedores to liverymen, from fishwives to housemaids. Of all these gainfully employed commoners, the women vendors of Lisbon provide an especially interesting example of the pattern of class and status within an occupational group. Moreover, their careers suggest that the stereotypic view of the Portuguese woman of that era as being a sheltered, demure creature has a distinct class bias to it, being probably more applicable to the wives of noblemen, *letrados*, and wealthy merchants than to average women.[84]

Generally, women vendors could not sell their wares without a license from the city council. During the 1690s, and probably before and after, quite a number of unlicensed women illegally hawked shellfish, sardines, and larger fish in the city squares and streets. Those women caught breaking the law were fined and jailed for up to thirty days.[85]

After the establishment of the monopolistic Junta do Tabaco in 1674, women tobacco vendors were exempted from *câmara* jurisdiction and became instead answerable to the crown's contractors who, in turn, were under the junta's control. During the years 1678 through 1682, at least seven of the outlets for the monopolized product were run by women.[86] In 1680, there were more than sixty tobacco shops (*estancos*) in Lisbon and its *termo*, but, according to the junta's officials, the outnumbered women were well suited to be tobacconists, even though they seldom possessed sufficient capital to run an *estanco* in their own names.[87] Nevertheless, there were apparently some women who independently ran prosperous tobacco shops. As we will see in a later chapter, women, especially nuns, also played an important role in the preparation and distribution of contraband tobacco.

One of the most interesting groups of vendors was the *medideiras*, the women who sold bread in the Terreiro do Paço, the major square in downtown Lisbon. In 1699, there were thirty-one licensed *medideiras*, but of these only eight to ten women had personal holdings of any consequence. Within this latter group, however there were five prosperous women (*mulheres poderosas*) who had gained a virtual monopoly over bread sales in the Terreiro. These women had outflanked their competition by sending their husbands out to meet wheat farmers bringing grain to market. The spouses bought up much of the wheat the *lavradores* had to sell, thereby cornering the market. In some instances, the husbands may even have waylaid the farmers, stealing their produce. Once the grain was secured, by fair means or foul, the five *medideiras*, it was alleged, sold their freshly baked bread at exorbitant prices.[88]

In attempting to combat the "bread oligopoly," the city council urged D. Pedro II to increase the number of vendor licenses. Quite understandably, consumers and other *medideiras* were not happy with the situation.[89] It is not certain how much success the complainants had, but it appears that they suspected some sort of collusion between the five *medideiras* and the *fidalgo* class since the latter always seemed to have an ample supply of bread. By 1703, the situation seems to have improved somewhat in the Terreiro, for bread was then in plentiful supply.[90]

As diverse groups in their own right, the winegrowers of the countryside and the women vendors of the city illustrated the variety within that mass of subjects known as *o povo*. Despite their diversity, all groups within both the agrarian and urban segments of *o povo* were suffused with a common understanding of the individual's place in society. Social advancement was usually confined to moving to the fore of an occupational group into which an individual had been born. Having made this advance, a select few might join the mercantile class, for example. Not surprisingly, the privileged estates shared the understanding of the individual's place. As António Oliveira has pointed out, even penniless titled individuals who had to rely on charity for their very existence steadfastly clung to their noble pretensions.[91]

Improvement in status was not necessarily contingent on personal wealth or accomplishment, as New Christian merchants well understood. Bloodlines and service to the crown were of overriding importance in most instances. But this last criterion, together with substantial wealth, sometimes opened the door of noble status, even to New Christians. In pursuit of that occasional opening for themselves or their descendants, merchants and *letrados* bought land in emulation of the nobility and guildsmen aspired to send their sons to the universities. The chance for noble status was far removed from most commoners, but some, like the five *medideiras* of Lisbon, became part of the *petite bourgeoisie*. Commoners rarely showed any inclination toward changing the social order of the Old Regime; instead, they sought to improve their own or their descendants' position in it. When rebellions such as the 1661 Oporto uprising occurred, they usually were aimed at the tax collector, not the social order.

Two further examples of this sort of uprising are the riots of 1684 in Sacavem and 1688 in Alcoutim. The first was precipitated when officials from Lisbon caught some fishermen using nets that had a smaller mesh than was allowed by the city council for fishing in the Tagus. The limit on mesh size had been imposed to prevent depletion of the river's supply of fish. The city officials, who were aboard a small frigate (*fragata*), followed three fishing boats into the small port of Sacavem and asked to see the suspect nets. What followed was a rock-throwing melee in which the fishermen, their wives, and other villagers pelted the hapless officials with rocks and insults, calling them thieves and adding that they killed thieves. All of the city officials received nasty wounds before retreating.[92]

Nearly a year later, the king's lack of concern over the whole affair was rather obvious, for no formal inquiry (*devassa*) had taken place and the city council was complaining that it was being made to look ineffectual. Apparently, this complaint fell on deaf ears since D. Pedro II did not even bother to respond.[93]

Although the outcome of the Alcoutim riot is less clear, the circumstances were similar. The *vila* of Alcoutim had apparently long been a center for smuggling between the Algarve and nearby Andalusia. In this case, the commodity in question was not fish but tobacco. The residents of Alcoutim were smuggling inexpensively prepared tobacco into Portugal from Spain and selling the contraband product throughout the province, thereby depriving the Portuguese contractor of business. In an attempt to stop the illicit traffic, a superintendent of the Junta do Tabaco had a search of the *vila* made. Substantial quantities of illicit tobacco and snuff were found, but at that point "the whole population rose in arms." The Junta's officials had to flee the area by back roads, being pursued, not only by enraged members of the popular classes, but by the governing officials of the town as well. According to the superintendent, only the intercession of the village prior prevented him and his fellows from being killed.[94]

Here again, the rioters vented their rage on government officials but not on the form of government itself. Moreover, there is no evidence available to suggest that the crown punished Alcoutim for its outburst. Perhaps the king understood that the violent outbursts of some commoners against government officials were the acts of unruly but loyal subjects.

The Lowest Strata

The lowest elements of the third estate (*a gente baixa*) were not regarded by contemporaries as members of *o povo* but as people apart and below. It is not altogether clear which groups were included in this category, but *a gente baixa* seems to have been a catchall term for the marginal elements in Portuguese society. The category included petty thieves and smugglers, drunkards, prostitutes, beggars, gypsies, idlers, thugs, and the like. Whether there was a clear distinction between criminal or socially reprehensible individuals and the destitute but law-abiding is uncertain, but the term *a gente baixa* appears to have referred primarily to unsavory and disreputable elements.[95] However, extremely poor people, orphans, and slaves will be included in this category in the present discussion.

The presence of dependent and criminal elements posed a challenge to other classes of the Old Regime. The sick and the destitute had to be cared for and the lawbreakers had to be punished if social order were to be preserved. Thanks to institutions such as the Santas Casas de Misericórdia (charitable brotherhoods), many poor, sick, and orphaned people received succor.[96] A document of 1673, for example, revealed that the Misericórdia of Lisbon took in between three and four hundred orphans every year.[97] But the charitable activities of Misericórdias and other philanthropic endeavors undoubtedly reached only a fraction of the needy, especially when war, disease, or hunger stalked the land.

After the Restoration campaigns of the 1660s, the demobilization of thousands of soldiers probably created considerable social and economic dislocation. Those soldiers who remained in uniform also created problems. In Lisbon soldiers repeatedly commandeered food and fuel without paying for them.[98]

The periodic depredations of soldiers were but part of a regime of chronic and pervasive criminality that plagued seventeenth-century Lisbon. Thieves and thugs victimized rich and poor alike, often with little fear of arrest and punishment. Thanks to the venality and corruption of police officials and jailors, the criminal element acted with impunity, knowing that even when they were picked up their chances of a quick return to the streets were good. Even if the police forces had been above reproach, their numbers were too small and they were so lacking in proper coordination that they stood little chance of success against the problem at hand. Moreover, dedicated officials were confronted by widespread disrespect for authorities such as themselves and not inconsiderable risk to their own lives (or the lives of would-be witnesses) when they attempted to carry out their duties. Further complicating the job of the police, the lack of street illumination allowed criminals to commit their crimes and slip away more easily into the night.[99]

An increase in begging also plagued postwar Lisbon. Beggars had become so numerous in the capital by 1671 that it was decided to lock them up when they did not have a license to beg. This policy seems to have stemmed in part from the fact that many able-bodied men, among them ex-soldiers, no doubt, had opted for begging instead of working or else were unable to find work. In 1685, a plethora of beggars still plagued the city and, reflecting on the practice of imprisoning panhandlers, the city council found it unsatisfactory. The prisons became overcrowded, the inmates were malnourished because the city could not afford to feed them all, and, as a result, they suffered from numerous forms of sickness. No acceptable solution was forthcoming, however, and the *câmara* could only recommend that the beggars be shipped to the colonies as settlers.[100]

Other problems of the poor periodically surfaced in the documents produced by the Lisbon city council. A 1670 *consulta*, for instance, reveals that there was an insufficient number of small-denomination coins in circulation for use by the poor. The lack of small copper and silver coinage caused additional difficulties for beggars since charitable passersby were less likely to part with larger coins. Three years after the 1670 *consulta* was submitted, nothing had still been done about the shortage and then, according to the *câmara*, the problem had become so acute that trade in less costly items was being impeded by the lack of small change.[101] Finally, in 1676, the Lisbon mint began to stamp out new low-denomination coins of copper, a metal chronically in short supply.[102]

Historians do not know to what extent the social deterioration of seventeenth-century Spain, which was characterized by population decline, begging, banditry, vagabondage, idleness, and the general impoverishment of the lower classes, was duplicated in the Portugal of D. Pedro II.[103] These problems and others were indeed present, but Portugal's somewhat healthier economy prevented a replication of the severe economic and social dislocation endured by commoners in Hapsburg Spain. Furthermore, as Aurélio Oliveira has shown, some regions of Portugal even prospered during the depressed 1670s.[104]

In other parts of the country, however, vagabondage, banditry, and smuggling were rife. The Luso-Spanish border was periodically crossed by bands of roaming gypsies, who were despised for their alleged thievery and deviousness.[105] The same border was penetrated by all manner of smugglers. In the Algarve, a province fraught with contraband trade, more than 120 smugglers of illicit Spanish tobacco were in jail in 1690.[106] Twelve years later, the usually crowded prisons of Lisbon were further jammed with men convicted of tobacco-related crimes.[107] Bandits prowled the highways and back roads of many areas, while petty thieves plagued the cities and *vilas* of the country.[108]

Despite the marginal and often risky lives led by the members of the lower strata of society, they enjoyed a modicum of respect as human beings and sympathy for their condition, even when in jail. The Church provided some of their numbers with charitable support and even sanctuary. The city councils of Lisbon and other cities, usually through the *juiz do povo*, sometimes interceded to alleviate the lot of the downtrodden. In 1669, for example, an impoverished widow over eighty years of age had broken one of Lisbon's city ordinances and thus was liable to the punishment of being flogged. The *câmara* appealed on her behalf to the crown, asking leniency. This was granted, and the old woman was spared the whip.[109]

The modest succor and personal recognition available to the poorer and even criminal classes were seldom to be had by those on the lowest rung of Portuguese society, the slaves. Before the law, slaves were usually regarded as little more than property and as such could not expect to find sanctuary in churches. When recaptured after an escape attempt, they were subject to brutal floggings of up to forty lashes.

During the mid-sixteenth century, approximately ten percent of the population of Lisbon were slaves.[110] During that same century, it has been estimated that ten percent of the population of the Algarve were also slaves.[111] The slave population was made up of blacks (*negros*), mulattos, Indians from the subcontinent, and Moors. By the seventeenth century, however, the number of Moorish and Oriental slaves had probably dropped considerably, thanks to legislation that constricted their importation into Portugal.[112] Occasional documentary references suggest, however, that the number of black slaves remained statistically significant. In 1687, the Lisbon city council complained about insolent slaves, especially those of the wealthy, who illegally bore arms and were the cause of constant disturbances.[113] During the same era, this time in 1689, there were complaints about *negros* drinking with working men in the beer taverns of Lisbon.[114] Some of these blacks, however, may well have been free laborers and not slaves.

The *negros* of Portugal and its island possessions, not to mention the thousands of black slaves in Brazil, could be found engaged in all sorts of activities, including farming, fishing, vending, domestic labor, and even artisanal occupations.[115] In Lisbon, for example, a group of black women regularly sold millet and rice in the Rossio.[116] Despite the well-known outrages of slavery, blacks and others held in this state had some legal protection from the excesses of slaveowners, and, moreover, they or their children could sometimes obtain their freedom through manumission.

In both Portugal and Brazil, numerous brotherhoods of free blacks and mulattos endeavored to buy the freedom of enslaved brethren. In Lisbon, the brotherhood of the Rosary of São Salvador petitioned the crown in 1688, asking that slaveowners be prevented from selling their *negros* outside the metropolis. Such sales frustrated attempts to free fellows who were being sold to foreigners or Brazilians. D. Pedro II responded favorably to the brotherhood's petition, ordering that Portuguese slaves not be sold outside the kingdom and that their selling price be set at the going market value, not the exorbitant rates some owners were attempting to exact from would-be black liberators. By the same decree, the king reconfirmed the Lisbon brotherhood's right to beg alms on Sundays, the accumulation of which often bought the freedom of black slaves.[117] But however freed, many *negros* in Portugal could do little more than subsist through back-breaking labor as stevedores and agricultural workers or as petty thieves, vagabonds, and prostitutes.[118]

The Portuguese of D. Pedro II's era harbored their share of prejudices against blacks and others, but they were certainly no more bigoted and probably more tolerant than other Europeans. Luso-Atlantic slaveowners could be both brutal and enlightened in their treatment of blacks and mulattos. In discussing the complex issue of race relations, C. R. Boxer related that, while Brazilian slaveowners could flog their *negros* to death for trivial offenses, they might also show genuine affection and generosity toward individual slaves. One spectacular, if highly unusual, display of the latter sentiment took place in Lisbon in 1708, when the Visconde de Ponte de Lima "appeared in the bull-ring . . . with a retinue of twenty husky Negroes, whom he had bought a few days previously, all of them richly dressed and with the certificates of freedom which he had given them tied to their arms."[119]

But this rather bizarre spectacle does not bely the existence of deeply rooted prejudices and presumptions about blacks and others. In addition to the cultural, psychological, religious, and other components of prejudice, there was an underlying economic aspect to it. At base, slavery was an institution predicated on exploiting black labor for economic gain. Many Portuguese believed that blacks were congenitally inferior beings and the economic benefits derived from enslaving them were instrumental in perpetuating this belief.[120]

Albeit to a much lesser degree, other groups also were victims of prejudice tinged with self-interest. Gypsies, for example, were regarded as an infestation of thieves and sharp traders that should be expelled. Since the early sixteenth century, periodic attempts had been made to expel them, apparently without much success. Responding to the complaints of property owners and tradesmen in 1654, D. João IV had moved to rid Portugal of the colorful nomads, ordering that they be rounded up and sent to the Maranhão. This order, however, also seems to have accomplished little since another expulsion edict was promulgated in 1665. In 1668, the popular estate of the Lisbon Cortes had called for more rigorous measures against the despised gypsies, unfairly blaming them for Portugal's shortage of copper coinage.[121] During the last quarter of the seventeenth century, a great number of gypsies were still in the country. Many lived in Lisbon and engaged in horse trading, which, according to one observer, was "the pretext for their thefts, selling in one region what they steal in another, going from fair to fair throughout the country using the same tricks."[122]

Despite various measures taken to rid the country of them, gypsies had become so numerous in Portugal that in 1689 it was decided that they should be gathered onto reservations and put to work at honest occupations. But this novel scheme also failed, and in 1694, 1707, and 1717 the crown issued further orders for their expulsion.[123]

In yet another instance in which intolerance intertwined with economic interest, the goldsmiths of Lisbon lobbied against the instruction of *negros*, mulattos, and Indians in the art of working gold, asserting that such a noble and sensitive occupation should not be opened to people who were by nature untrustworthy.[124] Given the goldsmiths' periodic attempts to limit competition, their argument rings rather hollow. Clearly, economic motives played a part in the expression of prejudice against other racial and ethnic groups. As we will see in the next chapter, a great deal of racist animosity was reserved for New Christians, especially those possessed of significant wealth.

Like other segments of Portuguese society, the lowest strata were a heterogeneous mixture composed of the poorest, most downtrodden elements of society as well as those who lived outside of the law. Even within the lowest classes, however, the common aspiration to status and position was surely at work. Though most sought simply to survive and gain the respect of their fellows, aberrations sometimes occurred. In 1687, for example, the Lisbon city council disgustedly complained that the *negro* slaves of the powerful had taken on the airs of their masters.[125] While extreme, this example suggests that the preoccupation with status was common to all classes of Portuguese society.

The Individual's Place and Social Equilibrium

Despite exploitation by the privileged and limited opportunities for social advancement, Portuguese commoners did not necessarily feel that they were the victims of an oppressive system. Instead, the social order was held together by the "motley feudal ties," to use Marx and Engel's expression, that bound all classes and groups together and through which the "right" of "natural superiors" to rule was understood and accepted by the commoners. The medieval relationship of ruler to ruled still had force in Portugal and, as Walter Ullmann put it:

We should not think that subjects in any way felt that they were oppressed or suppressed. The awareness of being suppressed presupposes considerable knowledge and critical judgement. Furthermore, the individuals and their aggregate, the people, had every opportunity of expressing their requests, petitions and aims; and in times of stress and tension the king was well advised to listen to the people.[126]

Popular sentiment had nudged Prince Regent Pedro toward a peaceful settlement with Spain in 1668, but there was no question that the decision was to be made according to his will and not in response to the wishes of petitioners and protesters. As it was suggested above, tbe unrest in Oporto, Sacavem, and Alcoutim, as well as other contemporary manifestations of social tension, were not challenges to the social order but angry outbursts against taxation and bureaucrats.

While acceptance of the status quo by the lower classes partially explains the longevity of the Old Regime, it should be reiterated that movement up the social ladder was possible, albeit usually quite limited. This possibility (together with the option of seeking one's fortune in the colonies) was an important factor in maintaining the fealty of the third estate and thus social equilibrium.

Commoners, of course, were usually less a threat to order in the Old Regime than a restive nobility. But like its counterparts most everywhere else in western Europe, the nobility of late seventeenth-century Portugal had lost its struggle to erode monarchical authority. Nevertheless, the nobility remained the dominant class. "The nobility paled like the stars of the morning before the rising sun of the monarchy, as the imagery of the day described it. But the stars continued to shine in the firmament."

The collaboration of the monarchy and a chastened nobility, which had emerged shaken but still intact after the economic and political setbacks of the decades prior to 1668, was yet another important factor in preserving the social order. Although the crowned heads of Europe never succeeded in bringing their nobles completely to heel, they could rely on them to maintain public order, to defend regions in which they owned property, and to carry the fight to domestic or foreign adversaries.[127]

Even though the struggle for the Restoration had undoubtedly caused much economic dislocation, the nature of production and ownership had not changed. Domestic agricultural production remained the mainstay of the economy. The nobility still controlled most of the land and the people who worked on it. Destabilization deriving from the emergence of new classes and modes of production was not present.

The only cloud that threatened to obscure the celestial scenario quoted earlier was the wealth and influence of the mercantile class. Merchant wealth was viewed as an ominous threat by many within the privileged classes, for it could (and often did) turn the head of a king and, through the burgeoning of international trade, threatened to change an economy rooted in agrarian production to one based on commercial capitalism.

The merchants themselves, however, aspired to the same honors, privileges, and status that the nobility enjoyed and thus converted substantial portions of their monetary wealth into land. "The bourgeoisie," according to Fernand Braudel, "knew what it was doing and no small measure of calculation entered into its purchases. It turned to land as a prime safe investment, thus reinforcing a social order based on aristocratic privilege."[128]

The resurgence of the Portuguese nobility after 1668 coincided with a decline of the merchants' influence. This occurred in part when individual merchants continued to "defect" from their class for the security of landed property and the status that went with it. But, since most of the members of the mercantile class were New Christians, the persecutions of the Holy Inquisition also had a hand in diminishing their presence in the social firmament.

CHAPTER IV

THE NEW CHRISTIAN CHALLENGE TO THE ESTABLISHED ORDER

> Those that favour the Jews pretend to do it for the good of the commonwealth, those that do not, for the good of the Church.
>
> Francis Parry, English envoy in Lisbon (1675)

> Aqui se diz pùblicamente que em Portugal e melhor ser inquisidor que rei.
>
> António Vieira, S. J., writing from Rome (1673)

During the early years of D. Pedro II's reign, the predominantly New Christian mercantile class made a concerted effort to obtain relief from the activities of the Holy Inquisition. The struggle that ensued lasted for more than a decade and was finally resolved in favor of the status quo. Though issues of race and religion characterized the debate that raged between pro– and anti–New Christian factions, class conflict lay at the root of the struggle. Conflict between the merchants and the privileged classes had gone on for centuries in Portugal and was to continue long after the death of D. Pedro II, but the suppression of the mercantile class during the first third of his reign marked an especially important victory for the established order. Nearly a century was to pass before the mercantile class again presented a significant challenge to the stability of the Old Regime.

Although questions of religious orthodoxy and racial purity obscure the underlying nature of the conflict from the present-day viewer, the combatants themselves, if asked, would surely have defined the struggle in terms of those same issues. Most clerics and *familiares* of the Inquisition, for example, undoubtedly believed that the New Christians posed an ever-present threat to the Catholic faith. Furthermore, the nobility's passion for purity of blood was not merely a cynical ploy for keeping New Christian merchants out of positions of prestige and influence. Despite a substantial portion of Jewish blood within their own ranks, many nobles were convinced that such ties were indeed "unclean." The lower classes harbored numerous prejudices and superstitions toward New Christians and, like the privileged estates, subscribed to the notion that businesspeople of Jewish ancestry were especially unscrupulous and greedy.

But these factors obscure the foundations of anti–New Christian sentiment in Portugal. Viewing the setbacks of the mercantile class after 1668 as the result of class conflict offers clearer insight into an important juncture in the development of Portuguese society. Previous use of this sort of analysis has been rather unsatisfactory. On the one hand, it has been burdened by rather simplistic application and, on the other, by admission of its at least partial validity, but little elaborative discussion. In an analysis in which the struggle was defined as being between the nobility and the bourgeoisie, António Saraiva attempted to show that New Christians had in fact been assimilated and had all but shed their Jewish beliefs by the late seventeenth century. Saraiva further argued that the Inquisition, in league with the nobility, perpetuated the myth of the crypto-Jew in order to suppress the predominantly New Christian mercantile class and, in the process, to fill its coffers with confiscated wealth.[1] Historians are presented with the spectacle of a parasitic, self-aggrandizing bureaucracy working in concert with the privileged estates to preserve the seignorial regime by falsely questioning the religious orthodoxy of businesspeople, even when their Jewish forebears were two or three generations removed.

The contention that New Christians had actually shed their attachment to Judaism and had been, for the most part, assimilated into the religious mainstream has been rather convincingly refuted by David Grant Smith, who has presented numerous examples of the persistence of Jewish belief in Portugal. During the seventeenth century, those subjects with Jewish ancestors were neither all converts to Catholicism nor all clandestine adepts of Judaism. There were "many

Jewish martyrs who submitted to death at the stake rather than confess the 'error' of their belief and adopt Christianity." Many others were, "to all appearances, sincere Catholics."[2]

Though Smith clearly showed the limitations of assimilation, his treatment of class conflict was less illuminating. At one point he noted that the Portuguese Consulado, a merchant organization patterned after the powerful Consulado of Seville, may have survived for only ten years after its establishment in 1592 because its "power began to pose too great a threat to the [Portuguese] nobility . . . ." In his discussion of the perpetuation of the distinction between Old and New Christian, he observed, "Exactly why Portuguese society went to such lengths to preserve and reinforce the distinction remains an unanswered question. Obviously, pure anti-Semitism was a major factor. Saraiva's explanation based on a theory of class conflict undoubtedly has a certain validity but it is far from wholly satisfactory."[3]

At these and other points in his study, Smith recognized the significance of class conflict in the changing fortunes of the mercantile community, but he never really pursued this line of analysis. His lack of follow-up is, to an extent, understandable, since available documentation does not readily lend itself to making a strong case for (or against) class conflict. One seldom finds, for example, nobles, clerics, or commoners arguing against New Christian pretensions in strictly economic terms. But one must ask whether "pure anti-Semitism" has a life of its own or whether it is symptomatic of underlying class antagonisms.

As one might expect, anti–New Christian writings focused on the alleged threat to the purity of blood and the faith and on the presumed perfidy of New Christians. An outpouring of such writings occurred during the 1670s, ranging from malicious graffiti scrawled on church walls to lengthy polemics. These expressions of hostile sentiment commonly portrayed the New Christians as enemies of the faith who used their wealth to buy off influential figures in the government and the Church. The last stanza of an anonymous poem written in 1673 captured the essence and tone of many of these anti–New Christian writings.

> A Divindade offendida,
> O Nosso Deos ultrajado,
> O Principe enganado,

> A Christandade vendida,
> A Igreja escurecida,
> O Triumpho da fé sem palma
> Desvalida a Lei dos Ceõs.
> Ai de ti, Reino sem Deos!
> Ai de ti, povo sem alma!

This same poem, which was composed in response to D. Pedro's favorable reception of a New Christian scheme to extend financial support to the crown in exchange for relief from inquisitorial persecution, also expressed the fear that Jewish blood would one day inundate the country. "In days less than a few," the anonymous poet proclaimed, "we shall all become Jews."[4]

The fear that an increasingly larger proportion of the population was becoming tainted by New Christian blood was not simply an expression of poetic license. Although historians do not know the percentage of the population that had Jewish ancestry, an English visitor to Lisbon in 1693 calculated that, despite continual persecution, New Christians and Jews comprised one-third of the population.[5]

The fetish for *limpeza da sangre* was such that it might take only one Jewish ancestor, even though two or three generations removed, to mark inalterably a family as New Christians. Thus, the proportion of New Christians in the population grew larger every time they married Old Christians and had children. During a session of the 1668 Cortes, an alarmed nobleman warned that

> this matter is extremely important, and of very ruinous consequences for the future. We already see that almost everybody in the kingdom is related to these people, which is a great pity, and that from hence forward there will be no one who has the purity of blood which is required for public duties and offices, not even for those of the Ministry of the Holy Office of the Inquisition.[6]

Like our unknown poet, the worried nobleman undoubtedly exaggerated the threat, but he was certainly correct in implying that many of the nobles themselves bore the stigma, however well disguised, of Jewish ancestry. After the prestigious Brotherhood of Nobles was established in 1663 to assure continuing purity of blood, it was discovered that a majority of noble families were unable to certify that their lineage was spotless.[7]

Some of those in the anti–New Christian camp were not content with mere railing against the seemingly ubiquitous presence of New Christian blood. They offered drastic solutions to the problem. A number of remedial measures were proposed in the *Perfidia judaica*, a carefully reasoned, if bigoted, tract written by Roque Monteiro Paim, an important figure in D. Pedro's government who later became the king's private secretary.[8] Paim advocated the expulsion of all individuals convicted of judaizing, as well as the imposition of harsh restrictions on the rest of the New Christian population, including deprivation of all honors and titles and the prohibition of mixed marriages. Paim shared the conviction that New Christian numbers were multiplying so rapidly that within a few years no Old Christians would be left to try them for apostasy and other crimes.[9] Though Roque Monteiro Paim and his fellows may not have simplistically equated purity of blood with purity of faith, they did believe that the tendency toward heresy and apostasy was endemic among those subjects who had Jewish ancestors.

Even though the vast majority of New Christians never penetrated the upper ranks of the mercantile class, they too fell victim to many of the biases directed at powerful merchants. To most Old Christians in seventeenth-century Portugal, whether aristocrats or commoners, the term *cristão-novo* would have conjured up a whole galaxy of presumed attributes and characteristics that would have immediately applied to anyone so designated. To [them] New Christians were secret Jews; they mocked the Church, they desecrated sacred images; they would not eat pork, rabbit, hare or shellfish; they became rich by dishonest selling practices and gouged Old Christians for taxes they farmed. The ignorant maintained fantastic beliefs about the monstrousness of New Christians: that [their] doctors and apothecaries systematically poisoned ... Old Christian patients, that their men menstruated, etc.[10]

Such beliefs, together with the fear of increasing New Christian numbers, should be regarded as symptomatic of a deeper conflict within Portuguese society. Fear and bigotry were expressions of an underlying confrontation between the status quo and the socioeconomic changes that undoubtedly would have occurred if New Christians, particularly the mercantile class, had been allowed to flourish unmolested. The nearly hysterical reaction to one episode of the merchant challenge, the details of which will be examined shortly, had its roots sunk deeply in the soil of class conflict. And such reactions most typically manifested themselves in virulent opposition to deviations from Catholic orthodoxy, the chief defender of which was the Holy Office of the Inquisition.

New Christians and the Holy Office

The influx of thousands of Jews into Portugal after their expulsion from Spain in 1492 was the principal justification for the permanent establishment of an inquisitorial tribunal in 1547. The fifty-five-year delay was, in part, the result of adroit lobbying in Rome by the Sephardic émigrés, their descendants, and others who opposed the activities of the Holy Office. An important argument used by the refugees was that most Jewish immigrants had been forcibly converted to Christianity in 1497. Opponents of the Inquisition could thereafter argue that Spanish Jews were being assimilated into Portuguese society as "New Christians."

The forcible conversion of Jewish émigrés was, in large measure, a rather shrewd maneuver on the part of the reigning monarch, Manuel I, to appease the intolerant Spaniards while keeping the influx of Sephardim, many of whom were prosperous and talented individuals, within Portuguese borders. Appeasement was necessary since D. Manuel, who entertained hopes of eventually inheriting the Spanish throne, had agreed to expel the Jews from Portugal as a condition of his planned marriage to the daughter of Ferdinand and Isabela. The king, however, probably never seriously considered the expulsion of the Jews since he had witnessed the social and economic dislocation that afflicted Spain after their eviction and appreciated the importance of skilled and wealthy subjects. Given time, it was believed that the *cristãos novos* would indeed be assimilated and become true Christians instead of nominal converts.[11]

Although the forced conversion of Jews, which included mass baptisms and efforts to prevent their leaving Portugal, alleviated the pressure for expulsion, anti-Semites still clamored for redress, claiming, no doubt correctly, that many of the immigrants had changed their faith in name only. The persistent presence of judaizers in Portugal became a powerful argument for the long-deferred establishment of the Holy Office in 1547.[12]

During the following decades, the Inquisition set up offices in various Portuguese cities. Eventually, three powerful tribunals, those of Lisbon, Évora, and Coimbra, held sway. Meanwhile, many New Christians were assimilated into Portuguese society and took their places in all classes. After making fortunes in commerce, some families even established *morgados* and settled down to life as minor landed nobility, successfully blending into the Old Christian aristocracy as time shrouded their Jewish origins.[13]

Whatever their class, numerous New Christians secretly clung to their Jewish beliefs, which, over time, evolved into a syncretistic mixture of Judaism and Christianity called Marranism. Although this hybrid faith was never formally organized and was by no means understood and practiced in the same fashion by all of its adherents, a distinguishing feature of Marranism was the unorthodox notion that personal salvation could be achieved by believing in Mosaic Law. Isolation from other Jewish brethren probably accounted for the Marranos' deviation from orthodox Judaism.[14]

The converts (*conversos*) of 1497 and their descendants fell into three general categories: those who were sincere believers in Catholicism, those who covertly practiced Judaism, and those whose convictions were so ill defined or loosely held that they could be readily changed in order to further economic or professional interests. Merchants of the latter type, for example, practiced Catholicism when in Portugal but joined with their Jewish brethren when in Amsterdam or some other center of tolerance.[15] Not unexpectedly, the activities of the latter two categories drew the Holy Office's greatest attention, but devoutly Catholic New Christians were also caught up in its net.

While ostensibly a judicial body concerned with matters of apostasy, heresy, witchcraft, sexual aberrations, various other deviations from orthodoxy, and censorship (a purview of obvious importance), the Portuguese Inquisition was also a powerful bureaucracy that had accumulated vast political and religious influence since its creation in 1547. The Holy Office acted as both a royal tribunal and a representative of papal authority, but neither king nor pope had real control over it. The crown-appointed inquisitor general headed a bureaucratic establishment that theoretically answered to two masters but, in reality, answered to neither. Thanks to this relative autonomy, the inquisitor general, together with a council of deputies that he named, enlarged the Inquisition almost unimpeded, appointing as many functionaries and *familiares* as they saw fit. Like any typical bureaucracy, the Holy Office sought to expand its size and field of action, an impulse facilitated by the lack of royal and papal restraint.[16] During the seventeenth century, at least, the behavior of the Portuguese tribunal strongly suggested that it enjoyed greater autonomy than its Spanish couterpart, which "was in every way an instrument of royal policy and remained politically subject to the crown."[17]

During its "golden age," which lasted from the mid-sixteenth century until the time of Pombal, the Holy Office derived its income and properties from a variety of sources. Periodic subsidies were granted by both the crown and the papacy to defray the costs of salaries and numerous other operating expenses. The costs of scaffolding, seating, decorations, refreshments, and salaries made autos-da-fé particularly expensive spectacles.[18] As one Portuguese historian put it, this "tribunal did not function cheaply."[19]

At some point during the Babylonian Captivity (1580–1640), the Inquisition significantly augmented its income by securing the right to keep for itself the confiscated wealth of its victims. Even before this, in an enabling *regimento* in 1572, the crown, for a reason not yet understood, abandoned its claim to the property of the convicted. In its connection with the Inquisition, the royal treasury became little more than the transit point for wealth destined for the Holy Office, a role that seems to have been firmly cast with the publication of another *regimento* in 1620. Securing this additional source of income was probably but one aspect, albeit an important one, of the consolidation and extension of inquisitorial power, a process that appears to have been facilitated by the absence of the Portuguese monarchy.[20]

The Restoration of 1640 was greeted with little enthusiasm by the Inquisition. The extent of its actual loyalty to Madrid is difficult to ascertain, but the well-known involvement of Inquisitor General D. Francisco de Castro in a plot to assassinate D. João IV in 1641 gave a clear indication of the tribunal's desire to eliminate threats to its expanding political and economic power. Eight years later, the inquisitors became infuriated by one crucial provision in the establishment of the Brazil Company. The property of New Christian backers of the company who faced arrest by the Holy Office was then exempted by law from inventory and confiscation unless the suspects refused to abjure alleged deviance from Catholicism. The Inquisition, of course, was not in business simply to shake down New Christians, but their loss of access to a valuable source of income was undoubtedly a crucial consideration in the inquisitors' extraordinary efforts to overturn the 1649 law. D. João IV's death in 1656 was quickly exploited by the inquisitors and their supporters and during the following year the controversial exemption was withdrawn.

The Holy Office's vehement reaction to what amounted to a perpetual pardon of many New Christian merchants suggested the tribunal's financial dependence on confiscated wealth. During the mid-seventeenth century, the Lisbon Inquisition was in especially difficult financial straits and was truly threatened by the ban on confiscations. In 1655, the Évora tribunal petitioned the crown for financial support, claiming that it was about to collapse for lack of funds. The Eborense inquisitors also made known their intention to defy the crown by continuing the prohibited confiscations.[21] It is indeed ironic that the Portuguese Inquisition depended on its despised victims for its very survival.[22]

In his Marxian analysis of the economic nature of the Holy Office, António Saraiva uncompromisingly argued that

the Inquisition was not a commercial enterprise, but a vehicle for distributing money and other property to its numerous personnel—a form of pillage as in war, albeit more bureaucratized. The inquisitorial army, whose members shared in the seignorial and warrior mentality of the *fidalgos* of India, maintained themselves by plundering the property of wealthy burghers.[23]

Although this rather narrow view of the Holy Office does not, for example, take into account the genuine religious conviction of many inquisitors, it focuses attention on the Inquisition's unquestionable interest in New Christian wealth. The numerous officials to whom the wealth of the bourgeoisie was redistributed included everyone from the inquisitor general himself to *procuradores*, notaries, and the already-mentioned *familiares*.

The *familiares* were of obvious importance for Saraiva's discussion of class conflict, for with the prestigious position of *familiar* the interests of the Holy Office and the privileged classes were most clearly joined. The element of prestige was indeed quite important in gaining the cooperation of the privileged classes in inquisitorial activities.

John Stevens, an Englishman resident in Lisbon during the era, observed, "This employment is accounted so Honorable, that Persons of the greatest Quality sue for, and are proud to be admitted to it."[24]

Besides enjoying an increment in personal status, those who became *familiares* played an important role in the activities of the Inquisition. Indeed, they did much of the Holy Office's "leg work," acting as spies, captors, and guards. When, for example, a *familiar's* report on a suspected judaizer resulted in an order for that person's imprisonment, the *familiar* and perhaps some colleagues arrested the accused. When autos-da-fé occurred, the *familiares* accompanied the procession of prisoners to the ceremony. Although *familiares* were paid no actual salary, they did receive a per diem of 500 reis when in service. They also wore a special habit while acting on behalf of the Holy Office and received a variety of privileges and exemptions in recognition of their status and presumed purity of blood.[25]

Toward the end of the seventeenth century, the number of *familiares* had grown to such an extent that D. Pedro II decided that the position should be held to 601 officeholders.[26] This limitation only served to make the position more prestigious. Even before the ceiling figure was imposed, the status attached to the office was such that almost all of the positions were filled by clerics, nobles, and *letrados*. As a result of this, an inordinate number of artisans and peasants were brought before the tribunal while privileged commoners and *letrados* were picked up only occasionally and nobles hardly at all.[27]

The principal victims of this class discrimination, of course, were individuals with Jewish ancestry, a group that constituted upwards of seventy-five percent of the mercantile class and probably a sizable fraction of prosperous elements within the artisan and peasant classes as well. As we saw in the case of Francisco Carlos, even those few New Christian merchants who attained noble status found that their elevated position did not always protect them from the inquisitors. New Christian merchants who had obtained some measure of privileged status thus seemed to be an exception to the Holy Office's discrimination against the lower classes.

Once a *familiar* or someone else had anonymously denounced an individual, the suspect was usually imprisoned and his (or her) properties were sequestered and inventoried. When the prisoner was adjudged guilty, his (or her) properties were sometimes let at public auction and portable wealth such as silver, gold, and gems was kept in the Santo Ofício's own treasury. When the prisoner owed debts, his (or her) creditors were allowed to come forward and claim the amounts due them. Confiscation applied not only to the net worth of the suspect upon the date of incarceration but also to income received during the period over which the crime was allegedly committed. Thus, sales or other transactions previously made could be annulled and the value of the exchange, or the items themselves, claimed by the Inquisition.[28] In 1671, for example, Pero Gomes de Lemos, a New Christian physician from Moura, had sold some ewes shortly before his imprisonment by the Évora tribunal. After a brief deliberation, the inquisitors determined that the price of the sale was owed to their treasury.[29]

During the following year, the Lisbon Inquisition confiscated properties from a New Christian merchant that were much more valuable than those of the unfortunate village doctor. This hapless merchant, Fernão Rodriques Penso, who fell victim to the same repressive wave that struck Francisco Carlos, lost properties that included a large home that fronted on the Rossio and the valuable furnishings and silverware inside the home. The inquisitors also confiscated a sack of uncut diamonds, numerous other gems, and items of silver and gold, as well as Penso's *quinta* in the suburb of Palhavã, his horses, coaches, and other possessions. The property taken from Penso, a very wealthy man but certainly not the only such captive of the Santo Ofício, was substantially greater in value than the annual operating expenses of the Lisbon city council.[30]

Once in the hands of the inquisitors, prisoners underwent a series of interviews in which they were urged to confess their transgressions even though the specific charges against them were not revealed. These interviews could drag on for months, and, when a prisoner's revelations were not deemed suitably complete, torture was used.

During the seventeenth century, the Portuguese Inquisition relied on two torture devices, the *polé* and the rack. The former was a simple contrivance of rope and pulley. With hands bound behind their backs and attached to the rope, prisoners were hoisted ceilingward and then dropped abruptly. The rope broke their fall just short of the floor but severely wrenched the prisoners' arms and shoulders, and the damage and pain increased with each successive drop. The injury that this yo-yolike contraption inflicted on its victims was such that the aged and infirm were gradually brought to the requisite levels of pain on the rack instead of the *polé*.

Besides torture, prisoners had to cope with elaborate spy systems in the Holy Office's prisons. Anything they said, no matter what duress they may have suffered, might be reported back to the inquisitors.[31]

Mounting a defense was usually a futile gesture, given the anonymity of the accusers and the inquisitors' own closemouthed contact with the prisoners. Not divulging specific charges was a rewarding tactic for the interrogators since the accused could not focus on any given instance of wrongdoing and instead felt greater pressure to tell all or even to incriminate themselves falsely.

Some of those who confessed to minor offenses were allowed to abjure privately before the inquisitors. But most were forced to undergo the embarrassment and humiliation of an auto-da-fé, during which they publicly acknowledged their religious, social, sexual, or doctrinal deviations. In many cases, the charges must have been groundless. Burning at the stake, the well-known fate awaiting prisoners judged to be irredeemable heretics, was not, as is commonly supposed, the centerpiece of an auto-da-fé. Instead, executions usually took place later as a subsidiary function, the condemned having been turned over to secular authorities since the Holy Office preferred not to be directly involved in the execution of prisoners. In many autos-da-fé, none of the convicted were sentenced to death but serious offenders who had fled the country might be burned in effigy. Moreover, many serious offenders were never brought to the stake because they died in prison.

Of the numerous autos-da-fé carried out in Portugal during the late seventeenth century, the ceremony that took place in Coimbra in 1699 was perhaps typical. Much of the historical knowledge of this particular auto-da-fé came from the account of an unnamed French Capuchin monk who was an eyewitness to much of the ceremony.[32] At six o'clock on the morning of July 14, a Sunday, the usual day for autos-da-fé, a procession of eighty-six prisoners, together with clerics and *familiares*, started on its way through the streets of Coimbra to the Terreiro de São Miguel, the principal square of the city. As in the case of other autos-da-fé, most of the prisoners (eighty-one) had been convicted of judaizing. Of the remaining five offenders, one had been found guilty of bigamy and one of blasphemy and three priests had transgressed by teaching quietism, a form of Iberian mysticism that challenged th Church's role as spiritual intermediary.[33]

Six of the convicted judaizers were sentenced to burning at the stake and the body of a prisoner who had died while incarcerated was also to be burned. The rest of the prisoners received sentences that included the wearing of tunics painted with large yellow crosses on front and back, jail terms, and banishment from the kingdom.[34]

Despite the solemnity of the typical auto-da-fé, there was a certain curious festiveness about such an event. The French informant disapprovingly noted that Englishwomen watching from their windows above the Terreiro de São Miguel laughed and jeered at the proceedings.[35] The costumes of prisoners were surprisingly colorful, being painted with symbolic figures and even portraits of the condemned. Michael Geddes, the Anglican pastor for the English colony in Lisbon who witnessed the auto-da-fé of 1682, reported that the procession to the Terreiro do Paço was led by Dominican priests and that behind them came the penitents,

all in black Coats without sleeves, and barefooted, with a wax candle in their hand; next comes the Penitents who have narrowly escaped being burnt, who over their black Coat have flames painted, with their points turned downward, to signify their having been saved, but so as by Fire.

Following the *penitentes* came heretics whose crimes were sufficient to warrant execution but, having abjured and professed fealty to Catholicism, might be spared execution or be strangled before their pyre was lit. This group was followed by the unrepentant. Geddes described the garb of these final marchers as follows:

Next come the Negative and Relapsed that are to be burnt, with flames upon their Habit, pointing upwards, and next come those who profess Doctrines contrary to the Faith of the *Roman* Church, and who besides Flames on their Habit pointing upward, have their Picture, which is drawn two or three days before upon their Breasts, with Dogs, Serpents, and Devils, all with open Mouths painted about it.[36]

The steps of these colorfully clad, steadfast heretics were dogged by priests who beseeched them to abjure. Last-minute conversions, as noted, could bring a less-agonizing death by strangulation. Jesuit fathers hovered about the six condemned judaizers in the 1699 Coimbra auto-da-fé, but they were violently repulsed by these resolute prisoners when they exhorted them to kiss crucifixes.[37]

Crowds attending autos-da-fé, especially those held in Lisbon, were quite large, numbering in the thousands. Perhaps as many as 12,000 attended the Coimbra auto-da-fé of 1699. But these large gatherings had a social significance that went beyond their principal raison d'être, the reconfirmation of religious orthodoxy. They were, in effect, elaborately staged events in which the established order ritualistically confronted its presumed enemies. The leaders of Portuguese society were themselves on display as monarchs, prominent nobles, ecclesiastics, and *letrados*, not to mention the inquisitorial bureaucrats, sat on elaborately festooned canopied platforms from which recitation of the crimes of prisoners could be heard and the supplication of penitents witnessed. The stairs up to these platforms were guarded to assure that only the privileged and distinguished were seated above the masses, who had not only come to see the public exhibition of those who allegedly held beliefs or committed acts that subverted the social order but to view their superiors as well.

Once the eighty-six prisoners (and one casket) of the Coimbra tribunal had entered the Terreiro de São Miguel, they were herded into an amphitheater adjacent to the central platform. The assembled dignitaries and foreigners and the milling masses then listened to a priest who sermonized against the four offenses represented by the prisoners: Judaism, bigamy, blasphemy, and quietism. Thereafter the three priests accused of quietism were brought before the pulpit and their offenses, which also included false miracles and quack cures, were described in detail. Some of their confessed acts, for one reason or another, sufficed to set the Englishwomen to laughing.

Later that day the cases (*processos*) of the condemned were read and then the six prisoners and the casket, which also had flames painted on it, were handed over to secular authorities. The *processos* of the seventy-four penitent judaizers, the blasphemer, and the bigamist were also read, an undertaking not completed until noon on the following Monday.

Late Sunday evening, the six prisoners and one painted coffin were taken to the execution site by their secular custodians. Their colorful tunics having been removed, the condemned, garbed only in white undergarments, were bound to the stake. The executioners also placed the remains of the dead prisoner on a wooden pyre. At midnight, the pyres below their feet were set to the torch and the six Marranos died, the flames that consumed them lighting the summer night.[38]

Sometime afterwards, the ashes of the deceased, together with those of the prisoner who had died before the auto-da-fé took place, were scattered to the wind. The habits worn by the six judaizers were probably kept and hung up like trophies in one of Coimbra's churches. In Lisbon, the west end of the Church of São Domingo was covered with habits bearing portraits of people who had died at the order of the Inquisition.[39]

The Coimbra auto-da-fé of 1699 was a costly affair. Expenses ran to 1,370,516 reis while confiscations from the prisoners amounted to only 219,547 reis, leaving a deficit of 1,150,969 reis. The Holy Office of Coimbra thus had to call on the crown for help in paying the outstanding balance, which comprised sums owed for salaries, materials, and refreshments.[40] Indebtedness such as this may have rendered the Inquisition more susceptible to royal influence, but, on the other hand, a financially pressed monarchy often found itself in the anomalous position of funding expensive spectacles in which members of Portugal's small but economically essential mercantile class were the most prominent prisoners.

Few New Christian merchants who underwent the public censure of an auto-da-fé were executed. But the drawn-out process, which typically extended from their arrest until completion of a term in prison, seriously disrupted their lives and commercial activities. According to David Grant Smith:

Anyone arrested by the Holy Office could expect to spend a minimum of two or three years in its prison, and not infrequently, prisoners remained incarcerated for more than ten years. For a merchant thus deprived of direction of his business affairs, such a period of inactivity would spell disaster.[41]

Although New Christians had previously thwarted the depredations of the Holy Office for brief periods by obtaining royal pardons or reprieves in 1604, 1627, and 1649, the leverage provided by their considerable wealth was never sufficient to withstand the vehement reactions to these exemptions. Unfortunately for most merchants, the strenuous protestations of the vast majority of Portuguese subjects, both the privileged and the commoners, was not the only factor working against the extension of their short-lived reprieves. New Christian merchants could never sufficiently mesh and coordinate their efforts to hold the inquisitors at bay since "their interests and convictions were simply too diverse to permit adherence to any single course of action."[42] Indeed, their awareness of being a distinct but beleaguered class was never strong enough to foster a concerted, unremitting defense of their shared class interests.

Father António Vieira and Jesuit Support of the Mercantile Class

New Christian merchants and their brethren in other classes were fortunate to have the strong support of the Jesuits, an order renowned for its organization, discipline, and erudition. Why the Jesuits had come to stand so staunchly with the New Christians against the Holy Office and most of the rest of Portuguese society is a subject in need of further research, but there is no doubt that the antagonism between the Inquisition and the followers of Loyola had much more to it than a struggle over the disposition of a despised minority. The rift between the Jesuits and the Holy Office arose, in large measure, after the Restoration of 1640.[43] In 1641, the inquisitor general, as was previously noted, was so opposed to the Restoration that he became involved in a plot to assassinate D. João IV; while in the same year the Jesuits, perhaps in conformity with the legal doctrine taught at their universities, emerged as ardent supporters of the new monarchy.

Another cause of the widening breach appears to have arisen from simple jurisdictional squabbles. The cities of Lisbon, Coimbra, and Évora, of course, were home to the three branches of the Portuguese Inquisition. The inquisitors shared the latter two cities with Jesuit-controlled universities, and Lisbon was the nerve center of the order's great missionary enterprise in the Portuguese world. An example of confrontation born of proximity occurred at a Jesuit-run trade fair in Évora in 1642. The Jesuit-appointed alderman (*almotacé*) who administered the fair had rendered a decision favoring a university student over a servant of a deputy of the Inquisition. The matter in question was the disposition of a basket of apples. The Holy Office called the *almotacé* before its tribunal, but he refused to appear and was subsequently arrested by two *familiares*. The Jesuits jumped into the fray in support of their official, but he was imprisoned, subjected to an auto-da-fé, and deprived of his office. Not unexpectedly, "the Jesuits and their friends were scandalized and privately censured the inquisitors."[44] This incident clearly suggests that there was an undercurrent of jurisdictional jealousy between the neighboring institutions.

Undoubtedly, the most eloquent spokesman for both the Restoration and the New Christians was the renowned Jesuit Father António Vieira, who has justifiably been called "the most remarkable man in the seventeenth century Luso-Brazilian world."[45] In his roles as missionary, orator, writer, diplomat, statesman, and economist, Vieira was truly Portugal's version of the Renaissance man. Born in Lisbon in 1608, Vieira accompanied his father, a colonial official, to Bahia when he was only eight years old. Seven years later, the young António joined the Jesuit order and subsequently refined his exceptional talents as a Latinist and preacher. When he returned to Portugal in 1641 as part of the delegation bringing news of colonial fealty to the newly acclaimed D. João IV, Vieira enjoyed great renown among his colonial colleagues. Once in Lisbon, the gifted Jesuit rapidly gained favor with the new monarch, becoming preacher of the royal chapel. Vieira attained considerable influence in matters of state and developed close ties with great nobles, such as the duke of Cadaval and the marquis of Gouveia. He also served stints as an adviser to Portuguese diplomats in Paris and the Hague. Next to D. João IV himself, Vieira was probably the individual most responsible for establishing the Brazil Company on a foundation of mostly New Christian money.

Although he could be a rough-and-tumble polemicist who argued on emotional rather than intellectual grounds, the great Jesuit was an extremely effective ally of the New Christians. His successful advocacy of the Brazil Company gave them a brief respite from inquisitorial confiscation. Vieira's rationale for such exemption (as we will see in the next chapter) was formulated primarily according to the cold logic of economic and imperial necessity. Suffice it to say for the present that Vieira regarded New Christian wealth and commercial activity as the key to preserving Portugal's national independence and maintaining its colonial empire. But fervent nationalist though he was, António Vieira genuinely sympathized with the plight of the New Christian merchants and did not simply regard them as wealthy tools with which to resurrect Portugal's imperial preeminence.

Thanks to his powerful and prolific pen, the backing of his order, and his close association with national and international leaders, the Jesuit repeatedly and effectively called into question the operations of the Holy Office in Portugal. For his trouble, Vieira was imprisoned by the Coimbra tribunal in 1665, ostensibly for writings that contravened Catholic doctrine. In a work entitled *Esperanças de Portugal, Quinto Imperio do Mundo* (1659), the great Jesuit, basing himself on the prophetic couplets of the Sebastianist poet Gonçalo Bandarra, had propounded a peculiar theory that foretold the establishment of a fifth universal monarchy to be led by the Portuguese.[46] The resurrection of the recently deceased D. João IV (who died in 1656) would inaugurate the biblical monarchy.[47] The Holy Office used this dubious bit of doctrine as the not altogether unjustified pretext for arresting its old enemy. An investigation of Vieira's lineage was made, and, while no evidence of Jewish ancestry was found, there was some question as to the purity of his mother's bloodlines. Moreover, the investigation revealed that a mulatto woman had a place on the family tree.[48]

After two years of harassment, which included incarceration in a drafty cell for a number of months, the charges against Vieira were suspended, but he was prohibited from public expressions of opinion, including sermons, and was remanded to the custody of his order. This state of affairs, however, changed considerably after D. Pedro's successul coup. Thereafter, many of Father Vieira's secular enemies within D. Afonso VI's government were removed and the Holy Office backed off, realizing that Vieira was well regarded by the usurpers. Even so, he never regained the influence that he had enjoyed during the reign of D. João IV. While initially amenable to curtailing inquisitorial excesses against the mercantile class, the new leadership soon retreated before the force of public opinion and sought alternatives to New Christian financing of economic projects.

Nevertheless, António Vieira was a man to be reckoned with as he carried his campaign against the Holy Office to Rome. His efforts to gain vindication against the charges leveled by the Coimbra tribunal met with resounding though belated success. In 1675, he gained an extraordinary papal exemption from any further molestation by the Portuguese Inquisition.[49] Vieira's campaign on behalf of New Christians, as we will soon see, also achieved success, albeit short-lived.

Moral considerations undoubtedly played a role in the Jesuits' advocacy of a liberalized policy toward New Christians. António Vieira led an exemplary struggle against the excesses of the Holy Office; and numerous other Jesuits, including D. Pedro's confessor, Padre Manual Fernandes, shared his indignation over the plight of New Christians. But, as it has already been suggested, Jesuit opposition to the Inquisition on this matter was probably but one aspect of a deeply rooted struggle between the two institutions.

Although probably not a vision shared by many of his Jesuit brethren, Vieira's dream of a Portuguese-led fifth imperium was suggestive of the sort of universalist ambitions his order harbored. Organized along military lines and seeking only the best candidates for its ranks, the Jesuit order had, since its founding in 1540, marshaled its small but talented forces on a global scale against Protestantism and for winning the souls of pagans. The Jesuits' great missionary enterprise in the Portuguese colonies, which far outstripped that of any other order at work in the empire, was complemented by their virtual monopolization of higher education in Portugal. It is difficult, however, to generalize about the world view of the Jesuits since some were associated with ultramontanism, the doctrine of papal supremacy, while others like Vieira steadfastly championed dynastic and nationalist aspirations.[50]

Whatever the aims of the order at large, António Vieira's unrelenting exertions on behalf of the mercantile class were part of his grand, if not fully articulated, scheme to restore Portugal's former greatness. Writing in 1643 in favor of allowing refugee New Christian merchants to return to Portugal unmolested, Vieira argued that if D. João IV saw fit to follow his advice, "Lisbon will again be a grand and wealthy emporium and very shortly the greatest opulence will arise throughout the kingdom."[51]

Both the Jesuits and the inquisitors regarded the mercantile class's wealth as a valuable resource with which to achieve their respective goals. Indeed, it has been suggested that the Jesuits' struggle with the Holy Office over this source of wealth was one "in which the New Christians were as much weapons as objects of benevolence."[52] Nevertheless, New Christians showed little reluctance to accept the support of António Vieira and his colleagues, backing that was to be sorely needed as the final round in the seventeenth-century confrontation between the mercantile class and the bulk of Portuguese society began.

The Climactic Decade, 1671–1681

The newly installed regime of D. Pedro and his noble cohorts must have been regarded with hopeful expectation by many New Christians. Despite continuing autos-da-fé and the hysterical rhetoric that issued from the 1668 Cortes, New Christians could look to powerful individuals within the new government for toleration, if not outright support, of their efforts to obtain relief from the depredations of the Holy Office. The duke of Cadaval, the marquis of Fronteira, the prince regent's Jesuit confessor, D. Luis de Meneses (third count of Ericeira), and other influential figures had evinced an interest in the New Christian cause. Whatever their personal feelings toward the merchants may have been, these and other well-placed individuals perceived the advantages to Portugal that would flow from greater mercantile activity.

Further hope arose from the knowledge that António Vieira, who had left Portugal for Rome in 1669, was then free to plead the New Christian case against the excesses of the Inquisition. In his communications with the papacy, Vieira stressed that other inquisitorial establishments, even that of Spain, took more care in establishing the guilt of alleged judaizers than the Portuguese Holy Office did by seeking testimony from sources other than the original informant(s). In Rome, efforts by the Jesuits on behalf of New Christian merchants were aimed largely at reforming the procedures used by the Portuguese tribunal to convict the accused.

Vieira's appeal to the papacy was complemented by the drawing up of a proposal for a general pardon of New Christians, which was later presented to the prince regent. Apparently, this plan grew out of meetings in Rome among Vieira, Padre Balthasar da Costa (the Jesuit provincial of Malabar who had recently returned from his post in the Far East), and Manuel da Gama de Pádua (an exceptionally wealthy New Christian merchant and confidant of Vieira who had journeyed to Rome to lobby on behalf of the mercantile class). The plan was essentially a reformulation of the proposal that had led to the establishment of the Brazil Company. In exchange for publication of an anticipated general pardon from the pope for any past judaizing by New Christians, the mercantile community agreed to finance an East India company that, it was hoped, would be the vehicle by which eastern possessions lost to the Dutch could be recovered and the once-prosperous trade of the *carreira da India* renewed. International developments seemed conducive to the success of such a plan, for Louis XIV was about to invade Holland and, according to Father da Costa, Indian rajahs were ready to turn against the Dutch interlopers.[53]

Portuguese merchants also may have been heartened by recuperation of some of the influence they had lost after the death of D. João IV. By 1670, they held two of the three seats on the Junta do Comércio, the only established institution through which merchants could wield influence on their own behalf.[54] In 1671, any expectations of relief from the ever-menacing Inquisition and its coterie of *familiares* were rudely shaken by an incident that catalyzed opposition to a general pardon.

On the night of May 10, a young peasant named António Ferreira had broken into the church at Odivelas, a small village a few miles to the northwest of Lisbon. Once in the church, Ferreira took various precious items from the altar and caused some damage before making good his escape. News of the robbery and desecration rapidly spread throughout Portugal and innumerable processions of penitent marchers soon wended their mournful way through city and town. And when word of Odivelas reached Bahia the following January, the governor ordered numerous exhibitions of mourning for the Brazilian capital.[55]

Speculation as to the identity of the perpetrators of the sacrilege fell squarely on the New Christians. Word was passed that on the morning following the incident a number of New Christians had set sail from Lisbon on a French ship. Rumors such as this provoked widespread outbreaks of riots and protests against the despised New

Christians. Anti–New Christian leaflets, some in clever verse, were soon printed and distributed; and *pasquins*, anonymously posted, often slanderous notices, were tacked up in public places.[56] The theory of a sinister plot was at one point given vent with the arrest of six New Christians in the city of Guarda, but these individuals were subsequently absolved of any role in the crime.[57]

The day after the outrage at Odivelas, the prince regent issued a royal letter calling for services of mourning in all the churches of Lisbon and demanding the harshest of penalties for the guilty parties.[58] Despite the fact that the identity of the culprit remained unknown, D. Pedro lost little time in jumping on the anti–New Christian bandwagon. During the next six weeks, he promulgated a series of laws that further penalized the stigmatized minority. The most drastic of the decrees ordered the expulsion of all New Christians who had abjured *de vehementi* during the most recent autos-da-fé in Lisbon and Coimbra and of all future penitents of this sort. (There were two degrees of abjuration, *de leve* and *de vehementi*, the latter being assigned to more serious offenses.) The order also extended to all individuals who had so abjured since 1604, the date of the last comprehensive pardon granted to New Christians and to their families and close relatives.[59]

Although this law had the practical effect of salving popular outrage over the events at Odivelas, it was not enforced.[60] Had it been enforced, the demographic damage wrought on Portugal would surely have been of significance since a sizable percentage of three generations of New Christians would have left the country. D. Pedro was not so unwise as to emulate Spain's economically damaging expulsion of Jews and Moriscos. If the crown had any serious notions about enforcing the decree, they were probably quickly dispelled by the Holy Office's strong opposition to the measure. The inquisitors argued that their investigative work would be seriously handicapped by the expulsion of so many potential witnesses and that many judaizers would escape punishment.[61] The Holy Office must have comprehended the adverse effect that the expulsion would have on its treasury.

It is not clear whether subsequent decrees against New Christians were rigorously observed or not, but it is likely that they were at least partially enforced since they had the backing of the Inquisition. The decrees of July and August 1671 prohibited the holding of public office by anyone of "impure" blood and forbade penitent lawyers and doctors from returning to their professions.[62] The following year, the Holy Office, by a decree of its own, further penalized all penitents. Thereafter, individuals convicted of judaizing were prohibited from holding royal contracts or honorific positions and from exercising any public functions. This same decree also struck at the galling frequency with which many New Christian *penitentes* reassumed the trappings of position and wealth after serving their sentences. After 1671, they were forbidden from riding horseback, going about in coaches or litters, wearing silks, or using precious metals or jewels.[63]

On October 18, 1671, António Ferreira was arrested while attempting another robbery near the scene of his sensational crime. To the undoubted satisfaction of many, it was discovered that both of Ferreira's parents were New Christians, confirming the popular belief that the sacrilege at Odivelas must have been the work of judaizers. Few, however, seem to have wondered why New Christians would have perpetrated a crime so antithetical to their own best interests. Some New Christians even argued that the crime was staged to further antagonize the public toward them.[64]

Ferreira, in fact, was a common thief whose motives had little relation to the sinister machinations attributed to him.[65] Nonetheless, the unfortunate youth—who was described as ignorant, lacking in judgment, and even crazy—did not escape the full wrath of the law. He was first tortured in order to obtain a full confession and then sentenced to die. On November 20, Ferreira was paraded through the streets of Lisbon to the Rossio, where the execution was to take place. Once in the square, he was handed over to the executioners, who chopped his hands off, burned his eyes out, and then hanged him from a tall pole. The hangmen then burned the body of the hapless burglar, and what few possessions he had were given to the church he had desecrated.[66]

The death of António Ferreira did little to lessen the anti–New Christian fervor sweeping Portugal. New Christians from all walks of life were arrested; but, most significantly, some of Lisbon's wealthiest merchants were apprehended and locked away in the dungeons of the Holy Office in late July 1672.[67] In addition to the previously noted Francisco Carlos and Fernão Rodrigues Penso, two of the

THE NEW CHRISTIAN CHALLENGE   93

crown's principal tax farmers (António Rodrigues Mogadouro and Diogo de Chaves) were caught up in the inquisitors' net, as were numerous smaller merchants. What little direct leverage the merchants could bring to bear from the board of the Junta do Comércio was eliminated with the arrest of Francisco Carlos and the effective neutralization of the holder of the other Junta seat in New Christian hands, António Correa Bravo, which followed the imprisonment of his brother and son. The jailing of Bravo's relatives and Carlos coincided with the issuance of a new *regimento* for the Junta do Comércio, which reduced the merchants' influence on that body by creating a five-man board on which merchants held only two seats, the remaining three being reserved for the president and two other noblemen.[68]

The year 1672 thus marked a nadir in New Christian fortunes. For those merchants arrested by the Holy Office the rigors of imprisonment must have been especially severe, given the fact that an inordinate number of them died while in jail.[69] Those who escaped imprisonment labored under the fear of their own arrest, knowing that what had befallen Portugal's wealthiest financiers could happen to them. Moreover, the increased suspicion and hatred that Odivelas had aroused undoubtedly made the pursuit of day-to-day business activities more difficult. Emboldened bands of zealots moved through the streets with impunity, plastering public areas with *pasquins* and menacing New Christian subjects. *Familiares* lay in wait for Marranos who incautiously practiced their sub-rosa faith. It was into this charged environment that the inflammatory proposal for a general pardon was introduced.

Although New Christian merchants probably had not relished the pardon scheme because of the great costs involved, the events of 1672 forced their hand. The threat of arrest, confiscation, and imprisonment, not to mention burning at the stake, confronted all New Christians no matter how wealthy. The only hope of relief lay in persuading the prince regent that a merchant-financed East India company would be of such benefit as to justify disregard of an already-ugly public mood.

In 1673, one of the formulators of the pardon proposal, Padre Balthasar da Costa, who was then in Lisbon, wrote to the royal confessor, Manuel Fernandes, detailing the plan. Fernandes presented the proposal to D. Pedro who, by all accounts, was favorably impressed. Though not all the specifics of the plan are known, the principal provision, as was previously indicated, called for the crown's assent to the promulgation of a general pardon to be issued by the pope in exchange for the establishment and funding of a commercial company for the defense and revitalization of the India trade. Following promulgation of the pardon, the New Christians stipulated the release of brethren held by the Inquisition and, from thence forward, the tribunal's conformity with the procedures of the Holy Office in Rome.[70]

In addition to putting up the money for a trading company, the New Christian merchants promised to finance the sending of a contingent of 5,000 men to India during the firm's first year of operation and 1,200 per annum thereafter. They proposed an annual contribution of 20,000 cruzados for the maintenance of these troops. Moreover, they offered to pay the expenses of future viceroys and governors sent to India. As an added incentive to the crown, the New Christians agreed to assume the costs of sending missionaries to the colonies and to contribute 200,000 reis per month for the expenses of Portuguese ambassadors in Rome.[71] Three exceptionally wealthy merchants, Manuel da Gama de Pádua, António Correa Bravo, and Pedro Álvares Caldas, stood ready to channel New Christian wealth toward those outlays and into the new Portuguese East India Company.[72]

What with these exceedingly attractive provisos, there is little wonder that D. Pedro seriously considered the 1673 proposal. But this was by no means the only instance in which the New Christian question had been argued, pro and con, before the young monarch. The 1668 Cortes, which had been convened to install D. Pedro and to approve increased taxes for national defense, also announced its wishes regarding the treatment of gypsies and New Christians. D. Pedro initially showed little inclination toward taking such unsolicited advice, but after Odivelas his decrees against New Christians largely followed those proposed by the Cortes.

The prince regent had also received communications arguing on behalf of New Christians. In 1670, for example, an unsigned paper was submitted to D. Pedro that emphasized the economic benefits to be derived from granting the New Christians relief from the Holy

Office's confiscations.[73] Given the shaky condition of the Portuguese economy after the struggle for the Restoration, the anonymous author probably hoped that his argument would hit a responsive chord. If the Inquisition's ability to confiscate property was made more difficult, it was asserted, many New Christians who had left Portugal would return, bringing their wealth back with them. Furthermore, those New Christian merchants living in Portugal would feel freer to retrieve money they had deposited outside Portugal in order to protect it from the inquisitors. In typically mercantilist fashion, the author stressed the drain of precious metals and the concurrent influx of false copper coinage as being at the root of Portugal's economic problems. To his mind, New Christian wealth and enterprise represented the best solution.

As further support for his argument, the writer noted that wealth confiscated from New Christians during the previous thirty years amounted to relatively little. Hence, the Inquisition's reliance on a few or even one accusation as a basis for arrest and confiscation had hardly been remunerative. Confiscations in Lisbon since 1640, according to the writer, had not reached 80,000 cruzados. Since much bullion was being sent out of Portugal by foreign merchants operating in Lisbon and other cities, the return of New Christians and their wealth would counteract these losses because their international dealings might allow precious metals to flow back into Portugal. Indeed, the author predicted that prosperity would return to the country within four years if his advice were followed.[74]

The response to this appeal for greater restrictions on the Inquisition was not slow in coming. In 1671, apparently prior to the robbery at Odivelas, the Supreme Council of the Holy Office submitted a lengthy *consulta* to D. Pedro that contained anti–New Christian arguments that were to be repeated again and again during the debates over the general pardon and whether the inquisitors should conform to the procedures of the Roman tribunal.[75] In arguing for the continuation of single testimonies as a basis for conviction, the inquisitors claimed that heresy would be given free rein if their activities were in any way curbed and that Portuguese Catholicism, which to their mind was the purest in all of Christendom, would be debased. Moreover, any moderation of inquisitorial procedures threatened the purity of

THE NEW CHRISTIAN CHALLENGE

the nobility as ever-larger numbers of heretics sought entrance into that privileged class. Here again was an expression of the fear of inundation by New Christian blood.

According to the inquisitors, permitting New Christians to return from abroad meant that individuals instructed in the synagogues of the world would teach "with greater authority, efficacy and persuasion those who live among us, and each one restored will be a source of dogma for the rest that live in Portugal, and with their industry and wealth they will corrupt the bulk of the population." The Supreme Council concluded by warning that any leniency in the area of confiscations would lead to the financial destruction of the Holy Office and the spiritual ruin of the kingdom.[76]

When word of the 1673 pardon proposal spread, numerous unfounded rumors also began to circulate. It was rumored that New Christians might be allowed to practice Judaism unmolested and that a synagogue would be built in the Vila Galega neighborhood (*bairro*) of Lisbon.[77] Word also spread that thousands of New Christian families would soon flood into Portugal and that rabbis would be accompanying them. Another rumor incorrectly had it that only Old Christians would be conscripted as soldiers for the new India Company's effort to regain lost possessions in the Far East, a project that would undoubtedly have cost many lives. Other erroneous tales spoke of the pardon being extended to future as well as past transgressions against the faith and of the certain retaliation of New Christians against their Old Christian enemies if it took effect.[78]

Distortions of the proposal continued until many thought that the prince regent had already accepted it and that his advisers, especially Padre Fernandes, had been bought off by agents of Judaism. Under cover of darkness, protestors streamed through the streets of Lisbon, posting *pasquins* and crying, "Long live the faith! Death to Judaism!" Not unexpectedly, the Holy Office did much to incite the noisy protests of the lower classes.[79]

Meanwhile, the question of inquisitorial excesses had reached a critical juncture in Rome. Padre Vieira and the New Christian contingent led by Manuel da Gama de Pádua had persuaded Pope Clement X that the alleged persecution of Portuguese New Christians should be investigated. Their case had been recently strengthened by the apparent excesses of the Évora tribunal. Two nuns who happened to be siblings and who belonged to a local convent had been burnt at the stake for judaizing even though they fervently maintained their innocence to the very last. When word of this incident reached Rome, Italian churchmen were scandalized. Additional unfavorable revelations about the tribunal's activities may also have induced the Vatican to pronounce ultimately in favor of the New Christians.[80] As further inducement for papal support, merchants had offered the Holy See 500,000 cruzados to aid Poland in its current struggle with the Turks, a war lasting from 1672 to 1676.[81] On October 16, 1674, some five years after António Vieira had arrived in Rome, the pope issued a brief that ordered cessation of autos-da-fé, sentencing, and compilation of *processos* while the activities of the Portuguese Inquisition were being reviewed.

The brief, however, was addressed to the duke of Aveiro, an inquisitor general who had died six months earlier. On the basis of this technicality, the Holy Office refused to obey the order, and in Coimbra plans were even made to carry out a previously scheduled auto-da-fé. After negotiations between the Coimbra inquisitors and the papal nuncio, the ceremony was permitted, but judaizers condemned to death were burnt in effigy. Similar restraints were imposed on autos-da-fé that took place in Évora and Lisbon in late 1674.[82] During the next seven and one-half years, the papal injunction held; no one was executed by the Holy Office during that period, but the merchants arrested after the robbery at Odivelas continued to languish in prison. Although New Christian merchants failed to obtain the long-sought-after general pardon, the decimation of their ranks by the Holy Office had been temporarily stopped.

In its confrontation with Rome, the Holy Office gained an unexpected ally in the prince regent. D. Pedro had first looked upon the general pardon with favor, then had vacillated, and finally had joined forces with the Santo Ofício and the three estates. The reasons for his turnaround are not altogether clear, but it is likely that an ominous event of 1673, the threat of being deposed by a countercoup, was the principal consideration. The prince regent had himself come to power on a wave of public sympathy and well knew the shakiness of a throne that had lost popular support.

Opposition to the ruler's suspected collusion with wealthy merchants had indeed gone beyond mere street protests and submission of antipardon opinions by inquisitors and representatives of the three estates. In late September 1673, a plot to assassinate D. Pedro, his wife Maria, and their daughter was uncovered. It is not known whether D. Pedro's favorable reception of the pardon proposal precipitated the plotting, but it is clear that the conspirators planned to restore D. Afonso VI, then imprisoned on the island of Terceira, to his throne after arranging a marriage between him and Mariana, queen mother of Spain.[83] The conspiracy involved at least fifty people from all three estates, including no fewer than eight nobles. Among these eight was António Cavide, D. Afonso VI's deposed secretary of state. Further investigation determined that the Spanish ambassador had played some role in the plotting. Money and arms apparently brought in from Castile were discovered. The prince regent expelled the Castilian envoy and recalled his ambassador to Madrid.[84] One of the conspirators, Francisco Furtado de Mendonça, the captain general of Mazagão, eluded capture. Due to the intercession of Charles II of England, which was apparently encouraged by his wife Catherine (Catarina), D. Pedro's sister, António Cavide was pardoned and put on an English ship in early January. However, eight of the principal conspirators were executed in the Rossio on May 10, 1674.[85] The hapless D. Afonso VI was later brought back to Sintra on the mainland, where he was confined until his death in 1683. Although the desire of diehard *afonsistas* to restore their leader may have been the primary impetus for the conspiracy, the plotters had clearly hoped to exploit the uproar caused by news of the New Christian general pardon plan.[86]

The ominous portent of the assassination plot also found expression in the stormy sessions of the 1674 Lisbon Cortes. This Cortes had been convened to approve changes in the laws of succession and to renew excise taxes on wine and meat agreed to by the three estates in 1668. These measures as well as retrieval of D. Afonso VI from Terceira were approved, but the delegates showed little inclination to simply rubber-stamp the prince regent's requests and instead attempted themselves to dictate policy. Acting as if it were a true parliament, the Cortes tried to tell D. Pedro how the tax on wine and meat should be spent.[87]

Anger over the incident at Odivelas had put the delegates in a dark and fractious mood. This, together with the suspicion that a general pardon from the Vatican was at hand, served to inflame their deliberations. Alluding to Odivelas, the clerical estate urged D. Pedro to have nothing to do with Rome's apparent willingness to grant the pardon. Preservation of the faith, not state finances, was to be uppermost in his mind.[88] In early May, the third estate sent the prince regent a *consulta* in which its violent opposition to the pardon was expressed. The representatives of *o povo* accused the Portuguese resident in Rome, Gaspar de Abreu de Freitas, of selling out to the New Christians and exhorted D. Pedro to send an ambassador extraordinary to the Vatican to champion the real interests of the Portuguese people.[89] The representatives of the third estate went on to warn darkly that New Christian greed would not be satisfied by the acquisition of additional money and property and would only be sated when all Old Christians were sold to the Moorish slavers at Algiers.[90] The third estate also took it upon itself to send a letter directly to the pope, voicing its opposition to the general pardon.[91]

The nobility was divided on the pardon issue. D. Pedro's staunchest supporters, who can be regarded as the progressive element in the nobility since they often advocated emulation of the socioeconomic policies of absolutist France, viewed the pardon scheme as a means of strengthening the state. Unfortunately for the New Christians, two of their strongest proponents in the noble estate, D. Rodrigo Meneses and the marquis of Minas, died in 1674, the latter succumbing while the Cortes was still in session. The inquisitors lost little time in ascribing their deaths to divine vengeance. António Vieira, however, voiced the suspicion that the Holy Office had had a hand in their untimely ends.[92]

The rest of the noble estate, which constituted a majority, joined clerics and commoners in opposing the pardon. This same group contained numerous individuals who favored closer ties with Spain, including perhaps some who had knowledge of, if not a part in, the recently discovered conspiracy.[93] In April 1674, all three estates of the restive Cortes informed the prince regent of their opposition to the general pardon. Because of the disorder and rebelliousness that had pervaded the proceedings of the three estates, D. Pedro, who by then had won their assent to his revenue requests, summarily dissolved the Cortes in June 1674.

The antipathy toward New Christian merchants did not subside, however. The return of D. Afonso VI in September provided some of the most fanatical anti-Semites with an occasion to further impugn the reputation of the wavering prince regent. Cries of "Viva D. Afonso! Death to the Jews!" were soon raised.[94] The dangerous implications of this slogan were surely not lost on D. Pedro. If the impassioned hatred for New Christians were linked with die-hard support for D. Afonso VI, the throne would indeed have been in jeopardy. Popularity based on his prowess at bullfighting and womanizing would do the prince regent little good if D. Afonso came to be regarded as the champion of Catholic orthodoxy. Except for a handful of nobles, merchants, and Jesuits, D. Pedro found himself all but isolated in his desire to launch the India Company. With an extensive assassination plot already uncovered and the unruly actions of the Cortes still fresh in mind, the prince regent reconsidered his position on the general pardon.

Other considerations may also have played a role in changing D. Pedro's stance. In 1673, the argument that confiscations brought in only small amounts was convincingly refuted. The bishop of Leiria reported that 500,000 cruzados had been confiscated during the wave of arrests of merchants in 1671–1672.[95] And, in the wake of the Cortes's overwhelming opposition to the pardon, the merchants had backed away from their generous East India Company scheme. Instead of a general pardon, they concentrated on obtaining the Holy Office's compliance with the practices of the Roman Inquisition. Through this moderate approach the merchants hoped that their imprisoned colleagues might be freed since many had been arrested with little attention to substantive proof of their guilt.[96] As one would expect, New Christian retreat from the company scheme removed a powerful incentive to royal support. Advances in Portuguese mercantilist thought that offered alternatives to New Christian-sponsored trading companies, a subject to be explored in the next chapter, may also have swayed the prince regent.

Royal retreat on the pardon question was counterbalanced by increasing papal pressure for the reform of the Portuguese Inquisition. Pope Clement X, who died in 1676, was succeeded by Innocent XI, a pontiff who proved more energetic in trying to determine whether the Holy Office was guilty of the irregularities of which it had been accused. The controversy moved to the *processos* of previously executed judaizers. Had these victims been executed with little regard for obtaining testimony that supported the accusations of single informants? In seeking the answer to this question, Innocent XI requested that a few *processos* be forwarded to Rome for inspection. The Holy Office balked at this request and instead offered to send copies, an offer that increased suspicion in the Vatican. Finally, on December 24, 1678, the pope instructed the inquisitor general to either deliver five of the original *processos* to the Lisbon nuncio within ten days or lose his office. The pope also threatened to suspend all Portuguese bishops if his order were disobeyed.[97] By a letter of the same date, Innocent XI informed D. Pedro of his ultimatum.[98]

Reaction to the papal order came swiftly. Mobs once again took to the streets and slanderous *pasquins* reappeared, one of which read as follows:

Who ever wants to be a Jew, heretic, sodomite, and marry three times, go speak with Padre Manuel Fernandes, confessor to His Majesty, and with Manuel da Gama de Pádua and Pedro Álvares Caldas, who have bulls from Padre Quental [the nuncio] for everything.[99]

D. Pedro, who apparently was surprised and angered by the unpopular ultimatum, hastily convened the Council of State and a panel of theologians to mount a counterattack. After due deliberation, the papal representative was informed that the Inquisition could be suppressed if the pope so desired but no changes in its structure or proceedings could be made without the permission of the prince regent. And D. Pedro forbade the inquisitor general to deliver the five *processos*.

Additional strengthening of the inquisitors' hand was to come from the Cortes of 1679–1680. The three estates jointly informed the prince regent of their wish that the powers of the Holy Office be returned to the status quo ante.[100] The pope then found himself in direct confrontation with the crown and the three estates, instead of the inquisitors.

D. Pedro had come full circle since the weeks following the robbery at Odivelas. The monarchy was once again in the forefront of the anti–New Christian forces. By attempting to force the issue, the pope had exacerbated resentment over the moratorium on inquisitorial activities.

The renewed rioting may have rekindled royal fears of a popular uprising if the pope was allowed to have his way. Given the *afonsista* plot of 1673 and the fractiousness of the 1674 Cortes, it must have been clear to D. Pedro that leaders of such an uprising could draw on considerable discontent. The crown had already seen the rise of a fanatical priest who had taken the name António das Chagas. Writing in 1675, António Vieira asserted that this charismatic renegade priest, who had been expelled from the Franciscan order but who later developed a strong following among the nobility, was quite capable of precipitating a popular revolt.[101]

News of another rabble-rousing cleric was relayed to the prince regent from the textile center of Covilhã in 1680. According to an anonymous informant, a Franciscan priest named Manuel de Jesús was going about openly exhorting people to burn, stone, and otherwise do away with New Christians, who evidently comprised the majority of Covilhã's population.[102] Word of this brazen call to vigilantism surely reminded an already-converted crown of the perils involved in brooking the wishes of anti–New Christian forces.

After the prince regent countermanded the papal demand for delivery of the five *processos*, it was only a matter of time before the Holy Office regained its old authority and independence. Resumption of overt power was abetted by disarray in the New Christian camp. Its lobby in Rome lost a powerful voice in 1675 when António Vieira, his papal grant of immunity from inquisitorial prosecution in hand, departed for Portugal, vainly expecting to wield influence at court on behalf of the mercantile class. In 1680, the forlorn cause was dealt a crippling blow with the death of Manuel da Gama de Pádua, the chief New Christian spokesman for the mercantile class. The merchant's death probably engendered a weakening of pro–New Christian sentiment in the Roman curia since the influx of monetary inducements with his death largely came to an end.[103]

With the incentive of merchant money gone and most of the leadership and population of Portugal insisting on a return to the status quo ante, the pope opted for a face-saving compromise. The Holy Office was allowed to submit two *processos* for inspection, documents that undoubtedly put the tribunal's procedures in the best light, and the pontiff, ostensibly deferring to the common desire of the Portuguese people, restored the Inquisition to its full functions in August

1681. The pope made some vague recommendations for reform in his enabling brief, but there was little alteration in the procedure required of the inquisitors.[104]

The Holy Office rapidly returned to its activities, arresting suspects and confiscating goods. The roundup of great merchants that took place in the early 1670s was repeated in 1681–1682.[105] During the first half of 1682, all three tribunals conducted autos-da-fé. The Lisbon auto-da-fé witnessed by the Englishman Geddes was an especially impressive ceremony. In order to assure its magnificence, prisoners were transferred to the capital by the other tribunals. D. Pedro, probably intent on polishing his tarnished public image, played an unduly prominent part in the proceedings.[106]

The chief Jesuit spokesmen for the New Christian cause, António Vieira and Manuel Fernandes, had long since lost whatever leverage they exerted at court. Fernandes was ordered to resign his post as confessor by the general of his order, probably in hopes that his departure would assuage anti-Jesuit sentiment. Vieira, who had received a frosty welcome from the prince regent after his return from Rome, departed for Brazil in 1681.

Finally, in 1683, a milder version of the 1671 expulsion law was promulgated, an act that apparently helped to calm anti–New Christian passions.[107] By this time, however, the expulsion edict probably came as but an anticlimactic blow to the mercantile class, for its inchoate challenge to the established order had already been repulsed. Not until the administration of Pombal did New Christian merchants obtain substantive relief from their inquisitorial nemesis.

The Triumph of the Established Order

The social firmament of late seventeenth-century Portugal had been clearly, if but temporarily, disturbed by New Christian efforts to remove the constant threat to their freedom and property and even their lives posed by the Inquisition. These efforts, as the inquisitors and their privileged cohorts sensed, presaged alterations in the status quo that ultimately undercut their preeminent position in society. Any moderation in inquisitorial rigor, according to the Holy Office, would have allowed Judaism—and the strength of the mercantile class—to increase.[108] Furthermore, it was feared, and not without some justification, that an expanding mercantile sector would increasingly infiltrate and thus sully the lineal purity of the entire noble estate, a privileged class already tainted by an embarrassingly large number of Jewish forebears.

The challenge posed to the established order by the mercantile class should not be regarded as a bid to seize power. Instead, Portuguese merchants, like their counterparts in other agrarian societies, generally "seem to have had the consuming desire to be like the members of the governing class, to be accepted by them as equals, and eventually, if possible, to become one with them."[109] New Christian merchants who covertly adhered to Marranism probably shared this desire.

But, as it was suggested earlier, the wealth of the merchants represented an ever-present threat to the privileged position of individuals who were heirs to an increasingly antiquated feudal social hierarchy. Ironically, the implications of the merchants' bid for leniency during the 1670s were probably more clearly understood by their privileged detractors than by the merchants themselves. This understanding derived in large measure from a greater degree of class consciousness among the privileged estates, especially the prominent nobility. On the question of class consciousness animating the aristocracies of precapitalist societies, E. J. Hobsbawm wrote:

> It is highly likely that even in such cases of "class consciousness" the criterion of self-definition will be primarily non-economic, whereas in modern classes it is primarily economic. It may be impossible to be a noble without holding land and dominating peasants, and abstaining from manual labor, but these characteristics would not be enough to define a noble to the satisfaction of medieval society. This would require also kinship ("blood"), special legal status and privileges, a special relationship to the king, or various others.[110]

Regardless of the nature of noble self-definition, knowing who they were and what they stood for gave the privileged classes an obvious edge in confrontations with the mercantile class.

Noneconomic characteristics such as those suggested by Hobsbawm tend to obscure the foundations of the privileged estates' opposition to the aspirations of New Christian merchants. Bloodlines and religious orthodoxy, not control of the economy or changes in the mode of production, were the issues that inflamed public debate. The bigotry, hatred, and superstition directed at New Christians from all quarters also beclouds the underpinnings of class conflict. Yet, if these and other noneconomic factors are regarded, at least in part, as symptoms of the collision of class interests, the nature of the struggle exacerabated by Odivelas becomes more understandable.

The fact that opposition to merchants was not uniformly deployed further obscures the bases of class conflict. The New Christians, who comprised the great majority of the mercantile class, bore the brunt of the privileged classes' antagonism and were the most prominent targets of the inquisitors. Old Christian merchants, though hardly viewed as allies by the privileged estates, were, on the other hand, given preference over their tainted brethren in appointments to positions in the royal bureaucracy, a policy that had the effect of undermining "any attempt to form a united front encompassing the entire mercantile class."[111] The availability of patents of nobility to both Old and New Christians, though certainly limited, especially for the latter, served to further dilute class solidarity. Fragmenting factors such as these undoubtedly did much to prevent the rise of class consciousness within the merchant community and thus reinforced the predominance of the privileged estates. Seen in this light, the uneven treatment of Old and New Christian merchants clearly redounded to the benefit of the established order.

But the "absence of class consciousness in the modern sense," as Hobsbawn suggested, "does not imply the absence of classes and class conflict."[112] Despite a variety of factors that becloud the issue, the struggle revolving around the question of inquisitorial excesses was essentially waged between the mercantile bourgeoisie and the landed aristocracy over whether the established social and economic order would be modified. Albeit a power in its own right, the inquisitorial bureaucracy, together with the *familiares*, acted as the diligent sentries of the status quo. The predominantly New Christian mercantile class lacked both unity of purpose and popular support but entered the fray with great wealth, which momentarily attracted royal and papal favor, and articulate Jesuit allies who drew attention to inquisitorial excesses and the economic benefits to be gained from greater security for the merchants. A small but enlightened cadre of nobles also recognized the advantages to the state inherent in expanded commerce. The bulk of the landed aristocracy, which was supported by the Holy

Office, the third estate, most of the clerical estate (itself a great landholder), and eventually the prince regent, held weapons that included overwhelming public support, control of the Cortes and municipal *câmaras*, and the weight of religious dogma.

The robbery at Odivelas, not in itself a truly significant event, supplied anti–New Christian forces with potent ammunition against a resurgent mercantile class. In a vain attempt to stem the reactionary assault that followed, the great merchants, acting in conjunction with their Jesuit allies, presented offers of extensive financial aid in Lisbon and Rome, which were to help pave the way for a general pardon. This maneuver temporarily blunted the onslaught, but it also further inflamed anti–New Christian passions. The Cortes became a forum from which to proclaim, usually by raising the banner of religious orthodoxy, "a longstanding anti-capitalist reaction" and "widespread hostility toward the merchant mentality itself."[113] Meanwhile, the Holy Office, resisting papal authority and fomenting popular agitation, spearheaded the privileged estates' final assault on the New Christian merchants, arresting scores of them after the 1681 renewal of inquisitorial activity.

The aspirations of the mercantile class were perhaps most seriously undermined by the concurrent resurgence of the noble estate. After enduring an erosion of influence during the first half of the seventeenth century, the aristocracy was embraced by a crown intent on refurbishing the Old Regime, albeit with itself then firmly in charge. This gave rise to a "baroque absolutism" in which the landed wealth of the aristocracy stood as the chief bulwark of a revitalized social order.[114]

The merchant's challenge to the established order had been beaten back, but in the process an opportunity to relieve Portugal's deepening economic difficulties was lost. Bullion flowed out of the country, while many of its most successful merchants languished in prison. The prince regent had successfully weathered the storm of protest that followed his flirtation with the East India Company proposal, but the financial problems that he faced in 1673 still afflicted the royal treasury.

In 1680, it was reported that D. Pedro did not wish to further burden his subjects with taxes but, nevertheless, still wanted "to return the kingdom to its old splendor."[115] With the principal social upheaval of his reign all but resolved in favor of the privileged classes, that goal could be better addressed, albeit without benefit of large infusions of New Christian wealth. If António Vieira's advocacy of merchant-funded monopoly companies, a typically mercantilist policy, was unacceptable, what then could be done to resuscitate the economy and Portugal's imperial glory? One answer to this question was to arise from an increasing sophistication in Portuguese mercantilist thought.

CHAPTER V

THE MERCANTILIST MIND IN SEVENTEENTH-CENTURY PORTUGAL

Quando [a] circulação do dinheiro se faz no Reino, serve de alimentar o Reino; mas, quando sai do Reino, faz nele a mesma falta que o sangue quando sai do corpo humano.

Duarte Ribeiro de Macedo (1675)

... ha mais prata, e ouro de Portugal nos Reynos estrangeyros, do que no mesmo Reyno de Portugal.

Roland Duclos (1679)

Portuguese mercantilist thought usually ran parallel to, if somewhat behind, that of the rest of western Europe. During the seventeenth century, Portuguese writers joined in the general movement away from so-called bullionism toward attempts at describing how a favorable balance of trade could be created through appropriate commercial policy.[1] (*Bullionism* was the simplistic belief that national wealth could be increased merely by accumulating precious metals and maintained by preventing their export.) During the last third of that century, Portuguese mercantilist writers and policy makers gave increased attention to improving the balance of trade by encouraging domestic manufacturing. This effort was primarily inspired by the example of French manufacturing. The aim of preserving and increasing the supply of bullion, however, had not changed. The approaches to this end only became more sophisticated. Though the mercantilist mind in Portugal was in the mainstream of European economic thought, its thinking was quite naturally conditioned by the problems, limitations, and potentialities of the Portuguese economy.

Although we cannot here wrestle with the thorny problem of defining *mercantilism*,[2] the following short definition provides a useful point of departure. "The term *mercantilism* denotes the principles of the mercantile system, sometimes understood as the identification of wealth with money; but more generally, the belief that the economic welfare of the state can only be secured by government regulation of a nationalist character."[3] The phrase "government regulation of a nationalist character" is suggestive, for it denotes the innumerable legislative and regulatory provisions that crowded the mercantilist era (1500–1800). In a narrow sense, mercantilism can even be viewed as a collection of legal proscriptions and incentives designed to improve the relative economic positions of competing nations.

Like their counterparts elsewhere in Europe, the mercantilist thinkers of seventeenth-century Portugal were intent on augmenting the state's power through the acquisition of wealth. In order to do this, the accepted wisdom dictated a twofold approach. First, a policy of protectionism was necessary in order to prevent an influx of foreign goods, the sale of which would syphon off precious gold and silver. Second, the connection between goods and money, the latter being virtually synonymous with national wealth, induced strong adherence to balance-of-trade theory. Its simultaneous functioning as a protectionist system and a monetary system thus characterize two important and complementary aspects of mercantilism.[4]

In his classic study of the subject, Eli Heckscher initially defined *mercantilism* as a body of political philosophy best understood in terms of power and unification. As an agent of unification, the mercantilism of national monarchies had as its first objective the subjection of the medieval forces of universalism and particularism (that is, the Church and fractious nobles) in order to " make the state's purposes decisive in a uniform economic sphere and to make all economic activity subservient to considerations corresponding to the requirements of the state." Once these medieval forces had been contained, the object of mercantilism was to use economic forces to further the interests of the state, primarily by employing them "to strengthen the state authority itself; it concentrated on the *power* of the state."

Heckscher added that this concentration was concerned "primarily [with] the state's external power, in relation to other states."[5]

In the case of Portugal, from the thirteenth through the fifteenth centuries, the crown gradually but steadily achieved greater independence from the universalist influence of the Roman Catholic Church. In 1361, for example, D. Pedro I forbade the publication of papal letters without his approval. Unlike Spain, and most of the rest of Europe for that matter, Portugal had largely overcome particularist forces by the end of the fourteenth century. The crown's crushing defeat of the old nobility and their Castilian allies at Aljubarrota in 1385, which was made possible by an alliance with the rising, energetic middle classes, heralded the success of the drive for internal unification.

As its internal predominance slowly emerged, the Portuguese state also moved to concentrate and expand its power in the international arena by use of force and trade. North African cities such as Ceuta and Arzila were seized, in part, for the additional wealth and resources they could provide. The great influx of wealth that followed the voyages of da Gama and Cabral furthered the quest for power.

It has been argued, however, that Heckscher overemphasized the role of power. The accumulation of wealth for its own sake has also been described as being of paramount concern to the mercantilists.[6] In a brief but suggestive passage, Jacob Viner asked:

What then is the correct interpretation of mercantilist doctrine and practice with respect to the roles of power and plenty as ends of national policy? I believe that practically all mercantilists, whatever the period, country, or status of the particular individual, would have subscribed to all the following propositions: (1) wealth is an absolutely essential means to power, whether for security or aggression; (2) power is essential or valuable as a means to the acquisition or retention of wealth; (3) wealth and power are each proper ultimate ends of national policy; (4) there is long-run harmony between these ends, although in particular circumstances it may be necessary for a time to make economic sacrifices in the interest of military security and therefore also of long-run prosperity.[7]

Though Portuguese mercantilists may not have directly addressed all four of these propositions in their writings, they, as Viner maintained, probably would have accepted them as reflective of their own views.

It seldom can be said that Portuguese thinkers were in the forefront of the development of mercantilist thought, but Portugal was a pioneer in establishing three principles of colonization that became basic to mercantilism. The first principle was that

colonies were to be exploited for the exclusive benefit of the mother country; the second was that all trade was to be regulated so that the metropolitan country would have an excess of exports over imports; the third was that national wealth was to be measured by the amount of bullion that a state had within its borders and therefore that precious metals should be accumulated at all costs.[8]

These principles were first put into practice within a commercial structure that gave heavy emphasis to the role of the state instead of private trading companies. State trading remained the predominant form in Portugal until the late sixteenth century, although a large proportion of Portuguese commerce was in the hands of private traders who operated illegally.[9] During the seventeenth century, some state enterprise continued in the form of commodity monopolies but private initiative then predominated.

It must be stressed here that many of the ideas and programs of Portuguese mercantilists had a limited and transitory impact on the economy and society of imperial Portugal. Specific proposals by mercantilist writers were often ignored by policy makers. Nonetheless, those members of the ruling elites who took the time to read the writings of mercantilist thinkers surely shared a common understanding of the national economy, although they may have disagreed as to how best to improve its performance. This is not to say that the average unlettered farmer or worker did not understand mercantilist principles. Quite often mercantilist writers merely described everyday realities of trade that were encountered by the common people, whether they were selling produce at a rural fair or buying Brazilian sugar or English woolens in Lisbon. Explanations for inflation, scarcity, and dependence on foreign producers were probably well known to anyone who participated in the market economy.

Although the level of comprehension quite naturally varied from one individual to another, Portuguese society, like the rest of western Europe, was characterized by a general understanding and acceptance of many basic assumptions of mercantilist thought. This nexus of common understanding, together with the more-penetrating analyses of economic thinkers, comprised the Portuguese mercantilist mind.

Precursors of Colbertism

Portuguese mercantilist thought passed through three distinct phases. The first extended roughly from the sixteenth century to the middle of the seventeenth century and was primarily influenced by Italian and Spanish thinkers. The second phase lasted from about 1650 to 1750 and was marked by French and English influences. Finally, during the last half of the eighteenth century, mercantilist doctrines came under fire as English liberal and French physiocratic thought became known in Portugal.[10]

During the first phase, the era of bullionism, the practice of state trading was complemented by prohibitions on the export of precious metals. In 1568, for example, the Portuguese crown forbade the export of gold and silver to England. The sixty years of Spanish domination over Portugal (1580–1640) saw little change in mercantilist thinking, or at least in its application. However, writers of the early seventeenth century were well aware of the socioeconomic crisis that then beset Iberia. In Castile, public-spirited men known as *arbitristas*, among whom the most notable were Sancho de Moncada and González de Cellorigo, offered a variety of proposals for regenerating Castilian society. "It was under the influence of the *arbitristas*," according to Prof. J. H. Elliott, "that early seventeenth-century Castile surrendered itself to an orgy of national introspection, desperately attempting to discover at what point reality had been exchanged for illusion."[11]

Although conditions in early seventeenth-century Portugal were probably better, thanks in part to the continuing expansion of Brazilian sugar production, the same introspective analysis was taking place. In his *Diálogos do Sítio de Lisboa* (1608), for example, Luis Mendes de Vasconcelos observed that the conquest of India had brought Portugal neither new fields to cultivate nor new pastures in which to raise cattle. Moreover, the Indian enterprise constantly lured people from the countryside to the city, further swelling the burgeoning population of Lisbon. From there many embarked to seek their fortunes in the Far East. Meanwhile, the exploding growth of the capital city was not counterbalanced by any increase in food production. In Mendes de Vasconcelos's mind, Portugal was paying a high price for imperial glory, for its agricultural sector was increasingly unable to meet the demands of a rapidly growing metropolis.[12]

Another writer, Duarte Gomes Solis, who is regarded as one of the five most important mercantilist thinkers produced by Portugal,[13] also addressed himself to the problems afflicting his native land. Indeed, much of what he had to say foreshadowed Portugal's later adherence to French mercantilism. Solis, a New Christian, was born in Lisbon around 1562 and, while still in his twenties, embarked for the Far East, where he became a trade official in China. At that point, Solis was himself part of the population drain of which Mendes de Vasconcelos was to complain. After years of business activity and numerous adventures, including shipwrecks and capture by the English, he returned to Portugal and later journeyed to the court at Madrid. He arrived in the Spanish capital in 1621 and, like the *arbitristas* he undoubtedly encountered there, began writing down his thoughts on the Iberian crisis. By the following year, he had completed his *Discursos*.[14]

This work was rambling, diffuse, and sometimes barely intelligible, and it was cluttered with data and observations about Iberia and its possessions. The aspects of decadence discussed by Solis include population decline, the lamentable state of peninsular agriculture and manufacturing, and the impoverishment of the peoples of Iberia.

Solis's description of Lisbon is especially revealing. According to him, the city had few public facilities, including only one slaughterhouse, one wheat warehouse, and one hospital. Public services in Lisbon, as we will see later, were little improved half a century later. Solis also related that perhaps 20,000 black and white women, many of whom were beggars, worked the streets of the city, trying to sell water, fruits, and fish. Many of these same women were widows who had lost their husbands at sea and were left with children to feed and clothe in a city where prices for staples such as wheat were among the highest in Europe. Lisbon and its environs produced insufficient food, necessitating costly cereal importation. To make things worse, the city's chief water supply, the Tagus, was polluted. In the midst of general deprivation, wealthy Portuguese and foreign merchants indulged themselves in conspicuous comsumption and a host of unproductive students, clerics, and court hangers-on taxed the already-constricted resources of the city.[15]

Problems of commerce, money, and credit dominated the economic writings of Solis. In 1628, he published his *Alegación*, a work that lent support to the establishment of the first Portuguese East India Company.[16] The *Alegación*, which is regarded as the most important of Solis's writings, went beyond mere advocacy of the soon-to-be-formed company. Echoing a theme present in earlier writings, Solis stressed the need to develop manufacturing so as to curtail the importation of foreign goods and thereby stem the outflow of silver bullion.[17] He gave particular emphasis to the revitalization of silk production, an industry that had flourished briefly in the fifteenth century and then languished during the years of imperial expansion and union with Spain.[18]

Solis understood Gresham's law and urged that the common practice of hoarding silver be curtailed by phasing out fractional copper coinage, using more silver in revalued smaller coins and allowing free exportation of bullion. Predictably, his advocacy of free commerce in unminted silver, a step too drastic for bullionist Spain, was rejected. Solis also offered a rather cynical solution for the chronic indebtedness of the Hapsburg government. If necessary, and it sometimes was, creditors could have been repaid in revalued currency.[19]

Such measures, however, were only stopgaps that did not get at one of the principal causes of the Iberian decline, the nobility's aversion toward commerce. According to Solis, this factor was largely responsible for the economic decadence of Spain and Portugal. Since the titled elite showed little inclination toward trading landed gentility for the vagaries of commerce, Solis urged liberalization of the restrictions against Jewish immigrants and New Christians.[20]

Deficiencies in the Iberian fleets were also scored by Solis. Many ships that voyaged to and from India, the *carreira da Índia*, fell victim to shipwrecks or pirates because of their huge, unmanageable size and chronic overloading. Many carracks were in excess of a thousand tons displacement and were made top-heavy by enormous castles fore and aft. Their cargoes were sometimes so overweight that the gunports were below the waterline. To compound the problem, the vessels were poorly armed and constructed, too few in number, and manned by inexperienced crews. As early as 1612, Solis proposed that shipbuilding be put in the hands of the wealthiest merchants, whom he felt could remedy the situation.[21] Had the crown embraced these and other proposals of Solis the slow but inexorable decline of the Iberian economy might have been stopped, if not reversed.

Although his writings did not enjoy wide circulation, Duarte Gomes Solis was one of the more prescient mercantilist thinkers of the early seventeenth century. He drew heavily on his business experience in the Orient to provide explanations for the Iberian decline and suggestions for its remedy. Had his writing style been less jumbled and confusing, and had he published for a wider readership, his influence would have been much greater.[22] Solis's successors found that the condition of the Portuguese economy had improved little since his death in 1630. If anything, it had grown worse.

The breakaway from Spain in 1640 compounded Portugal's economic difficulties and increased the vulnerability of its already beleaguered colonies. The supply of silver that Portugal obtained in trade with Spain or through illicit commerce in the Rio de la Plata region was constricted, as was the overland commerce with its Iberian neighbor. The threat to sugar shipments increased, and the slave trade suffered a crippling blow in late 1641 when the Dutch captured Luanda, the great slave port of Angola. During the following year, revenues for Portugal's defense were considerably below anticipated expenditures. One estimate showed a deficit of 394,425 cruzados.[23]

Confronted by such harsh realities, the new regime reacted with measures that departed from previous economic policy. Solis and other writers had steadfastly promoted policies that favored native merchant communities and domestic manufacturing. Despite numerous exceptions, the Spanish monarchy had adhered to policies that favored Old Christian merchant communities, especially that of the bustling entrepôt of Seville. But financial need forced Portugal's newly established government to rely on expedient solutions. Prominent among such solutions was the opening of Portuguese ports to foreign traders in early 1641. D. João IV invited all foreign merchants, regardless of their national or religious affiliations, to sell their wares in Portugal and to freely take the proceeds, paying only the standard duties.²⁴ Short-term measures such as this clearly ran counter to mercantilist doctrine aimed at fostering local manufacturing and encouraging national commercial enterprise.

The pressures of war and financial crisis were also felt by the mercantilist thinkers of the Restoration. The two most influential mercantilist writers of the Restoration era, António Vieira (1608–1697) and Manuel Severim de Faria (1583–1655), both concentrated on the economic difficulties that beset Portugal and its empire. Severim de Faria focused his attention on domestic problems, while the famed Jesuit laid greater stress on Portugal's Atlantic commerce.

Severim de Faria published his chief work, *Noticias de Portugal*, in 1655. His first *noticia*, "Two means by which Portugal can greatly increase its population, in order to augment military forces, agriculture and navigation,"²⁵ drew heavily on the writings of Mendes de Vasconcelos, Duarte Gomes Solis, and Giovanni Botero (1540–1617), an Italian mercantilist. It was from Botero that Severim de Faria derived his belief that insufficient population lay at the root of economic decline. As perhaps the most prescient of sixteenth-century Italian mercantilists, Botero had anticipated the Malthusian dilemma posed by limited food supply and population increase. In order to maintain and increase population growth, Severim de Faria proposed stimulation of the agricultural and manufacturing sectors to increase the food supply and employment. Like numerous other mercantilist writers, he anticipated policies that found their fullest expression in France under Colbert.

Severim de Faria depended so heavily on Botero that he reproduced entire passages from the Italian writer's chief work, *La Ragione di Stato* (1589), without attribution.²⁶ The Portuguese mercantilist, however, was no mere plagiarist. In his emphasis on the population problem, a question that was central to the thinking of many seventeenth-century Iberian writers,²⁷ he went beyond repeating the thoughts of a predecessor and analyzed circumstances peculiar to Portugal. According to Severim de Faria, depopulation had three main causes: the drain of manpower to the colonies, the lack of employment in Portugal, and the unavailability of cultivable land.²⁸

It is not clear how much influence Severim de Faria was able to exert on behalf of the "Atlantic first" policy lately pursued by Portugal, but his discussion of the matter encapsuled many of the reasons for relegation of the Indian enterprise to secondary status. Brazil, the colonies of the west coast of Africa, and the Atlantic islands, as Severim de Faria pointed out, were relatively close to Portugal, and the returns from these territories outweighed the losses of men and ships required for their preservation. On the other hand, the drain of men and wealth to the East rendered possessions there more costly than their financial return. Many men perished on the arduous voyages to and from India, and a large number of soldiers would have been needed to protect adequately a network of outposts that stretched from southeast Africa to China.[29] The salaries of existing garrisons already burdened the treasury of the Indian viceroyalty. Moreover, many of those who made it to the Eastern empire became free-lance fortune seekers who contributed little to the imperial enterprise. In order to cut losses in the Orient, Severim de Faria proposed a return to smaller, safer ships; better hygiene on board ship; and the creation of a militia with a predetermined number of companies.[30]

An insufficiency of gainful employment caused many people to leave Portugal to seek their fortunes in the colonies. Fear of being impressed into service against the Spanish or flight from the ubiquitous Inquisition impelled the departure of many others. The economic decline that set in after 1670 and the post-1690 gold discoveries in Brazil gave further incentive to would-be emigrants. During the last half of the seventeenth century, various laws were issued to stop emigration, but they did not stem the tide.[31] For those who did not leave, the lack of employment was such that many could not afford to marry and start families. In a passage reminiscent of Duarte Gomes Solis's *Discursos*, Severim de Faria spoke of men and women begging in the streets in such numbers as to constitute a small army.[32]

Severim de Faria proposed policies favorable to domestic manufacturing as a solution to unemployment and the depressed rate of population growth. He advocated diversified production of textiles, including luxury fabrics, as an especially effective means of putting people to work. Furthermore, he proposed exploitation of domestic iron deposits for use in arms manufacture.

A land tenure system that did not stress increased food production, according to Severim de Faria, further retarded population growth. Without land from which they could draw additional sustenance, not enough people in the lower classes felt secure in starting or enlarging their families. Most agricultural land, especially that in the fertile Alentejo region, was in the hands of a few great proprietors, who had their own ideas about how their land should be cultivated, if it was cultivated at all. Quite often, large feudal estates simply produced insufficient food, or the landlords exacted so much from their tenants as to discourage any substantial increase in population. In order to remedy this situation, Severim de Faria recommended the creation of agricultural colonies on unproductive but potentially fruitful land, the digging of wells, and the extension of privileges to settlers of the new communities.

Severim de Faria was an important spokesman for many of the policies advocated by his New Christian predecessor, Duarte Gomes Solis. It is not clear how much influence Severim de Faria had on government policy, but at the very least he kept alive arguments on behalf of manufacturing and reform of colonial administration. Probably his most original contribution to mercantilist thought in Portugal was his discussion of the relationship between land tenure, food production, and population size. He did not, however, face up to the problems caused by the depredations of the Inquisition against New Christians, which also contributed to the difficulties plaguing the Portuguese economy. Later mercantilist writers usually showed a similar indifference to the fate of New Christians, but Severim de Faria's famous contemporary, Father António Vieira, was more sympathetic.[33]

Not being one content to push positions exclusively through his extensive writings, Vieira often acted as an effective lobbyist for his own proposals. His successful promotion of the Brazil Company was undoubtedly his greatest achievement in the economic arena. The company played a significant role in the rescue of Pernambuco from the Dutch and did much to curtail the debilitating loss of Portuguese shipping.[34]

Insights into Vieira's economic thought were scattered throughout his writings, but the essence of his thinking appeared in proposals written shortly after the Restoration of 1640. In 1643, he addressed a brief discourse to D. João IV that stands as a condensation of many ideas that were to be elaborated in his later writings.[35] To Vieira, the solution of Portugal's economic woes lay primarily in the liberalization of commerce: "Portugal cannot be saved without a great deal of money, and there is no better means to obtain it than by commerce, and in commerce the New Christians have no equals in financial resources and industriousness." Relieving New Christian merchants from the persecutions and confiscations of the Holy Office of the Inquisition was the centerpiece of Vieira's program for commercial revitalization.

Vieira seems to have yearned for a return to the prosperous years of the sixteenth century, when the Portuguese virtually controlled the spice trade. In his 1643 proposal, he lamented that the "lack of commerce has reduced the grandeur and opulence of Portugal to the miserable state in which Your Majesty now finds it," and then he asserted that "renewal of commerce is the fastest route to the old and happy state of affairs."[36]

Father Vieira also urged imitation of the commercial practices of the Dutch. The Hollanders had created a trading company for the East Indies in 1601 and one for the West Indies in 1621. Both of these firms had wrought havoc with Portugal's far-flung empire, seizing valuable possessions in Brazil, Africa, and the Far East. In emulation of the Dutch example, Vieira called for the establishment of two great monopoly companies for trade and navigation, one to replace Solis's short-lived Portuguese East India Company and another for the Brazil trade. The capital needed to found these companies was to come from the New Christians of Portugal and from the Portuguese Jews scattered throughout Europe, especially those living in Holland.

If implemented, this program would have numerous benefits. Money needed to combat Dutch and Spanish aggression would then be available; the departure of Jews from Holland would cripple the Dutch trading companies, in which they had heavy investments; an increase in the size of Portugal's population would result; and foreign merchants would feel more confident about doing business in Portugal since New Christian colleagues there would be in less jeopardy of having their fortunes confiscated. Moreover, many Portuguese uncertain of their country's ability to prevent a Spanish takeover would embrace the national cause, and Portugal would benefit from the industry and intelligence of New Christians as well as from their extensive contacts in foreign commercial centers.[37]

In other writings, Vieira advocated the establishment of a commercial bank similar to that in Amsterdam. Jewish capital and financial experience would underwrite this project. In his later years, Vieira supported those who favored the development of manufacturing but remained preoccupied with the expansion of maritime commerce.[38]

In an unpublished document probably written by Vieira around 1643, the great Jesuit offered a five-point program for fending off the Castilian threat and revitalizing the Portuguese economy.[39] The first point was a call for the efficient administration of resources already available to Portugal. Vieira urged that essential goods be purchased when and where prices were cheapest. Soldiers should be well trained, and a good intelligence network should be built up throughout Europe, particularly in key Spanish cities. These defensive measures, the author argued, would save Portugal money in the long run. The use of mercenaries was also supported since Portuguese manpower was so thinly stretched in defending the colonies. In addition, it was suggested that admitting English Catholics to the colonies might not be a bad idea since they would marry and increase colonial populations.[40]

The second proposal called for the expansion and improvement of Portuguese shipbuilding. Minimum tonnage and armament requirements should be established.[41] Angolan slaves could be used to build caravels on the banks of numerous Brazilian rivers, using the sturdy woods found in Bahia, Rio de Janeiro, and Maranhão. Iron from São Paulo could be used for the artillery of the ships. With the building and putting into service of additional ships, royal revenues would climb and commodity exports would increase.

In the third point, the liberalization of restrictions against New Christians was advocated. In wording very similar to that of the *Proposta* of 1643, it was argued that Portuguese Jews dispersed throughout Europe should be encouraged to bring their wealth and commercial skills back to Portugal. Vieira asserted that the return of these potentially valuable subjects could be facilitated by the granting of a general pardon.[42]

The fourth measure proposed by Padre Vieira was the greater exploitation of the mineral wealth of the colonies.[43] The gold diggings of São Paulo and the Zambesi River basin were singled out as especially promising areas for prospecting. Emeralds and other precious stones rumored to abound in Brazil could also be exploited. The revenues received from colonial diggings might be used to pay for the arming of Portuguese ships and for the creation of a company of merchants. This suggestion is interesting for it shows that the Jesuit contemplated sources other than New Christian wealth for the financing of the trading companies he championed.

Finally, the document recommended a reduction of hostilities with Portugal's adversaries. Settlement of colonial disputes with the Dutch should be reached and some accommodation with Spain should be found in order to revive the slave trade with Peru.[44] This last proposition seems to coincide with Vieira's rather pessimistic estimation of Portugal's chances of defeating both its Dutch and Spanish enemies. He later advised D. João IV that Portugal should attempt to regain Pernambuco by offering the Dutch an enormous indemnity. If this should fail, the Jesuit proposed a drastic solution. In return for a strong and lasting peace, Portugal should recognize the Dutch claim to Pernambuco. Most Portuguese, however, strongly opposed appeasement.[45] Fortunately for Portugal, the tenacious battling of Brazilian colonists ultimately ousted the Hollanders and rendered Vieira's harsh solution unnecessary.[46]

António Vieira's economic writings were largely derivative and did not add a great deal to Portuguese mercantilist thought. Much of what he proposed had already appeared in the works of Duarte Gomes Solis and others. His emphasis on merchant capitalism instead of manufacturing suggests that he was somewhat out of step with other European mercantilists. However, it must be added that Vieira envisioned an economic regime on a global scale, instead of relying on the narrower nationalist approach of figures such as Severim de Faria. And, as we saw in the preceding chapter, Padre Vieira believed that Portugal would one day become the leader of a fifth universal monarchy. Thus, it must also be added that Vieira's often perceptive and practical proposals for improving imperial Portugal's economic condition were, to some extent, linked with something much grander than mere national prosperity. Perhaps the fifth biblical monarchy represented a synthesis of the thinking of Vieira the universalist Jesuit and Vieira the Portuguese nationalist.

Though he was not a seminal economic thinker, the talented Jesuit was a keen observer who appreciated the successful policies of the Dutch and others and urged their imitation. In Restoration Portugal, at least, Vieira's tireless promotion of religious toleration and merchant companies had greater impact than the writings of more penetrating mercantilist thinkers. The establishment of the Brazil Company and the vain but valiant struggle on behalf of New Christian merchants constituted twin monuments to his profound influence.

Mercantilism and Internal Development: The French Example

The power and opulence that António Vieira desired for Portugal were objectives fully in accord with mercantilist thought and policy, but one route toward these goals that he did not emphasize, that of manufacturing, had gained increasing application in seventeenth-century Europe. This was especially true in France, a country whose example was closely followed by the Portuguese after 1668.

Like other European nations, France had passed through a bullionist phase. The glittering river of silver flowing into Spain from the Indies had caused many of the French to believe that national wealth was contingent on how much bullion could be gathered and held within the country's own borders.[47] Laws to prevent the export of gold and silver were passed, but, since France did not have the easy wealth of the Americas at its fingertips as did Castile, alternative routes to greater national wealth and power also received attention. Besides bullionism, a policy that was never really abandoned during the seventeenth century, commerce and internal development became the principal avenues to a stronger French economy. The French policies for internal development had the greater influence on Portuguese mercantilists.

The internal development of France—which included attention to population growth, agriculture, stock raising, poor relief, mining, and manufacturing—received increased encouragement during the early seventeenth century. Under the leadership of Cardinal Richelieu (1624–1642), manufacturing enjoyed a brief flowering, even though the powerful minister probably gave greater emphasis to trading companies and France's colonies. Richelieu lent his support to a number of manufacturing endeavors, particularly the production of textiles. Other manufactures also won Richelieu's backing.

The glassworks of Picardy, for example, were granted letters of patent in 1627. Sugar refining, the manufacture of footwear, and iron casting are further examples of manufactures encouraged by the cardinal. The highly successful royal printshop (*imprimerie royale*) was founded by Richelieu in 1640. Unhappily for French industry, only the printing enterprise and a few other "enterprises established under Richelieu were of lasting or even temporary importance."[48]

The ministry that followed Richelieu's, that of Cardinal Mazarin (1642–1661), enjoyed the diplomatic triumphs of Westphalia (1648) and the Peace of the Pyrenees (1659). However, "in the field of industry, commerce, and economic expansion, the era . . . was one of stagnation and retrogession." Yet, commerce was given some encouragement during Mazarin's ministry and, to a lesser degree, so was manufacturing. An attempt to aid domestic production by raising tariffs was made, though the higher import duties actually caused a decline in the crown's customs. During the Fronde (1649), various *parlements* called for the protection of domestic textile production against the importation of Dutch and English cloth. Probably "the most important textile establishment of the period was that organized at Sedan for the manufacture of English, Dutch and Spanish-style woolens."[49]

These and other efforts were largely a continuation of the policies of Cardinal Richelieu. Although Mazarin's ministry was characterized by economic stagnation and a preoccupation with internal and external political struggles, the promising start made by Richelieu was passed along intact into the hands of Jean Baptiste Colbert, the chief architect of industrial mercantilism.

It was in the France of Louis XIV and Colbert that absolutism and mercantilism most successfully (if briefly) combined in the promotion of internal development. Virtually unchallenged in the political arena and secure in his alliance with a triumphant and cooperative nobility, Louis XIV turned his attention to consolidating control over the economy. Under the Sun King, "the state laid down regulations for the conduct of industry and consequently all marks of local and corporative control were replaced by others of the state."[50] Through this program, the guild system of the provinces was expanded and brought into conformity with that of Paris. The push for uniformity was complemented by an increasingly complex and detailed system of technical regulations (*reglements*), which Colbert began to erect in 1666.[51]

Colbert's interest in the internal development of France was most obviously manifested in his encouragement of manufacturing enterprises. The textile industry received special consideration. A variety of privileges were given to entrepreneurs willing to establish or expand factories, including exemption from inspection and regulation by the guilds. Increased manufacture of fine woolens, laces, silks, gold and silver cloth, tapestries, rugs, and numerous items of clothing followed. Colbert simultaneously sought to reduce consumption of foreign textiles and expand the export of French cloth. Through his influence, the Levant Company was founded in 1670 to promote exports of textiles. The fine cloths of Languedoc later gained a large share of the Levantine markets. Items of wool for the clothing of the general populace, especially stockings, were also produced and sold on a larger scale as a result of Colbert's efforts.

Manufactures other than textiles enjoyed similar encouragement and success. Mirror, glass, and earthenware production increased. Venetian glassmakers were induced to come to France and work in the newly established royal mirror company. By 1680, this company, the longest-lived of the enterprises founded by Colbert, was giving Venice serious competition on the French market. Tin plate, iron, brass, and copper production also experienced considerable stimulation under Colbert. He was especially anxious to reduce French dependence on foreign iron foundries in order to secure a reliable supply of armaments for the army and the navy. A miscellany of other products (for example, soap, leather, paper, and sugar) also attracted Colbert's attention.

As in the case of textiles, the production of such items did not originate with Colbert, but he, together with Louis XIV, gave such strong support to manufacturing that by 1683 France led the world in industrial production. From that year, the one in which he left office, until "the inauguration of the five-year plan by the Soviet government in Russia, no conscious and directed effort to develop a nation's industrial life was so prolonged, so thorough, so permeating, so far reaching as that of Colbert."[52]

The significance of the great minister's achievement is borne out by the fact that the term *Colbertism* stands as a synonym for industrial mercantilism. The ideas that propelled the resurgence of French internal development, particularly manufacturing, were by no means new, but the backing of a powerful, energetic minister and a supportive monarch were instrumental for its expansion and refinement. In order to increase French power and wealth, Colbert concentrated his efforts on expanding and improving domestic manufacturing, believing this to be the most effective way to keep bullion within French boundaries. The greater concentration on internal development differentiated French mercantilism from the lingering bullionism of Spain and England's emphasis on commerce and navigation.

Colbert's pivotal role in the flowering of French industry was not, by his own reckoning, that of a theorist. Instead, he considered himself

a doer who acted on grounds of well-established economic reasonings. . . . He probably derived his economic philosophy from discussion, and governmental precedents. It was in the very air about him in seventeenth-century France. Mercantilist thinking that had been burgeoning there for a half-dozen generations bore its fruit in Colbert, not because he was a thinker who saw more deeply into its problems or reasoned better from its premises, but because he was a man of action, vested with power, who accepted the mercantilist concepts as the only natural and logical way of attaining the end which he sought—a powerful and wealthy France, united under a glorious monarch.[53]

Unlike England, where vocal business interests used Parliament to promote a welter of often conflicting commercial, industrial, and agricultural legislation, absolutist France provided fertile ground for a coordinated approach to economic development. Unfortunately for French manufacturing, however, Colbert held sway only too briefly. With the outbreak of the Dutch war in 1673, Louis XIV withdrew his support for many of Colbert's projects. Within a few decades, the gains made were lost as courtiers of lesser capabilities in the economic arena succeeded the great minister. The revocation of the Edict of Nantes in 1685 forced the industrious Huguenots to leave, taking their wealth, business acumen, and manufacturing skills with them. Many of the exiles found refuge in England and Holland, where their talents gave impetus to the economies of those countries. By

1700, French finances were in near-chaotic condition.[54] But, during the years of Colbert's tenure (1661–1683), the advantages to be derived from expanded manufacturing and other aspects of internal development did not go unnoticed by foreign observers, including the Portuguese ambassador, Duarte Ribeiro de Macedo.

Portuguese Advocates of Colbertism

Duarte Ribeiro de Macedo (1618–1680) had first gone to France in 1659 as the secretary of a negotiating team headed by the count of Soure. The count's mission was to block the soon-to-be-consummated Peace of the Pyrenees between France and Spain. But the efforts of the count failed, and Spain, then freed of military entanglement with the French, could bring more forces up to the Portuguese frontier. Ribeiro de Macedo, who proved himself to be an effective member of the unsuccessful mission, returned to Portugal in late 1660 to resume a career in the bureaucracy.[55]

Born in the village of Cadaval in the province of Estremadura, Ribeiro de Macedo was a precocious youth whose intellectual abilities ultimately led him to a master's degree (*licenciado*) from Évora and a doctorate (*doutor*) in law from the University of Coimbra. Following stints as a judge (*juiz de fora*), crown magistrate (*corregedor*), and appellate magistrate (*desembargador dos agravos*), he joined the Soure mission. After returning from France, he assumed the position of *desembargador* on the High Court of Appeals (*Relação*) in Oporto. In 1666, he was promoted to a position on the High Court of Appeals in Lisbon, the Casa da Suplicação.[56] Two years later, Ribeiro de Macedo's rapid rise as a jurist was diverted toward diplomacy again, this time as Portugal's resident minister in Paris. Apparently, his support of the coup that had deposed D. Afonso VI in 1667 was an important consideration in his appointment.[57]

The first task of the neophyte diplomat was to smooth the presumably ruffled feathers of Louis XIV. The Portuguese worried that the French monarch was perturbed that an agreement had not been reached with him before the signing of the Luso-Spanish peace treaty of 1668. But the Sun King readily accepted Ribeiro de Macedo's solicitations, and the new envoy, who was to spend nine years at the French court, had equal success in subsequent negotiations for the marriage of his friend and supporter, the duke of Cadaval, to Mademoiselle d'Harcourt.[58] The most significant accomplishment of his years in France, however, came from Ribeiro de Macedo's observation of mercantilism as practiced under Colbert and his advocacy of a similar course for Portugal.

But, before he committed his thoughts on economics to paper, the ambassador had taken time to record his impressions of France. While Ribeiro de Macedo relayed the usual descriptions of diplomatic and ceremonial activity at court, he also found space to comment on Parisian society. In 1670, for example, he wrote to a friend, detailing the "libertine" behavior of French women. In a later letter, he strongly implied that French husbands were so lenient, and female liberties so extensive, that males could not maintain order in their own households without recourse to legal support.[59]

Ribeiro de Macedo also took careful note of innovations in municipal administration and services that might have application in Lisbon. At the request of the prince regent, who was interested in upgrading Lisbon's inadequate municipal services, the ambassador forwarded a report on street illumination and sanitation in Paris.[60] In this relation, he first commented on the vast improvement in the cleanliness of Parisian streets since 1660. By 1670, a large fleet of horse-drawn wagons patrolled twenty sanitation districts and was largely responsible for the cleanup. Parisians were obliged to place their trash in front of their doors for early morning pickup. Residents paid a tax every six months to cover outlays for the wagons' maintenance and the drivers' salaries. The Parisian city council paid for the cleaning of public squares, covered bridges, and wharves.[61]

In 1668, the problem of trash disposal in Lisbon was quite worrisome, for the streets of the capital were buried in rubbish that had piled up during the years of struggle with Spain. Not only did this accumulation of trash further congest Lisbon's already narrow streets, it posed a serious threat to public health as well. Yet, finding the money to pay for the cleanup was not an easy matter, given the postwar recession that was settling over Portugal. For the most part, the crown left it to the Lisbon city council to finance the cleanup but did give some support by decreeing that nobody, including recalcitrant nobles, was exempt from paying sanitation assessments.[62]

Although a lack of adequate street lighting also plagued Lisbon,

Ribeiro de Macedo thought that this problem could be inexpensively remedied. According to the ambassador, Parisian street illumination was largely necessary for reasons of safety, especially during the long winter nights in the French capital. In Paris, illumination was usually provided by lanterns suspended from cables strung between upper-story windows. At nightfall, residents appointed for the task lit candles of a standard size, which burned until about three o'clock in the morning. The Portuguese minister advised against the use of this form of lighting in Lisbon, noting that the French lamps were subject to breakage by rains, strong winds, and vandals. The form of lighting used in London—householders were required to burn lanterns in the niches above their doors from nightfall until two o'clock—Ribeiro de Macedo suggested could be instigated in Lisbon by appealing to the residents' strong sense of piety. If they could be persuaded to place candles with the numerous crosses that adorned the buildings along the city's streets, he reasoned, sufficient illumination would result. The envoy did not think that as many lights were needed in Lisbon as in Paris, where the winter nights were longer and darker and the sky so overcast that neither sun nor moon was visible for days on end.[63]

During his years in France, Ribeiro de Macedo repeatedly complained about the climate and its unhealthiness, about his lack of funds and the inevitable delay in their arrival, and of his homesickness (*saudades*) for Portugal. Moreover, the cost of living in France, which in his case included frequent moves to Versailles, Saint-Germain, and Saint-Cloud, was also a burden.[64] But, despite such annoyances, the envoy found time to write a number of memorials in which his ideas for improving Portugal's economic fortunes were set forth.

Although many of his contemporaries exalted the maritime commerce of Holland and England, Ribeiro de Macedo looked to France for his principal model of how mercantilist doctrine should be implemented. Spain, in his opinion, was a decadent nation whose example should be avoided at all costs.[65] Like Colbert, the Portuguese envoy was concerned with how best to attract and keep precious metals. He regarded the circulation of money within a national economy as virtually synonymous with the circulation of blood in the body. The ideal solution envisioned by him and other mercantilists was one in which money circulated within the national economy with as few obstacles to its movement as possible and in which more gold and silver flowed into the nation than out. As with his French and English counterparts, Ribeiro de Macedo took a strongly rationalist approach to economic analysis and sought to apply analogies from the natural sciences (for example, the circulation of blood) to society.[66]

The principal work in which Duarte Ribeiro de Macedo articulated his version of Colbertism was his *Discurso sobre a introdução das artes no Reino*, written in Paris in 1675.[67] The *Discurso* was divided into two parts. The first concentrated on the outflow of precious metals from Portugal, why this happened and what might be done to remedy the situation. The solution offered, of course, was emulation of Colbert's promotion of manufacturing. The second part of the *Discurso* elaborated on the advantages of manufacturing, discussed the Spanish economy as an example of the sort of decline that indifference to industry caused, and argued that royal revenues would rise if Colbertian policies were adopted.

According to Ribeiro de Macedo, national economies fell into three simplistic categories: wealthy (*rico*), middling (*medíocre*), and poor (*pobre*). Wealthy states absorbed more gold and silver than escaped, the middling gained about as much as they lost, and the poor experienced a constant "hemorrhaging" of the metals. The Portuguese ambassador placed his country in the *pobre* category because of its chronic loss of precious metals.[68]

Duarte Ribeiro de Macedo cited the importation of luxury goods into Portugal as the primary cause of the metal drain from his country. He recommended sumptuary legislation as a means of stemming the outflow of metals and proposed the establishment of domestic industries to meet metropolitan and colonial demand for foreign goods. Unlike the bullionists, Ribeiro de Macedo fully understood the futility of attempting to prevent the escape of precious metals with repeated legislative prohibitions and the searching of ships and travelers. Policies designed to produce a favorable balance of trade offered the best hope for retaining gold and silver in Portugal. The envoy recognized devaluation as another means of discouraging the export of coins, bullion, and even plate, but, like Colbert, he regarded this as an unsatisfactory expedient.[69]

The ambassador viewed Portugal's unfavorable balance of trade with England as exemplary of its disadvantaged economic position.

The Portuguese, for example, annually purchased 80,000 pairs of silk stockings from England, which, at 4 cruzados per pair, represented a drain of 320,000 cruzados. In addition to luxury items, Portugal imported great quantities of baize, serge, and other fabrics from the English. The export of primary products to England hardly balanced the influx of finished goods from that country. Although some salt, olive oil, and other metropolitan agricultural products made their way to the English market, the navigation laws had adversely affected Portuguese exports. Brazilian tobacco and sugar were also traded, but only in small quantities since both were then grown on English plantations in North America and the Caribbean. According to Ribeiro de Macedo, the disparity in the balance of trade was such that no English ship ever departed Lisbon "without taking a great sum of money."[70]

A similarly unfavorable balance characterized Portugal's trade with France. A variety of finished products produced by Colbert's factory system were imported, as were commodities such as wheat, barley, and even codfish, a dietary staple procured by Portuguese fishermen for centuries. Portugal, in turn, traded dyewood and speciality woods from Brazil, as well as a number of agricultural products. Some tobacco and sugar were exported, but, like the English, the French had erected trade barriers to these commodities since they could import them from their Caribbean possessions. Here again, the Portuguese had to make up a deficit with a trading partner by exporting scarce metal supplies. Ribeiro de Macedo observed wryly that the French took some Portuguese products more out of necessity than interest since it was not possible to get gold or silver for all their exports.

Portugal also obtained finished goods from Holland, Sweden, and Hamburg. Many armaments were imported from these northern trading partners, as were fittings, masts, and sails for ship construction. Oil paintings and other adornments for the households of metropolitan and colonial elites were purchased from the Dutch. As usual, Portuguese gold and silver filled the breach when northern merchants were on the favorable side of the trade balance.

Salt from the great deposits at Setúbal, a coastal city to the southeast of Lisbon, was the principal commodity exported to the northern markets. Since it was often purchased with silver, salt was a bright spot in the trade picture. Besides salt, the Portuguese exported agri-

THE MERCANTILIST MIND   131

cultural commodities, Brazilian woods, tobacco, sugar, and wine, a recent addition to Portugal's list of important export items. Precious stones borne to Lisbon on the *carreira da India* also were forwarded to the commercial centers of northern Europe, especially those of Holland.[71]

In his *Discurso*, Ribeiro de Macedo regarded Portugal's decline into the *pobre* category as a development of recent origin. According to him, the loss to the Dutch of key outposts in the Eastern empire had forced the Portuguese to use increasing amounts of bullion for trade with Europe instead of relying on their former near monopoly on Oriental products.[72] The concurrent erosion of Portugal's sugar monopoly compounded the problem. Although he did not say so, the envoy probably realized that the drying up of silver imports from Spain made matters even worse. To Portugal's illustrious diplomat, the route back to a growing stock of bullion, and thus *rico* status, was to be paved by sumptuary legislation, encouragement of domestic manufacturing, and better exploitation of the agricultural potential of Brazil.

Just before Ribeiro de Macedo was notified to leave France for another post, the second sumptuary pragmatic (*pragmática*) of the prince regent's reign was issued on January 25, 1677.[73] Previously, *pragmáticas* of this sort had been promulgated with the object of limiting luxury consumption and defining privileges of costume selection. The law of early 1677, however, was also aimed at fostering the growth of domestic textile production and sought to do so by proscribing certain items of foreign-made apparel. The pragmatic "prohibited the use and sale within the realm of French hats, ribbons and luxury lace, Italian brocades, and the more expensive English and Dutch cloths; the 'new draperies' (baizes and serges) and English stockings, which together made up the bulk of imports, were not affected."[74]

While Ribeiro de Macedo's writing on behalf of manufacturing surely played a part in the promulgation of the 1677 law and subsequent protectionist legislation, the envoy was hardly alone in promoting Portuguese industry. For example, D. Luis de Meneses, the count of Ericeira, who would come to be known as the Portuguese Colbert, strove to implement policies patterned on those of mercantilist France. Like his famous French counterpart, Ericeira was not a theorist but an energetic and effective proponent of domestic manufacturing. During his fifteen years as minister of the treasury (*vedor da fazenda*), he endeavored to give substance to the writings of Ribeiro de Macedo.

Ambassador Ribeiro de Macedo probably was not altogether satisfied with the thurst of the 1677 *pragmática*. Since the bulk of textile imports consisted of less-expensive fabrics, this was the market sector that should have been given greatest attention. Furthermore, he argued that the best course for Portugal was not to attempt to compete with foreigners in the production of luxury items. In his *Discurso*, the diplomat identified three types of manufacture. The first, that of luxury goods, included costly textiles, jewelry, and gilded coaches. These items might require as great an outlay for raw materials as for the labor to produce them. Despite the presence of a rudimentary sericulture in Portugal, the envoy apparently did not share French (or Severim de Faria's) enthusiasm for the production of expensive silk fabrics. The second category included those products for which the labor expended in production was greater than the value of the materials themselves. He cited flax, cotton, and wool textiles and iron implements as examples of this type. The third group consisted of especially cheap materials like wood, which could be used to produce paper.

The ambassador urged that Portugal concentrate on the production of goods in the last two categories since they were of common use, easier to make, and the most needed. Moreover, there was an abundance of natural fibers and dyestuffs in Portugal and its colonies that could readily be used in textile manufacturing. In the case of wool, Ribeiro de Macedo argued that it should not be exported in its raw state and then repurchased after being woven in French or English mills. Instead, garments produced by the inexpensive but experienced labor of Portugal's northern provinces could shortly fill domestic demand, and then surplus production could be sold on the Spanish market and in the colonies.[75]

In part two of the *Discurso*, Ribeiro de Macedo advanced five propositions as justification for the introduction of manufacturing. First, expensive and ostentatious display would be curtailed if those given to such behavior were limited to costumes and adornments made in Portugal. It was toward this end that the 1677 *pragmática* was in part directed. Furthermore, the living standard of the many, instead of just the privileged few, would rise. According to point two, this would happen when loafers, idlers, and the numerous unemployed were put to work producing goods to fill increasing demand. Ribeiro de Macedo noted that throughout Portugal there was considerable unemployment, or at least underemployment, especially among women. Third, gainful employment in manufacturing facilities and the resultant rise in the standard of living would induce an increase in population. The envoy observed that the population in French cities where silk production had been introduced earlier in the century had grown substantially. In the fourth point, it was asserted that Portugal, more than any other nation in Europe, could and should introduce manufacturing. If Portugal could complement the vast natural resources available to it in the colonies by establishing manufacturing, it could once again become one of the world's great centers of commerce.[76] Conversely, if Portugal did not keep pace with its European competitors, effective control of the colonial market, and thus of the colonies themselves, would be lost as foreign traders further insinuated themselves into the Portuguese empire. Finally, the establishment of industry would cause royal revenues to rise. The general economic expansion resulting from a larger, wealthier, more effectively employed population would naturally cause an increase in taxable income.[77]

All of these points repeated ideas already abroad in mercantilist Europe. Ribeiro de Macedo, in fact, may have derived some of his ideas from Thomas Mun's landmark work, *England's Treasure by Forraign Trade* (1664), a French translation of which was published in Paris in 1674. He may also have been influenced by other English writers, especially Sir Josiah Child and Samuel Fortrey.[78] The envoy had surely relied on the writings of Duarte Gomes Solis, Manuel Severim de Faria, and other Portuguese precursors, as well as those of Spanish *arbitristas* such as Sancho de Moncada. The policies of Colbert, of course, had greatly impressed Duarte Ribeiro de Macedo.

Despite the derivative nature of the *Discurso*, the work presented a well-organized, realistic evaluation of the liabilities and potentialities of the Portuguese economy. It was to become the manifesto of Portugal's subsequent venture into manufacturing,[79] a subject that we will investigate in a later chapter.

134   THE MERCANTILIST MIND

Though the *Discurso* proposed remedies for the economic malaise that afflicted Portugal, other writings of Ribeiro de Macedo focused on the more effective exploitation of the colonies, particularly Brazil. As a rationalist, the Portuguese mercantilist showed little of the "psychosis of the marvelous" that characterized the popular vision of Portuguese America.[80] Even though Brazil may have suggested a terrestrial paradise in its outward appearance, this was not to stand in the way of its systematic exploitation for the furtherance of Portuguese power and wealth.

In an unpublished memorial, Ribeiro de Macedo identified thirty-seven Brazilian products that were already consumed by the European market or that could profitably be introduced there.[81] With his *Observações sobre a transplantação dos fructos da India ao Brazil* (1675), the minister outlined a strategy for deriving greater returns from Portugal's immense colony. If, for example, cinnamon, a plant that had been taken from the Portuguese East to Brazil before the loss of Sri Lanka, the chief producing region, were grown on a large scale in the Maranhão, it could be could be marketed in Europe at prices much lower than those charged by the Dutch usurpers.[82] The envoy further asserted that cultivation of oriental plants in Brazil promised greater profits, at smaller outlays, than those extracted from the mines of Potosí.[83]

Ribeiro de Macedo wanted to expand and diversify the agrarian capitalism already existing in Brazil. Sugar, of course, had been a resounding success as a transplant, having first been introduced into the New World via Portugal's Atlantic islands. Ribeiro de Macedo singled out cotton as another successful transplant. Indeed, he may have hoped that it would be used in the weaving shops mentioned in the *Discurso*.[84] As a further example of the variety of plants that could be introduced from the Far East, the mercantilist writer cited the orange trees brought to Portugal from China by way of Goa in 1635.[85]

Apparently, Ribeiro de Macedo's plans for the systematic transfer of Asian plants to Brazil did not stem from his observation of French mercantilism. While serving as minister in Paris, he had read a translation of a history of the Royal Society of London.[86] The work's discussion of successes with oriental plants in North America prompted the diplomat to urge that the Portuguese do likewise before their English allies got the jump on them.[87] Ribeiro de Macedo went on to suggest to the prince regent that the prospects for success were excellent since no other monarch possessed so fertile and productive a colony as Brazil.[88] If his proposals were followed, the ambassador added, the revenues obtained would give Portugal the means to defend Brazil and its newly planted wealth.

In his *Observações*, Ribeiro de Macedo made clear, as he did in the *Discurso*, the belief that Spain's decline was the result of wrongheaded economic policy. While in Spain itself the principal failure was the neglect of manufacturing, the problem in the Spanish Indies was an overreliance on the silver mines of Mexico and Peru.[89] Development of agricultural exports had indeed languished in the Hapsburg Indies, although in New Spain, a land of great agricultural potential, the Castilian government had encouraged introduction of non-American products, especially during the sixteenth century. Basic needs for agricultural products were thereafter met, but New Spain's possibilities of gaining a respectable share of the European market were never realized.[90] In anticipation of the physiocrats, Ribeiro de Macedo saw that sustained prosperity lay in the productivity of the land. To his mind, the road to long-lasting wealth began in the plantation and factory, not the mine shaft.

The Portuguese mercantilist reinforced his case for a policy of systematic transplantation by noting the support of his illustrious friend and correspondent, António Vieira. The great Jesuit and Duarte Ribeiro de Macedo had exchanged letters for many years. Although the bulk of their correspondence contained news of diplomatic activity, they also discussed economic matters. After reaching his conclusions on the efficacy of transplantation, Ribeiro de Macedo communicated his views to Vieira. In early 1675, Vieira, then in Rome, wrote to voice agreement, adding that oriental transplants to Brazil made in the early sixteenth century had been so successful that D. Manuel I had ordered their destruction, fearing that his hard-won Indian enterprise would be jeopardized. Vieira also revealed that he had once advised D. João IV to adopt a similar transplantation policy, and, despite his earlier interest in the mines of Africa and Brazil, he admitted that agricultural products were "better and more certain mines than those of Rio de Janeiro."[91]

Vieira and Ribeiro de Macedo, however, never reached full agreement on other policies needed for revitalization of the economy.

Padre Vieira stuck to commercial expansion in emulation of the Dutch, while the author of the *Discurso* favored manufacturing on the French model. Unlike Vieira, he did not openly champion New Christian interests, despite the potentially valuable contribution that minority might have made toward development of Portuguese manufacturing. In part, this stance seems to have stemmed from the simple realities of his position. The secretary of state, Francisco Correia de Lacerda, to whom the *Discurso* had been addressed, was a staunch, even fanatical defender of the Inquisition. Lacerda was no doubt appalled by the 1674 papal suspension of autos-da-fé for which Vieira and powerful New Christian merchants such as Manuel da Gama de Pádua had successfully lobbied. Naturally, Ribeiro de Macedo did not wish to risk favorable reception of his program by bringing New Christians into the picture.[92] In his correspondence with Vieira, however, there were clear indications that the Portuguese envoy shared the Jesuit's tolerant sentiments toward New Christians.[93] Perhaps he also identified with the position of Colbert, who tried to protect Jewish businessmen.[94]

While in Paris, Ribeiro de Macedo not only saw to his diplomatic duties and economic writings, he also made specific policy suggestions in his correspondence with Secretary Lacerda. In late 1675, for example, he encouraged commerce in Brazilian cacao, noting that a royal agent in Rouen desired a sample of the product, apparently in anticipation of its sale there. Two years later, Prince Regent Pedro followed up with a royal order for the establishment of cacao plantations in the Brazilian captaincy of Pará.[95] This action on behalf of commercial agriculture in Brazil undoubtedly pleased the mercantilist writer.

Ribeiro de Macedo also kept an eye out for artisans skilled in textile manufacture, metallurgy, and other technologies. This had to be done surreptitiously, for the French sought to block establishment of competing manufactures in Portugal.[96] Only months before his departure, the ambassador proposed that a new armament factory be established in Portugal to produce bronze and iron artillery, with the use of the skills of an Italian arms expert he had recently encountered.[97] It is not clear whether anything came of this, but in 1685 a similar plan was launched when two Frenchmen were contracted to produce small arms in Portugal.[98]

At the orders of the prince regent, Duarte Ribeiro de Macedo journeyed to Madrid in 1677 to serve as ambassador extraordinary at the Spanish court.[99] His tenure there was brief. In 1680, he set out for Savoy to negotiate for the marriage of Pedro's daughter, D. Isabela Luisa Josefa. This mission was abruptly halted with the ambassador's death in the Spanish port of Alicante on July 10, 1680. The news of the envoy's untimely death was relayed to Lisbon by his assistant and traveling companion, Padre Rafael Bluteau, a member of the Theatine order. Responding to Bluteau's unhappy news, the count of Ericeira lamented the loss of his good friend and reported general distress at court over the death of Portugal's astute ambassador.[100]

Padre Rafael Bluteau (1638–1734) had come to Portugal in 1668 at the command of the general of his order. Writing half a century later, Bluteau stated that he assumed positions as preacher (*pregador*) of the royal chapel and qualifier (*qualificador*) of the Holy Office of the Inquisition.[101] He did not reveal, however, that, like Ribeiro de Macedo, he had acted as a Portuguese agent involved in covert attempts to lure foreign artisans to Lisbon.[102] Despite the strongly pro-French sentiment at court, Bluteau's initial sermons did not captivate the critical Lisboans. But one listener consoled him by noting that even the exhortations of Padre Vieira, whose eloquence in the pulpit was renowned on both sides of the Portuguese Atlantic, were not always received with enthusiasm.[103] In fact, a sermon given by Vieira in the royal chapel in 1668 was satirized by one noblewoman for its facile treatment of three topical issues: the first he understood but did not explain, the second he explained but did not understand, and the third he neither explained nor understood![104] Bluteau's (or Vieira's) talents as a sermonizer, however, will not concern us here. The French cleric is best remembered as the compiler of a multivolume dictionary[105] and as a spokesman for expanded silk production in Portugal.

One year before embarking on his tragic journey with Duarte Ribeiro de Macedo, Bluteau published an instruction manual on silk cultivation in which he frequently echoed the mercantilist views of the unfortunate envoy.[106] Like Ribeiro de Macedo, he strongly supported manufacturing. The cleric believed that mines and manufactures were the only true sources of national wealth. The latter, however, were less risky and less expensive. Of all the crafts, he regarded the weaving of silk as the most profitable. Portugal, according to Bluteau, was well situated to exploit the demand for silk, having a favorable climate and being closer to centers of consumption in northern Europe and thus less vulnerable to pirate attack than shipments of the fabric coming from the Mediterranean.[107]

Bluteau proposed that mulberry trees (silkworms feed on mulberry leaves) be planted in place of the olive and orange orchards that occupied much of the cultivable land in Portugal. Olive trees, he argued, took too long to mature and orange groves were often damaged by the weather. Additional cultivable land could be had by planting mulberries along the roadsides, as was done in Italy and France. According to Bluteau, a well-established sericulture offered the best prospect of increased wealth for the nobility, alleviation of poverty, employment of the idle, and an end to the bullion drain.[108] Padre Bluteau's enthusiasm for silk production seems to have been considerably greater than was Ribeiro de Macedo's.

Another proponent of sericulture was Roland Duclos, a French Jew who had received the contract for silk manufacturing in Lisbon in 1677.[109] Two years later, Duclos wrote a short paper that gave typically Colbertian arguments for the expansion of silk production.[110] The establishment of sericulture throughout Portugal, he asserted, would stem the outflow of bullion and attract precious metals from other nations. English and Italian merchants, according to an estimate of Duclos, annually took away more than one million cruzados for silk stockings alone.[111] Duclos added that the merchants of northern Europe would prefer to buy nearby Portuguese silk, which he called the best in the world, if sufficient quantities were available.[112]

Extensive cultivation of mulberry trees and the spinning of silk fibers could, as Bluteau also argued, help eliminate poverty. Duclos described the readying of fibers for weaving as a relatively easy but remunerative task that could be done by women, children, and the elderly.

Roland Duclos may have written his paper after reading Bluteau's manual, or he may well have helped the cleric complete that work. His brief document was significant in itself on two counts. First, it gave further evidence that the seed of Colbertism had been planted in Portugal. Second, Duclos had some practical suggestions of his own. He proposed, for example, the bringing of three or four weaving experts and their looms from the north so that similar machines could be constructed and operated in Portugal.[113] It is not known what influence this particular document may have had on contemporary policy, but, at the very least, it demonstrated concern over the beleaguered state of the Portuguese economy and proposed measures for its relief.

Duarte Ribeiro de Macedo stands as the most penetrating and systematic mercantilist thinker produced by seventeenth-century Portugal.[114] His *Discurso*, though largely derived from the ideas of contemporary European mercantilists, was an intelligent application of the basic tenets of Colbertism to the Portuguese economy. The work was complemented by his *Observacões*, which proposed transplantation of oriental flora as a means to better exploitation of Brazil's agricultural potential. Ribeiro de Macedo did not discuss in any detail the interrelationship between the agricultural and manufacturing regimes he envisioned for Brazil and Portugal, but it seems likely that he imagined Brazilian plantations producing a variety of products for use in Portuguese mills and factories. Such a scenario would have been in keeping with mercantilist thought.

The thinking of Ribeiro de Macedo and his fellow mercantilists had a definite impact on the economy and society of imperial Portugal. Eventually, attempts were made in the metropolis and the colonies to implement certain of their ideas, but what the mercantilist writers proposed and what happened were, of course, two different stories. The policies pursued by the imperial government were also shaped by fiscal needs, defense costs, and other contingencies. Moreover, the crown had to contend with landed nobles, inquisitors, foreign traders, and others who often did not support its economic programs. The smallness of Portugal's population and economic base greatly limited its ability to withstand the commercial expansion of more powerful European economies. Portuguese leadership was not altogether persuaded by some of the mercantilists' ideas. Despite the touted superiority of manufactures and commercial agriculture as sources of revenue, D. Pedro II still lent support to the expensive and uncertain quest for mineral wealth.

Social and economic obstacles thus lay in the course to power and opulence charted by Portugal's mercantilist writers. Their ambitious plans for stemming the outflow of precious metals were largely ignored after 1690, when economic conditions in Europe improved and great deposits of alluvial gold were discovered in Brazil. Portugal's most articulate mercantilist spokesman of the first half of the eighteenth century, D. Luís da Cunha, persisted in backing the ideas espoused by Ribeiro de Macedo and others, but he was a lone voice in the economic wilderness whose calls were not heeded until the coming to power of Pombal. Long before this occurred, however, the government of D. Pedro II took a number of steps designed to improve Portugal's economic fortunes. As we will see in the next two chapters, these steps included traditional monetary and fiscal measures as well as programs for internal development modeled largely after those of Colbertian France.

CHAPTER VI

PUBLIC FINANCE DURING AN ERA OF ECONOMIC DECLINE

V. Alteza tem alfandegas, tem consulados, tem almoxarifes, tem esta[n]cos, tem Mestrados, tem Reais de agoa, sizas, portos secos, e molhados, bens confiscados, e as rendas da Coroa, e outras miudezas, q̀ os Reys pacados não tinhão: e elles forão Ricos, e V. Alteza pobre.

António Vieira, S.J. (circa 1675)

From roughly 1670 to 1690, Portugal and its European neighbors experienced a general recession that adversely affected national economies and the collection of government revenues. During these years, price levels for most basic commodities dropped markedly, reaching their nadir in the late 1680s.[1] According to Frédéric Mauro, the period was characterized by an insufficiency of precious metals, capital shortages, and limited wars.[2] The cyclical nature of such recessions has been closely examined by Gaston Imbert, who discerned the movement of regular, long-term price cycles throughout the early modern era. The movement of one such cycle, as Imbert showed, was clearly downward during the late seventeenth century.[3]

Explanations advanced by Mauro, Imbert, and others to account for these cycles, particularly those of the seventeenth century, have usually emphasized the declining rate of population growth, economic setbacks caused by incessant warfare, capital shortages, and loss of New World bullion. These factors, especially warfare and demographic decline, were inextricably woven together. The slaughter of thousands of soldiers obviously played an important role in retarding population growth. However, epidemic disease and the lower average temperatures that Europe experienced during the "little ice age" of the seventeenth century (a cooling that adversely affected food production) also had noteworthy effects on the growth of population.[4] War, in its turn, laid waste to the fields and pastures from which both nobles and peasants drew their sustenance. There can be little doubt that the ravages of the struggle for the Restoration contributed to Portugal's subsequent economic woes. Moreover, inadequate supplies of precious metals and a concomitant increase in the circulation of debased currency undoubtedly had a role in the economic constriction that afflicted Europe after 1670. Economically disruptive as these factors may have been, they cannot individually or collectively account for the fundamental rupture in European life that has come to be known as the General Crisis of the seventeenth century.

In an article that still sparks controversy, Eric Hobsbawm suggested that the General Crisis was the "last phase of a general transition from a feudal to a capitalist economy."[5] Approaching the economic difficulties of the seventeenth century from this point of view has certain merits. According to Jan de Vries,

it directs attention away from explanations that rely on outside forces such as population pressure, bullion imports and warfare, and directs it toward the economy itself. It supplements the economic historian's typical preoccupation with measures that affect output with an analysis of the sources of demand for goods and services in the preindustrial economy. Finally, it focuses on the social structure that supports a given economic system and draws attention to the fact that changes in investment, production, and consumption do not occur in isolation from the social structure.[6]

If one sees that the transition described by Hobsbawn encountered resistance from the feudal regime, then the societal roots of the General Crisis can be more readily understood. The rapid economic expansion of the sixteenth century did not lead directly to modern capitalism since it took place within an essentially medieval social framework. The socioeconomic disruption that characterized the seventeenth century can also be attributed to the contradictory impulses of an emerging economic order and an increasingly outmoded power structure.[7]

Although Hobsbawm was not altogether clear as to the duration of the General Crisis, it is known that it occurred during the first two thirds of the seventeenth century. Thereafter, resolution of the challenge of mercantile wealth to traditional power followed two distinct paths. On the one hand, bourgeois elements in England and the Low Countries then enjoyed considerable political power with which to complement their accumulated wealth. On the other hand, most European societies, including Portugal's, "found an efficient and stable form of government in *absolutism* on the French model."[8] After Westphalia (1648), aristocrats throughout the continent began to align themselves more closely with their national sovereigns, discarding many of their disruptive particularist ambitions to help forge socioeconomic regimes that successfully constrained and co-opted the essential but dangerous mercantile class.

But what was the relationship of these developments to the economic downturn that occurred after 1670? This question is fraught with difficulty, but it can be tentatively suggested that European society was temporarily exhausted by the exertions of the previous decades. The monarchies, nobilities, and mercantile classes of Europe were recuperating from a struggle that was to be renewed in earnest late in the following century. This exhaustion surely had an adverse effect on production, investment, consumption, and the accumulation of capital at a time when warfare, population decline, bullion shortages, and dropping temperatures already depressed economic activity. Public treasuries were hard pressed to meet fixed expenditures, not to mention extraordinary outlays, and net government income showed little growth or even declined.[9]

Raising Taxes and Reforming Collection Procedures

The consolidation of absolutist government in Portugal came about during the reign of D. Pedro II and coincided with the suppression of the mercantile class's pretensions to greater economic, social, and religious freedom. Portugal's economy, which was already in a weakened state after a generation of warfare, was thereby further debilitated by the stepped up attacks on New Christian merchants. Moreover, the aristocracy's temporarily successful defense of the status quo did not fool its more perceptive members. Though in the minority, figures including the duke of Cadaval, the marquis of Minas, and others sought to restrain anti–New Christian fervor so that the wealth and commercial expertise of the merchants could be employed to Portugal's benefit.

The quantitative dimensions of the economic crisis besetting Portugal can be seen in price movements and chronic public deficits. The movement of most commodity prices shows that Portugal's late seventeenth-century recession followed the general trend, bottoming out around 1690. (See figure 1.) Wartime expenditures had financially weakened both the national treasury and local governing units. In 1645, the Cortes determined that an annual outlay of 2.15 million cruzados was needed for defense expenditures. Receipts for that year, however, fell short by 670,000 cruzados.[10] An accounting made a few years thereafter revealed a shortfall of 235,000 cruzados.[11] By 1668, the financial situation had become quite precarious and the government found itself having great difficulties in paying salaries of soldiers and officers already in arrears.[12] Count Schomberg, architect of the post-1660 reorganization of Portugal's army, was owed the princely sum of 10,000 cruzados.[13] Portugal also owed large sums to England, as stipulated in the Luso-English marriage alliance of 1662 (2 million cruzados), and to the Dutch, as specified in the 1669 treaty with Holland (3 million cruzados to be paid mostly in salt). Large floating debts were the order of the day.

In 1675, the Lisbon city council bemoaned the "numerous taxes with which this city is burdened, and the miserable state to which the necessities of the times have reduced the old prosperity of its residents."[14] Meeting in that same year, the Overseas Council (Conselho Ultramarino) lamented the depressed economic conditions that then afflicted Portugal's colonial empire. According to the councillors, declining sugar and tobacco exports, the loss of profitable Eastern commodities to the Dutch, and lower prices being paid for brazilwood gave little reason to expect an upswing in colonial revenues. The only ray of hope they could point to was a possible influx of precious metals from Africa and Brazil.[15] Given the crown's accumulated debts

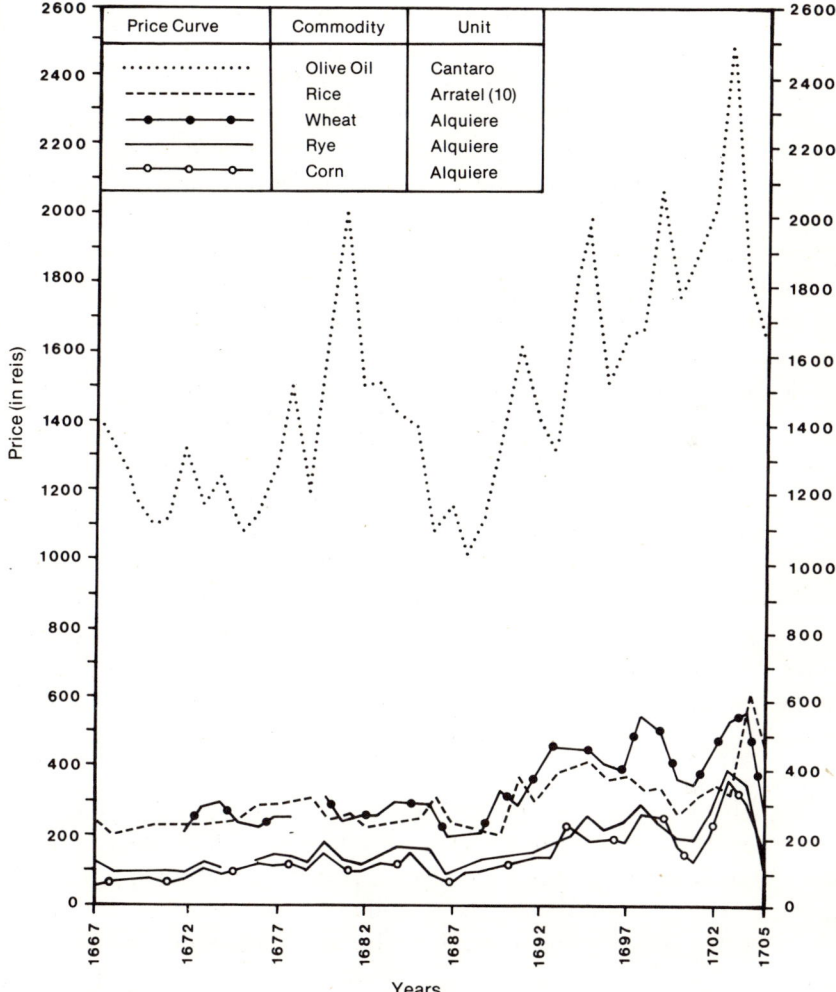

Figure 1. Selected commodity prices in Portugal, 1667–1705. (data from Serrão, ed., *DHP*, 4:505–9). The units used in the graph are measures of either volume or weight. The alquiere displaces about thirteen cubic liters, and the arratel is roughly equivalent to one pound. The price for ten arratels of rice was employed here for the sake of comparison, since that quantity is roughly equal to one alquiere. A cantaro (which is the same as one almude) is equal to three gallons. All prices are given in reis. It should be noted that Portuguese currency was devalued by twenty percent in 1688, thus fostering subsequent price increases. Four hundred reis (which equals one cruzado) in 1668 was approximately equal to three American dollars in 1980.

and the disappointing returns coming from the colonies, and despite repeated complaints against additional taxation by the Lisbon city fathers and others, the crown saw little alternative but to request periodically additional financial support from the three estates.

In 1668, representatives of the nobility and *o povo* had agreed to the imposition of additional taxes on the sale of wine and meat. These excise taxes, known collectively as the *real d'agua*, were hoped to raise 500,000 cruzados.[16] Of that amount, 400,000 was earmarked for maintenance of military garrisons, and the remaining 100,000 was needed to pay off war contractors (*assentistas*).[17] The newly augmented *real d'agua* was to be collected for a period of six years. The ecclesiastical estate, which still awaited Vatican recognition of Portuguese independence and selection of officials to fill many important Church offices, made its views known on various issues but did not participate to the extent of paying the added impost.

The fact that many of the unpaid *assentistas* were New Christians undoubtedly aggravated antimerchant sentiment in the 1668 Cortes. Yet, many of those who opposed the New Christians on this and other issues were themselves responsible for major drains on the treasury. The myriad privileges, exemptions, salaries, pensions, and other forms of income enjoyed by nobles and clerics imposed a constant burden on the crown's resources, especially during periods of decline.

By 1674, the year of the next meeting of the Cortes, the clerical estate, which had since been reconstituted, found itself and the other two branches being asked for even greater financial support. The prince regent then requested a million cruzados. The additional 500,000 cruzados were to come from increased taxes on tobacco. This sum was needed to meet growing defense expenditures.[18] The Junta do Tabaco, which was established shortly after D. Pedro abruptly disbanded the unruly 1674 Cortes, was to oversee collection of imposts on the crown-monopolized product. Unhappily for the government, the *real d'agua* of 1668 had not procured as much revenue as expected. The excise on wine and meat was, therefore, raised again.[19] Thanks to an enabling bull promulgated by the Vatican, the clergy was ordered to pay the sales tax. By 1680, a then-submissive Cortes approved renewal of the taxes on wine, meat, and tobacco.

In addition to the *real d'agua* and the excise on tobacco, the crown

Plate 1. Lisbon's Terreiro do Paço as portrayed by Dirk Stoop, 1662. (Reproduced from Virginia Rau, *D. Catarina de Bragança, Rainha de Inglaterra* [Coimbra, 1941].)

Plate 2. D. Pedro II, king of Portugal.
(Courtesy of the Biblioteca Nacional de Lisboa.)

Plate 3. A Portuguese noble couple of the seventeenth century. (Courtesy of the Biblioteca Nacional de Lisboa.)

Plate 4. Frei António das Chagas.
(Reproduced from Fernando
Castelo-Branco, *Lisboa Seiscentista*, 3rd ed.
[Lisbon, 1969].)

Plate 5. Padre António Vieira.
(Reproduced from Joel Serrão, ed.,
Dicionário de História de Portugal
[Lisbon, 1971].)

Plate 6. Fish vendors in Lisbon's Praça da Ribeira.
(Reproduced from Castelo-Branco, *Lisboa Seiscentista*.)

Plate 7. An auto-da-fé procession wending its way through Lisbon's Rossio.
(Reproduced from Damião Peres, ed., *História de Portugal*
(Barcelos, 1928–1966).

Plate 8. D. Nuno Álvares Pereira de Melo, first duke of Cadaval. (Reproduced from *Personagens Portuguesas do Século XVII* [Lisbon, 1942].)

Plate 9. D. Luís de Meneses, third count of Ericeira. (Reproduced from his *História de Portugal Restaurado* [Oporto, 1946].)

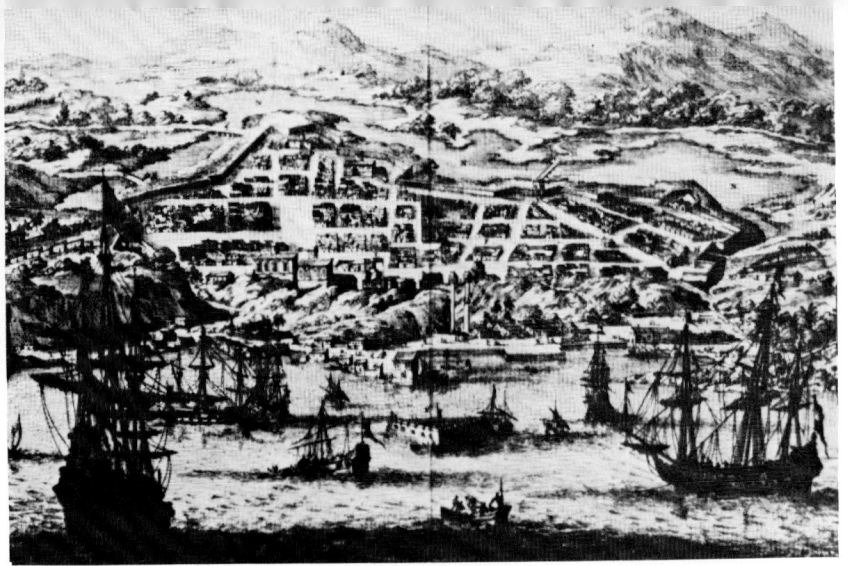

Plate 10. Salvador da Bahia de Todos os Santos (circa 1671), foremost entrepôt of the Portuguese empire. (Reproduced from Stuart B. Schwartz, *Sovereignty and Society in Colonial Brazil* [Berkeley, 1973].)

Plate 11. Manifest of the tobacco cargo borne by the Bahian *frota* of 1703. (Courtesy of the Archivo Nacional do Torre do Tombo.)

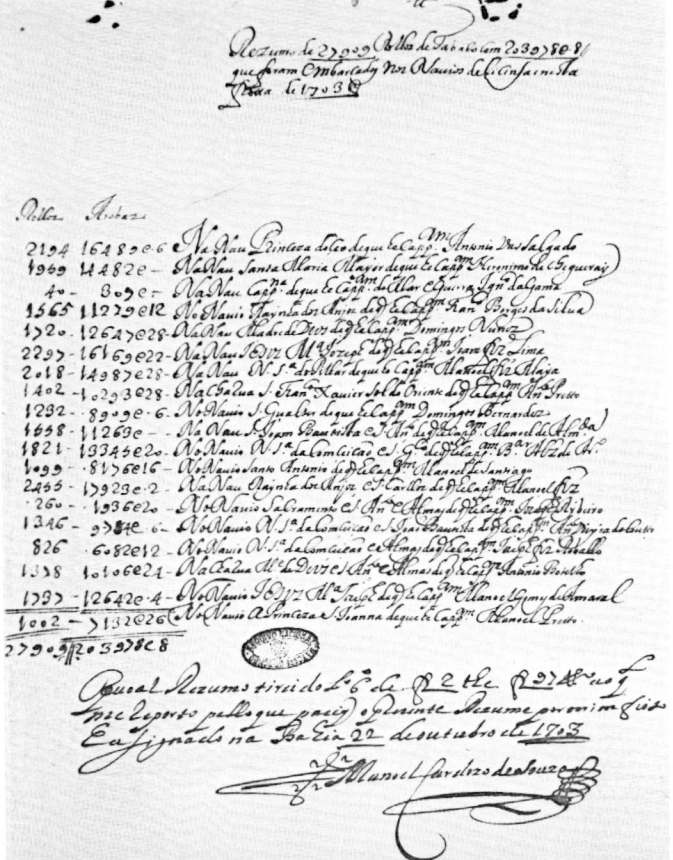

Plate 12. Lisbon harbor (circa 1700). (Courtesy of the Biblioteca Nacional de Lisboa.)

obtained income from a variety of other sources, including rents on royal landholdings, customs taxes such as the *décima* (a ten-percent ad valorem duty), payments from contractors and tax farmers, and the *quinto* (the royal fifth of all precious metals mined in Portugal and the empire). (For a detailed accounting of royal income in 1681, see table 3.) Through the revision of legislation concerned with certain of these taxes, it was hoped that the crown's income would increase.

A few months after D. Pedro had prevailed on the 1668 Cortes to raise the *real d'agua*, a move taken more out of financial desperation than reformist zeal, the government promulgated a new *regimento* for its coastal and border customs houses.[20] This was done because the crown was interested in renewing commercial ties with Spain. A detailed list of regulated prices known as a *pauta* was compiled that year, and a wide variety of goods was soon flowing across the border or entering Spanish ports after short voyages from Portugal.[21] The *décima* was assessed on all goods leaving and entering the country. Luso-Spanish trade increased during the following years. Though data on this commerce is scanty, historians do know that the seven customhouses (*alfândegas*) in the province of Beira collected over 38,000 cruzados in 1678.[22]

All such revenue did not go to the crown, of course, since tax farmers kept monies collected in excess of annual contract payments. In 1668, a merchant named Manuel da Costa Martins signed a three-year contract with the crown for the right to collect the *décima* at various coastal and border *alfândegas*. During the term of the contract, Martins agreed to pay 30,000 cruzados for the first year, 37,000 for the second, and 40,000 for the third. At the end of this period, Martins renewed the contract in concert with a partner, agreeing to pay 30,000 cruzados per annum for the next four years.[23] As was often the case with royal contracts, Martins may have lost money on the earlier agreement, necessitating the help of a partner and a reduction in the contract premium.

Though sluggish economic conditions may have played a part in reducing duty collections, the bane of contractors was usually the smuggler. Smuggling was rife along both the border and coastal regions near Spain, and all manner of items moved surreptitiously between the two countries. Not unexpectedly, this illicit commerce caused unremitting concern for the crown and its contractors since revenues and profits hung in the balance. In order to assure its return on contracts, the crown sometimes took rather draconian measures to discourage those who transgressed. In the 1668 contract for playing cards, for instance, it was noted that many contraband examples of these gaming articles were being smuggled off ships coming from India. Being arrested for this offense, or even buying or using the contraband, could lead to a four-year exile in disease-ridden Angola.[24]

Issuance of the *décima regimento* of 1668 was followed by further promulgations aimed at standardizing and modernizing Portugal's revenue collection system. In 1674, a new *regimento* was issued for the *sisa*, a ten-percent ad valorem duty on commercial transactions.[25] Like the *décima*, this duty provided the crown with a substantial portion of its income. It was hoped that by better codifying the *sisa* a number of procedural and jurisdictional questions that had hampered its collection could be resolved. Furthermore, the framers of the new *regimento* sought to eliminate abuses by tax farmers and to make certain that imposition of the levy did not vary unfairly from one region to another, a problem that had apparently been the cause of much complaint.[26]

In some instances, the crown moved to get rid of taxes when they impeded internal trade. Although most of the medieval tolls had been eliminated by the late seventeenth century, some still remained. The Lisbon *câmara* complained in 1675 that the *vila* of Benavente was exacting 50 reis on each moio of wheat passing on its way from the Alentejo to the capital.[27] (One moio is equivalent to twenty-four bushels.) During the following year, the holders of the contract to supply Lisbon with coal reported that the *vila* of Alcaçer do Sal was imposing a levy of the same amount on each sack of coal conducted through its jurisdiction.[28] In both cases, the prince regent agreed that these local tributes should not continue.

The crown also moved against the incompetence and dishonesty that characterized all too many tax officials. In 1691, for example, D. Pedro II established severe penalties for officials who diverted the crown's revenues to their own use. But apparently this did little good, for the wave of abuses grew, necessitating issuance of similar legislation in 1717.[29]

Devaluation and Protectionist Legislation: The First Steps

Measures to increase and streamline revenue collections were accompanied by calls for monetary adjustments and protectionist legislation. The Cortes of 1668 devoted much attention to a proposal for devaluing gold currency by twenty percent. This idea had largely been introduced as an expedient means of reducing the amount of bullion needed to pay the salaries and homeward passage of foreign mercenaries still on Portuguese soil. Since a good number of these fighting men were French and English nobles who had brought horses along for cavalry service, the Portuguese also faced the expense of transporting their mounts. Despite the great transport costs involved, the Portuguese were by then eager to be rid of the mercenaries since their salaries were totaling upwards of 100,000 cruzados per month.[30] If, as argued before the Cortes, the face value of gold currency were raised by the simple act of stamping coins with numerical values greater than their intrinsic worth, one-fifth of the precious metal going to the foreigners could be saved.

There were strong objections to this proposal. Despite earlier outcries by the *juiz do povo* and the Lisbon *câmara*, silver currency had been devalued by twenty-five percent in 1663 as a stopgap measure to meet the burgeoning costs of war. The *câmara* thereafter claimed that it took 160 reis to purchase an item in Portugal that could be had for 100 in England.[31] When devaluation was discussed in the 1668 Cortes, both the Junta do Comércio and the Treasury Council argued against the proposal. In their *consultas*, the junta and the council asserted that Portugal's dwindling stock of bullion would be further diminished as foreign merchants took advantage of the devaluation, selling ever larger quantities of imported goods and remanding even more silver and gold to their home countries.[32] The unfavorable opinions of the two royal ministries convinced the noble estate of the inadvisability of devaluation. Its representatives decided after "all due deliberation that the currency should in no way be altered, since the advantage is momentary and the harm is perpetual."[33]

Though devaluation of gold currency was found unacceptable by the Cortes, protectionist measures to constrict the influx of foreign goods did find some favor. It was on this issue, however, that many within the privileged estates and representatives of *o povo* parted company. To the dismay of domestic artisans, and despite economic recession, nobles and clerics consumed great quantities of imported items instead of products made in Portugal. Weavers, tailors, and other artisans felt that their very livelihoods were threatened by their privileged countrymen's penchant for foreign finery. With much justification, they contended that Portugal's unfavorable balance of trade could be attributed to conspicuous consumption of things such as English woolens, Italian silks, and French tapestries.

Conspicuous consumption had in fact been the target of sumptuary legislation issued by generations of Portuguese monarchs. During the reign of D. João IV, such legislation was made part of that ruler's wartime austerity program. But the need for repeated prohibitions on elaborate costumes, lavish personal adornments, gaudily appointed coaches, et cetera, clearly suggested that the privileged paid them little heed. Nevertheless, the crown, the popular estate, and a progressive element within the noble estate continued the effort to restrict consumption of foreign goods and thereby curtail the flight of precious metals.

Meeting in the 1668 Cortes, the third estate discussed legislation to limit purchase of imported textiles, which were regarded as the principal cause of the bullion drain. Significantly, delegates went beyond merely calling for yet another prohibition on consumption. In a *consulta* submitted to D. Pedro, they proposed that sumptuary legislation be linked to the crown's encouragement of domestic woolen production. The representatives further suggested that a minister of "intelligence and energy" be put in charge of this program and that looms and other weaving equipment be purchased abroad and put into operation in Portugal. Development of local woolen production, according to the delegates, "would enrich the realm."[34]

The third estate's *consulta* clearly anticipated the advocacy of textile manufacturing in Duarte Ribeiro de Macedo's 1675 *Discurso*. Although a concerted move toward manufacturing was still some years away, D. Pedro did respond rapidly to the call for sumptuary legislation. On June 8, 1668, he issued a *pragmática* against "the great superfluity and excesses which there are in dress, costumes, ornamentation and other things" and went on to proscribe a wide range of expensive apparel. On the following afternoon, D. Pedro was formally installed as prince regent, and, as if to emphasize his determination that the day-old law be enforced, he appeared dressed in an outfit of simple black silk, perhaps to the discomfiture of more luxuriously clad courtiers.

The 1668 *pragmática* was also aimed at curtailing the conspicuous consumption of certain wealthy members of the third estate. Well-to-do merchants and guildsmen aspiring to privileged status could ill afford to appear in clothing unbefitting individuals of such pretensions. Neither, for that matter, could their wives and children. The *pragmática* therefore repeated a traditional ban on the wearing of silk, a fabric reserved for the privileged, by members of the mechanical professions.[35] This prohibition was reconfirmed four years later in a newly drafted *regimento* for the city of Lisbon. In response to this latest prohibition, the *câmara* submitted a lengthy *consulta* to the prince regent, which noted rather coolly that widespread compliance with the 1668 *pragmática* was dependent on the example of the royal household. It may be that not all members of D. Pedro's inner circle shared his attachment to simple dress. The councillors also made the not unreasonable point that royal income from *alfândega* collections would decline commensurately with the desired drop in luxurious imports. Nonetheless, the *câmara* reaffirmed its support for the restrictions on sumptuous clothing and adornments. In one of numerous subsequent *consultas* urging greater enforcement of the ban on luxury items, the city council asked that the Venetian example of outlawing wigs be followed and that the prohibitions of the 1668 *pragmática* be formally repeated.[36]

In addition to its adverse impact on royal revenues (the enlargement of which, after all, was the principal purpose of the fiscal, monetary, and protectionist measures considered by the crown), sumptuary legislation had other shortcomings. Enforcement, for example, was a touchy problem since the crown placed itself in opposition to otherwise loyal supporters among the privileged who regarded consumption of luxury goods as a right and as a measure of their social standing. But perhaps the most fundamental drawback of such legislation was the attempt to curtail demand for foreign goods without a concurrent increase in domestic production of acceptable substitutes. It was to this problem that the third estate addressed itself when calling for establishment of a manufacturing program.

Observance of the 1668 *pragmática* apparently was wanting, for nine years later the crown issued another such prohibition. Even as a general recession spread across Europe, conspicuous consumption by the privileged few probably declined but little during the first decade of D. Pedro's reign. Streets once buried in refuse piled up during the war years were then crowded with richly dressed and magnificently transported noblemen, clerics, merchants, and others. But bullion continued to flow out of Portugal, and the state of the economy failed to improve significantly. Rejection of the New Christian proposal to finance an East India company blocked one possible avenue to commercial recovery; and, despite an emphasis on fiscal reform during the early years of D. Pedro's rule, Portugal's troubled economy failed to respond. Nonetheless, certain later steps taken in the realm of monetary policy helped improve the state of public finance.

Mounting Expenses and Monetary Reform, 1680–1688

D. Pedro's request that the 1679–1680 Cortes renew the *real d'agua* clearly suggested the anemic condition of the treasury. Collection of the million cruzados he had hoped to receive during the six years following the Cortes of 1674, half of it coming from imposts on wine and meat and the other half from an excise on tobacco, was falling short of expectations. In an effort to discover the causes of the shortfall, the crown had ordered the submission of a series of financial accountings. In 1678, for example, the prince regent asked the Lisbon city council for an accounting of its payments toward the *real d'agua* for the years 1668–1674. One year later, he requested that the *câmara* submit an accounting for the succeeding three years. The *câmara* thereafter reported that it would not soon be able to meet its share of the imposition, blaming other tax obligations for the shortfall.[37]

Given the deficiencies in revenue collections, the crown saw little alternative but to reconvene the Cortes. Besides its ongoing expenses for national defense, grants to the privileged, salaries for the royal bureaucracy, et cetera, the government felt compelled to make additional outlays, among which, for example, were funds to aid the Poles in their persisting struggle with the Turks.[38]

The principal reason for convening the 1679–1680 Cortes was neither renewal of the *real d'agua* nor aiding the Poles. Instead, the crown needed an enormous, one-time contribution of a million cruzados to cover the anticipated expense for the marriage of D. Pedro's daughter Isabel (1669–1690) to the duke of Savoy. Upon learning of this request, the Cortes delayed its response for a few days, during which time the noble and popular Estates attempted to foist the bulk of the outlay on one another. Thereafter, it was decided that a temporary tax on grants, pensions, and salaries be imposed and that the excise on tobacco be increased. The clergy, not having an enabling bull, was spared this latest tax increase.[39] The imposition on incomes, which was initially set at seven percent, was subsequently increased to ten percent when it was found that collection of the million cruzados was falling behind.[40]

Spending all of the extraordinary outlay on the imminent marriage soon became a moot question, however, for the duke of Savoy reneged on his pledge. To the great disgust of the Portuguese, this reversal occurred only after a costly expedition of twelve ships, convoying the duke of Cadaval as chief emissary, had sailed to Nice in 1682 and then waited for months in hopes of bringing the betrothed back to Lisbon.

The Savoyard leader had not reneged without considerable justification. His subjects, fearful of Louis XIV's well-known wish to annex Savoy, had prevailed on the duke to remain. Moreover, they were strongly opposed to a clause of the marriage agreement that would have made Savoy a virtual province of Portugal.[41]

As this diplomatic debacle was unfolding, it was decided that the *real d'agua* as renewed by the Cortes in 1680 would remain in force as long as D. Pedro felt it necessary.[42] The then-compliant Cortes was not to meet again until 1697. Compliance, however, did not guarantee delivery of the assessed revenue. Throughout the 1680s, especially during the rush to scrape together money for Isabel's wedding, the crown repeatedly ordered that accountings of revenues and expenditures be made in hopes of locating areas within the metropolitan and colonial economies where additional funds might be found.

Unfortunately, data on public revenues were often accumulated in rather slapdash fashion. In one extant accounting of the period, it was reported that the records on which it had to draw were poorly kept, that some data were missing altogether, and that other figures were out of place.[43] The incompetence and dishonesty of many tax officials surely lay at the root of this problem. Moreover, a French observer, the marquis of Torcy, reported in 1684 that the vast majority of revenues were encumbered and what little remained was poorly administered.[44]

Torcy was probably correct in noting that fixed expenditures drained away most revenues. It is known, for example, that in 1681 tax officials of the realm (in this case, *almoxarifes*) collected 196,608,488 reis. However, grants, pensions, salaries, and other obligations attached to this source of income totaled 211,693,542 reis, leaving a deficit of 15,085,054 reis, which had to be made up from other revenues.[45]

In 1681, the crown's total revenues amounted to at least 1.6 billion reis, and perhaps as much as 2.1 billion (table 3). Although it cannot be said with certainty what proportion of this income was already attached, it is likely that the government had little, if any, surplus with which to work and that this situation persisted during the following years. Moreover, income owed the crown was often in arrears, especially in the case of tax-laden Lisbon. Writing to the king in a *consulta* of late 1684, the Lisbon *câmara* blamed its continuing inability to collect sufficient taxes on clerical exemptions.[46] By 1689, D. Pedro II was again requesting an accounting from the city, this time for the years 1668 to 1688.[47]

As table 3 shows, the crown was heavily dependent on customs and commodity revenues. Returns from the tobacco monopoly were especially important, for they provided income in an era when the *carreira da India* was moribund and the demand for Brazilian sugar had substantially declined. Despite the inroads made by the post-1670 recession, the crown's revenues had grown over the years, albeit slowly. It is known, for example, that royal income in 1627 totaled less than a third that of 1681, being approximately 623 million reis.[48] Yet, when inflation and periodic devaluations are taken into account, it is unlikely that revenue collections rose substantially during the middle decades of the seventeenth century.

Although extant documentation only allows tentative conclusions as to the growth of royal revenues, information available to the crown during the 1680s must have presented a discouraging financial picture. Hikes in the rate of taxation and reform of revenue-collection procedures were designed, of course, to improve matters (for the crown, at least) but may actually have hindered commercial expansion.

TABLE 3
Two Computations of Royal Revenues in 1681
(in reis)

Source of Revenue	Computation Number 1	Computation Number 2
Almoxarifes (internal duties)	196,608,488	196,608,488
Almoxarifes of Lisbon	147,792,522	147,792,522
Alfândega of Lisbon	269,850,721	269,850,721
Other *alfândegas*	126,439,065	126,439,065
Dry ports	24,033,320	24,033,320
Angola contract		18,100,000
Terças (thirds) from councils	22,912,264	
Salt (Lisbon, Aveiro, Setúbal)	77,255,837	
Consulados	110,814,858	110,814,858
Monies from Lisbon	3,988,795	
Three estates	200,000,000	200,000,000
Bull of the Crusade	32,000,000	32,000,000
Playing-card monopoly	2,650,000	2,650,000
Tobacco	290,052,621	290,052,621
Chanceries	10,820,787	
New rights (increase in *real d'agua*)		14,000,000
Donations of monies for queen of England's dowry		8,000,000
Other treasury income		674,039,257
TOTALS*	1,665,388,077	2,114,380,852

SOURCES: Serrão, ed., *DHP*, 2:263; BNL, Fundo Geral, 1459, fls. 41–59. *The total given in computation number 2 is probably the more accurate one even though the document on which it is based (BNL, Fundo Geral, 1549, fls. 41–59) contains numerous errors. It is not clear whether the "other treasury income" in this computation includes income from the empire.

156 PUBLIC FINANCE

Under the count of Ericeira, D. Pedro II's chief minister, a number of monetary measures were taken to secure and increase Portugal's bullion stock. Among the earliest of these were attempts to prevent the clipping of coins in circulation. Individuals engaged in this illegal practice trimmed the edges of gold and silver coins, spent them at their face value, and, when enough clippings had been collected, melted them down and sold their ill-gotten metal. In the case of the *pataca* (which here denotes the Spanish piece of eight, a silver coin that circulated freely in Portugal), so much metal was sometimes cut away that its intrinsic weight amounted to only half of its face value.[49] Dwindling imports of silver from the New World kept the value of the metal at a premium, and a concurrent flood of ever-depreciating vellon coinage made the trimming of *patacas* and other coins a lucrative pastime for the unscrupulous. The fact that many coins of the era were crudely stamped, having irregular shapes and no serrations on their edges, made it relatively easy to pass on money from which slivers of silver or gold had been cut away. One step taken by Ericeira to curtail this practice was the introduction of a coining press in 1678 that produced a more uniform coinage that had milled edges.[50]

This measure, however, was not effective. In fact, the clipping of coins became increasingly widespread during the 1680s.[51] In July 1685, D. Pedro II issued a general decree against the clipping of coins, counterfeiting, and smuggling of bullion out of Portugal. With this same decree, he requested his ministers to advise him as to how the culpable could be most effectively and exemplarily punished, glumly noting that the bulk of silver and gold coins in circulation had been clipped. A few months later, the crown issued yet another law against clipping, this time ordering that coins newly minted on Ericeira's press were not to be circulated when they were below the legal weight. Anyone caught passing underweight versions of these coins, the trimming of which was easier to detect, would be fined and exiled to Angola for four years.[52] Concern over the clipping of coins was such that the king's secretary, Roque Monteiro Paim, whom we last encountered as the author of an anti–New Christian polemic, even went so far as to describe the problem as "being the most serious of the realm."[53]

During the next three years, additional edicts aimed at preserving the bullion stock were promulgated. In May 1686, the king decreed that older gold and silver coins received by royal offices must be weighed and the bearers credited according to the intrinsic value of the pieces. Thereafter, these coins were returned to circulation, but only after being stamped with an adjusted valuation and bordered with a milled edge.[54] In August of that year, legislation was issued that stipulated that owners of older gold pieces must bring them in for weighing, stamping, and milling within fifteen days of a nationwide posting of proclamations. Coins found in circulation after the deadline were to be confiscated.[55] Subsequent legislation, which included a new *regimento* for the Lisbon mint, also endeavored to bring the intrinsic and face value of gold and silver coinage into accord.[56] Ironically, however, the crown's countrywide program to reform the currency necessitated the expenditure of considerable sums of money to establish provisional offices for that purpose.[57]

Despite its expense, the reform program undoubtedly had a salutary effect, though it did not get at a fundamental discrepancy between currency valuation in Portugal and that in its neighbors, especially Spain. The monetary disorder that beset Hapsburg Spain during the latter half of the seventeenth century was characterized by periodic currency devaluations that followed speculative scrambles to convert oversupplies of vellon into silver. As in Portugal, silver coins were clipped, abraded, or even sweated as people sought to capitalize on the metal's periodically skyrocketing value. In 1680, strict limitations were placed on the supply of vellon, which had become so abundant that copper coins were being used for the casting of bells and other articles. These restrictions precipitated a sharp deflation and the latest speculative boom collapsed. But chaos in the monetary system still prevailed, finally leading to a twenty-percent devaluation of Spanish gold and silver currency in 1686.[58] This devaluation had the effect of making Portuguese currency (the relative intrinsic value of which then increased) all the more vulnerable to clipping and illegal export, a fact that led to the consideration of a similar action in Lisbon.

Devaluation, of course, had been considered by the Cortes of 1668 as a remedy for Portugal's bullion drain and thereafter was recurrently suggested as a possible course of action. In 1685, for example, Roque Monteiro Paim noted that Portuguese money was preferred by foreigners to that of Spain since the premium on silver (in terms

158   PUBLIC FINANCE

of vellon) was greater in Spain. This, according to Paim, accounted for the chronic lack of silver then afflicting the Lisbon mint. But, nonetheless, the secretary found devaluation an unsatisfactory alternative since foreign merchants would quickly raise the prices of their wares following devaluation.[59] Though local manufactures were beginning to make their presence felt in the market, the continuing heavy dependence on imported foodstuffs and finished goods threatened consumers with an intolerable jump in prices should a major devaluation take place.

The Spanish devaluation of 1686, however, forced the Portuguese to recognize their increasingly untenable monetary position. Despite the legislation of 1685 and 1686, old coins below the legal weight continued to circulate and bullion still flowed out of Portugal. The need for melting down circulating gold and silver and striking a new coinage became inescapable. On July 2, 1688, the count of Ericeira recommended that devaluation of Portuguese money take place, explaining that such a move was necessitated by changes in foreign currencies. The count also observed that Portugal had grown so dependent on the entry of Spanish gold and silver coins that internal commerce could hardly function without them. And, citing the hardships endured by producers as a result of an overvalued currency, Ericeira observed that "all those who are sustained by the fruits of their labors find themselves ruined by the low prices they receive."[60]

Two days after Ericeira submitted his recommendation and following

> a night of feverish discussion and military precautions [apparently to prevent rioting and to assure compliance], devaluation was decreed.... Pending collection and milling, the old coins were accepted on weight. Under popular pressure the Crown bore part of the loss, but it was estimated that private citizens incurred two-thirds of it. This general recoinage more than halved the quantity of money in circulation.

The mercantile community and others holding large quantities of coin lost considerable purchasing power after the reminting of underweight coins, and some went so far as to send old coins to Holland for stamping and milling before surreptitiously reintroducing the fraudulent pieces into circulation. In order to "counter this fraud, and under pressure of the Spanish devaluation, a decree of 4 August raised the nominal value of all gold and silver specie."[61] In conformity with the Spanish action of two years earlier, the Portuguese currency was devalued by twenty percent.[62] Shortly thereafter, the Lisbon *câmara* urged the crown to publish a *pauta* listing prices not to be exceeded when selling given units of merchandise. This measure, it was hoped, would prevent merchants from offering lesser quantities for the same price.[63]

Though fraud and profiteering accompanied the devaluation, its general effect on the Portuguese economy was salutary, endowing it with "a reliable currency that stood firm throughout the next decades."[64] Moreover, specie began to flow into Portugal as foreign traders found that they could get more for their money. In 1691, for example, a Genoese vessel entered Lisbon laden with 80,000 pieces of eight it had brought from Cadiz.[65] Indeed, the timing of the devaluation could hardly have been better, for it coincided with the beginnings of European economic recovery and placed Portugal's export sector on a strong footing. But, before this recovery took place, the crown's reliance on traditional monetary and fiscal measures to improve economic conditions had been joined by a venture into manufacturing, which was led by a minister of "intelligence and energy."

CHAPTER VII

ERICEIRA AND THE ECONOMY

> ... e conhecendo que o dinheiro era alma da republica, achou as minas de mayor segurança, que pudera descobrir a inteligencia dos homens fora o uzo de manufacturas, no qual artificiozamente todas as nações do mundo sabião conservar o dinheiro proprio e ainda justamente sabião adquirir o dinheiro alheyo.
>
> Gonçalo da Cunha Vilas Boas, Conservador das fábricas (1681)

> ... and I am obliged to consider him as the *Colbert* of his native Country. He was undoubtedly a very good Minister for *Portugal*, but a very bad one for *England*.
>
> Charles King, *The British Merchant* (1721)

Government involvement in the Portuguese economy expanded during the reign of D. Pedro II, and, in some respects, the state capitalism of the sixteenth century was revived. The 1672 reorganization of the Brazil Company as an organ of the royal bureaucracy and the establishment of the Tobacco Council (Junta do Tabaco) in 1674 were among the most important manifestations of increasing state involvement in the economy. The prince regent's serious interest in forming a privately financed East India company suggested, however, that the real aim of the crown's economic policy was the raising of capital from whatever source available, not expansion of the state's role in the economy. Given the widespread animosity toward the predominantly New Christian mercantile class, it is not surprising that the crown itself became more deeply involved in economic affairs during an era of decline. And, thanks to the strong French influence at court, as well as the third estate's advocacy of manufacturing, emulation of the policies of Jean Baptiste Colbert was perhaps predictable.

During the economically stagnant 1670s and 1680s, considerable emphasis was placed on the internal development of Portugal. The crown's venture into manufacturing signaled an important departure from traditional approaches to economic difficulties, such as increasing taxes, reforming revenue-collection procedures, and devaluing the currency. And, instead of simply issuing repeated proscriptions on the importation and consumption of foreign goods, as well as on the export of bullion and certain commodities, a notable effort was made to complement those steps with an expansion of domestic production. Hence, traditional measures were joined by government-backed programs designed to satisfy domestic demand for manufactured goods, particularly textiles, and thereby improve Portugal's balance of trade.

The Portuguese Colbert

Although numerous individuals played important roles in the genesis and implementation of an industrial program in Portugal, its establishment has been invariably linked to one of D. Pedro II's most influential ministers, D. Luís de Meneses, third count of Ericeira. It was under his aegis that the program achieved a modicum of success; and, after his untimely death in 1690, the venture encountered increasing difficulties.

Unlike many of the noblemen who supported the 1640 revolt against Spanish domination, Ericeira was not a member of the provincial aristocracy. Instead, his family had roots in Lisbon. The first two counts of Ericeira had served in the Castilian court before the Restoration, but D. Luís's elder brother, D. Fernando (1614–1699), the second *conde*, returned to Portugal from Madrid shortly after the acclamation of D. João IV and threw his support to the new dynasty.

D. Luís, who was born in Lisbon in 1632, distinguished himself in the subsequent struggle for independence as a general of artillery.

His skill in bringing cannon fire to bear on enemy forces played an important part in various Portuguese victories.[1] At a time when most noblemen preferred the more glamorous command of a cavalry officer, Ericeira devoted himself to the technology of warfare, a vocation that perhaps foreshadowed his later interest in manufacturing.[2]

In addition to his military service, Ericeira held various administrative posts before and after the ouster of D. Afonso VI, a deposition that he strongly supported. D. Pedro's rise to power soon catapulted the count into positions of increasing prominence in the new regime. In 1673, for example, he was appointed governor of arms for Tras-os-Montes, a province occupying the northeastern corner of Portugal. A largely unheralded appointment of the previous year, however, had much greater significance in fixing his place in Portuguese history and letters. The count had been granted use of documentation held by the Council of War in order that he might write a history of the Restoration campaign.[3] His lengthy account, though not always reliable, has remained the fundamental source on the struggle with Spain.

Today, Ericeira's loyalties in the conflict over the proposed pardon of New Christians are not altogether clear, but it is known that he harbored some sympathy for the merchants' cause. Like António Vieira, the duke of Cadaval, the marquis of Minas, and other enlightened (or at least pragmatic) individuals, he no doubt understood the importance of New Christian merchants and artisans to any concerted effort to revitalize the economy. Moreover, his correspondence with Duarte Ribeiro de Macedo suggested that he was primarily concerned with fortifying a beleaguered Portugal, not defending its religious orthodoxy.[4] It is unlikely that he lent much support to the anti–New Christian views of his brother D. Fernando, who, during the Cortes of 1674, voiced strong opposition to the general pardon or any changes in inquisitorial procedures.[5] Instead of becoming embroiled in the debate raging around the proposed East India Company and the general pardon, Ericeira apparently concentrated on writing his history of the struggle for the Restoration.

Completion of that work was to be long delayed, however, for D. Luís soon assumed duties that, as he explained, allowed him few free hours during which to write.[6] In 1675, Ericeira was appointed deputy of the Junta of the Three Estates and lord of the treasury (*vedor da fazenda*). In the latter position, he oversaw vital aspects of national defense and economy, including royal armories, maritime commerce, and currency. In addition, he was charged with developing national manufacturing.[7] It was in this last capacity that Ericeira, who formally received the title of superintendent of the workshops and factories of the realm, was to work most effectively for the internal development of Portugal and, in the process, achieve lasting renown.

Expansion of Textile Production

The nature of industrial activity in seventeenth-century Portugal was little different from that of centuries earlier, although considerable advances had been made in ship design and construction.[8] For the most part, basic industries such as metallurgical crafts, textile fabrication, and construction had experienced little technological change. The typical mode of production was still that of the cottage industry. Most work was done at home on a "putting out" basis; in workshops (*feitorias*) employing, at most, a few dozen laborers; or in the establishments of guildsmen, where the quantity and quality of production was carefully regulated. A variety of domestic resources, including wool, flax, silk, iron, and tin, comprised the raw materials available for manufacturing. These labor and resource factors provided a foundation on which industrial programs could be erected.[9]

The struggle for the Restoration forced Portugal to better exploit its productive capacity since resources usually obtained abroad were either prevented from entering the country or became too expensive for the beleaguered regime. Thus, for example, domestic production of iron and tin for the manufacture of ordnance received increased attention. One product not as obviously vital to the war effort, linen, was also the object of considerable attention. A new *regimento* for the linen *feitoria* in Coimbra, which had been established in 1625, was promulgated in 1658.[10] This *regimento* carried with it the idea that all available flax should be brought to the *feitoria* for weaving and that production, sale, and impost levying should be closely regulated.[11] A similar approach was followed in the development of manufacturing enterprise after hostilities with Spain had ended.

Although Ericeira was most closely associated with the manufacturing program of D. Pedro II's reign, its initial sponsor was the marquis of Fronteira, D. João de Mascarenhas (1633–1681). During his years in royal service, Mascarenhas held numerous important posts, including positions on the Councils of State and War and *vedor da fazenda*. In the latter capacity, Fronteira became "the first promoter of a coherent policy of ship and factory construction."[12]

Though Fronteira's policy was indeed coherent in the sense that establishment of industrial projects had the aim of stemming the outflow of bullion used to purchase foreign goods, his program apparently did not have the manufacturing priorities that emerged under Ericeira's aegis. Nevertheless, beginning in 1670, both domestic and foreign artisans and merchants joined their efforts in various industrial projects. Late in that year, Venetian master glaziers contributed their expertise to help two Portuguese entrepreneurs construct a furnace in Lisbon for the production of glassware, crystal, and plate glass. Father Rafael Bluteau, then in Turin acting as a clandestine agent for the Portuguese, may have been responsible for procuring the services of the Venetian masters. Once in Lisbon, these artisans undertook supervisory and technical work while the state provided the two entrepreneurs with a site, "advanced money, exempted them from duties on the imported equipment and materials, and from other taxes for ten years; the manufacturers, craftsmen and other staff received various personal privileges; and the undertaking enjoyed a monopoly throughout the kingdom and the Atlantic islands."[13]

While Father Bluteau covertly sought the talent of craftspeople in Italy, Duarte Ribeiro de Macedo used his position as Portuguese ambassador in Paris to recruit quietly English and French artisans. Probably thanks to his efforts, a master draper from Rouen and eight female workers entered Portugal in 1671, bringing with them looms to weave light woolens, such as serge and bolting cloth. They were soon at work in Estremoz, a *vila* in the Alentejo, which had an approximate population of 12,000 in 1640.[14] With abundant labor and a sizable local market for the state-founded enterprise, Estremoz was favorably situated, being only about forty miles from Portugal's eastern border and thus close to the superior wool produced in Spain. The *vila* also had water in plentiful supply, a prerequisite for textile manufacturing. It is not clear whether the *feitoria*, operated and equipped with French labor and machinery, was successful; but, after a short while, it was turned over to private enterprise.[15]

These and other efforts to establish manufacturing enterprises did not go unnoticed by foreign observers, who realized the unfavorable impact that an expansion of Portuguese industry would have on the balance of trade. In July 1671, the French ambassador to Portugal, the abbott of Saint-Romain, reported:

I learnt recently that the Portuguese, offended that we are imposing new taxes on sugar, were thinking more strongly than ever of ways and means of setting up factories to produce ribbons and most other goods in Portugal, and that Duarte de Ribeiro [de Macedo] has been ordered to find and send them again as many workers as he can for every kind of manufacture.[16]

During the following year, four Parisian hatters, who indeed probably were recruited by Ribeiro de Macedo, journeyed to Portugal to help establish a *feitoria* for the manufacture of beaver hats. Procured by French and English trappers in North America, beaver pelts were transformed into so-called castor hats, warm and fashionable headgear that had become extremely popular in Europe. The Portuguese attempt to establish domestic production of beaver hats ran into difficulties. Beaver skins had to be imported, a fact that handicapped the enterprise from the start since the Portuguese were dependent on suppliers whose governments had little interest in seeing the project succeed. Local dyes were found to be of poor quality, a shortcoming that caused repeated delays in production. Meanwhile, French emissaries, acting to subvert this latest imitation of Colbertism, managed to have two of the master hatters brought home, one in 1672 and the other in 1675.[17]

This setback did not discourage the Portuguese. As the second hatter was being ousted by his compatriots, a number of important developments were taking place that gave Portuguese manufacturing greater impetus and a clearer set of priorities. The depressed state of the economy, of course, gave those who supported manufacturing a powerful argument for implementation of their program. Another impetus, albeit an indirect one, was the social uproar caused by the 1674 papal moratorium on autos-da-fé in Portugal. Reliance on New Christian merchants to help shore up the economy was thus becoming an increasingly unacceptable route to recovery. The appointment of D. Luís de Meneses as *vedor da fazenda* in 1675 was of crucial importance, for development of domestic manufactures then came under the direction of an energetic and forceful minister. Duarte Ribeiro de Macedo's *Discurso* of 1675, by its emphasis on production using raw materials obtainable in Portugal (especially wool), suggested a more practical approach to manufacturing than had heretofore been taken. Not only should production be based on domestic resources whenever possible, but utilitarian items for mass consumption should receive greater attention than luxury articles. As we have already seen, Ribeiro de Macedo understood well that Portugal was in no position to compete effectively with long-established foreign manufacturers of luxuries. Although there is no way of knowing to what extent Ribeiro de Macedo's mercantilist tract affected the subsequent course of manufacturing in Portugal, his writing probably influenced Ericeira to make the manufacture of woolens the centerpiece of his program.

Despite the importance of wool, a commodity that was consumed by all classes, the production of silk (garments of which were legally if not actually restricted to the privileged classes) apparently got prior consideration. Indeed, apparently one of Ericeira's first priorities as superintendent was to develop an alternative supply of luxury fabric for the privileged and thus reduce the outflow of bullion going for foreign silks.

The *pragmática* of January 1677, as noted in chapter V, was promulgated to reduce importation of luxury items. Less expensive fabrics (for example, serges and baizes) consumed by commoners were not affected by the measure. The edict, however, was not so much an attempt to end the wearing of expensive materials as it was an effort to divert consumption to domestic production. Unlike the 1668 *pragmática*, the 1677 promulgation was accompanied by a broad program to revive domestic silk production and thereby provide the privileged with an alternative supply of fabrics regarded as emblematic of their elevated status. Revitalization of Portugal's moribund silk industry, moreover, would conform with Ribeiro de Macedo's advocacy of production based on locally obtainable materials.

Silk cultivation was probably introduced into Portugal by the Moors sometime before the middle of the thirteenth century. During the late fifteenth century, D. Afonso V sought to expand Portuguese sericulture, which had by then become well established in Lamego and Tras-os-Montes. This effort was made in hopes of sharing in the wealth enjoyed by Granada, a Muslim enclave that had prospered greatly from its silk production. But Portugal's imperial enterprise soon caused consumption of the domestic product to slacken as a myriad of luxurious materials, including silks, flowed into Lisbon from India after 1500. Silk production thereafter declined as imported fabrics flooded the metropolitan market.[18]

Sericulture continued to languish under Spanish rule, and the struggle for the Restoration further delayed any revitalization of production. Thus, as peace settled over the countryside, the interests of local artisans and the mercantilist views of writers such as Rafael Bluteau, who prepared his manual on silk production at Ericeira's behest, soon coalesced in policies aimed at reviving Portugal's centuries-old silk industry.

The basis for such a revival still existed in the northeastern province of Tras-os-Montes, especially around the *vila* of Torre de Moncorvo. There a few factories (*fábricas*) continued to produce quality fabrics.[19] Like most workshops in Portugal, these *fábricas* were modest affairs based on the "putting-out" system. Small establishments akin to those found at Moncorvo typified manufacturing enterprises put into operation during Ericeira's ministry.

The first steps to revive Portugal's sericulture were taken in late 1676. These steps, which included assessment of a tax on the production of mulberry trees, were rapidly followed by the *pragmática* of 1677.[20] In that same year, Roland Duclos, the French proponent of sericulture whom we met in chapter V, received the rights to silk manufacturing in Lisbon. Within two years, Duclos's establishment, which was situated near the then-standing Saint Catherine Gates, had fifty English looms in operation, most of which were run by foreigners. Nevertheless, over three hundred Portuguese, the great majority of whom probably were women, children, and the elderly working at home, were involved in spooling silk for the Lisbon *fábrica*. An impressive array of fabrics (including taffetas, satins, and grosgrains) was produced by the Duclos factory.[21] Sale of these and other fabrics was facilitated by the opening of a retail outlet in Lisbon by two Portuguese merchants, Francisco Lopes Franco and João Soares.[22] The effort to supply privileged consumers with domestically produced silks was clearly underway.

As *fábricas* were put into operation, measures were also taken to expand the production of raw silk. Royal orders went out to various officials commanding cooperation in a widespread program of tree planting. On October 25, 1677, for example, the prince regent sent a decree to the Lisbon *câmara* ordering it to do its utmost to see that mulberries were planted wherever possible within the city's jurisdiction.[23] A similar decree was sent to the marquis of Cascais, D. Luís Álvares de Castro, on December 4, requesting that officials under his control cooperate with teams sent out by Ericeira to plant mulberry trees.[24] According to Father Bluteau, this program was so successful that in the province of Entre-Douro-e-Minho alone over eighteen thousand trees were planted within one year's time.[25] Although this figure may be an exaggeration, a great number of mulberries were undoubtedly planted during Ericeira's years as *vedor da fazenda*.

Though difficulties in obtaining capital and equipment hampered the revitalization of Portuguese sericulture, the drive to expand production continued into the 1680s.[26] In 1680, for example, Ericeira reported that a *fábrica* for silk manufacturing was being established in the *vila* of Tomar and that the prince regent had himself put up the money for the venture.[27] Three years later, Benoît Duclos, a relative of Roland, received an exclusive ten-year contract for the finishing and dyeing of silk fabrics.[28] He thereafter "built a French-model calender for the finishing of raw silk and several machines based on French and Venetian models for the finishing of taffetas and linens, installed ten looms, and brought in foreign dyers."[29] Local construction of looms and other machinery suggests that, in part at least, the problem of obtaining equipment had been overcome.

As the first steps toward reviving Portugal's sericulture were taken, moves were also made to lay the cornerstone of Ericeira's woolen-manufacturing program. It was in this industrial activity that Ribeiro de Macedo's mercantilist thought found clearest expression, for an abundant domestic resource would be increasingly exploited to fill popular demand in both Portugal and its colonies.

Production of woolens in Portugal is undoubtedly much older than the country itself. At the time national independence was achieved during the twelfth century, simple woolen fabrics were already being woven in all of the Portuguese provinces. An early division of labor existed, which included the occupations of sheepshearer, wool spinner, and cloth weaver. Records from the thirteenth century indicated that looms and fulling mills were in operation in simple *fábricas* known as *lanifícios*. During the following centuries, diversification of labor and technological sophistication gradually increased, a process that culminated in the promulgation of the cloth manufacture *regimento* of 1573. Extending to some ninety-seven chapters, the 1573 *regimento* codified in close detail all stages of woolen and linen manufacture, as well as standards of quality and rules for the financing of production. This venerable document, which was in force during the whole of Ericeira's administration, was not revised and augmented until publication of the *regimento* of 1690.[30]

As in the case of silk manufacturers, the wool industry had fallen into decline during the six decades of Spanish domination. While the general economic malaise that characterized the later years of Castilian rule had much to do with this decline, the Spaniards compounded the problem by endeavoring to supplant local production with exports of their own wool and woolens. The debilitating struggle that ensued after 1640 probably further depressed domestic production. By 1668, a sizable share of the demand for woolens was filled by cloth coming from England and Holland. It was this state of affairs, of course, that the government of D. Pedro hoped to change.

The 1668 Cortes's call for domestic manufacture of woolens inaugurated Portugal's full-scale return to a field of enterprise that had then become extremely competitive. It has been said, in fact, that "the cloth markets of the seventeenth century formed something like a single theatre of operations within which technology, patterns and fashions were borrowed (or purloined), new raw materials bought, sold and smuggled, and finished products marketed, all on a massive scale."[31] Under the marquis of Fronteira, Portugal made its move into that theater with factories such as that established at Estremoz. Meanwhile, Portuguese agents and representatives, especially Father Bluteau, Duarte Ribeiro de Macedo, and Lisbon's ambassador in England, D. Francisco de Melo, showed considerable resourcefulness in clandestinely procuring skilled artisans and modern equipment with which to upgrade Portugal's rudimentary textile industry. But it would require more than adroit imitation and clever subterfuge to overcome the fierce competitiveness of the international textile trade and Portugal's late start in that arena, not to mention the handicaps imposed on the country's mercantile class.

Like Ribeiro de Macedo, the count of Ericeira was probably well aware of these sobering difficulties and thus focused his attention on expanding production of unpretentious, utilitarian woolens, especially baizes and serges. One of D. Luís de Meneses's first actions to stimulate the manufacture of such fabrics was the appointment of Gonçalo da Cunha Vilas Boas as judge (*juiz de fôra*) of Covilhã in 1676. This competent administrator, whose *Relatório* and correspondence are the source for much of what is known about manufacturing activity in Covilhã and elsewhere, encountered a variety of problems almost from the beginning of his appointment.[32]

As the most important of three major centers of woolen production—Estremoz and Portalegre being the other two—Covilhã was the focal point of the effort to modernize existing facilities and increase their output. Not unexpectedly, many of the problems confronted by Vilas Boas grew out of the attempt to increase production. One such problem stemmed from the granting of an exclusive contract to three Portuguese entrepreneurs, Luis Romão Sinel, Andre Nunes, and Jorge Frois. In October 1677, these three individuals obtained a monopoly on production of serges and baizes in Covilhã and the surrounding region. As part of their agreement, the contractors agreed to establish a *fábrica* with ten looms in the nearby *vila* of Manteigas. Moreover, they were to bring in foreign artisans to oversee the production process in the *lanifícios* of the area.

The monopoly contract drew almost immediate opposition from the traditional establishment in Covilhã, which feared that it would be squeezed out of the textile market. Wool traders, guild members, and an array of other people involved in local production resisted the attempt to centralize the purchasing, producing, and marketing of wool and wool products under control of the three entrepreneurs. Indeed, the contract was so unpopular that it provoked agitation by townsfolk, who, apparently for varying reasons, regarded the institution of a new mode of production with great alarm. In early January 1679, for example, protesters in Covilhã used the cover of darkness to go about venting their animosity toward the new regime at the local *lanifício*, shouting, "Long live the people, death to the *fábrica!*"³³

During the following year, outbursts against the *fábrica* continued. As Vilas Boas's *Relatório* revealed, the rabidly anti–New Christian priest of Covilhã, whom we encountered in an earlier chapter, raised his inflammatory preachings against the manufacturing establishments. Vilas Boas related that the possibly deranged cleric preached sermons in which he urged the torching of everybody and everything within reach, the *fábricas* included, and claimed that he had received this apocalyptic message from God Himself, who spoke to him through an animal. The ranting priest was eventually sent off to a monastery to atone for his outrageous behavior, but his exhortations to violence surely heightened existing antipathy toward New Christians and the manufacturing program. This held serious implications for local industry since many New Christians, including the contractors Nunes and Frois, were deeply involved in textile production.³⁴

The employment of foreign artisans at the Covilhã *fábrica* also caused difficulties for Vilas Boas. Even before the monopoly contract was granted to the three merchants, the government had procured the services of eleven English craftspeople. Thanks in part to the quiet support of D. Pedro's sister Catherine, queen of England since 1662, Ambassador Melo secretly dispatched the small contingent from London in the summer of 1677. Two weeks after arriving in Lisbon on August 8, they entered Covilhã.

The reception accorded the newcomers was not altogether warm. The city council greeted their arrival with enthusiasm, but the local guilds were not so forthcoming. Though Portuguese artisans had expected to benefit from protectionism and encouragement of domestic production, as the actions of the popular estate in the 1668 Cortes attested, the crown's reliance on foreign technicians and monopoly contractors threatened to exclude the local artisans from the anticipated advantages of industrialization. The appearance of foreigners to do work they regarded as their own was not well received by the guildsmen of Covilhã. The subsequent granting of the wool contract to the three entrepreneurs, two of whom, as noted, were New Christians, further antagonized the local artisans. Despite Ericeira's avoidance of the debate raging around the mercantile class, he perhaps signaled his position by contracting with members of the despised New Christian minority to help implement his program. This probably added to the rancor of the already-incensed guildsmen since, as the local Casa dos Vinte e Quatro argued, the contract was itself an infringement on traditional commercial freedoms enjoyed in Covilhã.

Local discontent was exacerbated by the unseemly behavior of the English artisans. Soon after their arrival, some of their number began complaining about the salaries they were being paid, which ran to 500 reis per day for the two married couples in the contingent and 200 reis per diem for the seven bachelors. In addition to receiving these salaries, which were generous by Portuguese standards, the artisans were allowed free exercise of religious belief, as was already the case for merchants in the English and Dutch factories of Lisbon and Oporto. Nevertheless, some of the artisans felt that they should be paid more for teaching the Portuguese their technical skills, especially those for increasing the number of threads per square inch and making individual threads more uniform. A small hike in pay was granted to those of the group who had converted to Catholicism, but few were satisfied. Using an age-old tactic, the Portuguese next attempted to defuse matters by encouraging the bachelors to marry local women. Two such marriages did take place in early 1678. But nuptials notwithstanding, the English craftspeople continued to grumble.

Meanwhile, problems had arisen in the production process itself. By December 1677, four looms had been put into operation in Covilhã. The eleven artisans had both assembled equipment slipped into Portugal and constructed machinery from local materials. But it was found that additional technicians expert in finishing and dyeing were needed to complete the manufacture of newly woven baizes and serges. The government again called on Ambassador Melo to procure the needed artisans. In late February 1678, three more skilled technicians made their appearance in Covilhã. A fuller, a dyer, and a master technician versed in all phases of woolen production joined the original eleven. Each of the new arrivals received 1,000 reis, a truly generous daily wage.

But the three experts proved themselves no less troublesome than the eleven who preceded them. The fuller was apparently not as expert as thought and proceeded to spend an excessive sum in putting his process into operation. The dyer, either out of malice or negligence, managed to set fire to twenty large pieces of fabric. Incidents such as these caused the three contractors to have second thoughts about their venture. To make matters worse, the disgruntled craftspeople attempted to escape their contractual obligations, sneaking out of Covilhã late one night in April 1678 and heading for the Spanish border. The runaway technicians were soon intercepted and brought back to the *vila*. After a brief stay behind bars, the experts agreed to go back to work. Nonetheless, the situation remained tense, and Vilas Boas found himself caught between the complaints of his foreign charges and the murmurings of resentful guildsmen who wanted to evict both the English workers and the contractors. Given the animus felt toward the monopoly contractors and the antics of the English, there is little wonder that the disturbances of 1679 and 1680 took place.

Apparently, however, some of the disruption was caused by English agents working out of Lisbon. The English merchants in the capital had quickly grasped the threat that domestic production of baizes and serges posed to their prosperous import business and sought at first to buy off the prince regent. They offered D. Pedro 2 million cruzados to desist, but the money was not accepted. Thereafter, it seems that the merchants moved to sabotage operations in Covilhã by stirring the passions of the disgruntled English technicians. The late-night flight of April 1678, according to Vilas Boas, was precipitated by a Portuguese working in the *fábrica* who was actually an agent of the English factory in Lisbon. After the failure of this ploy, the English hatched another scheme. In the spring of 1680, they attempted to undercut the sale of domestic woolens, especially those of a retail outlet in Lisbon that, like that for silk, had recently been opened. For two months, the English traders sold their imported woolens at drastically reduced prices in an unsuccessful effort to drive their Portuguese competitors out of business.[35] Meanwhile, a concurrent effort was being made to stem the flow of technicians out of England.

Despite the numerous difficulties Vilas Boas encountered, he managed to keep production going. Furthermore, the crown found additional contractors willing to establish new *fábricas*. In Vila do Melo, for example, a contractor from Covilhã, Felipe Cardona, launched an operation in which seven looms produced serges and baizes of excellent quality. Similar establishments also commenced operations in the *vilas* of Fundão, Tomar, and the already-mentioned Manteigas. And, in late 1680, Vilas Boas reported that seventeen looms were at work in Covilhã and that 415 people were employed in the production of woolens.[36] Although the English were then on guard against further expansion of the fledgling industry, their efforts to stop the importation of technicians and equipment were not fully successful. Historians know, for example, that an Irish Catholic named Curtin, together with a contingent of skilled workers, entered Portugal in 1681.[37] Additional skilled labor was occasionally found serving in the Portuguese military. In one such instance, three soldiers, two of whom were weavers and the third a cloth printer, were discharged and sent to work in Felipe Cardona's new *fábrica* at Vila do Melo in early 1681.[38]

A tendency toward concentration of equipment in large structures and labor in nearby lodging was at work in both the woolen and silk industries. The three entrepreneurs who held the Covilhã contract began their respective operations in separate facilities but soon consolidated their efforts. Large buildings were jointly built to house equipment for weaving, dyeing, and ironing, and housing for workers was provided near these edifices.[39] To what extent the hundreds, perhaps even thousands, of Portuguese employed by the *fábricas* of Covilhã and elsewhere relied on these workshops for their livelihood is not known, but it has been suggested that the more than 300 silk workers in Lisbon were largely dependent on the silk industry for their incomes.[40]

The trend toward industrial concentration is also suggested by the planned establishment of a large factory in Tomar, a *vila* that had five *fábricas* for woolen manufacturing in operation in 1680.[41] In late 1684, Vilas Boas informed Ericeira that adequate water was available for manufacturing woolens in the great *fábrica* envisioned for Tomar. Obtaining a site for the installation presented a problem, however, for the most appropriate piece of property was in the hands of clerics. The lack of sufficient firewood needed for the manufacturing process was also noted by Vilas Boas. Nevertheless, the judge felt that the *fábrica* could be built on the site of a then-defunct ironworks and that wood could be obtained a few miles away.[42]

Although evidence has not been found to show that the great *fábrica* planned for Tomar was actually built, the intention of doing so clearly suggests the capitalistic drift of the manufacturing program. In both silk and woolen production, technology accompanied by the hiring of relatively large numbers of workers, both for labor in workshops and at home on a piecework basis, was introduced. Moreover, entrepreneurs such as Roland Duclos, Felipe Cardona, and Jorge Frois invested in manufacturing monopolies and endeavored to gain control over wider markets.

This conjoining of technology, labor, and capital met strong resistance. English merchants, as we have seen, were bent on disrupting the Portuguese domestic manufacture of woolens since it harmed their profitable import trade; and Portuguese guildsmen strenuously opposed the threat that the new mode of production posed to their traditional monopoly. The weavers (*paneiros*) of Covilhã and other *vilas* repeatedly voiced their preference for the status quo ante. The commercial activities of Jorge Frois were a constant source of complaint for the *paneiros* of Covilhã, who claimed in 1688 that the New Christian contractor annually bought up large quantities of wool from Spain, the Alentejo, and elsewhere and then, having cornered the market on the fiber, sold it to small producers at inflated prices. The local artisans were further upset by the fact that Frois held the regional monopoly for brazilwood, which they used as a dyestuff. According to the weavers, the contractor often refused to sell the colonial commodity, keeping it for the baizes and serges of the Covilhã *fábrica*.[43]

Both foreign and domestic resistance to the expansion of *fábrica* production had manifested itself from the outset of Ericeira's manufacturing program, but industrialization moved forward during the depressed 1680s. The impact of manufacturing on the economy, or at least on the balance of trade, was apparently quite substantial. According to Gonçalo da Cunha Vilas Boas, English merchants involved in the import of woolens had sent 1.2 million cruzados out of Portugal by way of the *alfândegas* of Lisbon and Oporto in 1676. Yet, by around 1680, the *juiz de fôra* asserted, 1.6 million cruzados were being saved annually thanks to domestic woolen production.[44] These figures, if they were accurate, stand as impressive testimony to the initial success of the manufacturing program.

Mining, Metalworking, and Construction

In addition to silk and woolen production, Ericeira's program emphasized the development of mining, metalworking, and, to a lesser extent, construction in Portugal. Upon his appointment as *vedor da fazenda* in 1675, Ericeira found metallurgical activity well established in Portugal. Exploitation of tin and iron deposits were the most important aspects of this activity; but other metals, including lead, copper, mercury, and even some silver and gold, were also extracted. The skilled labor employed in mining and metalworking ranged from humble miners digging in isolated regions to the pretentious goldsmiths of Lisbon. Besides working metals extracted from Portuguese soil, artisans fashioned weapons, utensils, jewelry, plate, et cetera out of metals imported from Europe, Africa, the New World, and other places.

As in the case of Spain, metal extraction in Portugal had gone on for centuries before the establishment of national sovereignty.[45] After the Avis dynasty consolidated its control over the country, a series of laws regarding the extraction and sale of metals was issued. One of the most important of these edicts was the Mining Code of 1557, an act that remained in force until 1835. This law reaffirmed earlier legislation that stipulated that one-fifth of the precious-metal production, the famous *quinto*, belonged to the crown. Perhaps the most important revision embodied in the 1557 law was a clause that nullified the old requirement that common metals be sold to the crown to provision its armories. These metals could then be freely sold.[46]

Thereafter, the Mining Code was periodically revised by special legislation, the most notable additions being *regimentos* for mineral exploitation in Brazil (1618) and for the tin mines in Vizeu, Guarda, and Tras-os-Montes (1655).[47] The 1655 *regimento* for the mining of tin, which was one of Portugal's most abundant metallic resources, was largely necessitated by the embattled country's need for vastly increased supplies of ordnance. Tin was needed as an alloy for iron in the founding of artillery. With the 1655 *regimento*, D. João IV appointed a general administrator for Portugal's tin-mining regions and instructed him to increase production as much as possible. All the tin extracted was to be sent to the iron foundries. In the hope that additional tin deposits still lay undiscovered, the king offered a twenty-cruzado reward to any mine worker who found a productive vein. Workers were also exempted from military service, a privilege that was renewed in 1673.[48] Though tin does not seem to have played as significant a role in Portuguese industrial priorities after peace was attained in 1668, it was still an essential metal in armaments production.

The extraction and working of iron was considerably more extensive than that of tin. Workshops called *ferrarias*, many of which were located close to deposits of iron ore, could be found in many cities and *vilas*, including Elvas, Évora, Arruda dos Vinhos, Penela, Cardicais, Figueiró dos Vinhos, Barcarena, and Tomar. In addition, innumerable blacksmiths (*ferreiros*) fashioned a wide variety of implements and utensils from imported iron.[49] Much of this iron came from northern Spain.

As with tin, Portugal's supply of iron was found to be inadequate to meet the need for ordnance after 1640, especially since Madrid then sought to stop its export. Portugal was forced to better exploit its own ore deposits and revitalize ironworks that had languished during decades of Spanish rule. *Ferrarias* in Tomar and Figueiró dos Vinhos were reopened during the early 1650s. And, in late 1655, a *regimento* was promulgated for the two mining centers that, like that for tin, spoke to the need for increased production.[50] A French official named Dufour was soon put in charge of the foundries and forges at the two sites and his son arranged passage for four French ironmasters.[51] Almost ten years before Dufour assumed his duties, the Portuguese ambassador in Paris had contracted with a French expert named Pierre Courneaut to act as the crown's armorer at Barcarena. Courneaut later offered to search for additional iron deposits. After a stay of six years, he returned to France in 1652, but his son was then granted the position of armorer.[52]

Arms production at Barcarena, which probably started in the sixteenth century, was complemented by the manufacture of gunpowder. In a July 1640 report to Philip IV (Philip III of Portugal), the powder-making operation at Barcarena was described as being among the best in the Hapsburg empire.[53] The ingredients of black powder included sulphur, charcoal, and saltpeter, substantial quantities of the latter being brought from India. Carefully measured portions of these three components were mixed with water to form a paste, which was then dried and powdered. There were problems with this procedure, however. According to the 1640 report, the inexperience of the workers at Barcarena had been the cause of frequent fires, which left the facility in shambles. This necessitated the transference of operations to a nearby house that was itself dilapidated. The threat of fire continued to worry officials. In 1655, two Englishmen, Simon and John Mathews, were asked to relocate the operations in safer facilities.[54] By 1660, it appears that conditions had improved at Barcarena since the Superintendent Vicente Gonçalves Rebelo received orders to produce 300 pike heads and 400 musket balls.[55]

Exploitation of Portugal's deposits of lead, a metal with which musket balls and various other articles of warfare were made, also went forward. The absence of legislation concerning the metal suggests, however, that domestic production contributed only modestly to the struggle for the Restoration.[56] Nonetheless, the crown surely had a hand in such exploitation as occurred.

In an effort to lessen its dependence on the saltpeter of Portuguese India, which was then beleaguered by the Dutch, the government took steps to increase domestic production. In 1654, a detailed *regimento* was issued for the *comarcas* of Alenquer, Leiria, and Setúbal, the areas where most of Portugal's saltpeter was found. Administrative machinery for the three regions was established, and individual producers, like tin and iron miners, were exempted from military service. Five years later, the crown again promulgated legislation aimed at raising production of the mineral.[57] Despite increased attention to domestic saltpeter production, inadequate supplies of the mineral were to be a subject of concern for the rest of the century.

Of course, it is understandable that the production of common metals and minerals essential for national defense would be closely controlled by the state. The cannon, muskets, gunpowder, and other articles of warfare produced under state control during the Restoration years undoubtedly made a significant contribution to the defeat of Spanish forces. Moreover, the close connection between military need and metal production changed little after 1668. Hostilities with

Spain, or any other power, could break out with little warning. Arms were also needed to defend Portugal's colonies; for example, there was a reference in 1675 to the manufacturing of flintlocks in Portalegre, a center of armament production, for use in Brazil.[58] Portugal's battle-tested leadership frequently stressed the importance of having secure, readily available stocks of tin, iron, saltpeter, et cetera. As a former artillery general, the count of Ericeira was acutely aware of the relationship between national security and metal production. After examining a shipment of iron from the smelters of Figueiró dos Vinhos, which he found to be of superior quality, D. Luís confided to Father Bluteau that the "realm can receive no greater benefit than to have sufficient iron so as to dispense with that from abroad."[59]

Efforts to expand mining and metalworking, unlike those concerned with textile manufacturing, seem to have been primarily addressed to maintaining an adequate defense, not redressing the balance of trade. Nonetheless, domestic production of iron, tin, lead, and other metals also helped slow the outflow of bullion. And, in one instance in which the bullion supply may have been the paramount consideration, Father Bluteau himself was charged by Ericeira with examining silver deposits in Tras-os-Montes.[60]

Under Ericeira's leadership, a number of other steps were taken to expand mining and metalworking. Manufacture "of nails and wrought-iron articles in the *Ribeira* (port) of Lisbon began in 1680."[61] The practice of discharging skilled military conscripts to labor in workshops was used to facilitate *ferraria* operations. Thus, again in 1680, a young blacksmith was released from the Lisbon garrison and sent to finish his apprenticeship in the ironworks of Figueiró dos Vinhos.[62] During this same era, the important ironworks at Machuca were founded.[63] With both textile and metallurgical production at that time well underway, Ericeira could indeed note with satisfaction in 1681 that "all manufactures are rapidly moving forward."[64]

During subsequent years, additional measures were taken or considered in order to assure adequate iron supplies. The production centers of Tomar and Figueiró dos Vinhos were reorganized in 1687 and 1692, the latter change coming after Ericeira's death. Another center, "for casting ordnance, had already been set up at Arega, at the confluence of the Alge and Zêzere."[65] The need for artillery production grew more acute after Ericeira's death in 1690, for the imminent struggle for the throne of sickly Carlos II of Spain threatened to draw Portugal into war. Consideration was thus given to plans for moving the *ferrarias* of Tomar and Figueiró dos Vinhos to Alcobaça, where new iron deposits awaited exploitation and direct access to sea transport was available.[66]

A vitally important but seldom discussed aspect of internal development, that of construction, also progressed during Ericeira's tenure. It should indeed be noted that construction and textile production were perhaps the two most important industries of early modern Europe.[67] In Portugal, the construction industry was probably of greater economic consequence than that of textiles since so many fabrics were imported. Though textile manufacturing may have done more to reduce the outflow of bullion during Ericeira's administration, it is likely that construction involved greater levels of capital investment and employed more people. Construction, however, did not rely on technological innovation or capitalistic organization to the degree that Portugal's silk, woolen, and iron industries did. Instead, skilled artisans and gangs of workmen erected buildings, bridges, wharves, fountains, and other structures in accordance with time-honored practices, though materials and architectural styles varied.

Despite the economic downturn of the late seventeenth century, much construction activity was occurring in Portugal, particularly in Lisbon. One reason for this was a postwar mushrooming of traffic in the capital, which had led to intolerable congestion. The Lisbon *câmara* reported in 1676 that the city's streets simply could not handle the crush of carts, litters, and opulent coaches, not to mention pedestrians. A major project was launched in which both the Rua do Ouro and the Rua da Prata were widened and various gates within the city were enlarged or torn down altogether. Furthermore, at least twenty-six of the buildings along those streets were leveled.[68]

In Lisbon, a full-time architect earning an annual salary of 20,000 reis drew up plans for public edifices.[69] These included a new powderhouse and a tollhouse for collection of the *décima* levied on the catch of Portuguese fishermen. Reconstruction of a slaughterhouse in the Bairro Alto was also contemplated as a means of decentralizing the city's meat supply. The poor residents living in the Alfama district often found that the central market in the Terreiro do Paço had sold its entire stock to noble households.[70]

Larger public buildings in Lisbon were built according to the baroque style, but their facades were relatively free of the convoluted embellishments associated with that form. While most of the buildings were three stories in height, some rose to six floors.[71] Large private houses such as those owned by merchants residing around the Rossio or by nobles living in idyllic *quintas* in the countryside consumed large increments of capital and labor. The clerical estate also invested great sums for the construction of churches, monasteries, and chapels.[72]

The building and repair of waterworks further occupied the construction industry. In 1685, for example, work was completed on a large fountain in Lisbon. Known as the Bica das Fontainhas, the fountain provided a much-needed supply of water for the surrounding neighborhood. And, according to local witnesses, the water had health-giving properties.[73] But the finding and tapping of groundwater, as was done in the case of the Bica, was in itself insufficient to supply the needs of Lisbon. The polluted Tagus was of service to those living near its banks, but neighborhoods occupying high ground such as the Bairro Alto lacked an adequate supply of water.

From 1683 onward, proposals were made for the building of a large aqueduct to bring the needed quantities of water into the capital.[74] An individual named António de Miranda made such a proposal in 1688, but it was rejected as being too dubious an enterprise since a number of undescribed inventions were to be used in raising water to the needed heights. Moreover, the city found that Miranda was being pursued by creditors.[75] In 1700, a French nobleman named Theophile Dupineaut also proposed construction of a great aqueduct that would supply five fountains located in various parts of the city. Among the various advantages seen in such a work was the fact that water could be supplied to dyeworks then being run by John Bayle, an artisan of English origin, who produced scarlets. Worries about the great cost involved and damage to private property led to rejection of the Dupineaut proposal, but ultimately the immense project was begun in 1731 and largely completed during the administration of Pombal.[76]

It is not known what role, if any, Ericeira had in the genesis of the aqueduct scheme, but the fact that the project was first proposed during his administration is suggestive of the stress placed on construction during the late seventeenth century. Evidence of his involvement with other industrial activities such as shipbuilding and the manufacture of soap, pottery, tile, leather goods, et cetera, is also lacking, but it is likely that he favored their expansion.

Certain other aspects of internal development may also have had his support. Though little had been done to improve illumination in Lisbon following Ribeiro de Macedo's 1671 description of Parisian street lighting, the count may have had a hand in bringing the project under review again in 1689. The city council, however, balked at the idea, claiming that the project was too costly.[77] Ericeira did lend his support to Portugal's long-standing effort to convert marshlands into productive fields. In 1683, for example, he recommended that the count of Sarzedas be given the right to drain and plant marshlands near Vila França de Xira. In return for draining and planting the crown's unproductive property and keeping the majority of it under cultivation, Sarzedas was allowed to retain at least two-thirds of his annual wheat crop.[78] In these and other instances, Ericeira apparently followed the example of Colbert, supporting, in varying degrees, a multitude of projects for internal development.

The Impact of the Manufacturing Program

Though Ericeira probably sympathized with a wide range of measures for improving the performance of Portugal's economy, the principal thrust of his developmental program was directed at expanding basic manufactures. D. Luís did not attempt to expand the whole of Portuguese industry; instead, he concentrated on certain sectors.[79] Silk, wool, and iron, all of which could be obtained within Portugal's borders, were given highest priority. Increased production of silk and wool offered a means of improving Portugal's balance of trade, while iron was of prime importance for the country's defense. In the case of woolen manufactures, the industrial program indeed had a significant impact on the balance of trade.

Despite the attention given to it, the industrial program remained a relatively modest endeavor, employing directly or indirectly a few thousand people at most, while the vast bulk of the population continued to labor in traditional agricultural and pastoral pursuits. Individuals engaged in raising sheep or those who increased cultivation of mulberry trees obviously became more closely tied to the program, but the socioeconomic regime was but slightly altered by the expanding operations of *fábricas, lanifícios,* and *ferrarias.* Nevertheless, the manufacturing program of Fronteira and Ericeira represented the first coherent attempt to implant an industrial mode of production in Portugal.

In some respects, the manufacturing program was to have a distinct impact on Portuguese society. The protests of the Covilhã guildsmen attest to its disruptive impact on certain traditional modes of production. Furthermore, patterns of textile consumption underwent noticeable change. After production of serges and baizes was successfully underway, Ericeira sought to enlarge the scope of domestic textile manufacturing to include inexpensive druggets, fabrics that English merchants continued to import in large quantities.[80] In 1686 and 1688, additional sumptuary legislation was promulgated that placed further proscriptions on Portuguese dress.[81] As a result of this and earlier legislation, the origin and appearance of many of the Portuguese subjects' apparel changed, although in the latter instance perhaps not for the better for dress became increasingly drab and monotonous.[82] Yet, privileged and commoners alike resisted these prohibitions and still consumed restricted foreign products, though perhaps not so openly and ostentatiously.

Even as the market for domestic textiles was artificially enlarged by sumptuary legislation, Portuguese products encountered difficulties meeting local demand because of inadequate financing. Most nobles and merchants already had much of their capital invested in land or commercial ventures and showed little interest in financing an untried and not altogether popular program. The general recession then afflicting Europe further constricted potential sources of financing. The bullion drain, which Ericeira had hoped to stop, was itself a factor in reducing funding possibilities. At one point, D. Luís even sought financial backing from the Holy Inquisition.[83] And the crown, which, of course, was the most appropriate source of funds for a program that was, after all, its own, lacked sufficient revenues to underwrite generously Ericeira's plans for development. Ironically, Portuguese manufacturing, having withstood years of economic stagnation, was not to be favorably affected by the new prosperity that followed the devaluation of 1688. Before discussing that, however, we should first look to the commercial stirrings in Portugal and its Atlantic empire.

CHAPTER VIII

ECONOMIC EXPANSION AND FOODSTUFF SHORTAGES

> The Revenues of the Kingdom are so very great that did they all come into the King's hands, he would be one of the richest Princes in Europe.
>
> The Rev. John Colbatch, Chaplain to the English Factory in Lisbon (1700)

Three basic trends characterized the economy of imperial Portugal during the last years of the seventeenth century: the beginning of economic recovery after years of recession, the growing dominance of wine and Brazilian tobacco within the national economy, and the continuing shortages of basic foodstuffs. Economic recovery had become increasingly evident after the devaluation of the currency in 1688, though the production of wine and tobacco increased even during the depths of the 1670–1690 recession. These two products were to be among the most important contributors to a revitalized Portuguese economy. Yet, even as the metropolitan economy emerged from years of stagnation, Portugal still found itself very much dependent on other nations for such vital items in the national diet as wheat and codfish. As we will see in the next chapter, Portugal's post-1690 resurgence owed much to rising production in its Atlantic colonies, especially Brazil.

Portugal and the World Economy

The Atlantic economies controlled by Portugal, Spain, Holland, England, and France have been described as being "subsidiary to, a modification and enhancement of, the economies of individual countries."[1] This was certainly true, but the distinction between metropolis and colony here does not take cognizance of a larger context in which both were subsumed. Mother country and colony alike were part of an expanding capitalist economy, which Immanuel Wallerstein has described as the modern world system. Professor Wallerstein has persuasively argued that "capitalism as an economic mode is based on the fact that . . . economic factors operate within an area larger than that which any political entity can totally control."[2] Thus, it is the division of labor, rather than political demarcations or cultural homogeneity, that constitutes the boundaries of this larger arena. This division of labor is not

merely functional—that is occupational—but geographical. That is to say, the range of economic tasks is not evenly distributed throughout the world-system. In part this is the consequence of ecological considerations to be sure. But for the most part, it is a function of the social organization of work, one which magnifies and legitimatizes the ability of some groups within the system to exploit the labor of others, that is, to receive a larger share of the surplus.[3]

And, just as variance in the distribution of tasks is characteristic of the capitalistic world economy, so too is the differentiation between loci of economic power and less-advanced areas. Countries in which the integration of a strong state machinery and a national culture occurred during the period between 1400 and 1700 became the focal points of economic activity in the world economy. These "core states" remained surrounded by semiperipheral and peripheral areas, no matter how far their political hegemony may have extended.

During the late seventeenth century, the most readily identifiable core states were England, France, and Holland. Spain and Portugal which once themselves enjoyed quasi-core-state status, were then part of the semiperiphery, acting as intermediaries between the larger, more-advanced economies of northern Europe and much of the underdeveloped periphery. During this era, the most important peripheral areas were European colonies in the Americas, west Africa, and portions of eastern Europe. Standing outside the capitalist world economy were external areas (for example, India and China) with which nations of the world system traded but did not control.

When the modern world system is defined primarily in terms of its geographical scope and the division of labor, what were the parameters of the Portuguese portion of that system? The Portuguese subsystem (that is, the Luso-Atlantic world) was comprised of Portugal and its Atlantic colonies, an entity that we will call the Luso-Atlantic economy. Portugal's possessions in the Far East usually existed as little more than trading stations with populous, often aggressive native regimes. The principal components of the world economy under Portuguese rule were the metropolis itself and the Atlantic colonies, particularly Brazil. The division of labor within this area paralleled that of the world economy with the greatest levels of occupational skill and capitalization being concentrated in the major urban centers of Portugal and Brazil. The bulk of the labor force from which surpluses were derived worked in cities as a preindustrial proletariat, as peasants in rural Portugal or as slaves on Brazilian plantations.

Trade was the linchpin that held the Luso-Atlantic economy together. In conformity with mercantilist doctrine, Portugal sought to exploit the land and labor of its possessions for production of cash crops and precious metals while exporting domestic produce, finished goods, and technical and administrative expertise to colonial markets. The upswing in commercial activity after 1690 found the Luso-Atlantic subsystem contributing significantly to the expansion of the world economy. Indeed, the Luso-Atlantic economy played a vital role as supplier of various products then in short supply in northern Europe.[4]

Growing demand for the products over which Portugal exercised control in turn fostered expansion within the Luso-Atlantic economy. As economic conditions improved, increasing quantities of metropolitan and colonial products were funneled through Portugal and on to the European market. In exchange, products ranging from dried cod to Dutch paintings were sent to Portugal for domestic consumption or reexport to the colonies. This commerce, which generally favored the core states in the balance of trade, increased their socioeconomic ascendency over countries such as Portugal. As Professor Wallerstein put it, "the ongoing process of a world-economy tends to expand the economic and social gaps among its varying areas in the very process of its development."[5]

Portugal's venture into manufacturing, which necessitated the importation of technology and skilled labor, represented an attempt to reduce unfavorable trade balances with larger, more-advanced economies, but both foreign competitors and domestic interests resisted establishment of an industrial mode of production. Nevertheless, the hardships imposed by the General Crisis and cyclical decline had exacerbated the economic disadvantages of being on the semiperiphery and thereby lent greater attraction to an industrialization program for which the social order was not yet ready. Reprieve from this dilemma eventually accompanied economic recovery. The established order was soon revitalized by the growing demand for products over which it still exercised effective control. Commerce in a variety of commodities produced by Portugal and its colonies then engendered greater prosperity within the Luso-Atlantic economy, even as it contributed to the core states' predominance and the expansion of the modern world system.

The Growing Trade in Metropolitan Products

Revival of the world economy after 1690 was in part attributable to the fact that Europe enjoyed a relative degree of peace during the last two decades of the seventeenth century. Moreover, production in the French and English Caribbean had increased to meet a growing demand for sugar, tobacco, and other colonial products, all of which had become relatively scarce in northern Europe. The influx of Brazilian gold after 1700 added further impetus to the upswing as did the increasing production of silver and mercury in the Spanish Indies some years later.[6]

Growing consumption of products from the periphery was complemented by a rise in intra-European trade, a trend that Portugal was well positioned to exploit. Rising production of domestic commodities, together with an influx of wealth from the Atlantic possessions, attracted growing numbers of merchant ships to Portuguese shores. The increasing frequency of such visitations after the devaluation of 1688 stands as a measure of the recovery then underway. Though data are far from complete for the period, the information available on ship movements, like that for commodity prices, clearly illustrated the post-1690 upturn. (See figure 2 and appendix 3.)

But what were the products that brought these fleets of foreign vessels to Lisbon, Setúbal, Faro, and other Portuguese ports? In ad-

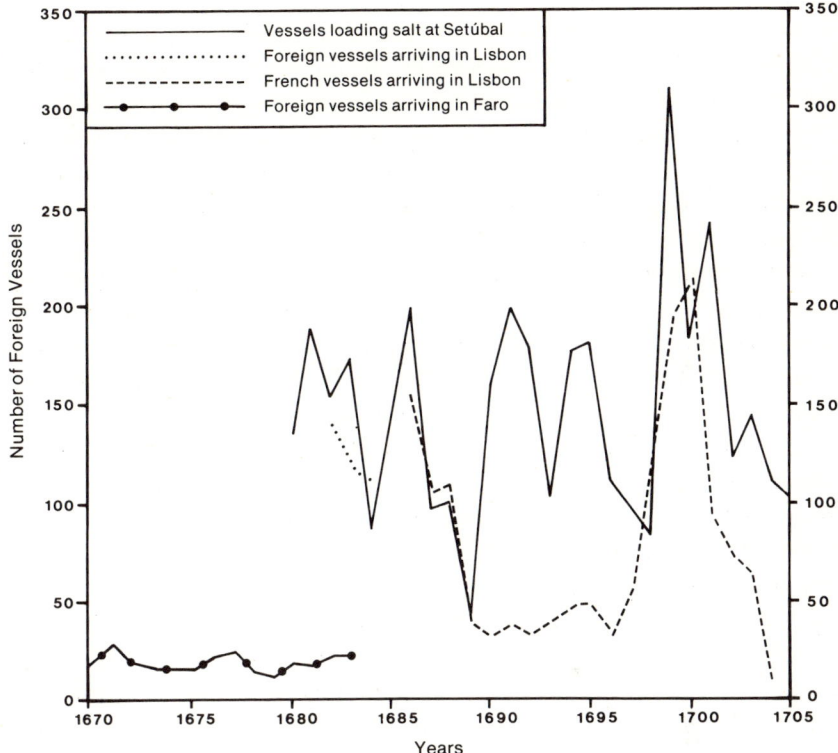

Figure 2. Some data on the number of foreign vessels arriving at Portuguese ports, 1670–1705 (data from Rau, "Os Holandes," pp. 68–196; idem., "Rumos e vicissitudes do comércio do sal português nos séculos XIV a XVII," *Revista da Faculdade de Letras* [Lisbon], 3rd series, 7 [1963]:21–22. [There is some variance in these two sources for the years 1680 (135 vs. 130), 1681 (184 vs. 189), 1684 (86 vs. 85), 1686 (143 vs. 199), and 1688 (101 vs. 98). In these instances, the larger number was used.] Idem., *Subsídios para o estudo do movimento dos portos de Faro e Lisboa durante o século XVII* [Lisbon: Academia Portuguesa de História, 1954], pp. 220 facing, 247; Nuno Daupiás de Alcochete, "Negócios da Feitoria francesa de Lisboa no Final do Século XVII," in *Actas* of the Fifth Colóquio Internacional de Estudos Luso-Brasileiros, 5 vols. [Coimbra: Imprensa da Universidade, 1965–1968], 2:156. Data on vessels coming from Portugal and passing through the Danish Sound can be found in Mauro and Parker, "Portugal," pp. 66–68).

dition to colonial commodities such as sugar, tobacco, hides, brazilwood, and gold, Portugal itself produced goods that, with the recovery, had become increasingly salable in Europe. Most important of these were agricultural products, especially wine and olive oil. Other such products for export included oranges, lemons, cork, and even wool, which, of course, was the keystone of Ericeira's manufacturing program.[7] Also important was salt, a product under royal monopoly, which had long been shipped to northern Europe for use in the drying of fish.

Documents from the medieval era have revealed that the exploitation of salt in Portugal had gone on in the northern part of the country since early in the tenth century.[8] The largest deposits, however, were found farther south along the estuary of the Sado River, which is about twenty miles from Lisbon. After this area was retaken from the Moors, extensive exploitation of salt began, and Setúbal, then a small fishing village, soon became the center of Portuguese production. By the mid-fourteenth century, extraction of salt from the area exceeded domestic consumption and export of the mineral to northern Europe began.[9] Smaller quantities of salt for export were also produced within the jurisdictions of Lisbon and Aveiro.

Most of the exported salt went to Holland; but other nations, including England, Sweden, Norway, Denmark, Spain, France, and Germany, also purchased quantities of the mineral. Though already Portugal's largest customer, Holland reinforced its predominance in the salt trade with the Luso-Dutch Treaty of 1669. In this peace agreement, the Portuguese pledged to pay the Dutch 3 million cruzados indemnification, but, in order to conserve its already-scarce supplies of bullion, Lisbon arranged to make payment in salt from Setúbal.

Under this arrangement, convoys of Dutch ships made their way to the saltpans of Setúbal, each vessel loading an average cargo of 600 moios (20,400 bushels). By a convention of 1677, the Dutch agreed to transport 85,000 moios annually, but the vicissitudes of war and weather precluded reaching this target figure in any given year. During the years 1680 and 1681, for example, a total of only 60,076 moios was loaded onto Dutch vessels. Furthermore, from 1680 to 1690, a total of 1,121 Dutch ships carried away 672,600 moios. During that same decade, 299 vessels from other nations also visited the salt deposits of Setúbal.[10] Between 1690 and 1705, however, the exportation of salt increased considerably (table 4).

The expansion of Portugal's salt trade was accompanied by numerous attempts to profit illegally from the new prosperity. In 1691, for example, the licensed salt producers of Lisbon complained that both foreign and Portuguese black marketeers were frequenting the local saltpans, buying up small quantities of the mineral, which were then put together for shipment to the north.[11] To counter this practice, the crown issued a law in the following year that required the Treasury

TABLE 4
Salt Exported from Setúbal, 1680–1705
(in moios)

Year	Quantity (1 moio = 24 bushels)	Price per Moio in Reis (400 reis = 1 cruzado)
1680	71,363.5	1,500
1681	98,273.0	1,500
1682	83,839.0	1,500
1683	—	—
1684	44,331.5	—
1685	73,109.5	—
1686	75,898.0	—
1687	—	—
1688	56,411.5	—
1689	22,278.0	—
1690	—	—
1691	98,625.5	—
1692	107,324.0	—
1693	73,311.5	—
1694	120,141.5	—
1695	120,151.5	788
1696	81,326.0	1,800
1697	67,478.5	1,500
1698	61,373.0	—
1699	227,901.0	—
1700	134,675.0	—
1701	179,249.0	—
1702	101,178.5	—
1703	102,437.0	—
1704	75,920.5	1,680
1705	65,005.5	—

SOURCE: Rau, "Rumos e vicissitudes," pp. 21–22. Also see Mauro and Parker, "Portugal," pp. 66, 68.

Council to hold annual hearings (*devassas*) on the problem. Anyone found guilty was summarily punished.[12]

More worrisome, however, was the possibility that Portuguese expertise in the production of salt might be transferred to other nations. It was then widely believed that the salt of Setúbal was superior to that of other sources because of the processes used in its extraction. So, in 1695, D. Pedro II ordered that no official engaged in the production of salt leave the realm for the purpose of instructing others in the techniques of its extraction. This order was prompted by the fact that some Portuguese experts had gone to Galicia to aid the Spanish in exploiting deposits there. Anyone apprehended for this crime was to be put to death and have all his property confiscated. An *alvará* of the following year prohibited foreigners from working the salt deposits of Portugal since they might spirit production secrets away to their home countries. Thereafter, any foreigner caught working in the salt industry was publicly flogged and sent to the galleys for five years.[13]

Little is known about the cargoes brought to Portugal by foreign salt ships. It seems, however, that they were usually laden with wood or codfish. Danish ships frequently brought loads of planking to exchange for salt.[14] Other customers undoubtedly purchased salt with specie, and it is possible that some of the salt ships visiting Setúbal, Lisbon, and Aveiro brought cargoes of wheat. The bad harvest of 1694 had left Setúbal with virtually no wheat reserves, a fact that induced the king to go along with the local *câmara's* request that one-third of the grain transiting the Sado estuary from fields upstream be earmarked for use by inhabitants of the area, as well as by crews of salt ships.[15] Since such shortages were common, it is likely that some enterprising foreigners took on cargoes of wheat before leaving for the saltpans of Portugal.

Besides supplying the European market, Portuguese salt was also exported to the Atlantic colonies. In 1631, the crown established a monopoly over all salt exports to Brazil. The trade had previously been handled by numerous private carriers, but the mounting costs of defending Brazil from Dutch interlopers prompted the government to take control of the traffic. After the Dutch were finally evicted from Recife in 1654, the monopoly continued. The crown was then loath to surrender this source of revenue, and its monopoly remained in force until 1801. As with other royal monopolies, the distribution rights for salt were sold to private contractors. Exclusive salt contracts often worked to the detriment of Brazilians, who repeatedly complained of shortages and high prices.[16] Mercantilist doctrine was clearly at work here, for peripheral areas of the Luso-Atlantic economy, which had saltpans of their own, were usually obliged to use the Portuguese product.

Valuable as salt was to the Portuguese, the burgeoning wine industry eventually assumed even greater importance. Like salt, wine had held a significant position in the export sector since the fourteenth century. It also found a receptive market in northern Europe. French wines, however, were the overwhelming favorites of European consumers. The heavier wines of Portugal and its Atlantic islands did not actually enjoy noteworthy popularity until the last years of the seventeenth century. Nonetheless, the transition from sugar growing to viticulture in certain Portuguese islands was well underway by the mid-seventeenth century. Expanding sugar production in Brazil had all but eclipsed the cane culture of Madeira, and its inhabitants turned to wine as a means of economic self-preservation.[17] By 1685, the Treasury Council reported that no sugar mills remained on Madeira and that wine had become the island's principal product.[18]

Exports from the mainland, especially of the wines produced in the Douro region, expanded considerably during this era and largely underwrote the growing prominence of the city of Oporto, from which thousands of pipes were shipped each year. Though consumption of Portuguese wines in Europe had been growing steadily throughout the reign of D. Pedro II, there were three vital catalysts for the vastly increased exportation. First, of course, the general recovery of the world economy fostered greater expansion of Portugal's wine industry. Second, the well-timed devaluation of 1688 added further impetus to consumption of Portuguese wines, for foreign merchants could purchase them at relatively cheaper prices. To some extent, however, this advantage was neutralized by the higher wages being paid agricultural workers. During the last decades of the seventeenth century, shortages of agricultural labor in Portugal became acute.[19] The rush to the Brazilian goldfields after 1700 further worsened the problem. Nonetheless, Portuguese wines held great attraction to foreign purchasers, particularly the English.

During D. Pedro II's reign, Portugal also benefited from the competition between core states. In 1672, for example, the Franco-Dutch conflict caused the merchants of Amsterdam and other commercial centers in Holland to turn increasingly to the wines of Spain and Portugal. From 1682 to 1685, the English placed the so-called Great Prohibition on all French goods, an act of retaliation for Louis XIV's invasion of the Spanish Netherlands. Consumption of Portuguese wines in England grew tremendously during the embargo. This expansion apparently caused labor shortages on the docks of Oporto, as evidenced by the fact that two ships from Pernambuco delivered cargoes of slaves to the city in 1686.[20]

After 1685, an uneasy truce between the two core states followed and sales of French wines rebounded, but the hiatus from conflict lasted only four years. In 1689, the War of the League of Augsburg broke out when the Sun King invaded Germany. This struggle, which lasted nine years and saw England place punitive imposts on French wines, provided a signal opportunity for the wines of the Upper Douro and other growing regions. Further impetus came in 1692–1693, when English duties on French wines were increased by twenty-five percent, and in 1696, when an additional levy of twenty-five pounds per ton was assessed.[21]

Portuguese wines again became attractive to both merchant and consumer in England, and by 1697 the English palate was becoming increasingly accustomed to a variety of Portuguese imports, ranging from young, sweet wines to heavy ports. After the war's end, English buyers again shifted a large share of their business to France. It was soon found, however, that cloth exports to Portugal, formerly a going concern despite sumptuary legislation, began to decline. Not wanting to jeopardize a good thing, English merchants once again increased their purchases of the by then extensively appreciated Portuguese wines.[22] This upward trend was soon reinforced by the War of the Spanish Succession, which again placed England at odds with France.

Research has yet to reveal annual figures on the total quantity of wine exported from Portugal during the reign of D. Pedro II. The fire that struck the archive of the Lisbon *alfândega* following the great quake of 1755 burned documents on wine shipments from the capital as well as vast quantities of documentation on other exports, imports, ship movements, et cetera. Figures on the importation of wine by

Portugal's chief customer, England, do remain, however (table 5). These data show the correlation between the Anglo-French conflicts and the increasing importation of wines from Portugal. Undoubtedly, the Portuguese crown's revenues grew commensurately with the ex-

TABLE 5
English Imports of Portuguese Wines and Duties Imposed
on Their Export by the Oporto Alfândega, 1675–1705

Year	Quantity Imported (in toneis)*	Per Tonel Duty (in reis)
1675	20	—
1676	83	—
1677	176	—
1678	199	240
1679	1,013	"
1680	1,003	"
1681	1,718	"
1682	13,860	"
1683	16,772	—
1684	1,611	—
1685	12,185	300
1686	289	"
1687	327	"
1688	540	"
1689	579	"
1690	1,115	"
1691	2,964	—
1692	6,054	417
1693	8,200	"
1694	9,454	"
1695	3,983	"
1696	6,668	"
1697	4,774	"
1698	4,057	"
1699	8,703	"
1700	7,757	"
1701	7,408	490
1702	5,924	"
1703	8,845	"
1704	9,924	"
1705	8,449	"

SOURCE: Borges de Macedo, *Problemas de História*, pp. 46, 53.
*The tonel is a measure of liquid volume equal to 848 liters.
†This is the median figure for the years 1692–1700.

panding exports and, as table 5 indicates, the government moved to increase its revenues further, gradually raising export duties.

Data on wine prices during the period are also incomplete, as, for that matter, is information on weather conditions, which, of course, had a critical bearing on the size of grape harvests. Nevertheless, it appears that wine prices in Lisbon gradually increased during the reign of D. Pedro II and were generally reflective of climatic fluctuations. Wine sold by the *canada* (three pints) ranged in price from forty-eight to fifty-two reis in 1663. In 1665–1666, the price in the capital rose to sixty reis per canada because of bad harvests. Between 1666 and 1681, weather conditions were generally good and the price hovered around forty reis. The harvest of 1678 was especially bountiful, but it increased the pressure to lower prices at a time when the growers were paying higher wages to workers. Due in part to labor shortages, the Lisbon *câmara* recommended that the already low price level not be reduced any further. Moreover, as the *câmara* pointed out, costlier wine coming from Oporto to help supply the Lisbon market could not be sold at lower prices. The *câmara* also warned that foreign merchants would buy up great quantities for sale in other European markets if the price dropped any further. Then, when periods of scarcity occurred in Portugal, these same merchants would sell foreign wines in Lisbon and elsewhere at high prices, further depleting the country's bullion stock. Scarcities did indeed follow, and, during the years 1681 to 1684, the price per canada rose to seventy-two reis. The harvest of 1684 was especially poor and exports declined considerably, as may be seen in table 5. Exports to England declined steeply with the lifting of the Great Prohibition in 1685, but this seems to have had little effect on Portuguese production since the grape harvest of 1686 was abundant. Production in the following year dropped precipitously, however, causing the price to be set at sixty-eight reis even though much of the 1686 vintage remained in stock. During the next decade, prices rose in conformity with increasing demand in Portugal, Brazil, and Europe. At the same time, costs of production and shipment also rose as the pace of economic recovery accelerated.[23]

Like the mainland, most of Portugal's Atlantic islands benefited from the post-1690 upturn in the world economy. The Cape Verdes, which existed primarily as an entrepôt for the Atlantic slave trade, experienced an economic upturn as the burgeoning American periphery of the world economy required ever-larger infusions of labor power. The discovery of great deposits of alluvial gold in the uplands of Minas Gerais vastly increased the demand for labor in Brazil. Although the Azores reaped little direct benefit from the slave trade, the islands were climatically well situated to produce wheat for sale in Portugal. Moderate temperatures and fertile volcanic soil usually provided the Azoreans with sufficient wheat with which to feed themselves as well as a surplus for export to the mother country. Nevertheless, the post-1690 recovery appears to have largely bypassed the Azores. The wheat surplus in 1701, for example, was approximately forty percent below that of 1680. In part, this may have occurred when corn replaced wheat as the dietary staple of the islanders.[24] It is also likely that emigration to the Brazilian goldfields was beginning to deplete the population of the Azores.

The economic situation in the Madeira archipelagoes was significantly different from that in the Azores. During the late seventeenth century, Madeira exported great quantities of wine, especially to English colonies in the Caribbean and North America. Before 1660, Madeira's largest customer had been Brazil, which preferred the island's wine to that of Portugal because Madeira wine, unlike the Portuguese product, was resistant to the heat that so often ruined wines from the mainland during shipment. Also, with British expansion into the Caribbean, especially after the taking of Jamaica in 1655, the merchants of Madeira found another market for their wine, though Brazilian imports probably continued to grow. It is perhaps ironic that the Madeiran economy, which had been greatly disrupted by the overpowering expansion of Brazil's sugar industry, benefited from its decline as Caribbean sugar began to supplant the Brazilian product in the world economy.

Promotion of wine exports from Madeira to the Caribbean plantations was largely in the hands of a prosperous class of English merchants residing in the islands' capital, Funchal. Like their counterparts in Lisbon and Oporto, these merchants enjoyed various privileges, including the right to practice their Protestant faith. But, unlike their fellows in Portugal, they did not have great success in promoting wine exports to England. Only after 1750 were significant quantities of Madeira wine consumed in the British Isles.[25]

Expansion of wine production was of keen interest to the Portuguese crown, for taxes on the beverage provided much needed revenue.[26] As it has already been noted, the crown hiked the duty on wine as its exportation increased. The *real d'agua* provided another source of revenue from wine sales, but this tax had been unpopular and difficult to collect since its inception in 1619. After the 1668 and 1674 Cortes increased the levy on wine and meat, the raising of which came to be known as the new rights (*novos direitos*), the grumbling about it grew. Moreover, the Lisbon *câmara* reported in 1678 that much wine was being smuggled into the city in coaches, litters, and other conveyances and then sold or consumed without payment of any tax. Sale and consumption of this contraband wine adversely affected *câmara* collections of the *real d'agua* and thus precluded the full delivery of the revenues owed to the crown. Perhaps more aggravating to the city council, however, was the open sale of untaxed wine in the convents and monasteries of the capital. When not retailing wine themselves, ecclesiastics sold their untaxed product to local taverns.[27] Periodic attempts by the crown to stem the illicit wine traffic appear to have done little good, even in times when a papal bull permitting payment of the *real d'agua* was in force.

Measures taken by the crown to improve collection of the wine tax took a variety of forms. In one instance, the prince regent ordered that shops and taverns along the Tagus board up all doors and windows facing the waterfront. It was hoped that this would curb the sale of untaxed wine to seamen.[28] In 1683, D. Pedro ordered that wines from Castile and Catalonia be prohibited from entering Portugal. Wine was temporarily plentiful in the country, and purchase of foreign vintages could only hurt domestic growers while worsening the bullion drain. Two years later, however, the king briefly relented, giving the Spanish ambassador permission to unload forty pipes of wine being shipped from Catalonia.[29]

As in the case of salt, the crown established annual *devassas* to investigate wine smuggling and avoidance of the *real d'agua*. By a decree of 1689, it was ordered that denunciations of individuals trafficking in untaxed wine and meat be heard each year and punishment meted out.[30] Apparently, however, this action had little impact on the black market, for the following year D. Pedro II felt compelled to increase the fines and jail terms imposed on those caught with untaxed wine and olive oil.³¹ Furthermore, the unpopularity of the *novos direitos* was such that when the Cortes reconvened in 1697–1698 (its first meeting in eighteen years), the crown, which needed an additional 600,000 cruzados for defense on top of the 1 million already assessed, agreed to moderate the despised excises on wine and meat. Most of the 1.6 million–cruzado tax burden then fell on tobacco.³²

A perhaps unexpected threat to the crown's revenues and to winegrowers arose in the form of beer. Growing numbers of northern Europeans coming to Portugal after 1640 fostered expansion of domestic brewing as the English, the Germans, and others sought out one of the comforts of home.³³ As demand for (and thus the price of) Portuguese wine increased in the world system, consumers of the lower classes turned increasingly to beer, which was less expensive. Attempting to slow this trend, D. Pedro II ordered in 1689 that beer be sold only in those taverns in which it was brewed or in designated eating houses (*casas de pasto*) that catered to foreigners.³⁴ This prohibition did not work very well, and it was reported a few years later that many Portuguese were frequenting these *casas*.³⁵ This and other threats to wine sales and revenues notwithstanding, the production of Portuguese vineyards led domestic economic recovery and later emerged as the principal bargaining chip in commercial negotiations with the English.

After salt and wine, olive oil was probably the most important export coming from Portugal during the late seventeenth century. This was especially remarkable since the Restoration campaigns had devastated the extensive olive groves in the province of Alentejo. Planting in other provinces, particularly the Beira Baixa, had slowed down during the war years. Yet, after 1668, replanting in the Alentejo went forward and spread northward during the rest of the century, "stimulated by demand from overseas and Baltic markets. In 1691 Lisbon alone sent to northern Europe (as far as Danzig) 10,000 pipes of olive oil, Oporto, 5,000—a sixth and a seventh respectively of the total volumes of exports from each port."³⁶

As with other profitable commodities, the smuggling of olive oil made inroads on the crown's revenues and also contributed to domestic shortages, even during years when production was high. Olive oil was especially scarce in Lisbon in 1702 and 1703, thanks in part to illegal exportation of the product to markets where greater profits were to be made. Perhaps despairing that the smuggling could not be substantially reduced, the Lisbon *câmara* urged that all exportation of olive oil be stopped. Not surprisingly, the crown ignored this plea since any such ban would have cost it considerable revenues collected as export duties.[37]

The crown's jealous protection of revenues coming from salt, wine, and olive oil also extended to smaller branches of the export sector. In 1671, for example, the prince regent prohibited the exportation of orange trees in hopes of preventing the foreign establishment of groves that would compete with those of Portugal.[38] Some idea of the amount of oranges exported to England was revealed in Duarte Ribeiro de Macedo's *Observações* of 1675. According to the mercantilist writer, England annually spent 50,000 cruzados on imports of or-

TABLE 6
Trade between England and Portugal, 1697–1715
(in thousands of English pounds)

Year	Imports from England	Exports to England	England's Export Surplus
1697	125	87	39
1698	365	155	210
1699	338	165	173
1700	336	279	57
1701	277	207	70
1702	460	194	266
1703	714	257	457
1704	781	331	450
1705	819	223	596
1706	763	242	521
1707	615	241	374
1708	538	272	267
1709	732	252	479
1710	615	192	423
1711	576	247	329
1712	565	202	362
1713	628	196	432
1714	794	281	512
1715	625	333	292

SOURCE: Fisher, *The Portugal Trade*, p. 142. (Tables showing the monthly rate of exchange between Lisbon and London from 1619 to 1775 can be found in McCusker, *Money and Exchange in Europe and America, 1600–1775* [Chapel Hill: University of North Carolina Press, 1978], pp. 108–14.)

anges from Portugal, while France, Holland, and other northern European countries also purchased sizable quantities of the fruit.[39] Though further data are lacking, it is likely that the production and export of oranges and other fruits rose to meet the growing European demand after 1690.

This was clearly true for cork, the production of which increased markedly around 1700 as demand for stoppers for wine bottles and other containers grew. Despite the emphasis on manufacturing in late seventeenth-century Portugal, little attention was given to production of corks until the marquis of Pombal assumed power. Before Pombal, the raw material was usually exported and made into corks abroad.[40]

Expanding exportation of Portuguese products spearheaded national recovery while helping fill demand in the world economy. Portuguese exports to England during this period, for which there are some figures, rose from a minimum value of 77,000 pounds in 1668–1669 to 155,000 pounds in 1698.[41] But this expanding commerce was heavily lopsided in favor of England, leaving Portugal with constantly unfavorable balances of trade (table 6). Indeed, these unfavorable trade balances with England were to persist throughout the eighteenth century, although much of the trade deficit was made up by the export of specie and bullion.[42] The principal reason for this state of affairs, which probably also characterized Portuguese commerce with other core states, lay in Portugal's continuing inability to provide itself with sufficient finished goods and foodstuffs.

Food Imports and the Trade Deficit

Despite Ericeira's manufacturing program and sumptuary legislation, the Portuguese continued to consume substantial quantities of English products, as table 6 suggests. This was to be expected, however, since the effort to industrialize was young, relatively small, undercapitalized, and opposed by foreign interests as well as many Portuguese consumers. Though textile purchases undoubtedly accounted for the lion's share of Portugal's unfavorable trade balance with England, long-standing structural weaknesses within the agricultural sector further frustrated mercantilist efforts at recasting the balance in Portugal's favor. Moreover, economic recovery only perpetuated those weaknesses.

Increasing cultivation of vineyards, olive and orange groves, as well as cork and mulberry trees produced commodities for which demand was then growing in the world economy; but, in the process, less land remained available for growing wheat and other essential foodstuffs. The privileged classes often preferred to raise only as much grain as was needed locally, reserving large tracts of their extensive holdings for production of cash crops for the export trade. At most, 900,000 hectares (around 2.5 million acres) were given over to cereal production. Wheat production averaged around 7 million bushels per year, most of which was produced in the Alentejo, the Tagus basin, and the province of Estremadura. In order to meet domestic demand, as much as one-fifth of that total (around 1.4 million bushels) had to be imported each year.[43] Central Europe, England, and the Azores supplied most of the needed grain.

The crown's efforts to ameliorate chronic grain shortages seem to have been mostly directed at augmenting storage facilities and not toward increased cultivation. During the mid-seventeenth century, numerous public granaries (*celeiros*) were established in the Alentejo. D. Pedro II continued this approach, granting licenses for construction of *celeiros* from which grain could be dispensed in years when harvests were poor. Thus, for example, permission to erect public granaries was granted to four *vilas* in the Alentejo: Mourão (1686), Terena (1687), Serpa (1690), and Mertola (1693).[44] In 1699, the king queried the Lisbon *câmara* about the feasibility of establishing a large *celeiro* in the capital. Citing drawbacks such as spoilage, costly outlays for employee salaries, and pricing problems, the city council urged instead that the Castilian system of carefully recording annual harvests be emulated. This, it was argued, would help prevent the hoarding and exorbitant pricing commonly attributed to powerful grain merchants when harvests were bad. Furthermore, the *câmara* believed that the smuggling of wheat to Spain might be curtailed if domestic production was better monitored.[45]

Much grain from the growing regions was indeed smuggled to nearby Spain, exacerbating the already chronic shortages in Lisbon and forcing the capital to depend all the more heavily on imports. These shortages, of course, were especially serious after bad harvests, for then growing regions were hard put to supply local needs, much less those of Spain or Lisbon. In 1692, a great drought hit Portugal, leaving little surplus wheat for shipment out of the Alentejo and other growing areas. Claiming that locally produced grain was needed by its inhabitants, the *vila* of Abrantes took drastic action in that year, blocking all wheat shipments to Lisbon.[46] During the next two years, there was widespread hunger in Portugal as the drought continued. At one point, the price of some wheat in Lisbon rose to 800 reis per alquiere.[47] In 1699, the weather again turned bad, causing the city of Évora to prevent the transport of sixty moios of sorely needed wheat to Lisbon.[48]

The king sometimes ordered local officials to desist in their efforts to block grain shipments to Lisbon, but this did little to increase total production. In isolated instances, the crown entertained schemes for improving the later stages of bread production. In 1703, for example, D. Pedro II granted an Italian inventor a ten-year contract to mill flour by a new process.[49] What became of this venture is not clear, but establishment of local granaries and occasional intercession between vying municipalities, not measures to increase grain production itself, seem to have been the typical means of coping with shortages. Although purchases of foreign grain undoubtedly worsened the bullion drain, they did allow the established order to ignore for the most part structural weaknesses in the agricultural sector that prevented Portugal from becoming self-sufficient in the production of cereals.

Another commodity in short supply was fish. Here again, imports filled the breach, especially cod caught by the English off the banks of Newfoundland. Though the Portuguese and French had pioneered exploitation of the Newfoundland fishery, the English had gained control of the distant banks during the six decades of Spanish rule in Portugal.[50] During this same period, the Portuguese fishing industry had fallen into decline. Why this happened is not altogether clear, but among the various causes were the depletion of local fisheries, labor and capital shortages, and, of course, formidable foreign competition. Moreover, Moorish pirates repeatedly preyed on the fishing fleet. In fact, it was claimed that the constant loss of fishing craft to the Moors was largely responsible for Portugal's inability to supply itself with cod and other seafood.[51] Many fishermen did little actual fishing and instead engaged their boats in the hauling of coal, foodstuffs, rocks for seawalls, and other items having little to do with their occupation.

Naturally, the decline of the fishing industry caused shortages of all types of fish, but most particularly of the less-expensive varieties such as sardines. In 1677, the Lisbon *câmara* complained that the city's poor could not purchase adequate rations of sardines since muleteers were buying up available quantities on the coast and transporting them to inland markets, where prices were higher. This commerce, according to the *câmara*, also deprived women vendors of their humble employment since sardines usually available for local sale were in short supply.[52]

English fishermen usually brought their catch directly to Portugal from American waters without going through customs in England. Approximately sixty English ships were involved in the Newfoundland-Portugal trade, as well as an unspecified number of vessels departing from England with fish caught in its coastal waters.[53] Few data on this trade are available, but it is known that much of the apparently lucrative fish trade to Portugal was handled by merchants based in the West Country of England. In 1667, for example, Bristol merchants paid over 40,000 pounds in duties on wine, oil, and fruits brought from Spain and Portugal, largely in exchange for cargoes of fish.[54] An anonymous Portuguese writer asserted in 1689 that between 600,000 and 700,000 cruzados worth of English codfish were introduced into Portugal each year.[55] In 1707, it was estimated that the value of Newfoundland cod sales to Spain and Portugal annually ran to 130,000 pounds.[56]

The Portuguese crown's response to deficient fish production was scarcely different from that accorded grain shortages. Laws proscribing the use of fine-meshed nets in the Tagus and other rivers in order to protect immature species had been promulgated, but such measures were seldom accompanied by efforts to better exploit the fisheries of the Atlantic.[57] Whaling in Brazilian waters did increase considerably after 1700, but this did little to supplement the Portuguese diet or improve the balance of trade.[58] As with cereals, the crown sought to maximize revenues collected from existing output instead of promoting expanded production. For example, in 1686, a law was promulgated that established a *devassa* to investigate nonpayment of the *décima* and *sisa* on fish. Six years later, a similar edict was issued, suggesting that the previous sanction had little impact.[59]

The Foodstuff Problem: Neglect and Dependence

Manufacturing had made some headway under the count of Ericeira as a means of redressing Portugal's unfavorable balance of trade, but no such program emerged during the era to promote the expansion of fish and grain production. Although the problems besetting the Portuguese fishing industry were legion, it is probable that some solutions could have been found if the privileged and mercantile classes had been more deeply involved in the industry. With the notable exception of Brazilian whaling, exploitation of the sea remained largely in the hands of small operators. Their share of the domestic market contracted as northern European competitors outstripped them in capital investments and gained control of the rich fisheries of the western Atlantic. Apt illustration of the state of the Portuguese industry can be found in the fact that in 1681 only 11 of the 206 able-bodied men available for militia duty in the fishing village of Cascais owned boats of any sort.[60]

As it was previously noted, many members of the landholding classes preferred to produce cash crops for export instead of staples such as wheat since the net return on the former was likely to be greater. Moreover, the price of grains coming from the Baltic and elsewhere was competitive with that produced by Portuguese workers, whose wages were increasing at the time. During the drought and hunger of the mid-1690s, foreign wheat sold for 600 reis per alquiere, a price substantially below the 750 and 800 reis being asked for the domestic product.[61] An inadequate and poorly maintained system of roads within Portugal added to already burdensome transport costs, thereby making seaborne grains all the more attractive.[62] Extortionate pricing by grain merchants when harvests were poor further exacerbated the foodstuff problem. To make matters worse, a long-standing and well-intentioned ban on wheat exportation discouraged expansion of production and even led to a reduction of the number of fields devoted to the growing of grain.[63] It is not surprising, as Father Rafael Bluteau reported in 1679, that much of the cultivable land in Portugal was already given over to olive and orange groves.[64]

Even as the economy recovered, neglect of vital sectors left Portugal heavily dependent on other states within the world system for foodstuffs that might have been produced domestically. Establishment of a manufacturing program similar to that proposed by Duarte Ribeiro de Macedo had shown its economic worth as the influx of imported goods declined. But a concurrent program of agrarian reform along the lines suggested by Manuel Severim de Faria was not attempted. Had his proposals for encouraging greater food production by landed estates and creating agricultural colonies also been adopted, D. Pedro II's effort to put Portugal on its economic feet and reduce dependence on imports would have been much better balanced.

Portuguese society, however, was far from ready for agrarian reform. It was much easier to manipulate the consumption patterns of the privilege classes than it was to alter a mode of production that they largely controlled. Seldom could nobles or clerics be induced to accept dictation of what was to be grown, much less the diversion of labor to agricultural colonies. The crown itself was greatly dependent upon duties imposed on exports and imports and so was usually unwilling to back basic reforms that might have jeopardized revenues. This reluctance was further abetted by rising income from the colonies, which allowed the government to all but ignore the structural weaknesses within the economy for decades to come.

CHAPTER IX

RECESSION AND RECOVERY IN THE COLONIES
(PART 1)

O Brasil se vay attenuando, e os Senores de Eng.ᵒˢ impossibilitando, que devem mais do que tem.

  Salvador Correia de Sá (circa 1669)

O estado esta tão mizeravel, que se V. Magᵉ não acudir como seu Real braco, será impossivel podello sustentar as Rendas.

  D. Rodrigo da Costa, Viceroy of India (1689)

Portugal's imperial enterprise existed both within and outside the world economy. Its outposts on the eastern coast of Africa, in India, and elsewhere throughout the East were, however, usually little more than points of commercial and cultural contact with regions external to the world economy. For example, the populous and wealthy states of India and China afforded the vastly outnumbered Portuguese little opportunity to institute thoroughly colonial regimes.[1] In the Atlantic islands, Brazil, and, to a lesser degree, west Africa, however, extensive colonization took place, a development that facilitated incorporation of Portugal's Atlantic possessions into the modern world system. The Portuguese found their Atlantic holdings less difficult to settle than those in the East. Distances were not nearly so great, and the aboriginals of Brazil, though often worthy opponents, could not mount the sort of resistance to intrusion that the Portuguese encountered in India, China, and Japan.

The colonial endeavor in west Africa occupied a position between that of the Eastern enclaves and the Brazilian settlements. Disease and the effective resistance of hostile tribes did much to retard Portuguese settlement. Instead of agricultural production (which brought white settlers and black labor alike to Brazil), slaves and ivory became the principal economic bases of Portugal's west African colonies. While west Africa held a middle ground between periphery and external areas, South America offered the most fertile ground for Portuguese colonialism. It was in Brazil that the Portuguese were most successful in reinforcing their economic and military dominance and maintaining cultural domination as well.[2]

Portugal's rule over its Atlantic domains was secured on two levels. First, laws were promulgated that legitimized metropolitan hegemony; and, second, the commercial intercourse between mother country and colony gave rise to political and administrative links that further strengthened the crown's control. Legislation frequently served to rationalize the relationship in conformity with mercantilist policies.[3] As these bases of imperial control were established, so too was the culture of the mother country impressed upon native populations, often by missionaries. Well after this process had begun, the Portugal of D. Pedro II launched a variety of programs aimed at rendering the periphery more prosperous and thereby furthering economic recovery in the metropolis.

Even as the manufacturing program and moves toward monetary and fiscal reform were underway in Portugal, the crown also sought to stimulate a greater infusion of wealth from its colonial possessions. Concerted efforts were made to discover precious metals in Portuguese Africa and Brazil and to gain access to the silver of Peru. Cultivation of oriental plants in Brazil, a program advocated by António Vieira and Duarte Ribeiro de Macedo, was encouraged in Maranhão and Pará. Toward the end of the seventeenth century, the Portuguese moved to expand their role in the African slave trade. These and other measures also had as their aim the revitalization of colonial economies, for the downturn afflicting the world economy after 1670 did not spare Portugal's Atlantic possessions. And, though its Atlantic colonies received a lion's share of the crown's attention, attempts were made to revitalize Portugal's decadent enterprise in the Far East.

Promoting Prosperity in the Eastern Empire

Things had gone badly for the Portuguese in the Far East. Thanks largely to Dutch intrusion in the Indian Ocean after 1600, the Portuguese had lost many wealthy outposts. The coup de grace to Portugal's once-prosperous Eastern empire had come with the loss of Ceylon and Malabar to the Dutch (1655–1663).[4] The Dutch depredations of the first two-thirds of the seventeenth century were followed with attacks by Arab powers, whose strength was then on the rise. Just as D. Pedro was beginning his reign as prince regent in 1668, the Arabs of Oman sacked the Indian enclave of Diu and then mounted an unsuccessful attack against Mozambique in the following year. In order to cement a vitally needed alliance with the English, the Portuguese ceded Bombay (and also Tangier) to England in 1662 as part of the Infanta Catherine's dowry.[5] In 1663, a Jesuit priest who had recently returned to Portugal from the Far East lamented that Portugal's once great empire was "reduced to so few lands and cities that it can be wondered if that State was smaller in the beginning than in the end."[6]

The sorry state of affairs in the Far East did not preclude attempts to revive Portugal's remaining possessions. C. R. Boxer has properly assigned most of the blame for the decay of the Eastern empire to the Portuguese themselves rather than to the Spanish regime in Portugal (1580–1640). However, he may have overstated the indifference of D. Pedro II's government to its Asian domains.[7] Despite its preoccupation with economic difficulties at home and its much greater concentration on the Atlantic colonies, the crown did make various attempts to revive the decadent East. The prince regent seriously entertained the idea of a new East India company as proposed by New Christian merchants, though he had to retreat in the face of virulent opposition to that scheme. In 1671 and 1672, the crown opened the east African coast to free trade for any subject willing to dispatch vessels to the area. This was done to stimulate trade and facilitate settlement of the region.[8]

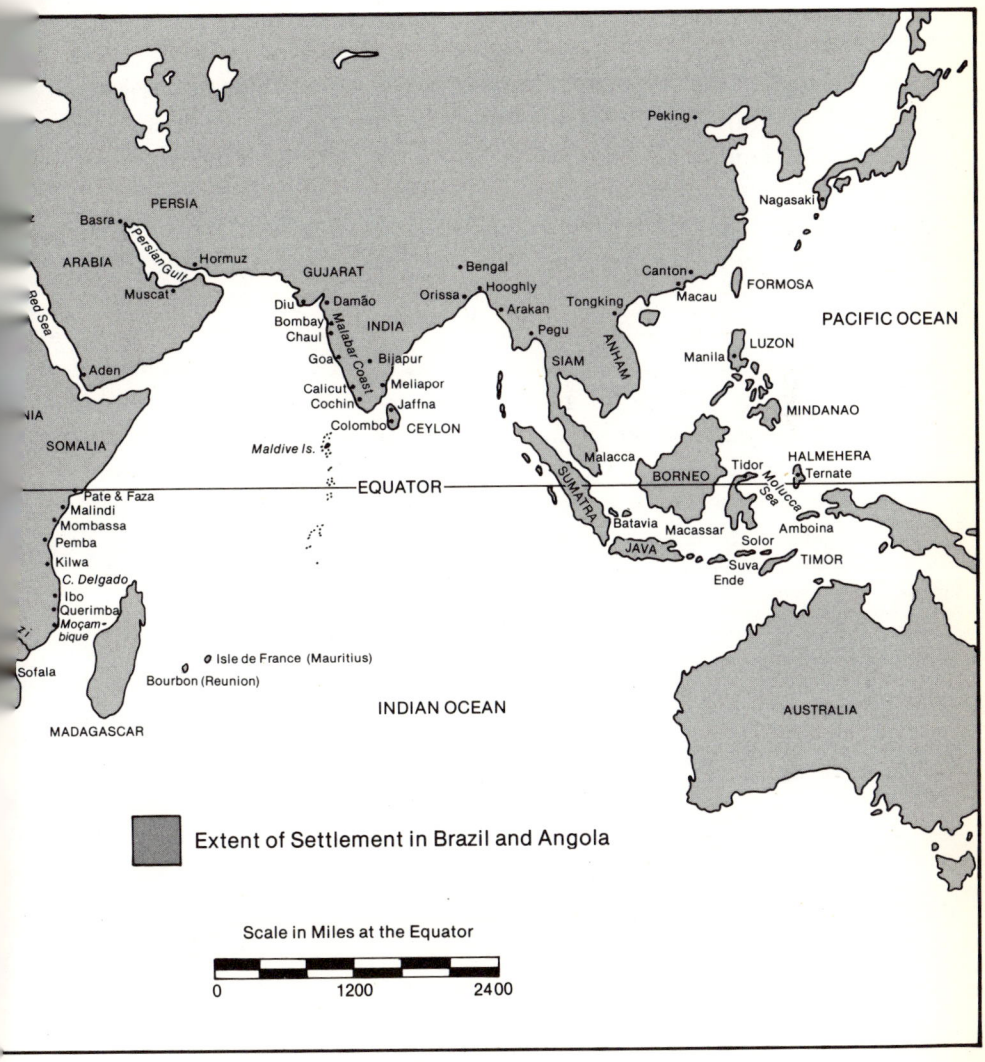

Within the next few years, plans were laid to send out a contingent of settlers to southeast Africa, a region reportedly possessed of great mineral wealth that required the protection that increased settlement would provide. In late 1677, an expedition of four ships carrying at least two thousand people left Lisbon on the long and arduous voyage to Mozambique. Finding that many people willing to embark on such a risky venture was no easy task. Consequently, the government scoured the capital for recruits, collecting many idlers, orphans, and prostitutes for the expedition. Many of the settlers undoubtedly believed that they would take part in the exploitation of great goldfields rumored to be in the territory of an African potentate known as the Monomotapa. But little came of the settlement scheme, and, instead of producing a torrent of gold, the settlers further burdened the already-strained finances of the colonial administration. In 1682, the governor of the region reported to the prince regent that "the settlers that Your Highness was pleased to send to these parts have done nothing but cause expense to your royal treasury, and bring discredit on the Portuguese nations from the evil practices of the women who came from the Kingdom."[9]

The failure of the settlement scheme was soon followed by increasingly serious threats to Portuguese outposts in both Africa and India from Arab invaders. Even Goa, the capital city of the Eastern empire, was threatened. In 1683 and 1684, thousands of Marathas moved south and laid siege to Chaul before attacking Goa.[10] This assault was repulsed, but Portugal's vestigial empire still remained endangered by Muslim attackers.

Even without this threat, the empire's potential for economic return was thwarted by the diversion of wealth into private and foreign hands. Many Portuguese who went out to India as soldiers left Goa to become free-lance traders over whom the colonial government had little control. Viceroys and governors themselves were often corrupt, sending home vast personal fortunes while doing little to improve collections for the treasury. Much wealth was also absorbed by commercially astute Jesuit missionaries, who spent it on ecclesiastical projects.[11]

Portuguese merchants in the Far East often traded directly with the English and other Europeans, thereby depriving the crown of substantial revenues. During the early 1670s, the Abbé Carré, an agent of Colbert assigned the task of furthering France's recently inaugurated trade with India, described the activity of the Martins brothers, two great merchants who specialized in the diamond trade. Carré reported that he

> was on board the *Caesard* [Caesar], in which were the two Martins and other rich Portuguese merchants. They took away immense sums of money, remitted to them from England in return for diamonds and precious stones which they yearly sold there. This is because it is a trade which they cannot handle with Portugal on account of the duties and strict prohibition against any Portuguese engaging in it, with the exception of those employed for this purpose on the king's behalf. Accordingly, the richest Goanese merchants avail themselves of the English ships, which never fail to call there about the months of November or December, in order to take in provisions.[12]

Great wealth was still to be had from Portugal's shrunken Eastern empire, but the difficulties involved in consolidating the crown's control over the activities of Portuguese subjects, not to mention the outlays needed to defend far-flung outposts from attackers, must have discouraged D. Pedro II and his ministers. Nonetheless, the crown continued its efforts to support its tottering enclaves. Following the Maratha assault on Goa, the king issued a number of laws designed to lend financial support to a beleaguered India. In late 1684, for example, he ordered that all revenues collected at the port of Aveiro be used for the sending of ships and financial aid in the next outward passage of the *carreira da Índia*.[13] Such aid was sorely needed since the Eastern possessions apparently were running annual deficits, as table 7 shows for 1684 through 1687.

In 1688, the governor of India complained that Portugal's possessions in southeast Africa had contributed little to royal revenues during the past three years. This shortfall could in part be attributed to the king's previous opening of the area to free trade by individuals under Portuguese sovereignty. Native merchants from India's Kannara coast had taken the liberalization to heart, flooding into the African outposts and selling goods at low prices, thereby forcing Portuguese traders to offer more goods in order to obtain a given amount of the gold then being extracted from the region. Furthermore, the English were illicitly trading with the African coast and thus depriving the Goan treasury of potential revenues. At the governor's urging, the king and the Overseas Council decided to end free commerce in the area and establish a company that would have a monopoly on the trade between Portugal's Indian and southeast African outposts.[14]

During the 1690s, such a company was formed, the needed capitalization coming largely from the wealthy merchants of Goa. These traders initially were reluctant to invest in the project, but, after certain conditions were met, they put up the required funds in 1694.[15] Establishment of the company marked the culmination of various proposals for similar enterprises, not the least of which was the New Christian scheme of 1673. D. Pedro II had himself recommended founding such a company to the viceroy of India in 1685, suggesting that it be modeled after those of England and Holland.[16]

This new firm, the Indian Commercial Company, which was formed for an initial term of twelve years, was granted a monopoly on the sale of cloth, cochineal, coral, emeralds, gold, and silver to Portugal. In India, it was to have exclusive control over the sale of

TABLE 7
Income and Expenditure of Various African
and Eastern Enclaves, 1684–1687
(in thousands of xerafins*)

Enclave	Income	Expenditure
Goa, Salsette, and Bardez	356.3	551.8
Chaul	15.4	44.7
Baçaim	173.0	107.5
Manora	4.9	5.9
Damão	103.0	41.2
Diu	62.3	65.5
Mombasa	34.2	24.6
Congo	44.0	6.4
Angediva	1.9	19.5
Mangalore	4.6	1.8
TOTALS†	799.6	868.9

SOURCE: ANTT, Convento da Graça, Misc. Manuscritos, *caixa* 6, *tomo* 3, fl. 276.
*The xerafin, the principal coinage of Portuguese India, was valued at 300 reis.
†All figures are approximate, having been rounded off to the nearest decimal. The actual income and expenditure figures were 799,407.3.09 and 868,571.1.50 xerafins.

pepper, cinnamon, indigo, raw cloth, and a variety of other items. Over the subsequent few years, the company turned a profit, but disaster in southeast Africa soon cut short its brief life.

During the mid-1690s, the African leaders who controlled the goldfields of southeast Africa formed an alliance against the Portuguese and Indian traders in the region, falling upon them in a series of raids. The resultant turmoil disrupted the gold trade and probably precluded exploitation of a silver mine that was discovered up the Zambesi around 1695. Attempting to explain this unfortunate turn of events to D. Pedro II, the Indian viceroy reported that

> it was the insolences of our people that caused these wars, because those who possess many Kafirs [Bantu slaves in this context] and have power are guilty of such excesses that the Kings and Princes, offended, break out in these disorders. Everybody in the Rivers [that is, the Zambesi drainage] wants to govern. And they say that if there cannot be somebody to tame and rule these potentates, then everything will be lost.[17]

Disruption in the region was soon followed by a development even more damaging to the success of the Indian Commercial Company. In March 1696, a force of about three thousand Arabs coming by ship from Muscat laid siege to Fort Jesus, the stronghold at Mombasa. During the next two years, a few hundred defenders valiantly but unsuccessfully struggled to prevent the capture of the African fortress. News of the siege did not reach Lisbon until 1698, but an expeditionary force of 900 men was dispatched in early 1699. By then, however, it was too late, for Fort Jesus had fallen on December 12, 1698.[18]

The fall of Mombasa led to recriminations against the recently founded Indian Commercial Company, including accusations that it was somehow culpable for the loss of the trading center. Such accusations were often merely a smoke screen thrown up by certain Goan merchants to obscure a long-standing desire to be rid of the company since, apparently, its activities had been cutting into their profits. Though the viceroy would have preferred otherwise, the clamor against the company was such that he disbanded it in late 1699. With the extinction of the short-lived company, hopes of establishing a great monopoly enterprise to oversee commerce within the Indian Ocean and between Goa and Lisbon were effectively extinguished.[19]

Despite the termination of a commercial venture that had shown promise, other companies were established after 1699. Meanwhile, the economic awakening then occurring in the world economy also reached Portugal's Eastern possessions. Larger and richer cargoes were embarked on the *carreira da Índia*. Tobacco and specie were the principal shipments on the *carreira*'s voyages to India, but Dutch woolens, coral, Italian paper, and various other luxury products were also on board. Diamonds, saltpeter, and oriental rugs were among the most important items brought on the return voyages. Other imports included porcelains from Macau, specie, indigo, pepper, calicoes, silks, damasks, and various other fabrics. Thanks to the expansion of commerce that came after 1690, the Eastern trade "was now regarded as flourishing."[20]

This trade, however, was but a shadow of its former self and really only an adjunct to Portugal's far more important commerce with its Atlantic possessions. This can be clearly seen in the long-standing decline in the number of ships voyaging to and from India each year, and even in the routes taken by the once-great *carreira*. From 1500 to 1519, 234 ships left Lisbon for the Indian Ocean; but, during the years 1630 to 1635, only 16 vessels embarked for the East.[21] During the remainder of the seventeenth century and throughout the following century, the slow rate of departure prevailed, and vessels were generally smaller than those used earlier. In any given year, only one or two, maybe three, ships made the arduous voyage to or from Goa. In 1672, for example, three ships from India made landfall in the Azores and then were escorted to Lisbon.[22] In some years the number might be slightly larger, but in others no vessels embarked (see appendix 4).

On the outward voyage, Indiamen followed the traditional route, swinging around the Cape of Good Hope before stopping in Mozambique to take on provisions for the relatively short leg to Goa. After 1600, however, the predations of Dutch warships made the return trip quite risky, especially after the Hollanders claimed the island of Saint Helena, another traditional provisioning stop, in 1633. By the 1660s, ships making the return voyage usually stopped at Bahia, where they were incorporated into the much larger fleets annually leaving the Brazilian capital for Portugal.[23]

While they were in Brazilian waters, portions of *carreira* cargoes were often sold illegally to colonials, thereby depriving the crown of additional revenues. But the sheer length of the return voyage frequently made provisioning stops in Brazil necessary; and, if not, resourceful captains or officials bent on a little illicit commerce found reason to call at Bahia or elsewhere.[24] In other instances, the India ships did indeed undergo torturous ordeals. Recognizing this, the crown relaxed a previous prohibition on *carreira* stops in Brazil in 1672.[25] After that, captains of ships in desperate shape need not have second thoughts about putting in at Bahia or elsewhere. But helpful as the relaxation may have been in saving men and cargoes, the lengthy voyage still took its toll. Father António Vieira reported, for example, that a ship reaching Bahia from Goa in 1691 had lost more than one hundred men during its five-month voyage.[26]

Despite the expense involved in maintaining Portugal's Eastern enterprise, the government of D. Pedro II did make repeated attempts to reinvigorate economic activity in its distant outposts. By 1700, economic conditions had improved, though the loss of Mombasa was a serious blow to the crown's efforts at preserving and revitalizing commerce in the East. Nevertheless, the Portuguese may have been fortunate to retain as much of the Eastern empire as they did. Sought-after products from external areas continued to reach Lisbon on the *carreira da Índia*, though then most frequently by way of Brazil.

The Decline of the Brazilian Sugar Economy

After the establishment of the Brazil Company in 1649, commercial intercourse between Portugal and its Brazilian colony was borne largely in great fleets (*frotas*) that annually made the voyage to and from the mother country. During the late seventeenth century, these fleets, which often comprised seventy to ninety vessels, included ships coming from Brazil's three principal ports, Bahia, Recife (Pernambuco), and Rio de Janeiro. Once laden with sugar and other commodities, these three contingents sometimes rendezvoused at sea or in the Azores and then proceeded together to Portugal.[27] Often, however, at least one of the three fleets departed late, voyaging to Portugal alone.

The value of sugar shipments coming from Brazil, a colony that D. João IV had once dubbed his "milch cow," began dropping sharply around 1650, with the serious decline continuing after 1670. One indication of this decline can be seen in the shrinking size of *frotas*. In 1657, for example, a great *frota* of 107 ships, 50 from Bahia, 33 from Pernambuco, and 24 from Rio de Janeiro, had borne 53,221 large wooden containers (*caixas*) of sugar to Portugal. Nine years later, however, both the number of vessels crossing the Atlantic and their cargo of sugar had declined by at least one-half.[28] In 1668, Bahia dispatched only eleven ships to Lisbon (see appendix 5).[29] This decline gives a clear indication of the crisis besetting the sugar economy, though falling valuation of the commodity, as shown in figure 3, offers a better illustration of the downturn in the sugar economy.

The fleets themselves soon adjusted to sugar's declining fortunes by carrying larger cargoes of other commodities, particularly tobacco, which growers probably planted in greater quantities as sugar prices continued to fall. The *frota* of 1669 consisted of fifty vessels.[30] In 1676, over forty ships left Lisbon for Brazil, while another twenty departed from Oporto for the giant colony.[31]

The initial threat to the sugar economy had come from the Dutch,

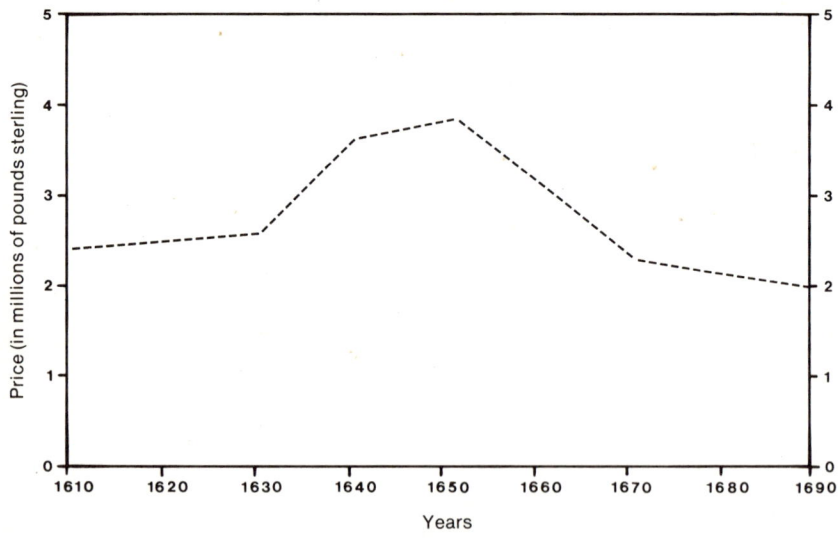

Figure 3. The rise and fall in the value of Brazilian sugar exports, 1610–1690 (in millions of pounds sterling) (data from Simonsen, *História Econômica do Brasil*, p. 382 facing). (Also see appendix 6.)

RECESSION AND RECOVERY IN THE COLONIES 217

who captured many of the rich plantations of Pernambuco after their occupation of Recife in 1630. Moreover, the Dutch had much success in waylaying sugar shipments from other Brazilian captaincies. Attacks on Brazilian shipping in 1647 and 1648 were so successful that they may have accounted for the loss of as many as 249 of the 300 vessels in Portugal's merchant marine.[32] Though these losses were probably exaggerated, they provided the principal impetus for the founding of the Brazil Company in 1649.

Financed largely by New Christian merchants and urged upon D. João IV primarily by António Vieira, the Brazil Company (Companhia Geral do Comércio do Brasil) was established to maintain a fleet of thirty-six warships, which would escort convoys of trade ships to and from Brazil.[33] In return for offering this protection, the company was granted a monopoly on supplying flour, wine, codfish, and olive oil to Brazil at prices that it would set. Furthermore, the Brazil Company was granted a monopoly on the import of brazilwood and was allowed to levy duties on cargoes of cotton, hides, tobacco, and sugar delivered to Portugal. Of perhaps equal importance to the firm's New Christian backers was, as we saw in an earlier chapter, a royal statute exempting their property from confiscation by the Inquisition "for the crimes of heresy, apostasy and Judaism."[34]

In addition to the inquisitors, whose protestations received a warmer reception after D. João IV's death in 1656, Brazilian colonists and merchant communities in smaller Portuguese seaports and the Atlantic islands also emerged as major opponents of the Brazil Company. Brazilian consumers complained of the shortages and inflated prices that accompanied the monopolization of supplies of basic foodstuffs. Representatives of smaller mercantile communities such as Aveiro, Viana do Castelo, and Vila do Conde bemoaned a loss of business since most shipping was then being funneled into Lisbon. These same merchants also railed against the exclusion of smaller, poorly armed vessels from the company's convoys.[35]

In addition to the antagonism of a multitude of detractors, the Brazil Company was, from its inception, plagued by a lack of capitalization. On its first convoy, the company was able to provide only eighteen of the stipulated thirty-six escort vessels. Largely because of financial problems and the increasingly effective tactics of its opponents, the company's stockholders were bought out and the firm was made part of the royal bureaucracy as the Junta do Comércio during the 1660s.[36] The work of the junta, which was itself abolished in 1720, was largely confined to the protection of merchant vessels engaged in the Brazil trade. In 1672, Prince Regent Pedro promulgated a *regimento* for the junta, which, besides reducing the New Christian influence on its governing board, streamlined its operating procedures.[37]

The brief interlude of commercial monopoly enjoyed by the Brazil Company was well timed, for it elicited capital (albeit less than anticipated) essential for the defense of trans-Atlantic shipping and the ultimate ouster of the Dutch from Brazil. But welcome as the 1654 recovery of Recife may have been to the Portuguese, the difficulties besetting the sugar economy only worsened. Indeed, the value of Brazilian sugar exports between 1650 and 1670 dropped by more than one-third. And, during the next two decades, as figure 3 shows, the decline continued.

The establishment of sugar production in the Caribbean was largely responsible for undercutting the market position of Brazilian sugar, which had held a virtual monopoly on sales to Europe during the first half of the seventeenth century. The rapid expansion of English, French, and, to a lesser degree, Dutch plantations in the West Indies after 1650 struck a devastating blow to the Luso-Atlantic economy. Duties collected at the Lisbon *alfândega* sagged, and the owners of sugar mills (*engenhos*) received so little for their production that many Brazilian plantations went bankrupt. Indeed, all sectors of the Luso-Atlantic economy were touched by the deepening crisis. Brazil remained the largest producer of sugar for the world economy, but its once overpowering hold on the market was gone.[38]

By 1670, the repercussions of expanding sugar production in the Caribbean were strongly felt in Portugal. Brazilian sugar piled up in the warehouses of Lisbon as tariff walls, particularly those raised by the English, French, and Dutch, effectively prevented entry of much Brazilian sugar into once profitable markets. In 1675, the crown reduced the established prices of various grades of Brazilian sugar by more than one-third in some cases.[39] Prices continued to fall as sugar surpluses grew.[40] (See appendix 6.)

Throughout D. Pedro II's reign, relatively little was done to resuscitate the sugar economy, even though Brazilian planters and their supporters complained loudly and bitterly about the crisis, usually singling out Portuguese duties on sugar as their principal affliction. These duties, like those imposed on English traders, comprised, at base, the *décima* (ten percent), the *sisa* (ten percent) and the *consulado* (three percent), which amounted to a twenty-three-percent imposition on sugar, tobacco, and other products shipped to Portugal and then reexported. It was argued that these and other taxes had so inflated costs that foreign sugar mills could profitably compete with Brazilian *engenhos* and were rapidly driving them out of business.[41] Taking up this argument, the Lisbon *câmara* addressed a long and forceful *consulta* to D. Pedro II in July 1689, blaming the heavy imposts on commodities (especially sugar, salt, tobacco, and pastel, a dyestuff produced in the Azores) for the economic difficulties confronting the producers.[42] The city council summed up its opposition to the ostensibly burdensome duties by declaring that "experience has shown that, being many the tributes, few are the revenues."[43] In a letter written one week after the *câmara* submitted its blunt opinion, Father António Vieira penned a famous, if rather exaggerated, lamentation about the sorry state of the Brazilian economy.

This year sugar mills ceased grinding cane, and next year only a few of them will be able to function. Prudent people advise us to dress in cotton, to eat manioc and to revert to using bows and arrows for lack of modern weapons; so that we will shortly relapse into the primitive savagery of the Indians and become Brazilian natives instead of Portuguese citizens.[44]

Complaints and advice notwithstanding, the crown had little latitude within which to act. D. Pedro II could do little about the escalating tariffs in Europe, much less the general decline of the world economy. Reduction of duties imposed in Portugal may have helped somewhat, but doing so entailed unacceptable risks to an already hard-pressed treasury. The crown, according to C. R. Boxer, "depended so heavily on the Revenue from its Customs that it could not forego the immediate yield for the uncertain prospect of a larger income in a distant future if taxation was drastically reduced."[45]

As was frequently the case with revenue-producing commodities, the crown devoted its attention to rendering existing sugar production more efficient and minimizing revenues lost to smuggling, fraud, and other such drains on the treasury. Measures to minimize losses to fraud included a 1687 order that all sugar brought to Brazilian warehouses be graded according to three standard classifications and that appropriate marks be burned onto their wooden *caixas* before shipment. This law was enacted to curtail the practice of falsely raising the grades, and thus the prices, of inferior sugar. The crown feared that the reputation of the finest Bahian sugar, which was then regarded as the best produced anywhere in the world, would be discredited if quality control were not maintained.[46] In an action taken in 1698, the crown limited the weight of *caixas* to forty arrobas (approximately 1,100 pounds). Laborers in the Lisbon *alfândega* were not showing up at work for fear of injuring themselves while attempting to manipulate the massive *caixas* that muscular slaves had loaded on ships in Bahia and other Brazilian ports.[47]

Certain steps taken by the crown were more supportive of the beleaguered Brazilian planters. In many instances, the government aided Pernambucan plantation owners in regaining their property after Recife was retaken from the Dutch in 1654.[48] This policy put owners back in control of their holdings but did little to improve the bleak financial prospects confronting many of them. However, D. Pedro II did issue laws that limited creditors of destitute planters to attaching only revenues produced by sugar plantations, and not the properties themselves.[49] Furthermore, the crown encouraged newly appointed governors to foster the establishment of additional sugar mills.[50]

On balance, however, little substantive action was taken to revive the sugar economy, and the crown instead concentrated on extracting what it could from a stagnating industry. Because of duties and other taxes on sugar, among which were levies for the 1662 dowry of Queen Catherine and the 1669 Dutch indemnity, the *câmaras* of Bahia and other Brazilian cities kept up a continuous chorus of woe. After reporting in 1691 that it had paid more than 100,000 cruzados in taxes and donations, th *câmara* of Bahia went on to remark bitterly that the crown ignored the city except in those instances when additional revenues were needed, "all to the damnation and ruination of this state which will be bled white as was India."[51]

The Portuguese devaluation of 1688 was especially upsetting to the colonists since supplies of gold and silver specie were already very low in Brazil. Just as precious metals drained out of Portugal to England and other core states, so did it leave Brazil for the mother country, which enjoyed a favorable trade balance with its principal colony. By devaluing Portuguese coinage to a level below that of Brazil, the crown had accelerated the flow of precious metals from colony to mother country after 1688. Following the devaluation, complaints against the measure flooded into Lisbon from all over Brazil. Much of the outcry had to do with the crown's order that the colony's already scarce specie was to circulate according to intrinsic weight, not face value. As with Portuguese coins, those of Brazil apparently suffered considerable clipping. At any rate, the devaluation had the effect of further weakening colonial specie vis-à-vis that of Portugal.

The *câmara* of Rio de Janeiro was especially incensed by the devaluation edict since holders of specie there lost an inordinately large share of their purchasing power. According to António Vieira,

money in Rio de Janeiro had declined so greatly that, in one day, computing that which was held relative to that which was lost, whoever had nine found himself with only five; and the worst of it is that what little remained was sent to Portugal, because they say it is worth more there.[52]

At one point, the governor in Bahia complained that there was no money in Brazil with which to make payments.[53] Ultimately, the unremitting protests of the Rio *câmara* and others had their effect. In late 1691, the crown finally devalued the currency of Brazil to conform with that of Portugal. In this instance, at least, colonial complaints had brought some relief from the crisis afflicting the sugar economy.[54]

Chronic shortages of specie in both Brazil and Portugal were, of course, symptoms of the Luso-Atlantic economy's unfavorable balance of trade with the world economy. Various proposals were made to remedy the shortage of precious metals in Brazil, including a scheme advanced by António Vieira. Writing to the duke of Cadaval in 1692, Vieira recommended that a colonial currency be instituted that would have an intrinsic value sufficiently low to discourage its exportation.[55] Resolution of the specie problem, however, eventually accompanied economic recovery, which was already underway. Though the sugar boom was long since over, other colonial commodities were emerging that, together with a still extensive cane culture, were to bring unprecedented prosperity to the Luso-Atlantic economy. Had he lived beyond 1697, Father Vieira may well have been amazed to learn that gold, once so scarce in Portuguese America, was being disgorged in vast quantities from mines in the Brazilian backlands.

Royal Efforts to Revitalize the Periphery

The golden bonanza discovered during the 1690s had not come easily, for a great deal of energy, capital, and even life had been expended in the quest for precious metals in Brazil. Indeed, this search, as well as a number of other steps, was taken by Lisbon after 1668 to revitalize economic activity on the periphery and thus increase the crown's revenues. Direct and sometimes forceful action was taken to find the reputedly vast reserves of mineral wealth suspected to lie somewhere in the hinterlands of Brazil. In order to attract trade in Peruvian silver, the government established the small settlement of Colónia do Sacramento on the Rio de la Plata estuary in 1680. And, as it has already been noted, the crown encouraged cultivation of crops transplanted from the Far East to the northern captaincies of Brazil. An attempt was also made to regain the monopoly contract for supplying African slaves to the Spanish Indies, the famed *asiento*, which had been revoked following the 1640 Restoration. Finally, establishment of the Junta do Tobaco in 1674 heralded an effort to better exploit a product that would help fill the void left by a contracting sugar economy. Even as this fivefold approach went forward, other less-emphasized sectors of the colonial economy, ranging from hide production to whaling, expanded as the world economy emerged from years of recession.

The quest for mineral wealth in Brazil had gone on for decades, and small, intermittent discoveries of precious metals and stones had kept alive both royal and colonial interest in finding bonanzas in the backlands. Much of the early mining activity was concentrated in southern Brazil, where placer mines exploited by Paulistas, inhabitants of the captaincy of São Paulo, produced undetermined quantities of gold. These same Paulistas later came to be known as *bandeirantes* in recognition of their path-breaking ventures into the Brazilian wilderness, usually in search of Indian slaves or, probably much less frequently, mineral wealth.[56]

D. Pedro II's first significant manifestation of interest in the mines

RECESSION AND RECOVERY IN THE COLONIES 223

of Brazil came in 1670 with the appointment of Afonso Furtado de Castro do Rio de Mendonça as governor-general of the colony. Unlike any previous governor-general, Mendonça received special authority over matters related to mining.[57] Furthermore, other officials (including the governor of Pernambuco, Fernão de Sousa Coutinho, who was himself appointed in 1670) were also enjoined to encourage the discovery of mines.[58] The administration of Mendonça (1671–1675) marked an era

of great activity in the search for gold, silver and emeralds. No other period in the history of Brazilian mining may be compared with it. Despite the repeated failures of past prospecting expeditions, the enthusiasm of the Governor was shared by the Home Government; and from both sides of the Atlantic, from Lisbon and Baia, the Brazilian colonists were incessantly urged to discover mineral wealth for the crown of Portugal.[59]

The periodic remission of precious metals and stones to the mother country had undoubtedly kindled the enthusiasm of the crown. One sample, an adulterated mixture of silver nuggets and an ore presumed to be silver bearing, was remanded to Lisbon by the governor-general as evidence of the potential wealth in the Bahian hinterlands. The sample never reached the capital, however, since the ship carrying it was wrecked off Portugal's northern coast. Nonetheless, news of the reputedly rich ore sample found a receptive audience at court.[60] In 1672, strikingly tangible evidence of wealth reached Lisbon from the Paranaguá diggings in southern Brazil. Though the documentary evidence is tantalizingly brief, from it it is known that a royal official named Diogo Carneiro Fontoura had brought 493.5 oitavas (approximately 1.85 kilograms) of gold from the placers of Paranaguá.[61] This small but encouraging influx of gold, which probably represented the fifth part (*quinto*) of precious metal production owed the crown, was, together with tales of great silver deposits in Bahia, undoubtedly an inducement to further exploration.

The crown soon began laying plans for a large, well-financed expedition to Brazil. Reaching silver mines reportedly located in the Itabaina Mountains of the Bahian interior would be the first priority of the venture. On June 28, 1673, D. Pedro entrusted leadership of the expedition to Dom Rodrigo de Castel-Branco, a Spaniard who had become one of the prince regent's gentlemen-in-waiting. Castel-Branco was, to some extent, qualified for the post since he had spent time in the silver diggings of Potosí.[62]

Despite the financial difficulties then plaguing the Portuguese treasury, the crown did not stint in its funding of the expedition. The not inconsiderable sum of 1,795,660 reis was laid out to cover the costs of salaries, transportation, and equipment.[63] Additional funding of up to 3.2 million reis was to come from money in Bahia's municipal treasury and taxes that the whaling monopoly paid the local *câmara*.[64]

After arriving in Bahia in late 1673, Castel-Branco readied his expedition and then set out for the backlands of the captaincy. For the next two years, he and his fellows searched in vain for the fabled mines of the Itabainas. Upon receiving word of this fruitless search, the crown ordered Castel-Branco to leave Bahia and proceed to the diggings at Paranaguá. He arrived there in late 1677 and began preparations for an expedition that had a twofold purpose. In addition to seeking out mines rumored to lie in the region of the Rio de la Plata estuary, it was to evaluate the military security of Brazil's southern border. One of Castel-Branco's lieutenants, Jorge Soares de Macedo, was to lead the reconnaissance. This added purpose, as we will see shortly, presaged the establishment of a Portuguese settlement in the poorly defined Luso-Spanish frontier along the Rio de la Plata drainage.

Meanwhile, Castel-Branco continued the search for mineral wealth in Brazil. From 1679 to 1682, the Spanish nobleman sought out deposits of gold and silver reportedly located in the southern region. But little was found, and even the placers of Paranaguá proved disappointing. In part, this may have stemmed from the Paulistas' unwillingness to reveal the true extent of their gold production since doing so would have necessitated full payment of the *quinto*. Whatever the actual scope of the Paulistas' *quinto* evasions, which may well have been substantial, the colonists had become incensed by Castel-Branco's presence. Apparently, the Spaniard's wasteful use of the crown's funds and his haughty bearing provoked the Paulistas. Furthermore, local monies were then being used to finance Castel-Branco's invariably unsuccessful forays into the wilderness. The nobleman was finally shot from ambush by local assassins in August

1682 while he was making yet another attempt to discover the elusive mines of the backlands.[65]

During the nine years the hapless Castel-Branco wandered in search of gold and silver, other lesser expeditions encouraged by the crown also sought out precious metals and gemstones. But here again, the efforts bore little fruit. Castel-Branco's experience in Potosí was probably of scant value in Brazil since the untapped wealth of the interior consisted of alluvial deposits of gold and diamonds, not veins of silver ore that he may have concentrated on finding. After his death, the crown's disappointment was strong, but standing offers of titles of nobility and other forms of reward acted as incentives to Paulista explorers, who ultimately tapped the great treasures of the Brazilian uplands.[66]

Besides this activity around São Paulo, establishment of a settlement on the Rio de la Plata estuary, called Nova Colónia do Sacramento, came as part of the crown's growing recognition of the failure of its effort to find mineral wealth within Brazil. As one opinion voiced in the Overseas Council in 1693 put it, "When hope was lost of finding mines in our Colony, it had seemed advisable to make way through Nova Colónia in order to profit from those of Castile."[67]

Nova Colónia do Sacramento, founded in 1680, not only gave access to Peruvian mines, it enhanced Portugal's claim to an area to which neither the Portuguese nor the Spanish held clear title. Moreover, the Rio de la Plata estuary had long been regarded by the Portuguese as the "natural" geographical limit to southern Brazil. There was considerable concern in Lisbon that the Spanish, through expansion of Jesuit missionary activity in the region, would soon acquire a stronger hold on the southern frontier. As early as 1672, the duke of Cadaval urged establishment of a settlement, noting that the time was ripe to exploit the economic and political weakness of Spain.[68] Even if the influx of silver expected from illicit trade in slaves and European goods with Buenos Aires and Spanish settlements upriver did not prove substantial, considerable income might be had by gaining access to the hundreds of thousands of wild cattle then roaming the plains of Uruguay and eastern Argentina. Acquisition of plentiful and inexpensive hides thus offered an added inducement to Portuguese expansion.[69]

The fledgling settlement at Colónia did not fare well, however. Only eight months after Jorge Soares de Macedo occupied the site in January 1680, the governor of Buenos Aires captured the contingent of settlers and destroyed the structures they had built. News of the governor's action provoked a sharp response in Lisbon, and the Portuguese began mobilizing for war with Spain. During the ensuing year, Spain and Portugal engaged in protracted negotiations over the latter's right to settle in the region. To an extent, as the Portuguese Council of State ruefully observed, the issue was thrashed out between the cartographers of the two countries, who produced historical and geographical testimony supporting the claims of each side.[70] Resolution of the issue, however, stemmed largely from Spanish weakness in the face of Portuguese saber rattling and pressure from other European governments, especially England and the papacy, which wanted to prevent war between the two Iberian powers, a conflict that would largely redound to the benefit of Louis XIV. In 1681, Spain and Portugal reached an agreement by which the settlement of Nova Colónia would be reestablished and the governor of Buenos Aires censured for his "excessive" reaction to the founding of the settlement. Portugal had achieved an impressive diplomatic victory at the expense of an impotent Spain.[71]

Financial returns coming from Colónia, which would again be briefly lost to Spain in 1705 during the War of the Spanish Succession, mounted during the final decades of the seventeenth century. As expected, considerable sums of Peruvian silver found their way to the rebuilt settlement and thence into circulation in Brazil and Portugal. The agricultural productivity of the rich Uruguayan soil soon was exploited as vegetable gardens, vineyards, and wheat fields were planted by the settlers. Salted meat (*tasajo*) was produced and exported to Brazil, becoming a staple in the diet of black slaves. Hides, however, became the principal product of the settlement and an increasingly important source of revenue for the Portuguese treasury. In 1694, it was claimed that cattle were so plentiful that their great numbers could never be extinguished and, given enough horses and carts, 20,000 to 25,000 hides could be brought to the coastal outpost and shipped each year. As it was, over 6,000 hides were shipped to Rio de Janeiro in that year, with 2,600 cruzados paid in duties.[72] Although syphoning off silver from the Spanish empire was probably the principal impetus for the founding of Colónia do Sacramento, cattle products proved to be the most important reward of the venture. There can be little doubt that the financial return on the settlement made the Colónia venture well worth while for the government of D. Pedro II.

Development of agriculture in the fertile soil of the Platine estuary had an exotic counterpart far to the north. In the captaincies of Maranhão and Pará, which had been administered independently of Bahia as the Estado do Maranhão since 1621, the Portuguese endeavored to cultivate plants brought from the Far East. Before 1640, the crown had generally sought to prohibit cultivation of Eastern plants in Brazil so as to preserve the integrity of its spice monopolies. After the Restoration, however, the government revoked some of the bans on the cultivation of oriental plants in Brazil. In 1642, for example, the Overseas Council allowed Brazilian colonists to plant ginger and indigo plants.[73] With this and other measures, the government of D. João IV was clearly shifting Portugal's attention from the Eastern colonies to those of the Atlantic.

The subsequent loss of important Eastern holdings such as Ceylon and the Moluccas lent special urgency to such endeavors, for Dutch interlopers then held control of commodities once virtually monopolized by the Portuguese. In their proposals for revitalizing the Luso-Atlantic economy, both António Vieira and Duarte Ribeiro de Macedo had urged introduction of plants from India and elsewhere into Brazil. Even before the latter mercantilist writer published his views on the subject, the Overseas Council had, in 1671, advised D. Pedro of the advantages of encouraging the cultivation of ginger. Like sugar, it had been introduced into Brazil during the sixteenth century and had soon spread rapidly.[74] A few months after receiving the council's advice, the prince regent renewed the 1642 concession for the product, reducing the export duties paid on Brazilian ginger by one-half for a period of five years.[75]

During the ensuing years, the crown encouraged the cultivation of other spices in the Amazon region. In 1677, Prince Regent Pedro wrote to the viceroy of India requesting that he send seeds and cuttings of certain valuable spice plants to Brazil, especially pepper, cinnamon, clove, and nutmeg.[76] The following year, the request was renewed, the prince regent directing that the project be undertaken with the greatest care and secrecy possible so as to assure the safe transit of seeds and cuttings and to prevent foreign competitors from discovering what was afoot.[77] Little came of this effort, however, since the viceroy, D. Pedro de Almeida, served such a short term (1677–1678).[78]

Nevertheless, the crown's interest in transplanting spices continued. In 1682, eight Indians believed expert in the cultivation of pepper and cinnamon were sent to Brazil to teach the specialized techniques needed for their successful cultivation. Seven years later, two more experts were dispatched from India to instruct colonials in the growing and harvesting of these two spices.[79]

This program met with disappointment, however. The quality of the spices produced in Brazil was generally inferior to that of those grown in the Far East. Furthermore, the Indian experts were apparently not as adept at spice cultivation as first believed. In fact, the work of the two individuals dispatched in 1689 was so disappointing that they were sent back to their homeland by way of Lisbon in 1693. The successful transfer of cultivation techniques remained a basic problem in the transplantation program, but further efforts were made. In 1707, for example, Father João da Assunção, a Franciscan priest reputedly expert in the growing of cinnamon, was sent from India to Bahia. But Assunção's cultivation attempts also met with failure when insect pests, particularly ants, attacked his plantings.[80] Ecological incompatibility may also have frustrated the efforts of Assunção's Indian predecessors, whose expertise was perhaps extensive when confined to their homeland but of little use in the new growing environment encountered in Brazil.

As Father Assunção's presence suggests, the crown's program for establishing production of Eastern spices in Brazil was tied to the ecclesiastical establishment in the colonies. Father António Vieira and his Jesuit brethren had experimented actively with plants from Europe, Asia, and the Americas at their college (*colégio*) in Bahia.[81] Numerous spices were cultivated there in the order's botanical garden, the Quinta do Tanque, whence seeds and cuttings were sent to other Jesuit *colégios* throughout Brazil.[82] It was at the Quinta do Tanque that the two experts dispatched by the viceroy of India in 1689 began their course of instruction. About one year before the Indian experts arrived, the Jesuits sent cinnamon from their Bahian station for

RECESSION AND RECOVERY IN THE COLONIES   229

planting at their *colégio* in Maranhão. Also in 1688, additional cuttings of cinnamon were forwarded from the Far East for use in the Jesuits' ongoing horticultural experiments. In the course of their work with cinnamon, the Jesuits produced enough of the spice to export small quantities to Lisbon.[83]

Despite the close alliance of crown and clergy in promoting transplantation, colonial resistance to cultivation of exotic crops and labor shortages frustrated the attempt to develop spice production in northeast Brazil. Even if the problems of transferring Eastern expertise and of dealing with agricultural pests had been overcome, establishment of oriental spices still would have required the cooperation of Brazilian growers, who were generally reluctant to abandon proven crops from which a steady income was obtained. For example, the governor-general of Brazil reported in 1693 that local growers were only interested in planting sugar, tobacco, and manioc.[84]

Chronic labor shortages also curtailed expansion of Brazilian spice cultivation, especially in the Estado do Maranhão. In fact, the whole region, like that surrounding Colónia do Sacramento, was underpopulated and in need of settlers whose presence would reinforce Portuguese authority in the Amazon basin.[85] Recognizing this problem, the crown had, in the years 1675 through 1677, promoted emigration from the Azores to Pará. During those years, two contingents totaling 457 people (about a hundred families) made the voyage from the island of Faial to the provincial capital of Belem.[86] Apparently, it was hoped that these emigrants would further development in the region as growers of both local and newly transplanted products. The burden of agricultural work itself, however, was largely borne by local Indians, whose exertions were overseen by European settlers and clerics.

The Jesuits and settlers of the Estado do Maranhão had long struggled with each other for control over the labor power of the forest Indians. The colonists wanted to enslave them for use in agricultural production, while the Jesuits sought to gather them into mission stations (*aldeias*), where the Indians could be proselytized and put to work in more humane fashion. Usually, the crown supported the Jesuits in their efforts to convert the Indians and minimize the excesses of colonial masters.[87]

After the Jesuits were temporarily expelled from the region in

1661, a period followed in which both the forest and mission Indians were shamelessly exploited by the colonists. In 1680, however, a new era was inaugurated as the Jesuits, thanks largely to the efforts of António Vieira and the duke of Cadaval, returned to Maranhão, bringing new powers for the control of Indian labor. The crown granted the order the exclusive right to seek out the forest Indians and convert them to the Christian faith. Instead of being enslaved, the Indians would be distributed from the *aldeias* to work for colonists and then returned to the supervision of their Jesuit tutors. It was hoped that this approach would eliminate earlier abuses while better utilizing Indian labor in tilling the soil and finding forest products ranging from medicines to dyewoods and foodstuffs.[88]

The colonists resisted this system of labor disbursement since it virtually abolished their status as slave masters. Other religious orders, particularly the Franciscans, resented the Jesuit monopoly over Indian labor. Further incitement to the colonists came in 1682 when the crown established a monopolistic company known as the Estanco do Maranhão e Pará. Although one of the purposes of this company was to supplement the labor needs of the settlers by supplying five or six hundred African slaves each year, the monopoly antagonized the colonists with its unreliable service and exorbitant prices charged for all trade goods, over which the company had exclusive control. The colonists finally rebelled in 1684, imprisoning local officials and abolishing the monopoly; though the evidence is incomplete, it appears that Franciscans encouraged the revolt. At any rate, the twenty-seven Jesuits of the Maranhão *colégio* were sent packing, being transported by two ships to Pernambuco. The uprising was soon quelled, but the rebellion spelled the end of the detested monopoly company, which was formally dismantled in 1685.

During the following year, the crown instituted a more acceptable program for the acquisition and distribution of Indian labor. On December 21, 1686, a famous *regimento* was promulgated that gave control of the Indians to both the Franciscans and the Jesuits, who had formally returned to the Estado do Maranhão in 1685. Efforts to meet the labor needs of colonists then hinged on more efficient and extensive use of Indians. This was to be accomplished by more expeditious disbursement of mission Indians and redoubled efforts to attract forest dwellers to the *aldeias*.[89]

RECESSION AND RECOVERY IN THE COLONIES

The success of the program was limited. It has been shown, for example, that "Maranhão e Pará suffered from perennial labor shortages during the first half of the eighteenth century."[90] Insufficient numbers of white settlers and the general poverty of the region precluded the institution of a labor regime based on black slaves. Hence, the establishment of a great spice culture in the Estado do Maranhão such as that envisioned by Duarte Ribeiro de Macedo and others was further undermined by shortages of labor power.

Labor shortage in Portuguese America were hardly restricted to the Amazon basin. Paulista expeditions into the hinterlands of Brazil frequently put the enslaving of Indians over the discovery of any mineral wealth as their primary objective. In those instances when mines were found, Indian labor was often procured to extract the buried wealth. In fact, the crown recommended in 1691 that *aldeias* be established near the mines of Paranaguá and Iguape in southern Brazil so that Indians could be spared the rigors of slavery while still providing the needed labor.[91] The once great sugar economy of Brazil had, of course, stimulated a vast trans-Atlantic traffic in African slaves needed to harvest and process the cane from coastal plantations.

During the first half of the seventeenth century, this traffic supplied the sugar economy with an abundance of labor power. Indeed, the rapid expansion of the Brazilian economy was largely borne on the backs of black slaves. Slaves coming to Brazil from Africa were taken from regions as far removed as Guinea and Mozambique, through most came from Angola during the heyday of the sugar economy. Carrying as many as six hundred slaves each, small vessels morbidly called *tumbeiros* (undertakers) made the voyage from Luanda, the Angolan capital, to Brazil in one to two months time.[92] Hunger, disease, suicide, and harsh treatment thinned the ranks of captives on board those floating morgues. Untold thousands of blacks died without seeing the cane fields in which most of their surviving brethren would lead short, brutalized lives. During the seventeenth century, the number of slaves surviving the voyage to Brazil has been estimated at 560,000.[93]

Black slaves were also transported to Spain's American colonies, where vast numbers of Indians already labored for their Iberian overlords. But, as in Brazil, millions of Indians were lost to disease, overwork, and other causes.[94] The loss of so many Indians, as well as the survivors' presumed unsuitability for certain tasks, necessitated the importation of black slaves, most of whom were transported by the Portuguese.

During the mid-seventeenth century, however, the Portuguese slave trade suffered numerous setbacks. Following the 1640 Restoration, Castile canceled the *asiento*, the lucrative license for delivering slaves to Spanish America long held by Portuguese contractors. The Dutch and other Europeans either captured Portuguese slave entrepôts on the west African coast or established their own. By 1650, only two important slave stations remained in Portuguese hands, Luanda, which had been recaptured from the Dutch in 1648, and the small, unfortified garrison at Cacheu, Portugal's last real foothold in Guinea after the Hollanders took the great fortress at Mina in 1637.[95] The impending decline of the Brazilian sugar economy, which depressed demand (or at least the ability to pay) for black labor, also adversely affected Portugal's trade in slaves. And, of course, the break from Spain in 1640 had entailed loss of the *asiento*.

From about 1642 onward, the Portuguese attempted to reconstitute their disrupted slave trade. After the Dutch capture of Mina in 1637 and the loss of Angola four years later, the crown sanctioned direct trade between Bahia and the Mina coast in 1644.[96] During the last decades of the seventeenth century, this commerce in fact proved quite remunerative for Bahian merchants, who traded tobacco to Dutch and other European intermediaries for black slaves. Beginning in 1649 and largely at the instigation of Salvador de Sá, the intrepid nobleman who retook Luanda from the Dutch, slave ships were sent to Buenos Aires, where their living cargoes were exchanged for desperately needed silver.[97] This commerce between adversaries was possible since the mines of Potosí had great need of black labor. Disruption of slaving in Angola continued, however, for the Portuguese became embroiled in warfare with local tribes, which lasted for the next three decades.[98]

Under D. Pedro II, steps were taken to end the fighting. In 1676, for example, the newly appointed governor of Angola, Aires de Saldanha de Meneses e Sousa, was urged to avoid conflict unless he had just cause, since the local struggles hurt trade and revenue collections.[99] By 1684, the Portuguese had all but overcome their tribal

RECESSION AND RECOVERY IN THE COLONIES 233

opponents, but the expected upswing in the slave trade did not occur. Indeed, the latest governor, Luís Lobo da Silva, reported after his arrival in that year that the colony had fallen into serious economic decline.[100] To make matters worse, an outbreak of smallpox around 1687 caused many vessels trading for slaves to go elsewhere, particularly the Mina coast.[101] Meanwhile, intermittent conflict with (and between) contentious tribes remained a disruptive factor. By 1690, however, Angola had entered an era of relative peace, which endured until the 1730s.[102]

This latest lull in the fighting did not immediately engender expansion of the slave trade. Whereas a century before approximately ten to fifteen thousand slaves were exported annually from Angola, the traffic then fell to a fraction of its former volume. In 1694, it was reported that the annual figure was 4,000.[103] Sixteen years later, only 3,549 slaves were embarked on the grim passage to the American colonies. Within the next sixteen years, however, this number doubled, the total sometimes approaching 8,500 slaves per annum.[104]

Despite Angola's former importance in the slave trade, the crown's major effort to revitalize the traffic came in Guinea. After 1640, the Portuguese tried to exclude Spanish traders from the region, but little came of this. The Portuguese in Guinea depended on the Spanish for capital, while Africans relied on them for trade goods. Not unexpectedly, this led to a flouting of the rules against Spanish traders.[105] Even so, the effect of the Restoration on the slave trade out of Cacheu appears to have been drastic; exports, which had annually run to nearly 3,000 captive *negros* before 1640, dropped to less than 600 around 1641.[106]

This state of affairs, together with the loss of Angola in late 1641, prompted a series of royal efforts to secure what was then its last real foothold in the slave trade. One obvious change came as slave ships from Guinea were sent directly to Brazil instead of stopping in Luanda, which had been usual before its capture. In the succeeding years, Cacheu was elevated to a full-fledged factor, having its own treasury representative (*provedor*), factor, and scribe. In 1646, the crown encouraged the slave station to engage in direct trade with the Spanish Indies, a policy that, as it has already been noted, was also implemented in Angola after Luanda was retaken. Cacheu was eventually fortified as the Portuguese moved to protect their outpost from possible invasion by European rivals. Ships coming from European possessions in the Americas frequented the outpost, often bartering goods and commodities for slaves in direct violation of the crown's orders, which required that only gold and silver be accepted. Despite efforts toward improvement, the slave port was still a marginal operation in 1670, and foreigners continued to trade contraband with the Portuguese garrison, much to the detriment of exports from the mother country.[107]

The need to curtail this illicit commerce, together with the need to finance construction at the outpost, gave impetus to schemes for establishing a monopoly company for the Cacheu trade. Creation of such a company also offered Portugal a chance to regain a share of the slave traffic to the Spanish Indies, now that peace existed between the two Iberian powers. From the early 1650s onward, company schemes had been contemplated, and, in 1664, a firm called the Guinea Coast Company was established for a term of eight years. This venture seems to have had little success, and, in the early 1670s, the Overseas Council began to push vigorously for creation of a company based in Cacheu. The principal opponents of this idea were the inhabitants of the Cape Verde Islands, whose livelihood depended heavily on reselling the slaves acquired from the African mainland. Despite the protestations of the islanders, the first Cacheu Company (Companhia de Cacheu, Rios e Comércio da Guiné) was formally established in May 1676.[108]

Formation of the company probably did have some role in the commercial decline that subsequently beset the Cape Verdes. During the last three decades of the seventeenth century, the number of slaves transshipped in the islands totaled approximately 5,250, about 1,500 less than for the previous thirty years.[109] But it is likely that the company's responsibility for this decline was minor and that the general recession between 1670 and 1690 had more to do with the islands' woes. Moreover, the Cacheu Company, though established for a six-year period, was in business only until 1680, when it failed and was incorporated into the Brazil Company.[110] Discouraging as this failure must have been to the crown, its program for revitalizing the slave trade stayed alive, and ten years later a successor company was formed.

While groundwork for estalishing a monopoly over the Guinea

trade was being laid in Lisbon, a plan for strengthening the royal tobacco monopoly was also being formulated. The crown had let monopoly contracts on the domestic sale of tobacco since the early 1630s. The first royal monopoly (*estanco*), which extended to Portugal and its Atlantic islands but not to Brazil or other colonial possessions, was briefly abolished in 1642 in hopes of generating greater revenues through liberalizing trade in the mother country and islands. But this approach proved financially disappointing, and the *estanco* was reestablished two years later.[111] An early effort to encourage expansion of Brazilian production came in 1647 when D. João IV prohibited the cultivation of tobacco in Portugal.[112] As with other European regimes during this era, monopoly control over tobacco was instituted by the Portuguese government primarily as a means of obtaining a share of the income produced from its sale. Actual distribution of tobacco was handled by private contractors.

With decline of the sugar economy, Brazilian tobacco became increasingly important as a revenue producer. To some extent, expanding consumption of tobacco in Europe cushioned the impact of the post-1670 decline on Portugal. In order to protect this vital source of revenue, the crown redoubled its efforts to secure the monopoly from inroads made by smugglers and ilicit growers of the plant.[113] In 1668, for example, the crown ordered stiff penalties for anyone planting tobacco without the permission of monopoly contractors.[114] Tobacco's importance to the treasury became clearly manifest in 1674 when the Cortes approved a 500,000 cruzado impost on its sale. Two weeks after D. Pedro abruptly dissolved that unruly Cortes, the Junta da Administração do Tabaco was established.

Soon after the junta was created, the government ended the practice of selling monopoly contracts for the whole of Portugal and its Atlantic islands. Instead, the junta, which acted as the bureaucratic overseer of all licit tobacco sales, sold regional contracts to private entrepreneurs.[115] As before, wealthier contractors subleased territories to smaller operators.

A president and three judges (*desembargadores*) headed the new junta, the authority of which reached throughout Portugal and its Atlantic islands. The newly organized monopoly gained an added measure of influence in 1678 when the powerful duke of Cadaval became its president, a post he held for twenty years.[116] In Portugal during that same year, five regional superintendents were empowered to carry out investigations of suspected contrabandists, including members of the privileged estates.[117] This authority sometimes led to the searching of monasteries, convents, and noble households for illegally grown and processed tobacco, including snuff, the return on which was especially remunerative to the crown and the contrabandist alike. Once apprehended, those contrabandists who did not enjoy privileged exemption were tried and sentenced solely by the junta. According to the Rev. John Colbatch, an English observer writing in 1700, "it became almost as great a crime in *Portugal*, for any to make snuff for themselves, as 'tis with us in England to Coin money, the People almost universally take it here."[118]

The treasury's dependence on tobacco revenues increased greatly after 1674 and, as table 3 in chapter VI shows, over 290 million reis were collected in 1681. The salaries of certain inquisitors were even paid out of tobacco revenues.[119] Reliance on tobacco, as it has been previously noted, was so heavy by 1698 that the Cortes approved greatly increased assessments on the product to meet mounting defense costs. This action, according to Colbatch, "was the ready way to destroy that Trade, and consequently the best and clearest part of the revenue."[120]

Although tobacco increasingly took up the financial slack as sugar revenues declined, its producers were also adversely affected by Caribbean competition. Tobacco grown in other areas of the periphery, especially the English colonies in North America, had done much to undercut sale of the Brazilian product on the world economy and prices dropped considerably after 1670. With entry into most large markets of northern Europe substantially blocked by tariffs, Brazilian tobacco was mainly consumed in Portugal, Spain, Italy, France, India, and Brazil itself and by blacks in west Africa. Brazilian planters, however, failed to recognize fully the realities of core-state competitiveness (or the post-1670 downturn) and instead blamed the junta for their problems.[121] Even so, the Brazilian tobacco industry expanded greatly during the last third of the seventeenth century, and by 1716 tobacco revenues had risen to 560 million reis.[122]

Establishment of the Junta do Tabaco, together with the other four programs (that is, mineral exploration, trade with Potosí, spice cultivation, and slaving) for rendering the Atlantic colonies more productive of revenues, were by no means the only aspects of the wide-ranging and even unorthodox mercantilism practiced during the reign of D. Pedro II. In 1672, for example, the crown issued legislation encouraging Brazilian commerce with Mozambique.[123] Though this attempt to foster intraempire trade, like that tried between India and southeast Africa, did not develop as hoped, it is clear that the government entertained a variety of measures for restoring colonial prosperity. In another instance, this time in 1673, the island of São Tome was granted the right to trade freely with Portugal's European allies for a period of five years.[124] The success of these and other efforts, however, ultimately hinged on an upswing in the world economy. Despite a wide range of mercantilist programs, the Portuguese Atlantic languished in the economic doldrums until about 1695. But, when recovery came, the energy and capital invested in some of these programs brought ample returns.

CHAPTER X

RECESSION AND RECOVERY IN THE COLONIES
(PART 2)

> ... não haverá quem possa duvidar de ser hoje o Brasil a melhor & mais util Conquista, assim para a fazenda real como para o bem publico, de quantas outras conta o Reyno de Portugal, attendendo ao muito que cada anno sae destes portos, que são minas certas e abundantamente rendosas.
>
> Antonil (Giovanni Antonio Andreoni, S.J.) (1711)

The post-1690 revival of the world economy owed some of its impetus to an influx of gold and other commodities from the Portuguese Atlantic. By the same token, growing demand (and so climbing price levels) in Europe contributed to a resurgence of prosperity in Portugal's colonies. This prosperity, however, was not distributed evenly throughout the Atlantic possessions. Rio de Janeiro, the hub of the expanding mining economy, was on its way to supplanting Bahia as the economic (and later administrative) center of Brazil. The locus of Luso-Atlantic slaving activities moved from Angola to the Mina and Guinea coasts. While the Atlantic islands, particularly Cape Verde, shared only marginally in the new prosperity, the economic weight once concentrated in the mother country was gradually shifting toward Brazil. Of those sectors of the colonial economy receiving special attention from the crown during the last decades of the seventeenth century, the tobacco industry, the slave trade, the production of hides, and the extraction of gold were in the forefront of commercial expansion.

The Resurgence of Colonial Prosperity

The growth of the tobacco trade played a crucial role in the recovery of the Luso-Atlantic economy, and thus in revitalizing an anemic treasury. This is borne out by a *consulta* of early 1684 in which the Junta do Tabaco reported with satisfaction that revenues collected on tobacco sales annually exceeded a million cruzados. Six months later, the junta noted that tobacco had become the chief source of royal revenue.[1] During the years between 1687 and 1695, returns from the tobacco monopoly rose considerably.[2]

The financial and bureaucratic influence of the junta grew in concert with the revenues it produced. In addition to tobacco, the junta also exerted control over much of Portugal's trade with India. The tobacco monopoly (*estanco*) in Goa exchanged snuff and smoking tobacco shipped from Lisbon by the junta for diamonds, saltpeter, and other items. In 1680 and 1681, ships of the *carreira da Índia* brought ten small sacks (*bizalhos*) of diamonds worth 135,352 cruzados as well as pepper valued at 11,509.5 cruzados.[3] After 1680, the junta rivaled the India House (Casa da India), the once great intermediary for the spice trade, as the financial and bureaucratic locus of commerce with Portugal's Eastern possessions.[4]

The growing importance of the junta stimulated rivalries with other bureaucratic entities. In 1687, for example, the Treasury Council unsuccessfully attempted to gain control of certain revenue collections under the junta's jurisdiction. Seven years later, the Évora Inquisition was rebuffed in an attempt to gain jurisdiction over tobacco-related crimes.[5] Evidently, D. Pedro II, not to mention the junta's president, the duke of Cadaval, saw little reason to tamper with the workings of such a valuable monopoly.

Expansion of the junta's influence was rooted in the plantations of Brazil, which began to remit vast quantitites of tobacco to Portugal during the late seventeenth century. In 1666, approximately 1,100 rolls of Brazilian tobacco reached Lisbon.[6] Two years later, eleven vessels coming from Bahia delivered 11,033 rolls to the capital (see appendix 5).[7] By the 1680s, annual shipments had grown even larger (see table 8). Neither Lisbon nor Oporto had adequate warehousing for the expanding tobacco production of Bahia, the chief producer, and other Brazilian captaincies. Even with construction of additional warehouses, tobacco stocks piled up, causing the junta's officials to worry about what to do with the rolls coming in the 1685 Pernambuco fleet.[8]

The diminishing (or at least stabilizing) demand among foreign and domestic consumers during the stagnant 1680s probably had a hand in creating the overstocked inventories. In Lisbon, the crown had to offer a reduction in price in order to induce buyers to purchase the excess quantities of the perishable product. In Oporto,

TABLE 8
Rolls of Brazilian Tobacco Shipped to Portugal,
1680–1704*

Year	Vessels	Rolls	Weight (in arrobas)
1680		9,191	
1681		18,134	
1682		22,872	
1683		18,713	
1684		21,922	
1685		22,016	
1686		30,413	
1689		22,000	
1699	23	28,258	206,774.16
1700	20	20,848	161,547.00
1701	21	30,920	238,768.18
1702	28	25,762	215,155.06
1703	19	27,909	203,978.80
1704	28	18,965	141,090.10

SOURCES: ANTT, Junta do Tobaco, Consultas, *maço* 3, May 2, 1687; numerous documents in Cartas do Brasil e India, *maços* 96 and 96A; Price, *France and the Chesapeake*, 1:182.

*Unfortunately, no data were found for the years 1687–1688 and 1690–1698. The figures for 1699–1704 are for Bahia and do not represent total shipments from Brazil during those years. Nevertheless, the Bahian data represent approximately ninety percent of Brazilian tobacco exports. When, for example, Bahia sent 27,909 rolls in 1703, it was reported that the fleet brought a total of 30,000 that year. da Silva, *Gazeta em Forma de Carta*, p. 11. Also see Price, *France and the Chesapeake*, 1:182.

3,066 rolls brought by the 1684 *frota* still remained to be disposed of in 1686.[9] A few years later, however, the inventory picture changed completely. The Portuguese devaluation of 1688, together with accelerating commercial recovery throughout Europe, led to an outburst of commodity buying. By August 1689, hardly "a single twist of tobacco remained in Lisbon and the price rose by more than thirty percent: an association of New Christians and rich merchants was soon formed which bought it up, good and bad, and controlled the entire market."[10]

The upswing in tobacco sales helped strengthen the economy of northeastern Brazil and thereby did much to fill the breach left by declining sugar sales. But the discovery of great deposits of alluvial gold in southern Brazil, to which we will turn in a moment, seems to have been a mixed blessing for the agricultural regions of the northeast. Fortune seekers from Bahia and Pernambuco flocked to the gold diggings, depleting the white population of those captaincies. Meanwhile, the northeast's labor pool probably contracted as the mining camps outbid plantations for black slaves. Yet, as recent studies have shown, the northeast did not, as had been generally assumed, fall into decline when both population and economic power moved south.[11] Since the burgeoning southern market was then consuming great quantities of tobacco, sale of the product there may have played a role in supporting continued, if diminished, economic activity in the northeast. Furthermore, the snuff trade to India was expanding. Rising prices in Portugal also fostered greater annual exports to the mother country; and, despite tariff walls, European demand for Brazilian tobacco climbed steadily.[12]

The French tobacco monopoly, which was established a few months after the Junta do Tabaco, was among the most important purchasers of Brazilian tobacco. By 1690, French consumption of tobacco from Brazil and the Estado de Maranhão may have exceeded 300,000 pounds annually. Ten years later, French purchases in Lisbon reportedly were in excess of five times that amount. Although Brazilian tobaccos were used primarily as chewing tobacco by the French, and thus were only marginally involved in the increasingly fashionable consumption of snuff, demand for the Brazilian product was such that supplies were limited when compared with those available from Dutch and English sources. Indeed, the quantity of Brazilian tobacco reaching Lisbon after 1700, as much as 7 million pounds, or 240,000 arrobas (table 8), was only about one-fourth of that imported by the English from their Chesapeake plantations.[13]

The expanding demand for slave labor in the mining camps led to greater exportation of tobacco to west Africa, where it was exchanged for black captives. The growing tobacco trade between Bahia and Africa's Mina coast was especially illustrative of this expansion. As table 9 shows, the number of vessels voyaging from the Brazilian capital to the Mina coast increased tenfold between 1681 and 1710. The Mina coast had in fact become the prime source of slaves shipped to Brazil. Loss of the great fortress of Sõ Jorge da Mina to the Dutch in 1637, together with the Hollanders' capture of Luanda in 1641, induced the Portuguese crown to sanction direct trade between Bahia and the Mina coast in 1644. Thereafter, growing Bahian commerce with Dutch intermediaries played a crucial role in ending the so-called Angola cycle of the Luso-Atlantic slave trade and launching the so-called Mina cycle.[14]

Despite the dissolution of the first Cacheu Company in 1680, the Portuguese had moved steadily to enlarge their share of the slave trade out of Guinea. Fortification of the trading station at Bissau was begun in 1687, and the crown's efforts to protect the tiny outpost at Cacheu continued. In 1686, D. Pedro II had expressed great concern about the status of Cacheu, noting that English and French slavers held an intolerably large share of the local slave trade.[15]

TABLE 9
Bahian Vessels Carrying Tobacco to Angola
and the Mina Coast, 1681–1710

Years	To Angola	To the Mina Coast
1681–1685	5	11
1686–1690	3	32
1691–1696	6	49
1697–1700	2	60
1701–1705	1	102
1706–1710	0	114
TOTALS	17	368

SOURCE: Verger, *Flux et Reflux*, p. 11.

An important step toward resolving this problem was taken when the Cacheu Company was reconstituted in 1690. One-third of the needed financing was put up by the crown. Working primarily out of the island of Principe, the newly revived company soon extended its activities to most of Portuguese west Africa and even to Angola, which its monopoly did not legally include. By 1692, the company obtained a contract to supply slaves to Maranhão. Meanwhile, the company moved to regain the famed *asiento* for carrying slaves to Spanish America. In February 1693, the firm made arrangements with the current holder of the *asiento*, the Spaniard Marín de Guzmán, to deliver annually 4,000 slaves to Cartagena de Indias. After a hiatus of more than fifty years, Portugal had again secured a share of the coveted *asiento*, which had been a virtual monopoly of Portuguese contractors until its revocation following the 1640 Restoration. Finally, in 1696, the Cacheu Company formally regained the *asiento* for Portugal, replacing the Guzmán operation and launching a brief but apparently profitable trade with the Spanish Indies.[16]

Two years later, the first shipments of company-transported slaves were unloaded in Cartagena (table 10). The profitability of this trade is suggested by the fact that one company ship, returning from Cartagena to Lisbon by way of Havana in 1698, carried 400,000 livres of silver.[17] (The livre, which was replaced by the franc when France adopted the metric system, was roughly equivalent to 0.075 pounds sterling at that time.) But the Cacheu Company's early success merely increased foreign jealously of the Portuguese contract. After the Bourbon dynasty was established in Spain in 1700, Louis XIV ex-

TABLE 10
Slaves Delivered to Cartagena de Indias
by the Cacheu Company, 1698–1701

Year	Shipments	Slaves
1698	19	2,886
1699	20	2,699
1700	12	2,600
1701	6	1,668
TOTALS	57	9,853

SOURCE: Palacios Preciado, *La Trata de Negros por Cartagena de Indias*, p. 99.

erted influence on his relative Philip V to turn the *asiento* over to France, which the new monarch did in 1701. Nevertheless, the Spanish agreed to pay the Cacheu Company an indemnity of 300,000 cruzados.[18] And, perhaps more important, the Portuguese were then "free to concentrate their trading efforts on Brazil alone."[19] Indeed, slaves were in great demand in Brazil at that time, especially in the mining economy of the south.

During the early 1690s, the modest Paulista diggings at Paranaguá and other sites in southern Brazil were all but forgotten after the discovery of extremely rich deposits of alluvial gold in the rivers of an upland region that soon became known as Minas Gerais (General Mines). Discovery of this unprecedented wealth had come at a singularly propitious time for both Portugal and the world economy. In Portugal, the influx of gold did much to alleviate the chronic problem of bullion shortages and underwrote a variety of expensive building programs, including construction of the great baroque monastery at Mafra.[20] And, with the post-1690 revival of Europe underway, the outpouring of Brazilian gold endowed the world economy, especially the core states and certain fortunate individuals, with great quantities of surplus wealth, thereby accelerating economic growth and the amassing of personal fortunes. Ultimately, the gold of Minas Gerais was to have a hand in underwriting the industrial revolution.

It may never be known who made the initial discovery of gold in Minas Gerais, but it is likely that a number of important strikes were made by Paulistas during the years 1693, 1694, and 1695. Ironically, a Paulista named Manuel de Borba Gato, who had been implicated in the 1682 ambush of D. Manuel Castel-Branco, probably made one of the initial strikes after escaping to the upland fastnesses of Minas Gerais.[21]

Word of the discoveries of Borba Gato and others soon leaked out and the great gold rush was on. It was not long before a motley assortment of fortune seekers crowded the few tracks into the wilderness. *Frotas* coming from the mother country annually brought great numbers of Portuguese (as well as foreigners who managed to secure passage) eager to share in the Brazilian bonanza. From all over Brazil, a wave of people left sugar and tobacco plantations, cattle ranches, and coastal settlements to converge on the diggings of Minas Gerais, over which neither the crown nor the Church as yet had much con-

RECESSION AND RECOVERY IN THE COLONIES 245

trol. Theft and murder abounded in the raw mining camps, while Church officials squabbled over which of their number had authority in the vaguely demarcated region. A fluid population of gold-hungry vagabonds and itinerants roamed the backlands. According to the classic contemporary account of the gold rush, written under the pseudonymn Antonil by a Tuscan Jesuit named Giovanni Antonio Andreoni, these restless adventurers moved "from one place to another like the children of Israel in the wilderness."[22]

The quantities of gold extracted from the sands of rivers and streams and, in a few instances, from subterranean mines were indeed spectacular. Tons of the yellow metal were soon accumulated and transported out of the backlands. Although many prospectors undoubtedly evaded payment of the royal fifth, a problem to which the crown soon addressed itself, great shipments of gold were dispatched for Lisbon (table 11).

The outpouring of precious metals from the placers of Minas Gerais gave rise to unprecedented prosperity in southern Brazil. Merchants and noblemen in Rio de Janeiro and Ouro Preto, the first capital of Minas Gerais, became intermediaries for markets hungry for European goods. Much of the gold mined in Brazil eventually found its way to England, Holland, and France, either legally or as contra-

TABLE 11
Shipments of Brazilian Gold to Lisbon, 1699–1705
(in kilograms)

Year	Quantity
1699	725
1700	1,475*
1701	1,785
1702	—
1703	4,350
1704	—
1705	7,258

SOURCES: Godinho, "Portugal, as Frotas," p. 83; Antonil, *Cultura e Opulencia*, p. 488; Cardozo, "The Collection of the Fifth," p. 372. For data that suggest that gold production during these early years was considerably less, see Mauro, *Le Bresil du XVe à la Fin du XVIIIe Siècle* pp. 146, 148–49.
*This figure, though a contemporary estimate for an unspecified year, has been assigned to 1700 since it seems an appropriate number for that year, given the quantities of gold reportedly shipped to Lisbon between 1699 and 1705.

band. Portugal also exchanged much of the gold debarked in Lisbon for European products, no doubt to the chagrin of those who followed Duarte Ribeiro de Macedo's mercantilist ideas.

Even as a socioeconomic regime based on gold was being born in Rio de Janeiro and Minas Gerais, which became a separate captaincy in 1720, other sectors of the Brazilian economy were also experiencing remarkable growth during the early decades of the eighteenth century. Cattle products, especially hides, became a major Brazilian export. Dried beef rapidly became a staple in the diet of both mining and agricultural regions. Great herds of cattle were driven from ranches in Bahia and other captaincies to the mining regions. And, as it has been previously noted, hides collected by the inhabitants of Cólonia do Sacramento and other southern outposts were shipped to Rio de Janeiro in great quantities. From there they were sent elsewhere in Brazil or embarked for Portugal. In 1699, 2,000 hides reached Lisbon from Cólonia by way of Rio de Janeiro. Four years later, at least 4,953 hides from Cólonia were shipped to the Portuguese capital.[23]

Great numbers of hides from Bahia also entered Lisbon, many of them as the wrappings of tobacco rolls. According to Antonil, 25,000 hides were sent annually from Bahia to Lisbon in this fashion. The Jesuit chronicler added that 2,500 hides encased tobacco rolls coming from Alagoas and Pernambuco. Growth in the traffic of leather products could also be seen in the expanding exports of tanned hides, which were in great demand in Portugal for shoe and boot manufacture as well as for fabrication of other items. Antonil related that after 1705 annual shipments of tanned hides from Brazil rose to 110,000 units.[24]

Another sector of the Luso-Atlantic economy that experienced accelerating growth in the post-1690 era was the whaling industry. Whaling, like most other economic activity in the world economy, had declined (or stagnated) during the latter half of the seventeenth century. In Brazil, however, an important cause for decline lay in the fact that cetaceans were becoming increasingly scarce in the Bay of All Saints, then the center of whaling in the colony. A diminishing number of whales and the smaller size of individual kills forced the crown to lower the price of whaling contracts, given the shrinking supply of the most lucrative and principal product of the industry, whale oil.

After 1700, however, the number of whaling stations along the Brazilian coast multiplied, and the Bahian center began a period of expansion that was to go on for the next fifty years.[25]

Data on the status of the production of brazilwood during this era are quite sparse, but, given the ever-diminishing quantity of trees remaining, it is likely that the growth of this sector of the Luso-Atlantic economy was hampered by increasing costs and shrinking supplies.[26] Nonetheless, exploitation of dyewood through the selling of monopoly contracts provided the crown with significant revenues during the whole of the colonial era. In 1602, for example, it is known that the brazilwood contract was sold to a private contractor for 21 million reis.[27] By 1627, the price had risen to 24 million reis.[28] In 1679, however, sale of the monopoly returned only 12 million reis to the treasury.[29] During most of the seventeenth century, the amount of brazilwood exported to Portugal appears to have averaged about 10,000 quintais (approximately 560 tons) per annum.[30] In order to tighten its hold on the dyewood traffic, the crown placed the monopoly under the control of the Junta do Comércio in 1697.[31] According to Antonil, the value of the brazilwood contract had reached 48 million reis by the early eighteenth century.[32] Revenues accruing to the Junta do Comércio from dyewood declined in 1719, however, falling to less than 30 million reis.[33] Yet by 1803, the crown's revenues from brazilwood stood at 120 million reis.[34]

Despite the various setbacks endured after 1650, the sugar industry, like other important sectors of the Luso-Atlantic economy, rebounded during the last years of the seventeenth century (see appendix 6). Recent research has shown that the negative impact of the gold discoveries on sugar production was not as great as it had been previously believed. The number of *caixas* of sugar exported from Bahia rose from around 11,000 in 1700 to approximately 16,000 in 1704. Indeed, "the first years of the eighteenth century were a time of prosperity for the sugar industry."[35] The flight of population from the northeast to the mining camps of Minas Gerais, though doubtless serious, has been overstated. When depression finally came in the 1730s, its principal cause was declining prices on the world market, not labor shortages.[36]

According to figures supplied by Antonil (table 12), the preeminent position of sugar in the Brazilian economy had not changed.

Nevertheless, its share of colonial production had been substantially reduced by rising tobacco, gold, and hide output. Though Antonil's figures must be regarded with caution since they apparently do not take into account gold and tobacco smuggling, they are clear evidence of the colonial contribution to economic revival in Portugal. After earlier programs to foster greater financial returns from the colonies had been so amply rewarded, especially those concerned with mineral wealth and tobacco production, the monarchy concentrated on protecting its growing revenues from inroads made by illegal commerce. In the process, the crown further consolidated its hold on colonial Brazil.

Controlling the Periphery

During the 1690s and early 1700s, the crown issued a plethora of legislation aimed at securing, to the maximum extent possible, revenues owed it from expanding commodity production in the colonies. Mechanisms necessary for this purpose were rapidly instituted or reinforced so as to reduce the alarming extension of illicit commerce

TABLE 12
Brazilian Commodity Exports to Portugal and
Their Estimated Value, circa 1700
(in reis)

Commodity	Estimated Value
Sugar	2,535,142.800
Tobacco	344,650.000
Gold	614,400.000
Tanned hides	201,800.000
Brazilwood (from Pernambuco)	48,000.000
TOTAL	3,743,992.800*

SOURCE: Antonil, *Cultura e Opulencia*, p. 488.
*This figure is equivalent to 9,359,982 cruzados. By way of comparison, it can be noted that in 1703 a *frota* of eighty-six ships reached Lisbon with a cargo valued at 14 million cruzados, including 40,000 caixas of sugar, 30,000 rolls of tobacco (27,909 from Bahia), and 17 arrobas (250.7 kilograms) of gold. This last figure, when compared with table 12, is much too low and probably represented the royal fifth. See da Silva, *Gazeta em Forma de Carta*, p. 11.

that accompanied the rising wave of prosperity then flowing out of Brazil. Although promulgation of laws had but limited impact against smuggling, tax evasion, fraud, et cetera, it did have the effect of reinforcing the crown's control over a colony whose path was gradually diverging from that of the mother country.[37]

Reducing the loss of revenues caused by smugglers, contrabandists, and even corsairs was a constant preoccupation of D. Pedro II's government. This concern appears to have passed through two phases. First, the crown attempted on a broad scale to curtail a welter of illegal activities that syphoned income away from the financially pressed treasury. Later, after the Luso-Atlantic economy had begun to regain its former prosperity, the government's focus narrowed somewhat as it concentrated on insulating exceptionally remunerative sectors, particularly gold and tobacco production, from the contraband trade.

Legislative proscriptions issued during the first two decades of D. Pedro II's reign addressed a broad spectrum of illicit commercial activities. One of the government's first acts was an edict promulgated in 1668 that sought to eliminate the black market in tobacco.[38] In an attempt to obtain scarce bullion during the depressed 1670s and 1680s, the crown had tried to stop the illicit exchange of European goods for slaves in its west African holdings while attracting sorely needed gold and silver. In 1676, for example, the prince regent ordered the newly appointed governor of Angola to refuse entry to slavers coming from Spain; but "as to those vessels coming from the Spanish Indies, the River Plate and Buenos Aires with silver, gold and other wealth, except goods from Europe or the Far East, I order you to give them entry and allow them to trade for slaves."[39] Other measures ranged from the already-noted prohibition on the exportation of Portuguese orange trees to an order of 1673 that forbade Brazilian governors from engaging in commerce on their own behalf. The business activities of these officials, which included the opening of unauthorized shops in their residences, infringed on the rights of royal contractors and thus reduced revenue collections.[40]

Given the pervasiveness of illegal commercial activities in the Luso-Atlantic economy, neither D. Pedro II nor his ministers harbored great hopes of eliminating them. Thirty years after issuance of the 1668 law against contraband tobacco, the Junta do Tabaco, responding to a royal request for more and tougher penalties against contrabandists, resignedly replied that "past experience has shown that the desire for profit is stronger than fear of the Law."[41]

In the case of Muslim pirates coming from north Africa, the crown encountered not only the profit motive at work but religious antipathy as well. Muslim depredations against Iberian shipping had gone on for centuries, but matters worsened considerably for the Portuguese in the decades after Spain expelled its Morisco population in 1609. Many of the exiles immigrated to Morocco, where they added their numbers to attacks on Atlantic shipping. All manner of shipping fell prey to these attackers, who not only took whatever booty they could find aboard ship but held Christian captives for ransom as well. In 1673, for example, a ship of the Rio de Janeiro *frota* was captured by Moors and the 140 people aboard were taken prisoner.[42] Many such captives were taken to Algiers, where they remained imprisoned until sufficient money was raised to buy their freedom.[43]

Pirates were in fact to be found lurking throughout the Portuguese Atlantic, off the Portuguese coast, near the Atlantic islands, up and down the African coast, among the islands at the mouth of the Amazon, and in the Rio de la Plata estuary. Many of these seaborne predators were not, of course, Muslims, but renegade Europeans, including Portuguese. Although the economic upswing that began after 1690 undoubtedly put more shipping within reach of pirates, efforts to curb their predations in Portugal's coastal waters may have become somewhat more effective. An important step was taken in 1675 when the prince regent ordered nine vessels to be outfitted to guard coastal shipping. This action may have been prompted by events of the previous year, when Muslim attackers captured a ship coming from Brazil, another from Angola, and numerous fishing boats.[44] The chartering of well-armed foreign ships and protection afforded by English escorts for the Brazilian *frotas* also discouraged pirates. Even so, they remained a constant threat to commerce. In 1698, for example, a slave ship of the Cacheu Company returning from Spanish America unloaded a cargo of money and Mexican dyewood in the Azores to prevent its capture by Algerian corsairs.[45] Although this particular cargo apparently eluded the Muslim pirates, their depredations accounted for a constant loss of shipments that otherwise would have paid duties. Moreover, seizure of Christian passengers and crews necessitated periodic outlays to secure their release.[46]

Unsettling as losses of shipping to pirates may have been, the crown was probably more concerned about revenues that went uncollected thanks to the illegal dealings of Portuguese subjects. The rampant smuggling of dyewood to European ports by such subjects was the main reason for placing the brazilwood monopoly under direct control of the Junta do Comércio in 1697. Before this change was made, dyewood could be carried in any of the ships sailing in Brazilian *frotas*. By one means or another, merchants, captains, crews, and probably *alfândega* officials colluded to avoid duties on brazilwood and then transfer it to foreign accomplices. After 1697, however, all dyewood was to be shipped in vessels of the Junta do Comércio, except when that body granted special exemptions to private carriers.[47]

Revenues from dyewood were soon surpassed by those being collected as the royal fifth on the recently discovered gold of Minas Gerais. But, like brazilwood, much gold escaped taxation, a loss that the crown sought to redress. Following word of the discoveries in Minas Gerais, a smelter was established at Taubaté in 1695, joining three already in operation in the captaincy of São Paulo. In 1694, a mint was opened in Bahia; it was transferred to Rio de Janeiro five years later. Though this mint was moved to Recife in 1700, another was in operation in Rio by 1702. The rationale for moving the first mint to Recife is not altogether clear, but it is likely that a significant decline in the *quinto* collected at the northeastern city prompted reestablishment of operations in Rio de Janeiro. Meanwhile, a smelting house was also opened in Rio to produce gold bars for those who preferred receipt of their metallic wealth in that form instead of coin.[48]

By law, miners and others in possession of unassessed gold were required to bring it to one of these smelters or mints, where the royal fifth was deducted and the metal was made into bars or coins. Once it was returned to its owners, they could use the gold as they wished, so long as they did not export it to foreign countries. Despite the crown's addition of mints and smelters for collection of the *quinto*, receipts were, and continued to be, disappointing. In part, this stemmed from the government's initial failure to recognize the true magnitude of the discoveries in Minas Gerais. Vast quantities of gold escaped taxation before the crown realized the extent of the bonanza it had hoped for so long to find. Furthermore, a series of inadequate policies, including failure to thoroughly search ships reaching Portugal from Brazil, made evasion of payment much easier. As it was shown in table 10, the amount of gold entering Lisbon during the early eighteenth century was enormous; but, of the approximately 16,000 pounds (7,258 kilograms) borne to the capital in 1705, only 740 belonged to the crown.[49] Moreover, it was estimated that less than one-third of the gold taken from Brazilian mines and placers was actually declared. Great quantities of gold, whether taxed or untaxed, found their way into circulation on both sides of the Atlantic.[50]

In addition to *quinto* losses caused by its own mistakes, the government also encountered financial difficulties while attempting to gain control of the gold traffic. Even as gold flowed into Portugal, the crown could not afford to establish sorely needed civil and military jurisdictions in Minas Gerais. In 1709, it was estimated that the cost of creating the administrative machinery necessary to bring the raw mining camps and boom towns of Minas Gerais under control would run to more than 1 million cruzados. Yet, *quinto* collections during the preceding years had never exceeded 200,000 cruzados.[51] And much of the *quinto* that was collected had been used to pay for Portugal's involvement in the as yet unresolved War of the Spanish Succession (1702–1714). Ironically, the crown lacked the funds needed to render unto itself its lawful share of the golden tide.

Nonetheless, the crown did take a number of steps aimed at strengthening its hold over the mining regions. In 1702, for example, a *regimento* for mining in Minas Gerais was promulgated. This code, which was based largely on one issued by the governor of Rio de Janeiro two years earlier, remained in force throughout the colonial era. Under the 1702 *regimento*, clearer definition was given to both the rights of miners and the crown.[52] During the following year, the assay house at Taubaté was joined by two additional points for controlling egress from Minas Gerais, one at Santos and the other at Paratí. Shortly thereafter, all personnel and equipment at Taubaté were transferred to Paratí and the São Paulo smelter house was moved to Santos.[53]

A further step was taken in 1705 when D. Pedro II ordered the expulsion of all regular clergy from Minas Gerais. This was done because unlicensed priests, large numbers of whom had flocked to Minas Gerais, frequently smuggled gold out of the region, relying on clerical immunity from search to get themselves past checkpoints. These same clerics evinced such indifference to their religious vows that many of them actively engaged in commerce and consorted with prostitutes who had made their way to the mining camps.[54] Lamenting the socioeconomic disruption that accompanied the scramble for mineral wealth, the Jesuit Andreoni wrote during the War of the Spanish Succession that "there is no prudent person who does not confess that God allowed the discovery of so much gold in Minas in order to chastise Brazil with it, just as an abundance of warfare is now chastising Europe with iron."[55]

Perhaps the most important impetus to the consolidation of the crown's control over Minas Gerais came with an outbreak of civil strife between Paulista prospectors and hordes of interlopers from Portugal and the Brazilian northeast. Most of these late arrivals had reached the goldfields by following the São Francisco River upstream, all but displacing the Paulistas from their diggings. Open warfare between the two factions broke out in 1708 and lasted until late in the following year. This so-called War of the Emboabas (*emboabas* was a derisive Indian word of uncertain meaning hung on the newcomers by the Paulistas) offered the governor of Rio de Janeiro, António de Albuquerque Coelho de Carvalho, an opportunity to extend the crown's influence into the mining camps. While arbitrating the dispute between the two sides, Albuquerque managed to establish military and administrative posts in the region, as well as to improve local administration and facilitate collection of the *quinto*.[56]

Despite persistent, if often ineffectual, efforts to better collect the royal fifth, the crown was probably even more interested in enlarging revenues from its single most important source of income during the late seventeenth century, the tobacco monopoly. This is suggested by the greater attention given to the workings of the monopoly in the official correspondence of the era.[57] Such an emphasis was probably a carry-over from previous years of recession, when tobacco revenues sustained the treasury. At any rate, this official attention was quite justified, for illicit production and sale of tobacco were rampant in the Portuguese world.

A constant stream of tobacco was smuggled out of Brazil for sale in Portugal, its Atlantic islands, Europe, Africa, and the Far East. Tobacco that had been legally shipped to Portugal often found its way onto the black market after being stolen from public or private warehouses. Much to the dismay of monopoly contractors in Portugal, smuggled and stolen tobacco, which was often ground into snuff, was openly sold at prices lower than those set by the crown. Tobacco was also smuggled out of Portugal to India, where its illegal sale undercut the local monopoly.[58] Sailors of the Brazil fleets often engaged in the contraband trade on a modest scale, secreting small quantities of tobacco in their footlockers and then selling it for a profit after debarking in Portugal. Though most crewmen who engaged in petty smuggling of this sort undoubtedly eluded arrest, it is known, for example, that in 1684 sixteen sailors of the *frota* were locked up in Oporto for tobacco-related crimes.[59]

Tobacco was also illegally grown and prepared in Portugal, often by clerics as well as by members of the nobility. Using its authority to search noble and clerical properties, the Junta do Tabaco carried out numerous raids against privileged contrabandists. In 1676, for example, junta officials raided the Lisbon monastery of São Bento da Sande, discovering equipment for grinding and sifting tobacco and two sacks of recently manufactured snuff. Clerical immunity prevented prosecution of the offenders, but some months later the abbot of São Bento was expelled from Portugal.[60] This small monastic operation, though perhaps typical of such clerical abuses, paled in comparison with the dealings of the sisters of the Santa Anna Convent in Viana do Castelo. In 1700, it was reported that these enterprising nuns (whose romantic liaisons were mentioned in chapter II) sold over 250 pounds of tobacco in one day and that a large field of the proscribed plant surrounded their convent. The scope of the contraband problem in Portugal is suggested by the junta's claim that in Oporto there was not a monastery or convent that did not engage in illicit tobacco traffic.[61]

One important step taken to constrict the supply of tobacco available to the black market was the creation of warehouses directly under the junta's control. After receiving a 1683 royal request for its views on the feasibility of erecting extra warehouses in Lisbon and Oporto, the junta urged the adoption of such a program, noting that much contraband tobacco originated in private stores.⁶² Lack of sufficient warehouse space had led the crown to put the growing influx of Brazilian tobacco in privately owned buildings where security was lax, if not lacking altogether. During the remainder of the seventeenth century, new facilities were built in Lisbon and Oporto and guards were posted to discourage theft.

While centralization of inventories in guarded warehouses was undoubtedly a step in the right direction, the sheer volume of tobacco entering Portugal precluded effective control of contraband traffic. In 1695, the junta described the three principal routes by which tobacco then found its way onto the black market. The first began when the Brazil fleets reached Portugal. Hidden caches of tobacco were covertly unladen from ships before searches could be made by the junta's officials. Moreover, legitimately transported tobacco rolls were stolen before they could be gotten into the crown's warehouses. The second route to the black market began when vessels other than those of the Brazil fleets, including foreign craft, surreptitiously introduced tobacco into Lisbon and other ports. A good deal of the contraband tobacco brought to Portugal by foreigners had been purchased from Brazilian slavers, who sold or traded it to them off the west African coast instead of exchanging it for slaves. Finally, much tobacco sent overland to Spain never reached its destination, being diverted onto the black market by highwaymen, muleteers, conniving officials, and others. Tobacco that did reach its Spanish destination was often smuggled back over the border after being reduced to snuff.⁶³

With the post-1690 economic revival then in progress, the crown launched a series of reforms designed to improve the collection of tobacco revenues. The principal impetus for these measures came out of the 1697–1698 Cortes, which, after lengthy debate over how the 600,000 cruzados needed for increasing defense costs was to be raised, agreed that the full burden should be placed on the tobacco monopoly.⁶⁴ In order to assure collection of this additional revenue, the rigid monopoly over tobacco's production and sale was relaxed in 1698 in hopes that a regime of "conditioned liberalization" would generate greater income. This reform proved unsatisfactory, however, and the monopoly system was reimposed in early 1700.⁶⁵

Even before the Cortes acquiesced to the additional excise on tobacco, D. Pedro II ordered the governor-general of Brazil, D. João de Lencastre, to institute a new system for the collection and exportation of tobacco. As it has been noted previously, an initial step was taken in 1696 when the size of tobacco rolls shipped on the *frota* was limited to no more than eight arrobas. Early in 1698, implementation of far more rigorous measures began. In compliance with a royal order of Janurary 30, Lencastre moved to tighten royal control over the movement of tobacco in Brazil.[66]

Tobacco superintendancies similar to those in Portugal were established in major Brazilian ports to help secure the monopolies of royal contractors. In order to prevent the hiding of tobacco in sugar *caixas* or barrels of molasses, apparently a favored means of concealment, planters were required to mark their wooden containers with distinctive brands, which would identify offenders if contraband were later discovered.[67] In Bahia, tobacco from outlying plantations was henceforth delivered to a single warehouse, where it could be graded, weighed, and stored. Premium tobaccos such as those grown in Alagoas were reserved for the European market, while inferior grades were sent to west Africa, usually well-soaked in molasses to suit the tastes of local consumers.

Meanwhile, the crown had decided that all tobaccos destined for Portugal should be transported in ships selected by the Junta do Tabaco. It was believed that concentrating tobacco shipments on fewer vessels would constrict the flow of contraband. The tobacco ships were to sail directly to Lisbon, using Oporto, Viana, and other ports only when necessary. However, the wealthy merchants of Lisbon protested against limiting shipments to designated vessels, and this restriction was soon dropped.[68]

Convinced that the new regime favored the interests of the crown and Lisbon merchants over their own, Bahian merchants and planters lost little time in complaining to the crown about the growing regulation of the tobacco industry.[69] But the die had been cast, and by September 1699 Governor-General Lencastre had compiled the new regulations in a twenty-six-point *regimento*.[70] While making smuggling more difficult, the new restrictions also reduced competition and allowed the merchants of Lisbon to charge higher prices for their tobaccos. Furthermore, the *regimento's* imposition of stricter quality controls enabled favored merchants to "offer premium tobacco for re-export. The more lucrative those re-export sales were, the more the crown's income from custom's revenue increased."[71]

The Bahian mercantile community was still smarting over the new tobacco regulations when the crown proposed that they finance a commercial company that would provide escort vessels for shipping between Brazil and Africa's Mina coast. The crown hoped that such a company would enlarge Portugal's share of the west African slave trade and thereby meet the growing labor needs of Brazil, especially those of the goldfields in Minas Gerais.[72] Typically, Bahian merchants dispatched two or three small, swift vessels (usually *sumacas* or *patachos*) to the Mina coast at bimonthly intervals. During the 1690s, the crown allowed a maximum of twenty-four ships to engage in this traffic, though special licenses could be obtained for vessels in excess of that number (table 13). This steady traffic apparently helped to stabilize slave prices at the four Dutch ports open to Bahian vessels—Whydah, Grand Popo, Jaquin, and Apa—but also made shipping more vulnerable to attack by the pirates who infested the African coast, as well as by the Hollanders who did not limit themselves to peaceful commercial intercourse.[73]

The Bahians were at first receptive to the escort scheme, but they balked at the idea when they learned that Portuguese merchants would be allowed to intrude on their near monopoly on trade with

TABLE 13
Tobacco Shipments from Bahia to
the Mina Coast, 1698–1704

Year	Vessels	Rolls of Tobacco	Weight (in arrobas)
1698	29	1,469*	—
1699	24	2,522	7,918.18
1700	—	—	—
1701†	24	4,318	10,898.29
1702	18	4,752	12,783.16
1703	—	—	—
1704	17	4,954	13,276.00

SOURCE: ANTT, Junta do Tabaco, Cartas do Brasil e India, *maços* 96 and 96A.
*This figure is for eight of the twenty-nine vessels leaving Bahia for the Mina coast in 1698.
† Shipments for August 30, 1700, to August 30, 1701.

the Mina coast. Moreover, the Bahians saw the scheme as a means by which the crown might curtail their shipping of contraband tobacco, sugar, gold, and other commodities to Dutch intermediaries. Though the crown persisted, the Bahians held firm, their resistance, it has been suggested, denoting a growing rivalry between themselves and the merchants of Libson.[74]

Efforts to impose greater control over the tobacco industry also included the appointment of a forceful new president of the Junta do Tabaco, D. António Luís de Sousa, second marquis of Minas.[75] In early December 1698, the aging but still alert duke of Cadaval retired as head of the junta. Though the reasons for this retirement are not altogether clear, the influential duke may have wished to devote more time to his job as president of the Desembargo do Paço (the Royal Council of Justice), to which he had recently been appointed.

The marquis of Minas proved to be an innovative administrator. In a long opinion submitted to the king upon his appointment, he suggested further measures for increasing revenues from the tobacco monopoly. These suggestions included hiking the prices of all grades of tobacco, tougher penalties for major contrabandists, and consolidation of tobacco distribution in Portugal and the Atlantic islands under a prime contractor. The last idea was broached since the present system, one of regional monopolies of varying profitability, was attracting only lukewarm merchant participation.[76]

The marquis of Minas's three recommendations were subsequently put into effect. An increase in penalties for contrabandists, which Governor-General Lencastre had also urged for Brazil, soon followed. The standard punishment imposed on offenders in Brazil, banishment to Angola for two years, was increased to five years and a fine of 3,000 cruzados was added. Penalties for individuals apprehended in Portugal were often more severe. In 1700, for example, it was ordered that, in addition to this banishment, all property of major offenders was to be confiscated.[77] And, on July 15, 1700, the crown signed a three-year contract with D. Pedro Gómez, a wealthy Spanish merchant, in which the latter agreed to handle the distribution of tobaccos in Portugal and its island possessions.[78] One year later, the crown issued a *regimento* that, as Minas had recommended, raised the price of all tobaccos, beginning on January 1, 1702.[79] The crown's measures for consolidating its hold over the tobacco industry ultimately were incorporated in a new *regimento* for the Junta do Tabaco, which was published in 1702.[80]

Despite the crown's extensive program to eliminate contraband, the profits of smuggling still attracted many individuals. The illegal trade between Brazilians and Europeans off the coast of west Africa, for example, probably accounted for a significant share of contraband foreign goods entering Portuguese America. This illicit traffic undoubtedly diminished Portugal's role as the middleman for European goods going to its colonies. In Portugal itself, unlawful traffic in tobacco remained widespread, especially among the clergy. Just two weeks after signing his comprehensive contract with the crown, D. Pedro Gómez received word that the nuns of the Esperançe Convent in Vila ca Viçosa were selling vast quantitites of tobacco.[81]

Efforts to stifle the contraband trade in Brazil and Portugal may not have met with resounding success, but they did much to reinforce royal authority over vital sectors of the Luso-Atlantic economy. Imposing such control was perhaps the logical outgrowth of the crown's various programs for gaining larger returns from its Atlantic possessions. This was done primarily by more closely regulating the commercial activities of colonials, especially those involved in mining and tobacco production. Although the crown may not have intended it so, imposition of additional restrictions on Brazilian commerce probably constrained particularist tendencies in the booming American colony. The growing absolutism of Portugal's government was making itself felt in Brazil. In Minas Gerais, for example, the crown's authority was to be consolidated during the early years of D. João V's reign (1706–1750).[82] Yet, even as the crown sought to tighten its grip on a prospering periphery, Portugal increasingly fell under the economic sway of England, a power whose rise to dominance in the modern world system was then well underway.

CHAPTER XI

CONCLUSIONS AND CONSEQUENCES

> The Great Empire will be by
> England. Great forces will pass by land and sea,
> The all-powerful for more than three hundred years;
> The Portuguese will not be pleased with it.
>
> > Nostradamus (1555)

> E a execução destes tratados [de Methuen] é soffrer Portugal o comercio passivo de todas as manufacturas, generos e fructos com que os inglezes tem exaurido e estão exaurindo todo o ouro potavel deste reino.
>
> > The Marquis of Pombal (1741)

Although the years between 1668 and 1703 mark an era of relative quiescence in Portuguese history, they also encompass a period during which the established order experienced significant challenges. Unsuccessful attempts by New Christian merchants to obtain relief from inquisitorial persecution constituted the most noteworthy challenge to a society built on landed property and inherited privilege. It may well be that this challenge hastened the emergence of an absolutist regime whose presence became increasingly apparent after 1680. As in most nation-states, the General Crisis that affected seventeenth-century Europe was clearly resolved in favor of absolutism in Portugal. Nevertheless, the onset of a lengthy period of cyclical decline, which had temporarily worked to the advantage of the mercantile class in its push for a liberalized regime, gave impetus to a manufacturing program that also threatened the status quo. Both guildsmen and privileged consumers found ample reason to complain about the industrial program. The importation of foreign workers and the promulgation of sumptuary legislation jeopardized jobs and limited options for consumers. Even so, the prolonged economic decline of the late seventeenth century imposed a measure of compliance with mercantilist policies designed to recapture the prosperity that had so long eluded Portugal.

After 1690, however, improving economic conditions within the world economy relieved much of the pressure on the established order. Spokespeople for the mercantile class and supporters of manufacturing then had little leverage with which to press their respective (and often complementary) causes. The well-reasoned arguments of António Vieira and Duarte Ribeiro de Macedo on behalf of New Christian merchants and domestic manufactures carried less weight and perhaps even seemed passé as enlarging revenue collections and incomes swelled the treasury of the crown and the purses of the privileged.

Chronic foodstuff shortages could be more easily relieved by imports as conditions in the Luso-Atlantic economy improved. Moreover, the resurgent demand for cash crops in northern Europe buttressed the position of Portugal's privileged estates, who saw little reason to increase cultivation of less remunerative grains when the market for wine, olive oil, and other exports was expanding so rapidly. As this occurred, the crown concentrated on improving the collection of taxes on key commodities such as wine, sugar, tobacco, and gold. Little attention was given to reducing Portugal's dependence on these products or on further diversifying economic activity in Portugal and its Atlantic colonies. Yet, thanks in part to royal initiatives taken after 1670, the Luso-Atlantic economy had in fact attained greater diversification and thus escaped its once-heavy dependence on sugar production. Commercial activity in formerly marginal regions quickened, and the Mina coast, Guinea, northern Portugal, and southern Brazil assumed greater economic importance. But even with its vast geographic scale and rising prosperity, the Luso-Atlantic economy became more heavily dependent on the core states of Europe for its economic sustenance.

Defense and Commerce: The Treaties of 1703

During the first few years of the eighteenth century, Portugal experienced heavy pressures from both England and France as the two powers vied for Lisbon's loyalty in their ongoing struggle for hegemony in Europe and the Atlantic. After the death of D. Carlos II of Spain in 1700, Philip of Anjou inherited the Spanish throne, styling himself Philip V. As a condition of his becoming monarch of Castile and all its possessions, Philip V renounced any claim to succeed his grandfather Louis XIV as king of France. Nation-states at odds with France, particularly England, insisted on the renunciation, fearing that the French and Spanish crowns would someday be united under one leader whose wealth and power would seriously threaten their own. The Portuguese, however, derived little comfort from Philip's renunciation, for it was strongly suspected that he might try to reclaim Portugal as a province of Spain.

Largely because of this suspicion, as well as lingering pro-French sentiment at court, D. Pedro II signed a series of treaties with Spain and France in June 1701 that supported Philip V's claim to the Spanish throne. Portugal agreed to bar the enemies of Louis XIV and Philip V (most notably, England and Holland) from using its ports for military purposes and acceded to the transfer of the Spanish *asiento* from Portuguese to French contractors. Furthermore, Lisbon agreed to prohibit the export of Portuguese tobaccos to Spain. In return, Portuguese sovereignty was guaranteed by the Castilians and, in time of war, Madrid promised to lift an embargo on the export of "corn" (actually grain) to Portugal then in force. Many Portuguese, including D. Pedro II himself, were not enthused about the treaties since they virtually destroyed the position of neutrality cultivated throughout the king's reign. Nonetheless, England's recognition of Philip V (April 13, 1701) as king of Spain left the Portuguese little choice but to reach an accommodation with the Bourbon camp.[1]

Yet, within two years the situation changed dramatically. England had second thoughts about the wisdom of recognizing Philip V and strongly supported the pretensions of Archduke Charles of Austria, the Hapsburg claimant to the Spanish throne. After months of cautious, noncommittal contacts with both the French and the English camps, the Portuguese began maneuvering their way back to a position of neutrality, letting London's envoy, John Methuen, know that they would gladly renounce the Bourbon pacts if England and its Dutch allies were to send a fleet into Portuguese waters. By doing this it was hoped that Lisbon would be given a pretext for abandoning its uncomfortable alliance if France and Spain were shown incapable of protecting Portugal from an Anglo-Dutch blockade. On the evening of August 19, 1702, an English squadron did indeed sail past the mouth of the Tagus, and shortly thereafter D. Pedro II voided his accommodation with the French alliance.[2] On October 19, 1702, the naval superiority of the English alliance was amply demonstrated when the Spanish silver fleet, together with its French escort squadron, was destroyed in Vigo Bay, an inlet on the Galician coast.

Though greatly impressed by this allied victory, the Portuguese clung to their recently regained neutral status. The principal proponent of the French alliance, the duke of Cadaval, had gradually been changing his mind in favor of the English, but he advised the crown to go slow on any commitments. In late 1702, he was particularly worried about any agreement that might get Portugal involved in a winter campaign against Bourbon Spain. Moreover, he was also concerned about the allies' ability to provision Portugal during a war that might last many years and about whether the English Parliament would remain faithful to any commitment made to the Portuguese. Apparently, Cadaval believed that playing for time was the best policy.[3]

During the following months, however, the desire to have Philip V deposed as ruler of Spain (and thereby thwart whatever plans the Bourbon leader may have had for annexing Portugal) and the realization that Portugal and its colonies were far more vulnerable to maritime attack than overland invasion finally induced Lisbon to seek an alliance with England and its Dutch and Austrian allies. A number of influential figures advocated this course, including the count of Castelo Melhor and D. Catarina de Bragança. Castelo Melhor, who had once been D. Alfonso VI's chief minister and who had fled to England following D. Pedro's 1667 coup, return to Portugal in 1690. Then reconciled with D. Pedro II's regime, he pressed for closer ties with England. In 1703, he submitted an opinion favorable to the English alliance, which may in fact have influenced the king's decision.[4] D. Catarina, Queen Catherine of England since 1662, returned to her native land in 1692 following the death of Charles II. Like Castelo Melhor, Queen Catherine favored an alliance with her adopted country and undoubtedly had a hand in her brother Pedro's decision to join with England and its allies.[5]

On May 16, 1703, Portugal formally joined the alliance, signing the Offensive Quadrangle Treaty and the Defensive Triple Treaty. In the first pact, the Portuguese agreed to carry the fight to Spain so that Archduke Charles of Austria might replace Philip V on the Spanish throne. The second agreement assured Portugal of English and Dutch support if attacked by Spain or France.[6] These accords completed the so-called Grand Alliance, which would oppose Louis XIV and his allies during the War of the Spanish Succession.

Less than eight months after joining the Grand Alliance, Portugal further committed itself to England by signing an extraordinary commercial document. On December 27, 1703, the marquis of Alegrate (Manuel Teles da Silva) and John Methuen signed the renowned commercial treaty that bears the latter's name. With the Methuen Treaty, the two nations agreed to lower or eliminate barriers to trade in Portuguese wines and English woolens. Remarkable in its brevity, the agreement contained only three articles, the last of which stipulated that the pact must be ratified by the English Parliament within two months of its signature. The two articles laying down the new commercial regime follow.

Article I. His sacred royal majesty of Portugal promises, in his own Name, and in the names of his Successors, that there shall be admitted at all times into Portugal, woollen cloths, and other woollen manufactures of England, no otherwise than they used to be, before they were prohibited by Pragmatical Sanctions, upon this Condition nevertheless:

Article 2. That her sacred royal Majesty of Great Britain be obliged in her own Name, and in the Name of her Successors, at all times to admit into England, Wines gathered from the vineyards belonging to the Portugal Dominions, as that at no time, whether there be Peace or War, between the Kingdoms of England and France, any more shall be demanded for such wines, directly or indirectly, on account of Customs or Impost, or upon any other Account whatsoever, than what shall, after deducting a third part of the Customs or Impost, be demanded from a like quantity of French Wine, whether such Wines shall be imported in Great Britain in Pipes, Hogsheads or any other Vessals; but if at any time this Diminution of Duties, to be made aforesaid, shall in any manner be attempted, and the same shall be infringed, it shall be right and lawful for his sacred Majesty of Portugal to prohibit again Woollen Cloths and other the Woollen Manufactures of England.[7]

Left unspoken in the treaty was the fact that Portugal's attempt to establish domestic manufactures, particularly textiles, had failed. Despite the determined efforts of the count of Ericeira and others, cloth was then in short supply in Portugal. Perhaps not surprisingly, Lisbon's forsaking its alliance with France was followed by the virtual abandonment of mercantilist policies fashioned after those of Jean Baptiste Colbert. Portugal then possessed an abundance of agricultural products to sell, and England offered a lucrative and expanding market for wine and other commodities. England, in turn, could supply the Luso-Atlantic demand for woolens and other finished goods. Furthermore, the Methuen Treaty reinforced England's position as Portugal's principal source of imported grains and codfish. For Portugal, the chief consequence of this emerging relationship was to be an increasing dependence on England as a market for agricultural exports and as a source of capital, manufactured goods, and foodstuffs. Before examining that relationship, however, the causes of Portugal's industrial collapse should be elucidated.

The Collapse of Colbertism

The rise of manufacturing in Portugal during the Ericeira administration was impelled by three crucial stimuli. First, the rebuff of the mercantile class's pretensions during the 1670s effectively constricted an important source of financial support, thereby lending greater attraction to manufacturing. Duarte Ribeiro de Macedo's silence on New Christian involvement in the program for recovery outlined in his 1675 *Discurso* carried with it the unwritten premise that Portugal's economic problems could be alleviated without undue reliance on the wealth of merchants. Revenues collected on the sale of domestic manufactures, together with an anticipated reduction in the bullion drain, appeared to offer the crown an alternative to increasingly impolitic dealings with New Christian merchants. Ironically, however, New Christian contractors in Covilhã and elsewhere played an important role in launching the fledgling textile industry.

The general economic downturn that began after 1670 was in itself probably a more important impetus to manufacturing in Portugal. Declining commercial activity and Portugal's chronically unfavorable trade balance lent urgency to the implementation of protectionist and sumptuary legislation, not to mention the expansion of domestic production. The crown could more readily justify restrictions on consumption to its privileged constituents by noting the economic problems then afflicting the country.

Finally, the influential position held by a progressive, pro-French faction within the nobility, of whom the count of Ericeira was probably the most forceful member, further stimulated emulation of Colbert's policies. The French example was indeed quite attractive to those in the nobility who most closely associated themselves with the crown's interests. D. Pedro II himself, from his installation as prince regent in 1668 onward, demonstrated an appreciation for the need to increase domestic production and curtail consumption of foreign products. He consistently backed Ericeira's efforts and, as Luís Dias wrote, was no "mere observer of the reforms of his Finance Minister."[8]

Criticism of Ericeira's program was muted during the economically depressed 1680s, but many of the privileged no doubt grumbled about the prohibitions on consumption of foreign luxury items that the *pragmáticas* of 1668 and 1677 imposed. Furthermore, many nobles, clerics, *letrados*, and wealthy merchants ignored these laws, continuing to purchase and wear forbidden fabrics and apparel. This is clearly suggested by the fact that in 1686 the crown felt compelled to issue yet another *pragmática* against conspicuous consumption. This latest edict, which noted an alarming rise in the consumption of luxury goods, ordered that transgressors, including native tailors who produced costumes in which scarce gold or silver was used as threads and adornments, be fined for the first offense and jailed for the second. The law also imposed greater restrictions in imports, prohibiting the use of "any type of black or colored fabric not manufactured in the realm."[9] Two years later, further dress restrictions were enacted as the crown again attempted to divert consumption to local products.[10]

As economic conditions improved following the devaluation of the currency in 1688, criticism of Ericeira's efforts on behalf of manufac-

CONCLUSIONS AND CONSEQUENCES   267

turing became more vocal. The increasing severity of sumptuary legislation on the one hand and the resurgence of prosperity on the other led many to question the wisdom of maintaining domestic manufactures. In a document apparently written in 1689, for example, an unknown petitioner suggested that bullion could most easily be retained in Portugal by simply registering the value of all imports and requiring that foreign merchants take payment in Portuguese goods, especially sugar and tobacco, instead of specie.[11] This requirement, it was believed, would allow Portugal to bypass the protectionist walls thrown up by the French, English, and Dutch against Luso-Atlantic products. Moreover, the author implied that registration of commercial transactions, which ostensibly would cost little or nothing to accomplish, was superior to the more expensive manufacturing program as a means of preserving domestic bullion stocks. In yet another implicit criticism of manufacturing, the writer urged that Portugal strongly promote export of cash crops since they were the principal resource of the economy.[12] Though exceedingly naive in its assumption that foreign merchants might go along with such a scheme, the registry proposal probably voiced the sentiments of many privileged individuals who were disgruntled by restrictions on consumption and regarded the manufacturing program as a threat to the status quo.

Opposition to sumptuary laws and domestic manufacturing may have influenced a loosening of restrictions after the 1688 devaluation. On August 9, 1692, D. Pedro II annulled certain provisions of the 1686 *pragmática*, thereby acknowledging that Portuguese production of hats, black cloth, glass, and other manufactured items was insufficient to meet demand. With this recision, the king also conceded that the crown's revenues deriving from taxes on restricted imports (which were needed to pay the salaries, pensions, and other expenses of the privileged) had failed to keep pace with the growth of such outlays.[13] Thus, while Portuguese industries, which were inadequately financed from the outset, failed to meet the domestic demand for manufactured goods, protectionist and sumptuary legislation designed to foster their development threatened traditional sources of the privileged classes' income.

Taken together, the disappointing progress of the manufacturing program and the growing criticism of its efficacy may have unnerved the count of Ericeira. Indeed, D. Louis de Meneses, according to some speculation, suffered from neurasthenia, an affliction that undoubtedly would have been worsened by denunciation of policies to which he had devoted years of effort.[14] Whatever the reasons, Ericeira had fallen into such a depressed state of mind that on May 26, 1690, he took his own life. Extant accounts of the suicide differ on various details, but one account has it that Meneses, feeling ill, had remained at home on the day of the Corpus Christi procession. As his wife, who had stayed with him, was offering prayers to the Virgin, the count opened a window and hurled himself to the garden below, dying shortly thereafter of massive head injuries.[15]

Ericeira's desperate act deprived Portuguese manufacturing of its most energetic promoter. Without his forceful presence at hand, Portugal's version of Colbertism slipped into decline. By the time the Methuen Treaty was signed in 1703, Portuguese industry was already in a moribund state. Though Meneses's death certainly had an adverse effect on the course of domestic manufacturing, other factors also contributed to its subsequent collapse.

Despite the importation of foreign expertise and equipment, the quality of Portuguese manufactures was generally inferior to that of nations with older, more firmly established industrial enterprises. The lifting of the prohibition on the importation of English beaver hats in 1692, for example, clearly belied an inability to produce acceptable substitutes. In 1681, Portuguese hatters had frankly admitted their competitive disadvantage, asking the crown for protection against inroads made on the local market by foreign products.[16] During the next decade, an ever-increasing variety of wares emerging from foreign mills and factories made it even more difficult for hatters, tailors, and other clothiers to suit the tastes of fashion-conscious nobles, clerics, and others.

Shortages of raw materials also contributed to the collapse of Colbertism. The great drought of 1692 through 1694, which, caused severe grain shortages and thus famine in Portugal, also killed innumerable mulberry trees. The cost of domestically produced silks soon rose as local supplies failed to keep pace with demand. Wool shortages, however, had a far more damaging impact on the manufacturing program, for production of woolens was at the heart of Ericeira's program. Writing to the king in 1699, the Lisbon *câmara* revealed that unscrupulous merchants were illegally exporting raw domestic wool to foreign markets, claiming that it was produced in Spain, not Portugal.[17] As with silk, the cost of wool used in Portuguese manufacturing undoubtedly rose.

Harmful as Ericeira's death, inclement weather, and the contraband trade may have been, the manufacturing program was probably most seriously damaged by the depredations of the Holy Inquisition. Reliance on New Christian merchants and artisans had helped industrialization off to a good start, but thereafter the Holy Office did much to cripple the program by arresting numerous individuals involved in the manufacture and sale of textiles. Fearful of imminent arrest, many New Christians connected with textile production fled the country, taking their skills and capital with them.[18] After visiting the manufacturing centers of Covilhã and Fundão in late 1704, an English officer, Colonel John Richards, attributed the decadent state in which he found the two *vilas* to inquisitorial predations.[19] In Covilhã alone, at least eighteen merchants were arrested by the Holy Office during the years 1700 to 1705.[20] D. Luís da Cunha (1662–1749), Portugal's ambassador to England at the time (who had boasted of wearing clothes of all-Portuguese manufacture upon his arrival at London in 1696) and the chief proponent of manufacturing after Ericeira's death, later confirmed that the Inquisition was largely responsible for the decline of woolen production in his country.[21]

When the Portuguese signed the Methuen Treaty in 1703, they were not so much abandoning domestic manufacturing as they were acknowledging its decadent condition. Moreover, the improving economic situation in the Luso-Atlantic world had the effect of calling into question the need for expanding Portugal's industrial capacity. As revenues from Portugal's export sector and colonial commodity production grew, the troubled manufacturing program lagged farther and farther behind. Contrary to one scholarly opinion, however, the effort to industrialize had been pursued as more than simply a stopgap measure employed during a lengthy recession that was thereafter sabotaged by big merchants and wine and olive growers eager to sell their products to the English.[22] Instead, the continued issuance of legislation favorable to manufacturing after 1690 suggests that the blame for the failure of industry should not be solely attributed to pressures exerted by certain growers and merchants, however, influential they may have been. It would seem more appropriate to recognize that Portuguese society as a whole had not yet advanced to the point at which an industrial endeavor could be successfully maintained. Furthermore, extensive commercial intercourse (both legal and illegal) with more-advanced economies, especially that of England, made the environment even less hospitable for Portuguese manufactures.

Portugal, England, and the Roots of Modern Dependency

The changing nature of Portugal's relationship with England, which reflected far-reaching transformations occurring within the structure of English society, also had a hand in the collapse of Colbertism in Portugal. The signing of the Anglo-Portuguese Treaty of 1654, which ended a brief conflict between the two countries, marked an important juncture in this changing relationship. Previously, the two allies had acted more or less as equals in their dealings with one another, but the 1654 pact with Cromwell's protectorate, which came at a point when Portugal was fighting for its very independence, weighted the balance heavily in favor of the English.

Perhaps most important, a secret article in the agreement stipulated that henceforth English goods could be taxed at no more than twenty-three percent, the combined total of the *décima* (ten percent), *sisa* (ten percent), and *consulado* (three percent) levies. This article thereby guaranteed that English merchants in Portugal would pay taxes lower than even those imposed on their Portuguese counterparts, an arrangement that would become especially valuable to the English after the Methuen Treaty removed legal barriers to woolen importation.[23] Although the 1654 accord had been reached at a time when Portugal was sorely pressed, and thus more readily taken advantage of by Cromwell (whose terms amounted to a virtual *diktat* "which set the pattern for the alliance for the next hundred years"), the agreement's lengthy tenure suggested something more fundamental at work than opportunistic exploitation of a beleaguered ally.[24]

During the reign of D. Pedro II, Portugal's relationship with England evolved toward one in which the division of labor between the two countries was firmly established. And, by specializing in commodities such as wine, olive oil, and tobacco, Portugal's less-advanced economy was, in the long term, consigned to what have been called the "less dynamic branches of production."[25] The Methuen Treaty clearly signaled that the Portuguese economy had become overwhelmingly devoted to the production of primary products, while its English counterpart moved increasingly toward a regime based on manufacturing. Thus, the relationship that emerged between the two countries "was one of strong dependence by Portugal on England, although it reinforced the Braganza House and the landed interests, thus the aristocracy and the Church."[26]

The causes of this emerging dependence were myriad and cannot be adequately explored here. Perhaps the most important single factor lay in the increasingly divergent nature of Portuguese and English society. Portugal, as we have seen, did indeed take tentative steps toward fundamental change; but, despite the best efforts of António Vieira, the count of Ericeira, and others, Portuguese society simply had not reached a stage in its development at which an unfettered mercantile class or an industrial mode of production could be tolerated or sustained. In both instances, incipient change was effectively blocked, giving obvious testimony to the tenacity of an established order when faced with such challenges to the status quo. As was the case in most of early modern Europe, Portugal's social foundations remained firmly embedded in privilege and landed property.

The old order as found in the Luso-Atlantic world remained quite adequate for containing the productive forces that, after 1690, brought renewed prosperity to Portugal. New relations of production had not emerged in Portugal, much less in its colonies.[27] Instead, the privileged classes' control of land and labor power and the effective social constraints on the mercantile class nurtured an emerging absolutist regime. And, as it has already been suggested, growing prosperity based on exploitation of primary products reinforced the social order after it had been mildly shaken by moves toward industrialization and greater freedom for the mercantile class.

Even as Portugal's old order was moving toward a prolonged tenure under an absolutist regime, English society was evolving new relations of production. Unlike Portugal, which despite renewed prosperity still needed to import essential foodstuffs and a wide range of

272 CONCLUSIONS AND CONSEQUENCES

finished goods, England had experienced a precocious transformation in its agricultural base that was characterized by an emerging symbiotic (that is, capitalistic) relationship between landlord and tenant, which led to greater productivity and an expanding domestic market for its manufactured goods. Moreover, the changing relationships in the countryside allowed increasing numbers of laborers to move from rural areas to jobs in English industry. According to Robert Brenner, England's industrial development was distinguished by

> its continuous character, its ability to sustain itself and to provide its own self-perpetuating dynamic. Here, once again, the key was to be found in the capitalistic structure of agriculture. Agricultural improvement not only made it possible for an ever greater proportion of the population to leave the land to enter industry; equally important, it provided, directly and indirectly, the growing home market which was an essential ingredient in England's continued industrial growth through the entire period of the "general economic crisis of the seventeenth century" in Europe. Thus during the sixteenth and seventeenth centuries, the prosperous class of tenant and yeoman farmers, as well as landlords, appears to have offered significant outlets for English goods.[28]

As Brenner also pointed out, continuing improvements in agricultural productivity during the late seventeenth and early eighteenth centuries

> combined with low food prices to give an extra margin of spending power to significant elements throughout the middle and perhaps even the lower class so as to expand the home market and fuel the steady growth of industry into the period of the industrial revolution. English economic development thus depended upon a nearly unique symbiotic relationship between agriculture and industry. It was indeed, in the last analysis, an agricultural revolution, based on the emergence of capitalist class relations in the countryside which made it possible for England to become the first nation to experience industrialization.[29]

The fundamental changes occurring in English agriculture not only put the country on the road to industrialization, they secured its position as the leading core state. Indeed, after 1707, England became the greatest commercial unit in the world economy, surpassing France, a nation possessed of a far larger population and a vast but unchanged agricultural base.[30] England's economic ascendancy over France, the premier absolutist regime in Europe, sprang primarily from "new superior relations of production" emerging in the English countryside.

Meanwhile, commercial relations between England and Portugal, the economy of which was much smaller than that of France and likewise had undergone no agricultural revolution, became, at base, the principal factor conditioning the relationship between increasingly disparate social orders. This emerging relationship is of signal importance in the evolution of the modern world system, for herein lay the roots of "modern" dependency.[31] *Modern dependency* is defined as those relations of dependence between core, semiperiphery, and periphery that emerged in the wake of England's precocious development of capitalistic agriculture and industrialization.[32]

By 1700, the Portuguese component of the modern world system (that is, the Luso-Atlantic economy) had clearly become entangled in a dependent relationship with England.[33] V. I. Lenin once observed that

not only are there two main groups of countries, those owning colonies, and the colonies themselves, but also the diverse forms of dependent countries which, politically, are formally independent, but in fact, are enmeshed in the net of financial and diplomatic dependence.[34]

Generations before the United States broke with England, and so became the first portion of the periphery to gain political independence, Portugal, a sovereign state with a far-flung empire, had fallen into a dependent relationship of the sort described by Lenin. Indeed, if modern dependency is understood as having arisen in concert with England's precocious transition to new modes of production, Portugal may well have been the first sovereign nation to become so ensnared.

Contemporary perceptions of this relationship, though not so formally defined as by Lenin, clearly fathomed the implications of dependency. Writing in 1710, an Englishman in Lisbon gave the following explanation of his country's trade with the Luso-Atlantic economy, which by then also relied heavily on England for its "corn" (grain) supply:

All their gold, sugars, and tobaccos are the returns of our own manufacturers, which our people give them upon credit, to be paid upon the return of the Brazil trade. Three parts in four of the corn expended here, and all the dyed cloth is imported by the English, so that 'tis plain these people live by us, and cannot live without us.[35]

Some thirteen years earlier, when the question of importing textiles from England was still at issue, a number of prominent English merchants in Lisbon (who had been barred from wearing their own cloth) voiced a perhaps accurate assessment of the local privileged classes' preoccupation with the latest fashions. Were English merchants allowed to wear the proscribed fabrics, one of their number asserted, "Ye Portuguese gentlemen will never bear to see us wearing fine cloth and they be denied it."[36]

Foreign observers also commented on the presumed lack of commercial acumen among the Portuguese, explaining that they did not regard trade as a gentlemanly occupation. According to a Frenchman of the late seventeenth century, the Portuguese

are not industrious and out of vanity they leave commerce as soon as they can; in addition, they find less profit than other peoples in business because they do not give themselves the trouble to get the goods for their shipments at first hand but buy in Portugal from other nations which profit from them.[37]

Such views, however, fail to take into account the socioeconomic constraints imposed on the Portuguese mercantile community. Living under the threat of inquisitorial persecution and having limited say in the formulation of government policy did not make for a notably venturesome or stable mercantile class. By contrast, entrepreneurs in northern Europe were spared Holy Office scrutiny and enjoyed great influence with the state, which often translated into strong support for their international commercial activities. Competition from growing numbers of foreign merchants and artisans in Portugal, many of whom held privileges equal or even superior to those of Portuguese subjects, also undermined the development of domestic enterprise. This trend became especially pronounced after 1700.[38]

Following the Methuen Treaty, England's dominance of the Luso-Atlantic economy was furthered by the demands of privileged consumers (as well as by those of wealthy merchants, *letrados*, and other influential commoners) who had considerable surplus income to expend on English manufactures, foodstuffs, and other products. This pattern was replicated in Brazil, where wealthy colonial elites also consumed vast quantities of English goods. By the mid-eighteenth century, however, Luso-Atlantic prosperity had started to wane and D. Luís da Cunha's advocacy of domestic industries, which had long been ignored, began to attract increasing attention. The marquis of Pombal, who assumed power in 1750 as the chief minister of D. José I, shared da Cunha's views, believing, as the following passage shows, that Portugal's largely unrestrained trade with England was at the root of his country's growing economic problems.

The English . . . have conquered [Portugal] without the inconveniences of a conquest. . . . In 1754 Portugal scarcely produced anything for her own support: two-thirds of her physical necessities were supplied by England . . . [and] all the trade of the country was carried on by [English] agents. The English monopolized even the commerce of Brazil. . . . These foreigners, after having acquired immense fortunes, disappeared, carrying with them the riches of the country.[39]

Although Pombal, following Ericeira's example, inaugurated a variety of programs designed to give Portugal a measure of economic independence, he, too, failed. Portugal had yet to undergo a socioeconomic transformation such as that experienced in England. No agricultural revolution had occurred, and, consequently, Portuguese society was insufficiently advanced to sustain industrial development and thus escape a dependent relationship with an ascendant England.

The years between 1668 and 1703 comprised an era of relative quiescence in Portuguese political history, but a tentative movement toward significant transformation of the socioeconomic order was experienced. The mercantile class pressed for greater influence even as the establishment of an industrial mode of production was begun. But the foundations of the Old Regime were little disturbed by these movements toward fundamental change. Portugal was still far from a position in which the elements necessary for capitalist production prevailed. A social regime favoring privileged landholders and guildsmen still held firm. What was needed, as William Shaw put it, was

. . . a population of free laborers, stripped of both feudal encumbrances on their labor power and means of production sufficient for their independent subsistence, and monetary accumulations capable of being converted into the means necessary for industrial production.[40]

Furthermore, capitalist development in Portugal required "a correlative growth of a class of purchasers of labor power."[41] But neither a class of propertyless wage laborers nor a class of capitalists who might employ them and sell goods to them had yet emerged in sufficient strength to effect a transition from feudal to capitalist modes of production.

After 1690, movement toward a more advantageous position in the international division of labor was all but engulfed by a rising tide of prosperity flowing out of the vineyards of Portugal and the mines and plantations of Brazil. Instead of making way for expanding middle classes, a transformed agricultural base, and industrial growth, the old order found refuge in absolutism and dependency, relying on cash crops and mineral wealth for its sustenance. When the prosperity of the first half of the eighteenth century had passed, the old order, then abjectly dependent on England, was confronted by its own increasing obsolescence. Thanks to the great Lisbon quake of 1755 and the subsequent actions of the marquis of Pombal, the foundations of the Old Regime were again shaken and undoubtedly crumbled a little more.

APPENDIXES

APPENDIX 1

Persons Tried and Sentenced to *Autos-da-fé* by the Portuguese Inquisition, 1682–1691

Year	Tribunal	Principal Groups				Total Number Tried	Minimum Number Executed
		Merchants*	Craftsmen	Women	Others		
1682	Lisbon	28	4	43	27	102	4
	Évora	2	16	68	28	114	—
	Coimbra	2	9	15	5	31	—
1683	Lisbon	15	5	29	13	62	—
	Évora	12	25	79	44	160	—
	Coimbra	28	26	65	38	157	—
1684	Lisbon	20	2	19	14	55	3
	Évora	5	3	25	8	41	0
	Coimbra	4	11	38	12	65	0
1685	Lisbon	2	1	1	2	6	0
	Évora	4	5	27	6	42	—
	Coimbra	15	49	85	25	174	—
1686	Lisbon	6	1	4	4	15	3
	Évora	3	4	17	10	34	—
	Coimbra	0	1	3	1	5	0
1687	Lisbon	—	—	—	—	—	—
	Évora	8	6	31	7	52	—
	Coimbra	0	1	0	0	1	—
1688	Lisbon	7	2	13	6	28	1
	Évora	1	2	15	3	21	—
	Coimbra	0	0	3	0	3	—
1689	Lisbon	0	1	1	3	5	—
	Évora	1	12	30	10	53	—
	Coimbra	3	2	8	2	15	1
1690	Lisbon	0	1	1	1	3	—
	Évora	0	3	14	2	19	0
	Coimbra	4	0	3	1	8	0
1691	Lisbon	—	—	—	—	—	—
	Évora	2	1	7	2	12	—
	Coimbra	13	2	26	5	46	6
	TOTALS	185	195	670	269	1,329	18

Sources: Azevedo, *História dos Cristãos Novos*, p. 492; Almeida, *História da Igreja*, 3 (pt. 2): 292; Geddes, "A View of the Court," pp. 447–48.
*This category includes goldsmiths.

APPENDIX 2

"Whereas the Portugal Trade is very advantageous to this Nation"*

(A discourse on its advantages, with a view to the reduction of Customs duties—London, circa 1678)

WHEREAS the *Portugal* Trade is very advantageous to this Nation, because it doth annually consume a great quantity of our Manufacture, Fish, *&c*. And of late declines; because the Sugar, and other Commodities of that Country, are either so fallen in price, or grown so scarce, so that the Merchants, trading thither, cannot procure wherein to have Returns, nor the People of that Country wherein to make satisfaction for the Goods they take, which hath occasioned the Setting up of Fabricks of their own, and the prohibiting of some of our Commodities; to prevent the said inconveniency, being that Country abounds with several sorts of good *Wine*, and is capable to afford great Quantities thereof, which are in manner totally prohibited from being brought into this Kingdom, by the great Custom charged on them, of Sixteen pounds Eighteen shillings and Eleven pence *per* Tun, as on *Spanish* Wine; whereas their Use, nor Goodness, doth nor render them capable of paying more than the *French*.

It is humbly conceived, it may be the Interest of this Nation, That by Act of Parliament, the Custom of the said Wines be abated, and that being the fraight from *Portugal* is 40 *s. per* Tun, more than from *France*, That the Custom may be less than what is charged on the French Wine for these Reasons following.

  I. The abating of the said Custom would certainly introduce the Expence of the said Wine, and make them serve to supply the great want of Returns, at present Experimented in that Trade, and consequently be a great means to increase the Consumption of our Manufactory in that Country.

  II. It would diminish the importation of French Wine, which, it is well known, we purchase with our Money, whereas it is probable, these will always be purchased with our Manufactory, and it may be convenient to encourage the growth of Wine in *Portugal*, thereby to diminish the *French* Trade.

III. Whereas the Prince of *Portugal* did about Twelve Months since, make a Sumptuary Law, to prevent the wearing of Foreign Cloath, Gold and Silver Lace, and some other Commodities, and did also Set up Fabricks of Bayes and Serges in that Country; because they have not effects to ballance their Importation, which hath already proved of great prejudice to the said Trade, and may prove very fatal if pursued. It may be hoped, That by thus introducing the Expence of their Commodities, and the Taking of them in Exchange for our Manufactures, they may be brought to neglect the Observation of the said Law, and the said Fabricks, because the occasion of them will be taken away.

IV. It may advance his Majesties Revenue; for the present extraordinary Custom is little less than a total Prohibition: So that the said Wines yield at present very little to his Majesty; whereas if the Custom be abated, they may yield a considerable Sum, and whatever may be received less on the *French* Wine, will be advanced on these, and probably more; because of their Variety and Goodness, and also because a great quantity of the Wines of that Country are not so strong as the *French*.

*BL 8.6.m.11(9110). Contrary to previous conjecture, this short pamphlet, which apparently was prepared at the instigation of English cloth merchants, was probably published in 1678, not 1695. Internal evidence, particularly Reason III, clearly suggests that the pamphlet appeared about a year after the *pragmática* of January 25, 1677. The establishment of woolen manufactures in Portugal coincided with the promulgation of the *pragmática* (see chapter VII).

APPENDIX 3

Vessel Arrivals in Oporto, 1657–1698

Year	Provenance						Brazil				Other and Unidentified	Total
	England	Newfoundland	Holland	France	Hamburg	Spain	Pernambuco	Bahia	Rio de Janeiro	Paráiba	Pará		
1657	9	5	6	1	3	1	......	......	......	......	......	7	32
1658	15	7	7	5	6	1	......	......	......	......	......	6	41
1659	3	13	5	9	7	1	......	......	......	......	......	1	39
1660	7	3	9	4	5	1	......	......	......	......	......	1	30
1661	9	......	4	2	4	......	......	......	......	......	......	......	19
1672	22	1	4	10	8	......	......	......	......	......	......	11	56
1673	8	4	3	11	12	13	......	......	......	......	......	7	58
1674	31	14	8	6	14	12	......	......	......	......	......	9	94
1675	28	8	14	12	6	6	......	......	......	......	......	6	80

Year													
1676	18	13	..	8	8	7	..	..	..	..	..	5	68
1677	22	8	9	10	9	4	..	..	..	..	..	7	69
1678	10	11	9	9	8	5	..	..	..	..	..	4	56
1679	34	14	9	24	9	2	..	..	..	..	..	8	111
1680	19	14	20	28	17	3	..	..	..	..	..	6	106
1681	12	20	19	45	19	3	..	..	..	..	..	11	144
1682	22	16	34	26	13	2	..	..	..	..	..	12	106
1684	21	8	15	13	10	6	13	..	..	..	..	6	82
1686	24	23	18	20	11	9	..	14	2	..	..	6	136
1690	23	7	14	6	9	4	..	..	..	..	1	15	80
1691	39	12	16	13	9	8	5	..	..	..	..	11	113
1692	67	5	20	10	12	11	1	3	1	..	..	14	157
1693	57	14	33	8	4	7	1	1	2	..	..	23	140
1694	52	21	22	22	6	7	7	7	3	..	..	16	143
1695	28	4	15	10	9	6	7	7	5	..	..	23	112
1696	47	13	26	11	6	9	10	6	5	2	..	21	155
1697	32	14	25	12	7	5	9	..	..	1	..	29	146
1698	31	8	16	10	6	8	7	10	1	..	1	46	145

Source: Pinto Ferriera, *Visitas de Saúde*, pp. 108–515.

APPENDIX 4

Ships of the *Carreira da Índia* Reaching Bahia, 1663–1703

Year	Provenance					Total
	India	Mozambique	Portugal	Brazil	Not Specified	
1663		2				2
1664	1	1	2		1	5
1665	2				1	3
1666	1					1
1667	2					2
1668	1					1
1669	2					2
1670	1					1
1671	1					1
1672			1			1
1673	2		1			3
1674			2			2
1675	2				1	3
1676	1					1
1677	1					1
1678	1					1
1679			2(?)			2(?)
1680	1				1	2
1681	1				1	2
1682	1					1
1683	1					1
1684	1					1
1685	1					1
1687					1	1
1688	1					1
1689	2					2
1690	1					1
1691	1		1			2
1692	1				3(?)	4(?)
1696	1					1
1697	1					1
1698	1					1
1699	1		1			2
1700	1		1	1*	1	4
1701	2					2
1702	1					1
1703	1					1
TOTALS	39	3	9–11	1	7–10	59–64

SOURCE: Amaral Lapa, *A Bahia*, pp. 309, 333–36.
* This ship joined the *carreira* after being built in Brazil.

APPENDIX 5

The Bahian *Frota* of 1668

Ship (and type)	Captain (and home port)	Tobacco (rolls)	Cargo Sugar* (in *caixas/fechas*)			Hides		Brazil wood (*quintais*)	Ivory (tusks)
			branco	*mascavado*	*panella*	*meio sola*	*em cabello*		
Nossa Senhora do Livramento e Almas (*caravella*)	Francisco Cardozo Pereira (no port given)	825	507/3	....	....	805	....	....	....
São Francisco Xavier (*fragata*)	Domingos Escorcio (Madeira)	906	334/24	506	....	60	80	140	....
São Joachim (*fragata*)	António Francisco Aires (Lisbon)	813	337/21	82	....	305	....	....	....
São Antonio (*patacho*)	Francisco Franco Coresma (Peniche)	386	904/9	32	....	609	....	....	....
Nossa Senhora de Rosário e Almas (*fragata*)	João Ruis Samamede (Viana)	434	320/26	74	....	314	75	....	....

(APPENDIX 5, *continued*)

Ship (and type)	Captain (and home port)	Tobacco (rolls)	Cargo Sugar* (in *caixas/fechas*)				Hides		Brazil wood (*quintais*)	Ivory (tusks)
			branco	*mascavado*	*panella*	*meio sola*	*em cabello*			
São Francisco (*fragata*)	Manuel da Silva (Lisbon)	1,459	337/11	38	......	352	65	......	......
São Pedro (*não*)	João Fereira (Lisbon)	1,551	230/15	94	......	117	......	......	......
Nossa Senhora da Salvação e Chagas de Jesus (*navio*)	Antonio Rodrigues (Lisbon)	555	255/16	41	6	445	......	......	......
Santo António (*fragata*)	António Monteiro (Viana)	659	451/31	116	......	979	130	......	......
Santa Anna Maria (*não*)	Domingos Franco Bauptista (no port given)	2,609	490/41	99	......	83	100	......	......
Nossa Senhora da Conceição (*não*)	Manoel Álvares Maia (Lisbon)	836	508/21	82	......	320	80	140	30
	TOTALS	11,033	4,673/218	1,164	6	4,389	530	140	30

SOURCE: AHU, Bahia, Papéis Avulsos, *caixa* 10, manifests of June 23–27, 1668. This source also reveals that at least two ships from India accompanied the *frota* to Lisbon.

* Sugar figures are quite low, probably because of droughts: See Mauro, *Le Portugal*, p. 239.

APPENDIX 6

Prices and Estimated Annual Production of the Best White Bahian Sugar, 1655–1710

Year	Price (per arroba)	Quantity (in caixas)
1655	1,500 reis	
1656	1,000	
1660	1,090	
1665	1,100	
1666	1,300	
1669	1,200	
1675–76	1,000 (in Lisbon)	
1677	1,160	
1680	1,060	
1682	1,200	
1683		less than 10,000
1687	1,160	14,500–15,500
1688	800 (in Lisbon)	
1691	1,200	
1693		14,500
1697	1,500	
1698		14,000+
1699–1700	2,200	
1702	1,800	15,000
1703	1,600	
1704	1,600–1,700	
1705	1,600	
1707	1,350	
1708	1,350	14,000+
1710	1,350	15,000

Sources: Flory, "Bahian Society," pp. 26–27; Alfândega de Lisboa, *Reflexos Aduaneiros*, pp. 42, 46.

APPENDIX 7

A Note on Currency, Weights, and Measures

In the text and notes of this volume, I have provided equivalent values of units of currency, weight, and measurement as they were mentioned. For further information on currency, weights, and measures, see the following sources: Boxer, *The Golden Age of Brazil*, pp. 354–57; Russell-Wood, *Fidalgos and Philanthropists*, pp. 376–82; Lopes Sierra, *A Governor and His Image*, pp. 182–83; Serrão, ed., *DHP*, 3:369–74; and Simonsen, *História Econômica do Brasil*, pp. 462–64. An extended discussion of Portuguese currency during the latter half of the seventeenth century can be found in Teixeira de Aragão, *Descrição Geral*, passim (particularly 2:5–67). Full citations for these studies are given in the Bibliography.

NOTES

ABBREVIATIONS

AHMF	Arquivo Histórico do Ministerio das Finanças
AHU	Arquivo Histórico Ultramarino
ANTT	Arquivo Nacional da Torre do Tombo
BACL	Biblioteca da Academia das Ciências de Lisboa
BA	Biblioteca da Ajuda
BL	British Library
BNL	Biblioteca Nacional de Lisboa
DHP	*Dicionário de História de Portugal*
HAHR	*Hispanic American Historical Review*

NOTES

Chapter I

1. Edward Gaylord Bourne, *Spain in America, 1450–1580* (New York: Harper and Brothers, 1904), p. 128.
2. H. V. Livermore, *A New History of Portugal* (Cambridge: Cambridge University Press, 1969), p. 1.
3. Traditional estimates have given a population of between 1.1 and 2.0 million in 1640. Joel Serrão, ed., *Dicionário de História de Portugal (DHP)*, 4 vols. (Lisbon: Initiativas Editorais, 1971), 1:797. Recently, it has been estimated that the number was 1.3 million inhabitants. Joaquim Verissimo Serrão, *Uma Estimativa da População Portuguesa em 1640* (Lisbon: *separata* from *Memorias da Academia das Ciências*, vol. 16, 1975), p. 217.
4. It has been estimated that, during the seventeenth and early eighteenth centuries, a stream of people ranging in number from 2,000 to 10,000 annually flowed out of Portugal, mostly to Brazil. Vitorino Magalhães Godinho, *Estrutura da Antiga Sociedade Portuguesa*, 2nd ed. (Lisbon: Arcádia, 1975), p. 57.
5. One authority has estimated that toward the end of the Old Regime eighty percent of the active population was engaged in agricultural pursuits. Albert Silbert, *Le Portugal Méditerranéen à la Fin de l'Ancien Régime, XVIII^c—Début du XIX^c Siècle*, 2 vols. (Paris: S.E.V.P.E.N., 1966), 1:121.
6. An excellent discussion of Portugal's chronic grain shortages can be found in Vitorino Magalhães Godinho, "Le Problème du Pain dans l'Economie Portugaise. XV^c–XVI^c Siècles. Blé d'Europe et Blé des Iles," *Revista de Economia*, 12 (*fasc.* 3) (September 1959): 87–113.
7. Serrão, ed., *DHP*, 3:618–19.
8. João Pinto Ribeiro, *Uzurpação, Retenção, Restauração de Portugal* (Lisbon: Lourenço de Anvers, 1642), p. 4.
9. The most valuable account of the struggle for the Restoration remains the contemporary chronicle of D. Luís de Meneses (Count of Ericeira), *História de Portugal Restaurado*, 4 vols. (Oporto: Livraria Civilização, 1946). Other useful studies of the Restoration era not specifically cited in the present volume are: Eduardo d'Oliveira França, *Portugal na Época da Restauração* (São Paulo: Universidade de São Paulo, 1951); Edgar Prestage, *The Diplomatic Relations of Portugal with France, England, and Holland from 1640 to 1668* (Watford: Voss and Michael, Ltd., 1925); Hipólito Raposo, *Dona Luisa de Gusmão, Duquesa e Rainha (1613–1666)* (Lisbon: Empresa Nacional de Publicidade, 1947); and Theresa M. Schedel de Castello Branco, *Vida do Marques de Sande* (Lisbon: Livraria Ferin, 1971). Also see Biblioteca Nacional de Lisboa, *Exposição Bibliográfica da Restauração*, 2 vols. (Lisbon, 1940–1941).
10. António H. de Oliveira Marques, *History of Portugal*, 2nd ed., 2 vols. in 1 (New York: Columbia University Press, 1976), 1:332–33.
11. It should be emphasized, however, that in addition to sugar other Brazilian commodities, particularly tobacco and dyewood, accounted for sizable revenues. See Vito-

rino Magalhães Godinho, "Création et Dynamisme Économique du Monde Atlantique (1420–1670)," *Annales: ESC* 5 (January–March 1950):35–36.

12. Frédéric Mauro, *Le Portugal et l'Atlantique au XVIIe Siècle (1570–1670)* (Paris: S.E.V.P.E.N., 1960), pp. 512–13.

13. During D. Pedro II's reign, the Cortes met in 1668, 1674, 1679–1680, and 1697–1698. It was long assumed that the Cortes was also convened in 1677, but that assumption has been convincingly refuted in Luís Ferrand de Almeida, "Cortes de Lisboa em 1677?," *Revista Portuguesa de História* 12 (1969):383–88.

14. For a discussion of Vieira's importance as a literary figure, see Hernâni Cidade and Carlos Selvagem, *Cultura Portuguesa*, 18 vols. (Lisbon: Imprensa Nacional de Publicidade, 1967–1977), 9:76–92.

15. Ibid., 9:146–48; 10:43–44.

16. Irving A. Leonard, *Baroque Times in Old Mexico* (Ann Arbor: University of Michigan Press, 1959), p. vii.

17. A recently published and otherwise valuable survey of Portuguese history, for example, devoted only three pages to the period. See Marques, *History of Portugal*, 1:381–83. The following three studies by Vitorino Magalhães Godinho, though brief, are landmark explorations of the period: "Portugal, as Frotas do Açucar e as Frotas do Ouro (1670–1770)," *Revista de História* (São Paulo) 7 (1953):69–88; "Portugal and Her Empire," *The New Cambridge Modern History*, 14 vols. (Cambridge: Cambridge University Press, 1957–1970), 5:384–97; "Portugal and Her Empire, 1680–1720," ibid., 6:509–40.

Chapter II

1. Karl Marx, *Pre-Capitalist Economic Formations*, ed. Eric J. Hobsbawm, trans. Jack Cohen (New York: International Publishers, 1964), pp. 137–39. Further discussion of the "crisis" that befell the aristocracy can be found in François Billacois, "La Crise de la noblesse européene (1550–1650): Une Mise au point," *Revue d'Histoire Moderne et Contemporaine* 23 (1976):258–77; and Charles Jago, "The Crisis of the Aristocracy in Seventeenth Century Castile," *Past and Present* 84 (1979):60–90.

2. For a brief survey of the rise of absolutism in Europe, see Max Beloff, *The Age of Absolutism, 1660–1815* (New York: Harper and Row, Torchbooks, 1966). For a discussion of absolutism in Portugal, consult Eduardo d'Oliveira França, *O Poder real em Portugal e as origens do absolutismo* (São Paulo: Universidade de São Paulo, Faculdade de Filosofia, Ciências e Letras, 1946); and Serrão, ed., *DHP*, 1:8–14.

3. This summary account of the swearing-in ceremony is taken from the *Auto do Iuramento que o serenissimo Principe Dom Pedro Nosso Senhor Fez aos Tres Estados destes Reynos, de os Reger, e Governar no impedimento perpetuo d'El Rey Dom Affonso VI* (Lisbon: António Craesbeeck de Mello, 1669), which can be found in BA 44–XIII–42, fls. 236–264v. Another description of the baroque splendor of the Paço da Ribeira can be read in John Villiers, "Portuguese Society in the Reigns of D. Pedro II and D. João V 1680–1750" (unpublished Ph.D. dissertation, Cambridge University, 1962), pp. 91–93. Descriptions of the seating assignments for joint sessions of the Cortes can be found in Alexandre da Paixão, *Monstruosidades do Tempo e da Fortuna* (1662–1680), 4 vols. (Barcelos: Companhia Editora do Minho, 1938–1939), 1:58–60.

4. Damião Peres, ed., *História de Portugal*, 7 vols. in 8 with supplement and indexes (Barcelos: Portucalense Editora, 1928–1966), 1:116–17.

5. Henrique Schaeffer, *Historia de Portugal*, 13 vols. (Lisbon: José Baptista Moranda, 1842–1847), 13:210–11.

NOTES TO CHAPTER II 293

6. Harold V. Livermore, *A History of Portugal* (Cambridge: Cambridge University Press, 1947), pp. 321–22.

7. Presently, there is but one book-length biography devoted to D. Pedor II, and that is a slim, unsatisfactory study. See Luís Chaves, *D. Pedro II* (Lisbon: Empresa Nacional da Publicidade, 1959).

8. António Caetano de Souza, *Historia Geneologica da Casa Real Portugueza*, 12 vols. (Lisbon: José Antonio da Silva, 1735–1748), 7:433.

9. Villiers, "Portuguese Society," pp. 83–84.

10. "Memoire touchant le Portugal," BL, MS Sloane 2294, fls. 1–5. This anonymous account is translated in A. D. Francis, *The Methuens and Portugal, 1691–1708* (Cambridge: Cambridge University Press, 1966), pp. 26–28. In at least two instances, D. Pedro also became involved with D. Maria's ladies-in-waiting. See Afonso Eduadro Martins Zuquete, *Nobreza de Portugal*, 3 vols. (Lisbon: Editorial Enciclopédia, 1960), 1:559.

11. Pedro de Azevedo, *Doença e Morte de Dom Pedro II* (Oporto: n.p., 1911), passim. An English diplomat of the period observed that D. Pedro II was the only modern sovereign for whom good sex caused so much suffering. See Edgar Prestage, *Memórias sobre Portugal no reinado de D. Pedro II* (Lisbon: Archivo Histórico de Portugal, 1935), p. 9, n. 3.

12. Quoted in Francis, *The Methuens*, pp. 27–28. Another contemporary portrait of D. Pedro II's character can be found in Joaquim Verissimo Serrão, "Uma Relação do reino de Portugal em 1684," *Boletim da Biblioteca da Universidade* 25 (Coimbra, 1962):83–86.

13. Discussion of corporatism in medieval and early modern Portugal can be found in Howard J. Wiarda, *Corporatism and Development: The Portuguese Experience* (Amherst: University of Massachusetts Press, 1977), pp. 15–17, 29–43.

14. Godinho, *Estrutura*, p. 106.

15. Antonio Domíngez Ortiz, *Las Clases Privilegiadas en la España del Antiguo Régimen* (Madrid: Ediciones ISTMO, 1973), p. 27.

16. Earl J. Hamilton, *El Florescimento del capitalismo y otros ensayos* (Madrid: Revista de Occidente, 1948), p. 128.

17. Godinho, *Estrutura*, p. 86.

18. It should be noted here that the estimated number of nobles in Portugal is meant to include all individuals who claimed (though not necessarily correctly) noble status. Further, it has been assumed that the ranks of the nobility grew in relation to the size of the general population during the early modern era. This assumption, however, must remain tentative until quantitative analysis has been brought to bear on the problem. During the fourteenth century, it has been estimated that the nobility did not exceed five percent of the population. Serrão, ed., *DHP*, 3:149.

19. Godinho, *Estrutura*, p. 97.

20. Godinho, "Portugal and Her Empire, 1680–1720," p. 537.

21. Ibid., p. 538. It should be noted that there were also definite constraints on colonial *donatários*. At first sight, their holdings appear analogous to feudal properties, but there were significant differences. *Donatários* in Brazil and the Atlantic islands, for example, were not permitted to strike their own coinage or raise independent armies. Serrão, ed., *DHP*, 1:476.

22. Godinho, "Portugal and Her Empire, 1680–1720," p. 538.

23. Ibid.

24. Ibid., pp. 538–39.

25. Ibid., p. 539.
26. Serrão, ed., *DHP*, 3:154.
27. Villiers, "Portuguese Society," pp. 98–99. For one of various contemporary genealogies of the Portuguese nobility, consult Francisco Coelho, *Thesouro da Nobreza* (Lisbon, 1675), a copy of which exists in ANTT, Livraria (no. C3 E2 P7).
28. Villiers, "Portuguese Society," pp. 100–101.
29. Ibid., p. 114. Villiers noted, however, that in the eighteenth century restrictions on induction into military orders, particularly that of Christ, had become so lax that commoners with pretensions to noble status, including merchants, surgeons, and others had attained membership. Ibid., p. 115. For a highly favorable view of the Order of Christ, see Vieira Guimarães, *A Ordem de Cristo* (Lisbon: Imprensa Nacional, 1936). A far more useful discussion of the order can be found in Francis A. Dutra, "Membership in the Order of Christ in the Seventeenth Century: Its Rights, Privileges, Obligations," *The Americas* 27 (1970):3–25.
30. Serrão, ed., *DHP*, 3:154–55.
31. Ibid., p. 155.
32. Ibid.
33. Angel Sánchez Rivero, ed., *Viaje de Cosme de Medicis por España y Portugal (1668–1669)* (Madrid: Centro de Estudios Históricos, 1933), p. 254.
34. Serrão, ed., *DHP*, 1:425–26. Two years earlier, the crown had demonstrated its regard for the young marquis by exempting him from payment of the *décima militar*, an extraordinary tax on both nobles and commoners levied by the Cortes in 1641. See José Justino de Andrade e Silva, *Collecção Chronologica da Legislação Portugueza (1603–1702)*, 10 vols. (Lisbon: F. X. de Souza, 1854–1859), 6:316; and Serrão, ed. *DHP*, 1:788–89.
35. Virginia Rau, "Large Scale Agricultural Enterprise in Post-Medieval Portugal," in *Contributions to the First International Conference of Economic History* (Stockholm) (Paris: Mouton, 1960), p. 430. Professor Rau noted in this study that she was preparing a larger work on the Melo family and its landed property, but apparently it was not completed before her death in 1975. Her pioneering scholarship is outlined in Charles Verlinden, "Virginia Rau and the Economic History of Portugal," *Journal of European Economic History* 4 (1975):243–45.
36. For short biographical sketches of D. Nuno (who, like D. Pedro II, awaits a biographer), consult Serrão, ed., *DHP*, 1:425–27; and J. M. Esteves Pereira and Guilherme Rodrigues, *Portugal: Dicionario Historico, Biografico, Bibliografico, Heraldico, Chorografico, Numismatico e Artistico*, 7 vols. (Lisbon: João Romano Torres, 1904–1915), 2:590–91. A brief evaluation of Melo's influence is in Francis, *The Methuens*, pp. 32–33.
37. Villiers, "Portuguese Society," p. 135.
38. Francis A. Dutra, "Duarte Coelho Pereira, First Lord-Proprietor of Pernambuco: The Beginning of a Dynasty," *The Americas* 29 (1973):415.
39. C. R. Boxer, *Salvador de Sá and the Struggle for Brazil and Angola, 1602–1686* (London: Athlone Press, 1952), pp. 139–40.
40. Ibid., pp. 152–54, 196.
41. Virginia Rau, "Fortunas ultramarinas e a nobreza portuguesa no século XVII," *Revista Portuguesa de História* 8 (1959):5–7.
42. Additional information on Teles da Silva can be found in Boxer, *Salvador de Sá*, passim. A useful prosopographical study of colonial governors, which showed that most were drawn from the nobility of the sword, is Ross L. Bardwell, "The Governors of

Portugal's South Atlantic Empire in the Seventeenth Century: Social Background, Qualifications, Selection and Reward" (unpublished Ph.D. dissertation, University of California, Santa Barbara, 1974).

43. For a brief discussion of the attitude of contemporary Spanish nobility toward commerce, consult Jaime Vicens Vives, *Historia Social y Económica de España*, 4 vols. in 5 (Barcelona: Editorial Teide, 1957–1959), 3:292–94.

44. Rau, "Fortunas ultramarinas," pp. 7–8. Moreover, the stigma placed on noble involvement in commercial activity, even in Spain, was fading by 1700. Henry Kamen, *The Iron Century: Social Change in Europe, 1550–1660* (New York: Praeger, 1972), pp. 135–36.

45. BNL Fundo Geral 510, fls. 157v–158.

46. Charles Jago, "The Influence of Debt on the Relations between Crown and Aristocracy in Seventeenth-Century Castile," *Economic History Review*, 2nd series, 26 (1973):233–34.

47. Godinho, *Estrutura*, pp. 85–86.

48. Ibid., p. 88.

49. Ibid., pp. 87–88.

50. C. R. Boxer, *The Golden Age of Brazil, 1695–1750* (Berkeley: University of California Press, 1969), p. 282.

51. Stuart B. Schwartz, "Free Labor in a Slave Economy: The *Lavradores de Cana* of Colonial Bahia," in Dauril Alden, ed., *Colonial Roots of Modern Brazil* (Berkeley: University of California Press, 1973), p. 178.

52. Villiers, "Portuguese Society," p. 149. (1 cruzado = 400 reis. One real was the basic unit of Portuguese money of account.)

53. Ibid., p. 138.

54. Ibid., p. 157.

55. Ibid., p. 138.

56. Godinho, *Estrutura*, p. 86.

57. Fortunato de Almeida, *Historia da Igreja em Portugal*, 4 vols. in 6 (Coimbra: Imprensa Academica, 1910–1922), 3 (pt. 1):521–22.

58. Villiers, "Portuguese Society," p. 157.

59. Almeida, *Historia da Igreja*, 3 (pt. 1):522. Expansion of the clerical estate did not go unimpeded, however. In 1654, for example, D. João IV resolved that no new *conventos* be built. Andrade e Silva, *Collecção*, 7:293. Furthermore, D. Pedro II tried to hold creation of new monastic communities to a minimum. See promulgations approving three such establishments in ibid., 10:207–08, 265, 397. It was during D. Pedro II's reign that the Oratorian order entered Portugal. Almeida, *Historia da Igreja*, 3 (pt. 1): 486–89.

60. Andrade e Silva, *Collecção*, 8:183.

61. Ibid., 9:30–31.

62. Almeida, *Historia de Igreja*, 3 (pt. 1):205–6.

63. Andrade e Silva, *Collecção*, 10:190.

64. BA, 44–XIV–1, fls. 167–167v.

65. ANTT, Gaveta 23, *maço* 8, nos. 18, 19.

66. Andrade e Silva, *Collecção*, 10:477, 499.

67. Ibid., 10:266.

68. Aurélio de Oliveira, *A Abadia de Tibães e o Seu Domínio (1630–1680)* (Oporto: Faculdade de Letras do Porto, 1974). It should be noted that Oliveira's work is well complemented by a recent study of a Brazilian convent. See Susan Soeiro, "A Baroque

Nunnery: The Economic and Social Role of a Colonial Convent: Santa Clara do Destêrro, Salvador, Bahia, 1677–1800" (unpublished Ph.D. dissertation, New York University, 1974).

69. For a map locating the Benedictine monasteries active in 1763, see Serrão, ed., *DHP*, 1:327.
70. Ibid., 1:739.
71. A map showing the abbey's holdings can be found in Oliveira, *A Abadia de Tibães*, p. 60, facing.
72. Ibid., pp. 60–61.
73. Ibid., p. 84.
74. The origins and nature of the *prazo* system are discussed in Pereira and Rodrigues, *Portugal*, 5:1044–45.
75. Oliveira, *A Abadia de Tibães*, pp. 125, 188, 194.
76. Ibid., pp. 149–65.
77. Ibid., pp. 265–66.
78. Ibid., pp. 213–15, 225.
79. Serrão, ed., *DHP*, 1:739.
80. Villiers, "Portuguese Society," p. 159.
81. Serrão, ed., *DHP*, 1:591.
82. Ibid.
83. Villiers, "Portuguese Society," p. 166.
84. For a discussion of the church at Tibães, see particularly the following two works by Robert C. Smith: *Cipriano da Cruz: Escultor de Tibães* (Oporto: Livraria Civilização, 1968); *A Igreja de S. Bento da Vitória a Luz dos "Estados" de Tibães* (Oporto: Fernando Machado, n.d.).

Chapter III

1. A comparable percentage for an earlier era can be found in António H. de Oliveira Marques, "Estratificação Económico-Social de uma Vila Portuguesa da Idade Média," in *Ensaios de História Medieval Portuguesa* (Lisbon: Portugália Editora, 1965), p. 174.
2. Kamen, *The Iron Century*, p. 199.
3. Ibid., pp. 166–67.
4. Ibid., p. 167.
5. For a list of officials on the Lisbon city council payroll in 1661, see Eduardo Freire de Oliveira, *Elementos para a História do Município de Lisboa*, 17 vols. (Lisbon: Tipografia Universal, 1882–1911), 6:279–81.
6. Godinho, *Estrutura*, pp. 102–3.
7. Kamen, *The Iron Century*, p. 188.
8. Godinho, *Estrutura*, p. 103.
9. This subject is treated at length in Koenraad W. Swart, *Sale of Offices in the Seventeenth Century* (The Hague: Martinus Nijhoff, 1949).
10. Freire de Oliveira, *Elementos*, 8:424. This was neither the first nor the last time such a decree was deemed necessary. In 1644 D. João IV decreed against the accumulation of offices. Andrade e Silva, *Collecção*, 6:255. D. Pedro's first decree apparently did not sufficiently curtail the widespread practice, for a similar order was issued in 1686. Freire de Oliveira, *Elementos*, 8:424, n. 2, 562–63.
11. Ibid., 8:583.
12. António de Oliveira, *A Vida Económica e Social de Coimbra de 1537 a 1640*, 2 vols. (Coimbra: Imprensa da Universidade, 1971–1972), 1:377.

13. This term, which is nearly interchangeable with *legistas*, is commonly associated with graduates in law. Serrão, ed. *DHP*, 2:710-11.

14. Stuart B. Schwartz, *Sovereignty and Society in Colonial Brazil* (Berkeley: University of California Press, 1973), p. 14.

15. Stuart B. Schwartz, "Magistracy and Society in Colonial Brazil," *HAHR* 50 (1970):715. Much work remains to be done on the *letrado* class in Portugal. But, for a valuable discussion of their counterparts in Spain, see Richard L. Kagan, *Students and Society in Early Modern Spain* (Baltimore: Johns Hopkins University Press, 1974), pp. 77-105.

16. Pereira and Rodrigues, *Portugal*, 3:501.

17. BNL Fundo Geral 1532, fl. 149.

18. Freire de Oliveira, *Elementos*, 8:370.

19. Oliveira, *A Vida Económica e Social de Coimbra*, 1:381-83.

20. Quoted in Villiers, "Portuguese Society," p. 175.

21. Freire de Oliveira, *Elementos*, 6:280.

22. Schwartz, *Sovereignty and Society*, p. 15.

23. Frédéric Mauro, "Mercadores e Mercadores-Banqueiros Portugueses no Século XVII," in *Nôva História e Nôvo Mundo* (São Paulo: Editora Perspectiva, 1969), pp. 132-33.

24. Ibid., p. 133.

25. Ibid. It should be noted, however, that during the first half of the seventeenth century the great merchant banker families of Lisbon moved closer to purely banking activities, especially in their dealings with the Castilian crown. See James C. Boyajian, "The Portuguese Bankers and the International Payments Mechanism, 1626-1647" (unpublished Ph.D. dissertation, University of California, Berkeley, 1978), passim.

26. António Saraiva, *Inquisição e Cristãos-Novos*, 3rd ed. (Oporto: Editorial Inova, 1969), pp. 197-99.

27. David Grant Smith, "Old Christian Merchants and the Foundation of the Brazil Company, 1649," *HAHR* 54 (1974):233-59; "The Mercantile Class of Portugal in the Seventeenth Century: A Socio-Economic Study of the Merchants of Lisbon and Bahia, 1620-1690" (unpublished Ph.D. dissertation, University of Texas, 1975).

28. Smith, "The Mercantile Class," pp. 18-19. Smith also estimated that the Lisbon mercantile class numbered about two hundred in 1650. But this figure, which is admittedly hostage to extant documentation, seems too low. Also, it should be noted that there were many foreign merchants (and their descendants) in Portugal. If one were to speculate as to the size of the mercantile community in late seventeenth-century Portugal, it would probably exceed fifteen hundred.

29. Smith, "The Mercantile Class," pp. 31-32.

30. João Lúcio de Azevedo, *História dos Cristãos Novos Portugueses*, 2nd ed. (Lisbon: Livraria Clássica Editora, 1975), p. 21.

31. Smith, "The Mercantile Class," p. 32.

32. Ibid., pp. 25, 31.

33. Saraiva, *Inquisição e Cristãos-Novos*, p. 192.

34. Smith, "The Mercantile Class," pp. 138-39.

35. Ibid., pp. 54-64.

36. Ibid., p. 103.

37. Rau, "Fortunas ultramarinas," p. 8. Frédéric Mauro, however, is not convinced that Portugal was comparably afflicted by the "betrayal of the bourgeoisie" and rightly asserts that more research needs to be done before the question can be adequately

answered. "Mercadores e Mercadores-Banqueiros," p. 132. A discussion of the bourgeois "betrayal" can be found in Fernand Braudel, *The Mediterranean and the Mediterranean World in the Age of Philip II*, 2 vols., trans. Siân Reynolds (New York: Harper and Row, 1972), 2:725–31. Also see Kamen, *The Iron Century*, pp. 196–98.

38. Smith, "The Mercantile Class," p. 117.

39. Ibid., p. 102. Smith observed that Mauro's categories are to be used with caution when applied to any given merchant at any given time since they may simply denote stages in an individual's business career. Ibid., p. 73.

40. Ibid., p. 71.

41. According to Smith, the assets of Gaspar Vaz de Siqueira, a medium merchant who specialized in textiles, especially those of English manufacture, totaled about 10,000 cruzados in 1652. Ibid., pp. 74–76.

42. Eulalia Maria Lahmeyer Lobo, *Aspectos da Influencia dos Homens de Negócio na Política Comercial Ibero-Americana (Século XVII)* (Rio de Janeiro: n.p., 1963), p. 50.

43. Oliveira, *A Vida Económica e Social de Coimbra*, 1:390–91.

44. Serrão, ed., *DHP*, 1:399–400.

45. For brief discussions of *barqueiros* and *almocreves*, see ibid., 1:119–20, 301–2.

46. Ibid., 1:400.

47. Ibid., 3:44. In some instances, artisan groups scattered throughout Lisbon were ordered to congregate together. In 1706, for example, gauze workers faced a fine of 4,000 reis if they failed to move their shops to an assigned street. Freire de Oliveira, *Elementos*, 10:326–28.

48. Serrão, ed., *DHP*, 3:45.

49. Numerous works on the Casas dos Vinte e Quatro have appeared, among the most useful of which are: Marcelo Caetano, *A História da Organização dos Mesteres da Cidade de Lisboa* (Lisbon, 1959); António Cruz, *Os Mesteres do Porto*, vol. 1 (Oporto, 1943); Franz-Paul de Almeida Langhans, *A Casa dos Vinte e Quatro de Lisboa* (Lisbon, 1948), and *As Corporações dos Ofícios Mecânicos*, 2 vols. (Lisbon, 1943–1946); J. Pinto Loureiro, *Casa dos Vinte e Quatro de Coimbra* (Coimbra, 1947).

50. Serrão, ed., *DHP*, 1:515. A document of 1788 shows that at least sixty-five different artisan groups were recognized and formally organized in eighteenth-century Lisbon. Langhans, *A Casa dos Vinte e Quatro de Lisboa*, p. 39.

51. Langhans, *As Corporações*, 1:xlix. Prof. Harry Bernstein recently completed a manuscript entitled, *The Portuguese Juiz do Povo* (Lisbon, forthcoming), which covers the period between 1640 and 1834. This study should add considerably to knowledge of the Lisbon casa.

52. ANTT, Corpo Cronológico, part 2, *maço* 373, doc. 148.

53. Serrão, ed., *DHP*, 1:515.

54. Fortunato de Almeida, *Historia de Portugal*, 6 vols. (Coimbra: Imprensa da Universidade, 1922–1929), 5:127.

55. BNL, Fundo Geral 851, fls. 173–74.

56. Cruz, *Os Mesteres do Porto*, 1:xlviii–1.

57. Langhans, *As Corporações*, 1:xlviii.

58. Ibid., 2:484. Additional reasons for the revisions may have been the superabundance of *sapateiros* in Portugal, a temporary shortage of shoe leather, and inroads made by foreign imports. Freire de Oliveira, *Elementos*, 9:280–81, 557.

59. Langhans, *A Casa dos Vinte e Quatro de Lisboa*, p. 128.

60. Cruz, *Os Mesteres do Porto*, p. 43.

61. Andrade e Silva, *Collecção*, 10:374–75. For a discussion of the distinction between *regimento* and *compromisso*, see Langhans, *Corporações*, 1:xxxix.

62. Andrade e Silva, *Collecção*, 10:461.
63. In 1693, John Methuen, the English ambassador extraordinary, had petitioned D. Pedro II, complaining that Portuguese coopers were exacting exorbitant prices for barrels and attempting to prevent English merchants from procuring them outside their monopoly. Freire de Oliveira, *Elementos*, 9:313–14.
64. Langhans, *As Corporações*, 1:lxxiii.
65. ANTT, Corpo Cronológico, part 2, *maço* 373, doc. 148.
66. Smith, "The Mercantile Class," pp. 43–46.
67. Artur de Magalhães Basto, "A 'Nobreza' do Oficio de Ourives," *Estudos Portuenses* 2 (Oporto, 1963):211–13.
68. Freire de Oliveira, *Elementos*, 8:388, 421, n. 1.
69. Ibid., 9:203–4.
70. Cruz, *Os Mesteres do Porto*, pp. 209–11.
71. Freire de Oliveira, *Elementos*, 9:406–8.
72. Ibid., 8:285.
73. Serrão, ed., *DHP*, 3:458.
74. Langhans, *As Corporações*, 1:113.
75. Andrade e Silva, *Collecção*, 10:17–18.
76. Ibid., p. 456.
77. Ibid., pp. 414–15.
78. Joel Serrão, ed., *Alterações de Évora (1637)* (Lisbon: Portugália Editora, 1967), pp. xvii–xviii. However, the recently completed studies of António and Aurélio Oliveira have added much to historical knowledge of the lower classes in Portugal.
79. Serrão, ed., *DHP*, 1:31.
80. Godinho, *Estrutura*, p. 104.
81. Freire de Oliveira, *Elementos*, 8:15.
82. Ibid., pp. 124, 130, 132.
83. Data on the wide variety of popular-class employments in the capital can be found in Maria Lourdes Akola de Cunha Meira do Carmo Silva Neto, "A Freguesia de Sta Catarina de Lisboa no I.º Quartel do Século XVIII" (unpublished Ph.D. dissertation, University of Lisbon, 1956), pp. 124–31.
84. This is not to say, however, that lower-class women were any less subject to antifeminine constraints, beliefs, and prejudices than their upper-class counterparts. Women of lower social standing worked to make ends meet, not because they were career minded. Undoubtedly, most would have exchanged their jobs for the sheltered, leisurely lives of privileged females. The only group of women who seem to have enjoyed a measure of personal independence and influence were widows. For a discussion of the inferior status of women in Portugal and its empire, see C. R. Boxer, *Women in Iberian Expansion Overseas, 1415–1815* (New York: Oxford University Press, 1975), especially pp. 53, 60, 101–2. Also see Schwartz, "Free Labor in a Slave Economy," pp. 178–79.
85. Freire de Oliveira, *Elementos*, 9:520.
86. ANTT, Junta do Tabaco, Receita e Despesa, *maço* 201. The rules governing the operation of tobacco shops, which were published in 1676, can also be found in this *maço*.
87. "... he ocupação mais pertence a mulheres, he preciso em muitos dellas, acetar maridos por fiadores, por não haver outros." Ibid., Consultas, *maço* 2, September 6, 1680.
88. Freire de Oliveira, *Elementos*, 9:551, 556. The wealthy residents and ecclesiastics of Lisbon apparently employed much the same tactic, sending servants to buy up food-

stuffs for the *quintas* and *conventos* before they reached the city. Ibid., p. 553, n. 2.

89. Ibid., pp. 567–70. The French consul also complained that merchants from his country resident in Portugal who imported bread into Lisbon were being damaged by the sharp practices of the *mulheres poderosas*. Ibid., p. 576, n. 1.

90. Ibid., p. 551, 10:188–90.

91. Oliveira, *A Vida Económica e Social de Coimbra*, 1:351. Furthermore, as John Villiers astutely observed, "the status of 'nobreza' penetrated very far down the social scale while the stigma of 'mecanica' applied surprisingly far up it." "Portuguese Society," p. 174.

92. Freire de Oliveira, *Elementos*, 8:525–28.

93. Ibid., pp. 546–47.

94. ANTT, Junta do Tabaco, Consultas, *maço* 3, October 11, 1688.

95. Serrão, ed., *DHP*, 3:458.

96. The best short survey of imperial Portugal's far-flung Misericórdias is in Serrão, ed., *DHP*, 3:76–80. Further information on the charitable institutions can be found in the sources cited there and in A. J. R. Russell-Wood, *Fidalgos and Philanthropists: The Santa Casa da Misericórdia of Bahia, 1550–1755* (Berkeley: University of California Press, 1968).

97. Freire de Oliveira, *Elementos*, 7:370.

98. In 1675, for example, soldiers violently seized a shipment of coal and then sold it off to the highest bidders. Ibid., 8:107.

99. Fernando Castelo-Branco, *Lisboa Seiscentista*, 3rd ed. (Lisbon: Gráfica Santelmo, 1969), pp. 201–13.

100. Freire de Oliveira, *Elementos*, 8:551.

101. Ibid., 7:255, 408–9, 452–53.

102. A. C. Teixeira de Aragão, *Descrição Geral e Histórica das Moedas Cunhadas em Nome dos Reis, Regentes e Governadores de Portugal*, 2nd ed., 3 vols. (Oporto: Livraria Fernando Machado, 1964), 2:308.

103. Vicens Vives, *Historia Social y Económica*, 3:322.

104. Oliveira, *A Abadia de Tibães*, pp. 52, 215.

105. F. Adolfo Coelho, *Os Ciganos em Portugal* (Lisbon: Imprensa Nacional, 1892), passim.

106. ANTT, Junta do Tabaco, Consultas, *maço* 4, August 29, 1690.

107. Ibid., Decretos, *maço* 51, March 21, 1702.

108. " . . . nesta cidade andan de noite com grande devassidão e ousadia, muitos ladrões, fazendos varios roubos, e outros insultos." Andrade e Silva, *Collecção*, 6:227. This 1644 description of the situation in Lisbon probably applied equally well a generation later.

109. Freire de Oliveira, *Elementos*, 7:171.

110. Mauro, *Le Portugal*, p. 147; Godinho, *Estrutura*, pp. 84–85. It remains to be shown, however, whether this oft-repeated percentage remained as high a century later.

111. Joaquim Romero Magalhães, *Para o Estudo do Algarve Económico durante o Século XVI* (Lisbon: Edições Cosmos, 1970), p. 69.

112. Serrão, ed., *DHP*, 2:79.

113. Peres, ed., *História de Portugal*, 6:373–74.

114. Freire de Oliveira, *Elementos*, 9:132–33. Foreigners also noted their presence, often referring to their involvement in criminal activity. See, for example, Castelo-Branco, *Lisboa Seiscentista*, pp. 212–13.

115. Godinho, *Estrutura*, pp. 84–85.
116. Freire de Oliveira, *Elementos* 10:330–32.
117. Andrade e Silva, *Collecção*, 10:154. Upon his death in 1706, D. Pedro II freed the slaves in his household. This apparently became rather common practice during the reign of his son, D. João V. Villiers, "Portuguese Society," pp. 197–98. For a discussion of the brotherhoods of Brazil, see A. J. R. Russell-Wood, "Black and Mulatto Brotherhoods in Colonial Brazil: A Study in Collective Behavior," *HAHR* 54 (1974):567–602.
118. Serrão, ed., *DHP*, 2:79.
119. C. R. Boxer, *Race Relations in the Portuguese Colonial Empire, 1415–1825* (Oxford: Oxford University Press, 1963), p. 123.
120. Ibid., p. 29.
121. BA, 44–XIII–43, fls. 128–128v.
122. Quoted in Serrão, ed., *DHP*, 1:583. Despite the general resentment felt toward gypsies and the constant effort to rid Portugal of them, some performed valuable service for the crown. During the Restoration campaign, about 250 served in the king's frontier forces and were exempted from an expulsion order. Andrade e Silva, *Collecção*, 7:26–27. In 1646, one gypsy, Jeronimo da Corta, was even commended to the king for his valiant service. BNL, Fundo Geral, mss. 13, no. 18.
123. Peres, ed., *História de Portugal*, 6:371–72.
124. " . . . e como tães e razão que não aprendam nem usem do dito officios negros, mulatos, nem indios . . . por razão dos grandes furtos, falsidades e enganos que poderão fazer e usar em officio de tanta importancia e credito . . . por serem os tães negros, mulatos e indios do ordinario ladrões por natureza, e de pouca verdade e confiança, como a experiencia tantas vezes tem mostrado." Freire de Oliveira, *Elementos*, 10:170.
125. Ibid., 9:18.
126. Walter Ullmann, *The Individual and Society in the Middle Ages* (Baltimore: Johns Hopkins University Press, 1966), pp. 22–23.
127. Braudel, *The Mediterranean*, 2:709–10.
128. Ibid., 2:732. In the case of Portuguese merchants, it has been suggested that they had little alternative but to "defect." Smith, "The Mercantile Class," pp. 181–84.

Chapter IV

1. Saraiva, *Inquisição e Cristãos-Novos*, passim. See especially pp. 208, 317–19.
2. Smith, "The Mercantile Class," pp. 195–205.
3. Ibid., pp. 163, 209.
4. Paixão, *Monstruosidades*, 3:61–62. The quoted stanza was left in Portuguese since it does not readily lend itself to translation in verse.
5. William Bromley, *Several Years Travels through Portugal, Spain, Italy, Germany, Prussia, Sweden, Denmark and the United Provinces* (London: A. Roper, 1702), p. 6.
6. BA 44–XIII–43, fl. 117v.
7. Saraiva, *Inquisição e Cristãos-Novos*, p. 200.
8. Roque Monteiro Paim, *Perfidia judaica, Christus Vindex, Manus Principis Ecclesiae ab Apostatis liberata* (Madrid, 1671).
9. Azevedo, *História dos Cristãos Novos*, p. 296.
10. Smith, "The Mercantile Class," pp. 208–9.
11. Serrão, ed., *DHP*, 3:776.
12. The standard work on the founding of the Portuguese Inquisition is Alexandre

Herculano, *History of the Origin and Establishment of the Inquisition in Portugal*, trans. John C. Branner (New York: AMS Press reprint, 1968).

13. Smith, "The Mercantile Class," p. 204.

14. I. S. Révah, "Les Marranes," *Revue de Etudes Juives*, series 3, tome 1, vol. 118 (1959–1960):53–55. Further discussion of the nature of Marrano belief will be found in Cecil Roth, "The Religion of the Marranos," *Jewish Quarterly Review* 22 (1931):1–33.

15. Révah, "Les Marranes," p. 53.

16. Saraiva, *Inquisição e Cristãos-Novos*, pp. 237–39.

17. Henry Kamen, *The Spanish Inquisition* (New York: New American Library, 1965), p. 138.

18. A scholarly study of the financial operations of the Portuguese Inquisition has yet to be written, but an auto-da-fé was certainly its most expensive ceremonial activity. The cost of the 1646 Lisbon auto-da-fé, for which there is a detailed breakdown of expenditures, ran to 208,664 reis, about 522 cruzados. António Baião, *Episódios Dramáticos da Inquisição Portuguesa*, 2nd ed., 3 vols. (Lisbon: Seara Nova, 1936–1938), 3:210–14.

19. Almeida, *História da Igreja*, 3 (pt. 3):244.

20. Saraiva, *Inquisição e Cristãos-Novos*, pp. 253–54.

21. Azevedo, *História dos Cristãos Novos*, p. 259.

22. Even though the Holy Office, as noted above, had jurisdiction over many areas besides that of judaizing, it is suggestive that the vast bulk of records (in this case, *processos*), over 40,000 of which are preserved in the Torre do Tombo in Lisbon, were concerned with "the prosecution, if not the persecution, of apostate New Christians." Smith, "The Mercantile Class," pp. 215–16.

23. Saraiva, *Inquisição e Cristãos-Novos*, p. 257.

24. John Stevens, *The Ancient and Present State of Portugal* (London: W. Bray, 1713), p. 136.

25. Saraiva, *Inquisição e Cristãos-Novos*, pp. 240–41. It seems, however, that individuals of sufficient influence could become *familiares* despite their having questionable backgrounds. Villiers, "Portuguese Society," p. 338.

26. BNL, Fundo Geral, 6504, fls. 99–100v; Andrade e Silva, *Collecção*, 9:319–20.

27. Villiers, "Portuguese Society," p. 339.

28. Saraiva, *Inquisição e Cristãos-Novos*, pp. 253–54.

29. BNL Fundo Geral 730, fl. 168.

30. Saraiva, *Inquisição e Cristãos-Novos*, pp. 255–56. The revenues of the Lisbon city council in both 1669 and 1670 were around 27,000 cruzados. Oliveira, *Elementos*, 7:136, 204.

31. For a firsthand account of life in the prison of the Lisbon tribunal during the early nineteenth century, which was probably similar to that of D. Pedro II's reign, see "Extracts from a Narrative of the Persecution of Hippolyto Joseph da Costa Pereira Furtado de Mendonca, a Native of Colonia-do-Sacramento, on the River La Plata," in Philip Limborch, *The History of the Inquisition* (London: printed for W. Simpkin and R. Marshall, 1816), pp. 521–30.

32. "Impressões dum Auto-da-fé Celebrado em Coimbra, nos Fins do Século XVII," in Baião, *Episódios Dramáticos*, 3:147–54.

33. A brief discussion of quietism (or more appropriately *molinosismo*, after its chief proponent, the Aragonese priest Miguel de Molinos [1640–1696]) can be found in Serrão, ed., *DHP*, 3:523–26.

34. "Impressões dum Auto-da-fé," p. 148.

35. Ibid., p. 153.
36. Michael Geddes, "A View of the Court of the Inquisition in Portugal with a LIST of the Prisoners that came forth in an Act of the Faith Celebrated at Lisbon, in the Year 1682," *Miscellaneous Tracts*, 3 vols. (London: printed for A. and J. Churchill, 1702), in vol. 1, pp. 389–448.
37. "Impressões dum Auto-da-fé," p. 149.
38. Ibid., pp. 152–54.
39. Geddes, "A View of the Court," 1:416.
40. Baião, *Episódios Dramáticos*, 3:184–85.
41. Smith, "The Mercantile Class," p. 232.
42. Ibid., p. 251.
43. The best available discussion of the antagonism between Jesuit and inquisitor can be found in I. S. Révah, "Les Jésuites portugais contre l'Inquisition: La Campagne pour la fondation de la Compagnie Générale du Commerce du Brésil," *Revista do Livro* (Rio de Janeiro) 3–4 (1956):29–53. The most convincing argument for inquisitorial opposition to the Restoration is in Serrão, ed., *DHP*, 3:621–24.
44. Saraiva, *Inquisição e Cristãos-Novos*, p. 249.
45. C. R. Boxer, "A Great Luso-Brazilian Figure, Padre António Vieira, S.J., 1608–1697," *Diamante* 5 (1957):4. The venerable but still most satisfactory biography of the illustrious Jesuit is João Lúcio de Azevedo, *História de António Vieira*, 2nd ed., 2 vols. (Lisbon: Livraria Clássica, 1931).
46. The origins of *sebastianismo*, the belief that young King Sebastião, who had perished in battle against Moslems in North Africa in 1578, would one day return, are examined in João Lúcio de Azevedo, *A Evolução do Sebastianismo*, 2nd ed. (Lisbon: A. M. Texeira, 1947). Also see Serrão, ed., *DHP*, 3:810–17. For a discussion of Bandarra, consult ibid., 1:288–89, and the sources listed there. Vieira's *Quinto Imperio do Mundo* can be found in his *Obras Inéditas*, 3 vols. (Lisbon: Seabra and Antunes, 1856), 1:83–131.
47. For a discussion of the origin and development of Vieira's prophetic thought, consult Robert Ricard, "Prophecy and Messianism in the Works of António Vieira," *The Americas* 37 (1960):357–68; and Raymond Cantel, *Prophétisme et Messianisme dans l'Oeuvre d'Antonio Vieira* (Paris: Ediciones Hispano-Americanas, 1960).
48. Azevedo, *História de António Vieira*, 2:74.
49. This exemption is printed in Vieira, *Obras Inéditas*, 1:175–78.
50. Jesuit loyalties remained divided in the following century. See Magnus Mörner, ed., *The Expulsion of the Jesuits from Latin America* (New York: Alfred A. Knopf, Borzoi Books, 1965), p. 21.
51. Vieira, *Obras Inéditas*, 2:36.
52. Smith, "The Mercantile Class," p. 251.
53. Azevedo, *História de António Vieira*, 2:122–24.
54. Smith, "The Mercantile Class," p. 175.
55. Juan Lopes Sierra, *A Governor and His Image in Baroque Brazil: The Funeral Eulogy of Afonso de Castro do Rio de Mendonça*, ed. Stuart B. Schwartz, trans. Ruth E. Jones (Minneapolis: University of Minnesota Press, 1979), pp. 50–52.
56. Paixão, *Monstruosidades*, 2:121–22.
57. BNL, Fundo Geral, 851, fl. 183v; Paixão, *Monstruosidades*, 2:132.
58. Andrade e Silva, *Collecção*, 8:190.
59. Ibid., p. 191.
60. Paixão, *Monstruosidades*, 3:5–6. The law of July 22, 1671, as well as those

304 NOTES TO CHAPTER IV

anti–New Christian edicts that followed, largely conformed to measures advocated by the 1668 Cortes. Azevedo, *História dos Cristãos Novos*, p. 289.

61. Azevedo, *História dos Cristãos Novos*, p. 293.
62. Andrade e Silva, *Collecção*, 8:191–92.
63. Azevedo, *História dos Cristãos Novos*, pp. 292–93.
64. Azevedo, *História de António Vieira*, 2:119; Paixão, *Monstruosidades*, 3:36.
65. Paixão, *Monstruosidades*, 3:11.
66. Numerous accounts of Ferreira's sentence and execution have been preserved. For example, see: BNL, Fundo Geral, 589, fls. 88–91v; BL, Additional, 20,958, fls. 131–135; Paixão, *Monstruosidades*, 3:12–18.
67. These arrests of important merchants were not the first to follow Odivelas. The hapless Fernão Rodrigues Penso, as well as Miguel Lopes de Leão, Diogo Rodrigues Marques, and Gregório Gomes Henriques, all of Lisbon, and Manuel Mendes Soares of Guarda were jailed as suspects in the 1671 robbery shortly after it took place. They were subsequently released when it was determined that the accusations against them were groundless. BNL, Fundo Geral, 851, fl. 183v.
68. Smith, "The Mercantile Class," p. 175. The full text of the junta's 1672 *regimento* appears in Andrade e Silva, *Collecção*, 8:207–20.
69. Smith, "The Mercantile Class," p. 240. According to Smith, at least seven of the ninety merchants imprisoned in 1671–1672 died in jail. Ibid., pp. 239–40.
70. Azevedo, *História dos Cristãos Novos*, p. 295.
71. BNL, Fundo Geral, 868, fls. 468–468v; Paixão, *Monstruosidades*, 3:66–67.
72. Smith, "The Mercantile Class," p. 247. The brief life of the first company was thoroughly examined in A. R. Disney, *Twilight of the Pepper Empire: Portuguese Trade in Southwest India in the Early Seventeenth Century* (Cambridge: Harvard University Press, 1978), pp. 71–148. Also see Chandra Richard da Silva, "The Portuguese East India Company, 1628–1633," *Luso-Brazilian Review* 2 (1974):152–205.
73. "Paracer a favor dos XXNN davo a El Rei d. Pedro 2º sendo Principe Regente," BNL, Fundo Geral, 868, fls. 443–446v. A careful reading of this document suggests that it may be the work of António Vieira.
74. Ibid., fls. 444–444v.
75. "Consulta que o Supremo Conselho do S. Officio fez a S. Alteza," BNL, Fundo Geral, 868, fls. 449–462.
76. Ibid., fls. 458, 462.
77. Paixão, *Monstruosidades*, 3:50.
78. BNL, Fundo Geral, 868, fls. 469v–470.
79. Azevedo, *História dos Cristãos Novos*, p. 295.
80. Ibid., pp. 306, 309–10.
81. ANTT, Papeis dos Jesuitas, *caixa* 2, no. 11.
82. Azevedo, *História de António Vieira*, 2:121.
83. " . . . e cazar El Rei com a Rainha viuva de Castella." BNL, Fundo Geral, 851, fl. 184v.
84. Manuel Pinheiro Chagas, *História de Portugal*, 14 vols. (Lisbon: Livraria Moderna, 1899–1909), 6:119.
85. BNL, Fundo Geral, 851, fl. 184. The fact that Cavide escaped execution is confirmed in Paixão, *Monstruosidades*, 3:145–46. Also see Oliveira, *Elementos*, 7:465–66; Andrade e Silva, *Collecção*, 8:230.
86. Azevedo, *História de António Vieira*, 2:145. In a letter to his friend and confidant in Paris, Duarte Ribeiro de Macedo, Portuguese ambassador to France and mercantilist

writer, António Vieira suggested that the Holy Office had a part in the conspiracy. António Vieira, *Cartas*, 2nd ed., 3 vols., ed. João Lúcio de Azevedo (Lisbon: Imprensa Nacional, 1971), 2:658.

87. Oliveira, *Elementos*, 8:8, n. 1.

88. BNL, Pombalina, 67, pp. 130–134.

89. Freitas did in fact favor the pardon, but he seems to have done so on the merits of the India Company proposal and not out of cupidity. Azevedo, *História dos Cristãos Novos*, p. 301.

90. BL, Additional, 20,844, fl. 310v. This particular bit of rhetoric bespoke the constant concern of the Portuguese over the fate of Christians captured by the Muslim pirates who infested Portugal's coastal waters. This subject is discussed in chapter X.

91. BL, Additional, 20,844, fl. 327; Azevedo, *História dos Cristãos Novos*, p. 306.

92. Azevedo, *História de António Vieira*, 2:166–67; Vieira, *Cartas*, 3:87. Vieira later lamented the misfortune that had befallen supporters of the New Christian cause. Besides Meneses and Minas, the wife and son of the duke of Cadaval had died, as had the wife of the marquis of Fronteira. Belief that heavenly wrath was at work, according to Vieira, explained Fronteira's subsequent defection to the antipardon forces. Ibid., p. 88.

93. According to a French observer writing in 1684, pro-Spanish sentiment remained strong among substantial numbers of the nobility. J. V. Serrão, "Uma Relação," p. 83.

94. Mendes dos Remedios, "Depois da Restauração de D. João IV," *Biblos* 4 (Coimbra, 1928):97.

95. Paixão, *Monstruosidades*, 3:99.

96. Azevedo, *História de António Vieira*, 2:167.

97. ANTT, Papeis dos Jesuitas, *caixa* 2, no. 74.

98. The letter is printed in Paixão, *Monstruosidades*, 4:67–69.

99. Ibid., 4:66.

100. BNL, Fundo Geral, 868, fls. 481–482. Also see ANTT, Papeis dos Jesuitas, *caixa* 2, no. 78.

101. Vieira, *Cartas*, 3:143–44. Also see António das Chagas, *Obras Espirituais do Espiritual, e Veneravel Padre Frey António das Chagas* (Lisbon: Miguel Deslandes, 1701).

102. ANTT, Papeis dos Jesuitas, *caixa* 2, no. 81. One estimate suggests that Covilhã was a *vila* of respectable size, having about 5,000 inhabitants in 1640. J. V. Serrão, *Uma Estimativa*, p. 259.

103. Azevedo, *História de António Vieira*, 2:210.

104. Ibid., 2:211; idem, *História dos Cristãos Novos*, p. 322.

105. Smith, "The Mercantile Class," p. 249. During the years 1682 through 1684, at least 120 individuals identified as New Christian merchants underwent autos-da-fé in Portugal. Azevedo, *História dos Cristãos Novos*, p. 492. For a tabulation of individuals undergoing autos-da-fé from 1682 to 1691, see appendix 1.

106. Azevedo, *História dos Cristãos Novos*, p. 323.

107. Ibid., pp. 326, 329.

108. BNL, Fundo Geral, 868, fl. 455.

109. Gerhard Lenski, *Power and Privilege: A Theory of Social Stratification* (New York: McGraw-Hill, 1966), p. 255.

110. Eric J. Hobsbawm, "Class Consciousness in History," in István Meszaros, ed., *Aspects of History and Class Consciousness* (New York: Herder and Herder, 1972), pp. 8–9.

111. Smith, "The Mercantile Class," pp. 183–84.

112. Hobsbawm, "Class Consciousness in History," p. 11.

113. Godinho, "Portugal and Her Empire, 1680–1720," p. 511.
114. José Antonio Maravall, *La Cultura del Barroco: Análisis de una estructura histórica* (Barcelona: Ariel, 1975), pp. 71–74.
115. Visconde de Santarem, *Quadro Elementar*, 18 vols. (Paris: J. P. Aillaud, 1842–1854; Lisbon: Academia Real das Sciencias, 1858–1876), 4 (pt. 2):672.

Chapter V

1. Eli Heckscher, *Mercantilism*, 2nd ed., 2 vols., trans. Mendel Shapiro (New York: Macmillan, 1955), 2:296.
2. The best exposition of this controversy is in D. C. Coleman, ed., *Revisions in Mercantilism* (London: Meuthuen, 1969), pp. 1–18.
3. Quoted in ibid., p. 1.
4. Heckscher, *Mercantilism*, 1:26–27.
5. Ibid., 1:22, 24.
6. This position is the one usually taken by Marxian writers. See, for example, Maurice Dobb, *Studies in the Development of Capitalism* (New York: International Publishers, 1947), p. 209.
7. "Power versus Plenty as Objectives of Foreign Policy in the Seventeenth and Eighteenth Centuries," D. C. Coleman, ed., *Revisions in Mercantilism*, p. 71.
8. Shepard B. Clough and Richard T. Rapp, *European Economic History*, 3rd ed. (New York: McGraw-Hill, 1969), p. 206.
9. Heckscher, *Mercantilism*, 1:341–42. Extensive treatment of this subject will be found in Vitorino Magalhães Godinho's monumental *L'Economie de l'Empire portugais aux XVᵉ et XVIᵉ Siècles* (Paris: S.E.V.P.E.N., 1969), especially pp. 683–98, 794–812.
10. Serrão, ed., *DHP*, 3:37.
11. J. H. Elliott, *Imperial Spain, 1469–1716* (New York: New American Library, Mentor Books, 1966), p. 296. For a discussion of the efforts at reform in Spain during the period examined in the present study, see Mario L. Sánchez, "The Attempts at Reform in the Spain of Charles II: A Revisionist View of the Decline of Castile, 1665–1700" (unpublished Ph.D. dissertation, University of Notre Dame, 1976).
12. António Sérgio, *Antológia dos Economistas Portugueses (Século XVII)* (Lisbon: Sá da Costa, 1974), pp. 69–73.
13. The others were Manuel Severim de Faria, Duarte Ribeiro de Macedo, Alexandre Gusmão, and D. Luís da Cunha. See Moses Bensabat Amzalak, *Do Estudo da Evolução das Doutrinas Económicas em Portugal* (Lisbon: Oficina Gráfica do Museu Comercial, 1928), p. 25.
14. *Discursos sobre los Comercios de las Indias* (Madrid[?], 1622). A second edition was edited by Moses B. Amzalak (Lisbon: n.p., 1943).
15. Amzalak, *Do Estudo*, pp. 57, 67–68.
16. *Alegación en Favor de la Compañía de la India Oriental y Comercios ultramarinos que de Nueuo se Instituyó en el Reyno de Portugal* (Lisbon: 1628). A second edition of this work was also edited by Moses B. Amzalak (Lisbon: Editoria Império, 1955). For a discussion of Solis's role in the formation of the company, see Silva, "The Portuguese East India Company," pp. 155–56; and Disney, *Twilight of the Pepper Empire*, pp. 73, 90.
17. José Calvet de Magalhães, *História do Pensamento Económico em Portugal* (Coimbra: Imprensa de Universidade, 1967), pp. 211–12.
18. José Acursio das Neves, *Noções Historicas, Economicas e Administrativas sobre a Producção e Manufactura das Sedas em Portugal* (Lisbon: Impressão Regia, 1827), pp. 8, 12–14.

19. Magalhães, *Pensamento Económico*, pp. 201, 208, 205.
20. Ibid., pp. 213–14.
21. Ibid., pp. 217–18. Also see Moses B. Amzalak, *Uma Carta de Duarte Gomes ao Duque de Lerma* (Lisbon: Gráfica Lisbonense, 1943).
22. Magalhães, *Pensamento Económica*, p. 223.
23. Vitorino Guimarães, *As Finanças na Guerra da Restauração (1640–1668)* (Lisbon: Tipografia da L.C.G.G., 1941), p. 29.
24. Andrade e Silva, *Collecção*, 6:87.
25. This section appears in Sérgio, *Antológia*, pp. 119–63.
26. Magalhães, *Pensamento Económico*, pp. 223–25.
27. René Gonnard, *Les Doctrines Mercantilistes au XVIIe Siècle en Portugal* (Paris: Librairie de Sciences Economiques et Sociales, 1935), p. 8.
28. Sérgio, *Antológia*, pp. 127–29.
29. For an introduction to the literature on the tragic voyages of Portuguese Indiamen, see James Duffy, *Shipwreck and Empire, Being an Account of Portuguese Maritime Disasters in a Century of Decline* (Cambridge: Harvard University Press, 1955).
30. Sérgio, *Antológia*, pp. 131–37.
31. Joel Serrão, "Conspecto histórico da emigração portuguesa," *Analise Social* 8 (Lisbon, 1970):601.
32. Magalhães, *Pensamento Económico*, p. 229.
33. Ibid., pp. 232–234, 237.
34. Charles R. Boxer, *The Dutch in Brazil, 1624–1654* (Oxford: Clarendon Press, 1957), pp. 237–41.
35. "Proposta feita a El-Rei D. João IV, em que se lhe representava o miserável estado do Reino, e a necessidade diversas partes da Europa," *Obras Escolhidas*, 12 vols. (Lisbon: Sá da Costa, 1951–1954), 4:1–26.
36. Ibid., 4:14–15.
37. Magalhães, *Pensamento Económico*, pp. 247–48.
38. The crown did in fact take steps to establish such a bank, but nothing came of them. See Andrade e Silva, *Collecção*, 7:107, 371; Magalhães, *Pensamento Económico*, pp. 251–52. Also see, Ivan Lins, *Aspectos do Padre Antônio Vieira*, 2nd. ed. (Rio de Janeiro: Livraria São José, 1962), pp. 117–25.
39. "Meos para Portugal se fazer opulento e poderoso," BNL, Pombalina, 738, fls. 258–262v. Paleographic and textual examination of this undated, unsigned document strongly suggests that Vieira wrote it at about the same time as his 1643 *Proposta*.
40. "Meos," fls. 58–59v. Vieira may have had in mind a scheme similar to that of Peter Suthmann (sp?), an Irishman who contracted in 1643 to establish a colony of 130 refugees from Protestant persecution in Pará. Suthmann's death a few years later evidently put an end to the project. See BNL, Fundo Geral, 7627, fls. 78–96, 99; Lobo, *Aspectos da Influencia dos Homens de Negócio*, p. 54.
41. In 1648, a law setting a tonnage minimum (350 toneladas) was passed for ships being built for trade with the colonies. This was done to limit the number of small, easily captured vessels at sea. The law also contained specifications for sturdier construction. Andrade e Silva, *Collecção*, 7:3. More on shipbuilding in Brazil can be found in Boxer, *Salvador de Sá*, pp. 307–10, 330–32. For a discussion of Vieira's views on black slavery, see António José Saraiva, "Le Père Antonio Vieira S.J. et la question de l'esclavage de Noirs au XVIIe siècle," *Annales: ESC* 6 (1967):1289–1309.
42. "Meos," fls. 260–62.
43. Ibid., fl. 262. Vieira, however, had few illusions about the reliability of colonists

NOTES TO CHAPTER V

as miners since they often used prospecting expeditions as a cover for enslaving Indians living in the Brazilian backlands. Speaking of Maranhão, he observed in 1661 that "enslaving Indians and drawing red gold from their veins was always the mine of that state." Quoted in Boxer, *The Golden Age of Brazil*, p. 277.

44. "Meos," fl. 262.
45. Boxer, "A Great Luso-Brazilian Figure," p. 14.
46. The literature on the Dutch foothold in the Brazilian northeast is quite extensive, but probably the best studies are Boxer, *The Dutch in Brazil, 1624–1654*; and Evaldo Cabral de Mello, *Olinda Restaurado: Guerra e Açucar no Nordeste, 1630–1654* (Rio de Janeiro: Editora Forense-Universitaria, 1975).
47. Charles W. Cole, *French Mercantilist Doctrines before Colbert* (New York: Richard R. Smith, 1931), pp. 214–15.
48. Charles W. Cole, *Colbert and a Century of French Mercantilism*, 2 vols. (New York: Columbia University Press, 1939), 1:164, 160–61.
49. Ibid., pp. 209, 230, 234–36.
50. Heckscher, *Mercantilism*, 1:139.
51. Ibid., p. 158.
52. Cole, *Colbert*, 2:314, 362.
53. Ibid., 1:355. Furthermore, Colbert regarded the course of economic life as being characterized by perpetual strife (*un combat perpétual*). Pierre Clement, ed., *Lettres, instructions et memoires de Colbert*, 10 vols. (Paris: Imprimerie Impériale, 1861–1882), 6:269.
54. David Ogg, *Europe in the Seventeenth Century* (New York: Collier Books, 1968), p. 286.
55. Moses B. Amzalak, *A Economia Política em Portugal: O Diplomato Duarte Ribeiro de Macedo e os seus Discursos sobre Economia Política* (Lisbon: Academia das sciencias de Lisboa, 1922), p. 5.
56. An excellent description of the Portuguese system of royal and ecclesiastical courts is presented in Schwartz, *Sovereignty and Society*, pp. 5–21.
57. Serrão, ed., *DHP*, 2:863–64.
58. Further details of this marriage can be found in António Álvaro Dória, *A Rainha D. Maria Francisca de Sabóia (1646–1683)* (Porto: Livraria Civilização, 1944), p. 295.
59. Virginia Rau, "Cenas da vida parisiense na correspondência de Duarte Ribeiro de Macedo (1668–1676)," *Bulletin des Études Portugaises*, new series, 30 (Paris, 1969):102–3.
60. "Governo de Paris, sobre a limpeza da cidade, e luzes para de noyte," BNL, Pombalina, 67, pp. 135–142. This relation, which is a copy of the original document, is neither dated nor signed, but internal evidence shows that it is probably the report requested by D. Pedro. See Rau, "Cenas," p. 106, for information that suggests that the document was written and remitted to Lisbon in late 1671.
61. "Governo de Paris," pp. 135–38.
62. Freire de Oliveira, *Elementos*, 7:442.
63. "Governo de Paris," pp. 138–40.
64. Rau, "Cenas," pp. 115–16, 97.
65. Despite his disenchantment with the economic regime in Spain, Ribeiro de Macedo did study the writings of Spanish mercantilists, especially Sancho de Moncada. See José Larraz, *La Epoca del Mercantilismo en Castille (1500–1700)*, 2nd ed. (Madrid: Atlas, 1943), p. 174.
66. Magalhães, *Pensamento Económico*, pp. 263–65, 267.
67. Various editions of this essay have been published, but the most accurate and

accessible is that contained in Sérgio, *Antológia*, pp. 165–229. Subsequent references to the *Discurso* will be given from this edition.

68. Sérgio, *Antológia*, p. 171. The precious metal shortage grew especially acute after 1665. Arrivals of American silver at Cadiz continued to decline as production in the Spanish colonies fell off. This worked an especial hardship on Portugal, which depended on trade with Spain for much of its silver. Portugal's chronically unfavorable balance of trade made matters even worse. By 1675, perhaps one-third of Portugal's imports had to be purchased with specie. Godinho, "Portugal and Her Empire, 1680–1720," p. 511.

69. Magalhães, *Pensamento Económico*, pp. 271–72.

70. Sérgio, *Antológia*, p. 172.

71. Ibid., pp. 172–73.

72. Ibid., p. 181.

73. Peres, ed., *História de Portugal*, 4:401.

74. Godinho, "Portugal and Her Empire, 1680–1720," p. 513.

75. Sérgio, *Antológia*, pp. 189–91.

76. Ibid., pp. 201–12. The emporium ideal, that is, assuming the role of a major international commercial intermediary, was probably irresistible to all mercantilist writers. Magalhães, *Pensamento Económico*, p. 297.

77. Sérgio, *Antológia*, pp. 224–25, 227.

78. Child, *Brief Observations Concerning Trade, and the Interest of Money* (1668); Fortrey, *England's Interest and Improvement* (1663). The genesis of Child's pamphlet, which later appeared as *A New Discourse on Trade* (1690), is examined in William Letwin, *The Origins of Scientific Economics: English Economic Thought 1660–1776* (London: Methuen, 1963), pp. 5–42.

79. Ibid., p. 260.

80. Sérgio Buarque de Holanda, *Visão do Paraíso: Motivos Edênicas no Descobrimento e Colonização do Brasil* (Rio de Janeiro: José Olympio, 1956), p. 201.

81. "Trinte e sete generos que se tem descoberto no estado do Maranhão e Pará," BNL, Fundo Geral, 3542.

82. Duarate Ribeiro de Macedo, *Obras Ineditas* (Lisbon: Impressão Regia, 1817), p. 106. The story of Portugal's loss of Sri Lanka is expertly told in George Davison Winius, *The Fatal History of Portuguese Ceylon* (Cambridge: Harvard University Press, 1971).

83. Ribeiro de Macedo, *Obras Ineditas*, p. 108.

84. Sérgio, *Antológia*, p. 189.

85. Ribeiro de Macedo, *Obras Ineditas*, p. 118.

86. Two translations of this work by Thomas Sprat were then in print: *L'Histoire de la Société Royal de Londres* (Geneva, 1669) and *Histoire de l'Institution dessein et Progrès de la Société Royal de Londres* (Paris, 1670). The famous society included among its earliest fellows António Álvares da Cunha (a Portuguese nobleman), Giuseppe de Faria (Pedro II's ambassador), Gaspar Meres de Sousa (a Portuguese mathematician), Robert Southwell (ambassador to Portugal, 1665–1668), and a merchant in the Portugal trade named Goodwyn. See Thomas Birch, *The History of the Royal Society of London*, 4 vols., introduction by Rupert Hall (New York: Johnson Reprint Corporation, 1968), 1:xxxvii–xxxviii, xliii.

87. Ribeiro de Macedo, *Obras Ineditas*, pp. 120–22, 114–15. Ribeiro de Macedo's promotion of transplantation may also have been prompted by conversations with the French and Dutch ambassadors in Paris in 1670. On this see Visconde de Santarem, *Quadro Elementar*, 18:112–13.

NOTES TO CHAPTER V

88. Ribeiro de Macedo, *Obras Ineditas*, p. 124.
89. Ibid., pp. 140–42.
90. Charles C. Cumberland, *Mexico: The Struggle for Modernity* (New York: Oxford University Press, 1968), pp. 96–100.
91. Vieira, *Cartas*, 3:152, 154.
92. Magalhães, *Pensamento Económico*, pp. 302–3.
93. Ibid., pp. 301–2. Among other important figures who opposed the inquisitors were the duke of Cadaval, D. João Mascarenhas (the marquis of Fronteira), and D. Rodrigo de Meneses. Mascarenhas and the count of Ericeira jointly headed up the treasury as *vedores da fazenda*. See Saraiva, *Inquisição e Cristãos-Novos*, p. 299. Ericeira was himself no friend of the Holy Office.
94. Cole, *Colbert*, 1:362.
95. Virginia Rau, *Política Económica e Mercantilismo na Correspondência de Duarte Ribeiro de Macedo (1668–1676), separata* from *Do Tempo e da Historia* II (Lisbon: n.p., 1968), pp. 31–32.
96. Godinho, "Portugal and Her Empire, 1680–1720," pp. 512–13.
97. Rau, *Política Económica*, p. 42.
98. Sousa Viterbo, *A Armaria em Portugal* (Lisbon: Academia Real das Sciencias, 1907), p. 67.
99. The envoy's orders to depart from Paris arrived on February 9, 1677. His post was filled by Salvador Taborda Portugal. Ribeiro de Macedo had not been in Madrid long before he was nominated to represent Portugal at the negotiations for the Treaty of Nijmwegen (1678), but he declined the position. Visconde de Santarem, *Quadro Elementar*, 4 (pt. 2):653–54, 668.
100. Ericeira to Bluteau, July 23, 1680, BNL, Fundo Geral, *caixa* 64, no. 8.
101. *Prosas Portuguesas* (Lisbon: José Antonio da Silva, 1728), p. 319.
102. Godinho, "Portugal and Her Empire, 1680–1720," p. 512. For further biographical information on Bluteau, consult *Grande Enciclopedia Portuguesa e Brasileira*, 40 vols. (Lisbon: Editoria Enciclopedia, Ltda., 1936–1960), 4:784; and the sources listed there.
103. Diogo Gomes to Bluteau, n.d., BNL, Fundo Geral, 7701, n.p.
104. BNL, Fundo Geral, 589, fl. 82v; Azevedo, *História de António Vieira*, 2:348.
105. Rafael Bluteau, *Vocabulario Português e Latino*, 8 vols. (Coimbra: Collegio das Artes da Companhia de Jesu, 1712–1721); *Supplemento*, 2 vols. (Lisbon: José Antonio da Silva, 1727).
106. *Instruccam sobre a Cultura das Amoreiras e Criação dos Bichos da Seda* (Lisbon: João da Costa, 1679).
107. Ibid., pp. 4–5, 20–21.
108. Ibid., pp. 45–48.
109. Godinho, "Portugal and Her Empire, 1680–1720," p. 513.
110. Roland Duclos, "Alvitre que se deo no anno de 1679 sobre tres conveniencias para o nosso Reino," BNL, Pombalina, 67, pp. 143–50. This document is an incomplete copy written in an eighteenth-century hand.
111. Ibid., p. 144. If this amount and Ribeiro de Macedo's earlier figure were correct, it would seem that English merchants controlled about one-fourth of the Portuguese market for silk stockings during the 1670s. See Sérgio, *Antológia*, p. 172.
112. Duclos, "Alvitre," p. 145.
113. Ibid., pp. 147, 149.
114. Magalhães, *Pensamento Económico*, p. 303.

Chapter VI

1. Fernand Braudel and Frank Spooner, "Prices in Europe from 1450 to 1750," *The Cambridge Economic History of Europe*, 8 vols. (Cambridge: Cambridge University Press, 1966), 4:470.
2. Frédéric Mauro, *L'Expansion Européene (1600–1870)*, 2nd ed. (Paris: Presses universitaires de France, 1967), pp. 312–13.
3. Gaston Imbert, *Des Mouvements de Longue durée Kondratieff* (Aix-en-Provence: Pensée Universitaire, 1959), pp. 402–5.
4. For discussion of the so-called little ice age, see Emmanuel LeRoy Ladurie, "Climat et récoltes aux XVIIe et XVIIIe siècles," *Annales: ESC* 15 (May–June 1960):434–65.
5. Eric J. Hobsbawm, "The Crisis of the Seventeenth Century," in *Crisis in Europe, 1560–1660*, ed. Trevor Aston (New York: Basic Books, 1965), p. 5. Various other views on the nature of the General Crisis can be found in Aston, ed., *Crisis in Europe*, passim. A strong, if unconvincing, critique of Hobsbawm's thesis is presented in A. D. Lublinskaya, *French Absolutism: The Crucial Phase, 1620–1629* (Cambridge: Cambridge University Press, 1968), chapter 1. A useful discussion of certain aspects of the General Crisis (which shows that similar political disruption occurred in the mid-sixteenth century) appears in J. H. Elliott, "Revolution and Continuity in Early Modern Europe," *Past and Present* 42 (February 1969):35–56.
6. Jan de Vries, *The Economy of Europe in an Age of Crisis, 1600–1750* (Cambridge: Cambridge University Press, 1976), pp. 24–25.
7. Recently, it has been suggested that the economic crisis that beset most of Europe during the seventeenth century "was in the last analysis a crisis of agrarian productivity, resulting ... from the maintenance of relationships of property or surplus-extraction which prevented any advance in productivity." Robert Brenner, "Agrarian Class Structure and Economic Development in Pre-Industrial Europe," *Past and Present* 70 (February 1976):66.
8. Hobsbawm, "The Crisis of the Seventeenth Century," p. 12.
9. Unfortunately, documentation on the annual net income of the Portuguese crown during this period is quite sparse. However, data on the income of the English government show that, after exceeding 2 million pounds in the mid-1660s and again in the early 1670s, revenues sagged below that figure until the mid-1680s. See C. D. Chandaman, *The English Public Revenue, 1660–1688* (Oxford: Clarendon Press, 1975), pp. 333–35.
10. Guimarães, *As Finanças*, p. 38.
11. "Relação dos efeitos que contribui o Reino para a despesa da guera da Restauração," BNL, Fundo Geral, *caixa* 2, no. 25.
12. Guimarães, *As Finanças*, pp. 54–56.
13. Freire de Oliveira, *Elementos*, 7:368. Schomberg's activities in Portugal were examined in C. R. Boxer, "Marshal Schomberg in Portugal, 1660–1668," *History Today* 26 (October 1976):653–63.
14. Freire de Oliveira, *Elementos*, 8:101.
15. João Lúcio de Azevedo, *Épocas de Portugal Económico* (Lisbon: Livraria Clássica, 1929), p. 211.
16. Lisbon's *real d'agua* was imposed in 1619, raised in 1630 and hiked again in 1636. BNL, Fundo Geral, 2632, fl. 284v. The text of the latter edict can be found in Andrade e Silva, *Collecção* 4:101–9. As Joel Serrão pointed out, the 1636 hike played a key role in precipitating the Évora riots of 1637. *Altercações de Évora*, p. xxxiv.

312   NOTES TO CHAPTER VI

17. A breakdown of the assessment appeared in Andrade e Silva, *Collecção*, 8:153–54; and Freire de Oliveira, *Elementos*, 7:70–71.

18. For a breakdown of these expenditures, which also included the cost of embassies, see Paixão, *Monstruosidades*, 3:118–24. After garrisoning Lisbon with a large standing force in 1673, D. Pedro pressed for further increases in military strength, including raising the number of men serving in the Alentajo *terço* to 450 in that year and increasing the size of the Setúbal *terço* from eight to ten companies in 1675. ANTT, Conselho da Guerra, Decretos, *maço* 32, doc. 22; ibid., *maço* 35, doc. 24. Further discussion of military reforms carried out during D. Pedro's reign can be found in Gastão Mello de Matos, *Notícias de Terço da Armada Real (1618–1707)* (Lisbon: Imprensa da Armada, 1932), pp. 77–95.

19. The *regimento* detailing the manner in which the 1674 *real d'agua* was to be levied in Portugal and its Atlantic islands can be found in BNL, Pombalina, 473, fls. 402–416; BA, 44–XIII–60, fls. 76–89.

20. This *regimento* can be found in Andrade e Silva, *Collecção*, 8:154–63. For a brief discussion of *alfândegas*, see Serrão, ed., *DHP*, 1:94–95.

21. BA, 44–XIII–42, fls. 445–494v.

22. BA, 50–V–37, fls. 18–18v.

23. BA, 44–XIII–42, fls. 389, 429. For a similar contract, see João Mascarenhas, *Contrato dos rendimentos dos consulados das alfandegas da cidade de Porto, Vianna, Aveyro, Buarcos, e As mais de Barlovento do Tejo pera o Norte entrando Peniche, que se fez com Simão da Sylva de Govea, e seus companheiros* (Lisbon, 1675).

24. BA, 44–XIII–42, fls. 342–344.

25. The complete *regimento* appears in Andrade e Silva, *Collecção*, 8:232–54. The best brief discussion of the impost is in Pereira and Rodrigues, *Portugal*, 6:980–82.

26. Andrade e Silva, *Collecção*, 8:232.

27. Freire de Oliveira, *Elementos*, 8:107–8.

28. Ibid., 8:153–54.

29. Virginia Rau, *A Casa dos Contos* (Coimbra: Imprensa da Universidade, 1951), pp. 130–31.

30. BA, 44–XIII–43, fls. 85v–86v.

31. Teixeira de Aragão, *Descrição geral*, 2:36.

32. The two *consultas* can be found in BA, 44–XIII–43, fls. 86v–96v.

33. Ibid., fl. 97.

34. BNL, Fundo Geral, 275, fls. 9v–10.

35. Andrade e Silva, *Collecção*, 8:147–49.

36. Freire de Oliveira, *Elementos*, 7:393–97, 403.

37. Ibid., 8:260, 338–39.

38. This request for money to help the Poles was turned down by representatives of the three estates, who almost uniformly cited Portugal's economic woes as justification for their refusal. Luis Ferrand de Almeida, "As Cortes de 1679–1680 e o auxílio à Polonia para a guerra contra os Turcos," *Biblos* 27 (Coimbra, 1951):101–9.

39. Paixão, *Monstruosidades*, 4:76–77.

40. Freire de Oliveira, *Elementos*, 8:432.

41. The best account of the unsuccessful marriage negotiations is in Dória, *D. Maria Francisca de Sabóia*, pp. 304–38. A detailed breakdown showing how the outlay of 1 million cruzados for the marriage was to be assessed can be found in BNL, Pombalina, 475, fls. 277–87. For a discussion of Cadaval's disappointing mission to Savoy, see

BL, Additional, 15,169. In 1687, D. Pedro II remarried, his wife Maria having died in 1683. Despite the great cost of the festivities that accompanied the arrival of his new bride, Maria Sophia Isabel de Neubourg, the financial blow was softened somewhat by the fact that she brought a dowry of 100,000 florins. Freire de Oliveira, *Elementos*, 9:6, n. 1; 15, n. 2; 16, n. 2.

42. Ibid., 9:251.
43. BNL, Pombalina, 475, fl. 256v.
44. J. V. Serrão, ed., "Uma Relação," p. 135.
45. BNL, Fundo Geral, 1459, fl. 41.
46. Freire de Oliveira, *Elementos*, 8:534.
47. Ibid., 9:123–24.
48. ANTT, Convento da Graça, *caixa* 5, tomo 2, fl. 80v.
49. Teixeira de Aragão, *Descrição geral*, 2:60.
50. J. M. Esteves Pereira, *A Industria Portuguesa (Séculos XII–XIX)* (Lisbon: Imprensa do Occidente, 1900), pp. 31–32. The housing of this minting machine, which produced coins until 1837, is now in the Museu do Carmo in Lisbon.
51. Teixeira de Aragão, *Descrição geral*, 2:53.
52. Andrade e Silva, *Collecção*, 10:41, 47–48.
53. BA, 50–V–37, fl. 85v.
54. Teixeira de Aragão, *Descrição geral*, 2:53.
55. Andrade e Silva, *Collecção*, 10:63–64.
56. The 1686 *regimento* for the mint is in ibid., 10:67–80.
57. Teixeira de Aragão, *Descrição geral*, 2:54.
58. Earl J. Hamilton, *War and Prices in Spain, 1651–1800* (Cambridge: Harvard University Press, 1947), pp. 30–32. For a further discussion of decline in Spain, see Henry Kamen, "The Decline of Castile: The Last Crisis," *Economic History Review*, 2nd series, 77 (1964):63–76; António Domínguez Ortiz, "La Crisis de Castilla en 1677–1687," *Revista Portuguesa de História* 10 (1962):435–51.
59. BA, 50–V–37, fls. 86–86v.
60. BNL, Fundo Geral, 748, fls. 266–267.
61. Godinho, "Portugal and Her Empire, 1680–1720," p. 514.
62. The August decree, as well as a table showing the denominational revaluation of Portuguese gold and silver coins, can be found in Andrade e Silva, *Collecção*, 10:163–65.
63. Freire de Oliveira, *Elementos*, 9:84. For a clerical view of New Christian opposition to the 1688 devaluation, see BNL, Fundo Geral, *caixa* 199, no. 46.
64. Godinho, "Portugal and Her Empire, 1680–1720," p. 514.
65. Ibid.

Chapter VII

1. Serrão, ed., *DHP*, 3:27.
2. During the late seventeenth century, study of the fine points of military technology, especially the design and construction of fortifications, became an increasingly important part of a nobleman's education. For a contemporary Portuguese work on the subject, see Luís Pimentel Serrão, *Methodo Lusitanico de Desenhar as Fortificacoens das Praças Regulares e Irregulares, Fortes de Campanha, e Outras Obras Pertencentes a Architectura Militar* (Lisbon: António Craesbeeck de Melo, 1680).
3. ANTT, Conselho da Guerra, Avisos, *maço* 3, February 29, 1672.

4. Virginia Rau, "Um 'Trabalho divertido' do Conde da Ericeira: A História de Portugal Restaurado," *Aufsätze zur Portugeisischen Kulturgeschichte*, 10 (1970):305.
5. BNL, Fundo Geral, 1538, fls. 504–506.
6. Meneses, *História de Portugal Restaurado*, 1:8.
7. J. V. Serrão, ed., "Uma Relação," pp. 100–101. The Treasury Council itself had great responsibility, as the following passage indicates: "The council of finance directed the financial, economic and mercantile administration. It was headed by three Vedores (Superintendents), all noblemen, representing specific interests. It consisted of three to five legally trained Councillors, a Procurator Fiscal, and Four Secretaries. Subordinate to this council were the Court of Accounts, the *Casa da India*, the mint, civil shipyards, and depots, consulates, the customs and other branches of the revenue, and the Brazilian Trading Company with its successor, the *Junto do Comércio do Brasil*." Godinho, "Portugal and Her Empire," p. 391. The most powerful council, however, was the Council of State. Its singular influence is discussed in Edgar Prestage, "The Mode of Government in Portugal during the Restoration Period," in *Mélanges d'Études Portugaises offerts à M. Georges Le Gentil* (Lisbon Instituto para a Alta Cultura, 1949), pp. 265–70.
8. Advances in Portuguese shipbuilding are detailed in Eugénio Estanislau de Barros, *Traçado e Construção das Naus Portuguesas dos Séculos XVI e XVII* (Lisbon: Imprensa da Armada, 1933). Also see Mauro, *Le Portugal*, pp. 29–52.
9. The background of industrial activity in Portugal is outlined in Serrão, ed., *DHP*, 2:525–34.
10. Andrade e Silva, *Collecção*, 8:7–18.
11. Jorge Borges de Macedo, *Problemas de História da Indústria Portuguesa no Século XVIII* (Lisbon: Associação Industrial Portuguesa, 1963), p. 31.
12. Godinho, "Portugal and Her Empire, 1680–1720," p. 522. Though he was correct on this point, Professor Godinho erred in giving the impression that Fronteira, who died in 1681, was still on the Treasury Council after that date. A similar mistake was made on the year of Ericeira's death, the count having died in 1690, not 1692.
13. Ibid.
14. J. V. Serrão, *Uma Estimativa*, p. 255.
15. Godinho, "Portugal and Her Empire, 1680–1720," pp. 512–13.
16. Quoted in ibid., p. 512.
17. Ibid., pp. 512–13.
18. Neves, *Noções Históricas*, pp. 2, 8, 13–15.
19. Ibid., p. 17.
20. Ibid. The mulberry tax, a 500-reis levy on each tree's production, was imposed, perhaps unwisely, before substantial output had been achieved. In another of his works, Neves argued, albeit unconvincingly, that there was no connection between the attempts to expand silk production and the promulgation of the *pragmática* of February 1677. *Variedades sobre objectivos Relativos às Artes, Commercio e manufacturas*, 2 vols. (Lisbon: Impressão Regia, 1814–1817), 2:320.
21. Neves, *Noções Históricas*, p. 19.
22. Borges de Macedo, *Problemas de História*, p. 32.
23. Freire de Oliveira, *Elementos*, 8:232–36.
24. BNL, Fundo Geral, *caixa* 14, no. 148.
25. Neves, *Noções Históricas*, pp. 21–22.
26. One such difficulty arose when English officials blocked an attempt by the Portuguese ambassador in London, D. Francisco de Melo, to ship looms for the manufacture of silk stockings to Lisbon. Neves, *Variedades*, 2:317.
27. Ericeira to Bluteau, July 5, 1680, BNL, Fundo Geral, *caixa* 64, no. 8.
28. Serrão, ed., *DHP*, 3:825.

29. Godinho, "Portugal and Her Empire, 1680–1720," p. 513.
30. Serrão, ed., *DHP*, 2:656–57. The linen industry, as noted above, received a new *regimento* in 1658.
31. Charles Wilson, "Cloth Production and International Competition in the Seventeenth Century," *Economic History Review*, 2nd series, (December 1960):209.
32. Vilas Boas's *Relatório*, on the woolen industry at Covilhã, as well as his letters to Ericeira, which span the years 1677 to 1687, were published in Luiz Fernando de Carvalho Dias, *Os Lanifícios na Política Económica do Conde da Ericeira*, 2 vols. (Lisbon: Tipografia da Sociedade Industrial de Imprensa, 1954), 1:82–111, 2:3–106. Further documentation on the manufacturing program, which came to my attention as this volume was going to press, may be found in Library of Congress, Portuguese Manuscripts, pp. 325–35.
33. Ibid., 1:96.
34. Ibid., 1:101.
35. Ibid., 1:50–59. The English reaction to the manufacturing program is further elucidated in chapter XI and appendix 2.
36. Dias, *Os Lanifícios*, 1:97, 103–4.
37. Neves, *Variedades*, 2:320. In 1683, however, the English consul in Lisbon, Thomas Maynard, reported that Curtin and another Irishman had been arrested. C. R. Boxer, "Vicissitudes of the Anglo-Portuguese Alliance, 1660–1700," *Revista da Faculdade de Letras* (Lisbon), 3rd series, 2 (1958):32, n. 1.
38. ANTT, Conselho de Guerra, Decretos, *maço* 40, doc. 1, February 2, 1681.
39. Dias, *Os Lanifícios*, 1:54–56.
40. Neves, *Noções Históricas*, p. 19.
41. Ericeira to Bluteau, July 5, 1680, BNL, Fundo Geral, *caixa* 64, no. 8.
42. Dias, *Os Lanifícios*, 2:100.
43. Ibid., 2:102.
44. Ibid., 1:86–95. In 1685, it was reported that the total value of imports from England had fallen to 400,000 pounds. Bento Carqueja, *O Capitalismo Moderno e as Suas Origens em Portugal* (Oporto: Livraria Chardron, 1908), p. 120.
45. The beginnings of mining in Portugal have been explored in John C. Allan, "A Mineração em Portugal na antiguidade," *Boletim de Minas*, 2 (3) (Lisbon, July–September 1965):139–75.
46. Pereira and Rodrigues, *Portugal*, 4:1120. For a general view of mining in Portugal during the early modern era, see Alfredo Augusto de Oliveira Machado e Costa, "A Mineralogia quinhentista," in *Congresso do Mundo Portugues*, 19 vols. (Lisbon: Bertrand, 1940), 5:295–311.
47. Andrade e Silva, *Collecção*, 2:330–32, 7:366–69.
48. Ibid., 7:367, 8:228.
49. Borges de Macedo, *Problemas de História*, p. 25.
50. Andrade e Silva, *Collecção*, 7:328–29.
51. Godinho, "Portugal and Her Empire, 1680–1720," p. 513.
52. Viterbo Sousa, *A Armaria em Portugal*, pp. 49–50.
53. ANTT, Corpo Cronológico, part 1, *maço* 120, doc. 65, July 16, 1640.
54. Freire de Oliveira, *Elementos*, 1: li.
55. Viterbo Sousa, *A Armaria em Portugal*, p. 69.
56. For a brief discussion of lead production in Portugal, see Serrão, ed., *DHP*, 1:570–72.
57. Andrade e Silva, *Collecção*, 7:321–29, 8:27.
58. AHU, Bahia, Papeis Avulsos, 1st uncatalogued series, *caixa* 12, *consulta* of August 3, 1675.

59. Ericeira to Bluteau, July 5, 1680, BNL, Fundo Geral, *caixa* 64, no. 8. Gonçalo Cunha das Vilas Boas also spoke highly of Figueiró's iron, noting that foreigners were quite impressed by its quality. Dias, *Os Lanifícios,* 1:86.
60. *Grande Enciclopedia Portuguesa e Brasileira,* 4:784.
61. Godinho, "Portugal and Her Empire, 1680–1720," p. 513.
62. ANTT, Conselho da Guerra, Decretos, *maço* 39, doc. 6, May 20, 1680. A decree of eighteen years later showed that the practice of transferring skilled conscripts to manufacturing enterprises continued after Ericeira's death. In this instance, a young soldier of the Lisbon *terço* was sent to help with mining operations at Vila Viçosa. Ibid., *maço* 57, doc. 2, April 4, 1698.
63. Pereira, *A Industria Portuguesa,* p. 32.
64. Ericeira to Bluteau, April 21, 1681, BNL, Fundo Geral, *caixa* 64, no. 8.
65. Godinho, "Portugal and Her Empire, 1680–1720," p. 513. The *regimento* detailing the 1692 reorganization can be found in Andrade e Silva, *Collecção,* 9:290–98.
66. Borges de Macedo, *Problemas de História,* p. 39.
67. Domenico Sella, "European Industries, 1500–1700," in *Fontana Economic History of Europe,* 6 vols., ed. Carlo M. Cipolla (New York: Barnes and Noble, 1977), 2:355–56.
68. Castelo-Branco, *Lisboa Seiscentista,* pp. 57–58.
69. Freire de Oliveira, *Elementos,* 8:281.
70. Ibid., 8:163, 299–300; 7:248–49.
71. Castelo-Branco, *Lisboa Seiscentista,* p. 76.
72. An extended discussion of post-1640 ecclesiastical architecture can be found in George Kubler, *Portuguese Plain Architecture: Between Spices and Diamonds, 1521–1706* (Middletown, Connecticut: Wesleyan University Press, 1972), pp. 146–71.
73. Jorge das Neves Larcher, *Memória Histórica sobre o Abastecimento de Água a Lisboa até ao Reinado de D. João V* (Lisbon: Centro Tipográfico Colonial, 1937), p. 39.
74. Freire de Oliveira, *Elementos,* 8:494.
75. Larcher, *Memória Histórica,* p. 43.
76. Ibid., pp. 44–49, 59. Dupineaut also took an interest in the Portuguese fleet. See Teófilo Dupineaut, "Memoire touchant la Marine de Portugal (Memoria sôbre a Marina Portuguesa no reinado de D. Pedro II—Notas de Prof. Edgar Prestage e do Comte Quirino da Fonseca)," *Arquivo Histórico da Marinha* 4 (Lisbon, 1936):267–75.
77. Freire de Oliveira, *Elementos,* 9:159–60. Lisbon in fact did not enjoy street illumination on any real scale until the 1780s. Ibid., p. 161, n. 1.
78. BNL, Fundo Geral, 7982, July 30, 1683. (This *códice* has no pagination.) It is of interest to note that the renowned Salvador de Sá received a similar grant to cultivate land near Santarem. Ibid., March 28, 1647.
79. Borges de Macedo, *Problemas de História,* p. 31.
80. Dias, *Os Lanifícios,* 1:63.
81. Andrade e Silva, *Collecção,* 10:64–65.
82. Francis, *The Methuens and Portugal,* p. 13.
83. Borges de Macedo, *Problemas de História,* pp. 30–31.

Chapter VIII

1. Ralph Davis, *The Rise of the Atlantic Economies* (Ithaca: Cornell University Press, 1973), p. xiii.
2. Immanuel Wallerstein, *The Modern World-System* (New York: Academic Press,

1974), p. 348. For Portugal's crucial role in the rise of the "modern world system," see pp. 38–50.

3. Ibid., p. 349.

4. Godinho, "Portugal and Her Empire, 1680–1720," p. 519.

5. Wallerstein, *The Modern World-System*, p. 350. As a corollary to this, periods of decline (for example, 1670–1690) tend to increase concentrations of capital in economically stronger core states. Immanuel Wallerstein, "Underdevelopment and Phase-B: Effect of the Seventeenth-Century Stagnation on Core and Periphery of the European World Economy," in Walter L. Goldfrank, ed., *The World-System of Capitalism: Past and Present* (London: Sage Publications, 1979), p. 75.

6. Mauro, *L'Expansion Européene (1600–1870)*, pp. 313–14.

7. It should be noted that barrels and other containers for wine, olive oil, and other such products also had a place in the export picture and their manufacture increased as commodity shipments rose. This, as discussed in chapter III, led to conflict between prosperous coopers trying to corner the market on wood and their less fortunate brethren. Andrade e Silva, *Collecção*, 10:461. For a contemporary view of Portuguese commerce (which is especially valuable for the wide range of imported products it lists), see Florentino Bonaccorsi, "O Comércio dos portos de Lisboa, Setúbal e Pôrto nos fins do século XVII, conforme um documento italiano da mesma /epocaχ‡σλ†Boletim da Sociedade de Geografia de Lisboa, series 53, 9–10 (September-October, 1935):337–45.

8. Virginia Rau, *A Exploração e o Comércio do Sal de Setúbal* (Lisbon: Instituto para a Alta Cultura, 1951), p. 29.

9. Ibid., pp. 44–45, 95.

10. Virginia Rau, "Os Holandes e a exportação do sal de Setúbal nos fins do século XVII," *Revista Portuguesa de Historia* 4 (1950):60–65.

11. Freire de Oliveira, *Elementos*, 9:231–32.

12. Andrade e Silva, *Collecção*, 10:275–76.

13. Ibid., 10:364–65, 383.

14. Rau, "Os Holandes," p. 66.

15. Andrade e Silva, *Collecção*, 10:344. The Lisbon *câmara* wasted little time in complaining about this *alvará* since wheat was also in short supply in the capital. D. Pedro II, however, told the city council to mind its own business. Freire de Oliveira, *Elementos*, 9:413–16.

16. Myriam Ellis, *O Monopólio do Sal no Estado do Brasil (1631–1801)* (São Paulo: Universidade de São Paulo, 1955), pp. 47–51, 145–51.

17. Joel Serrão, "Em Torno da economia madeirense de 1580 a 1640," *Das Artes e da História da Madeira* 1 (1) (1950):22–23.

18. BA, 44–XIV–1, fl. 274. Sugar cultivation for local use continued, however, and surpluses were usually exported to France or the Netherlands. T. Bentley Duncan, *Atlantic Islands* (Chicago: University of Chicago Press, 1972), p. 72.

19. Fortunato de Almeida, *História de Portugal*, 6 vols. (Coimbra: Imprensa da Universidade, 1922–1929), 5:325–26.

20. J. A. Pinto Ferreira, *Visitas de Saúde às Embarcações Entradas na Barra do Douro nos Séculos XVI e XVII* (Oporto: Câmara Municipal, 1977), pp. 320–21. Although slaves were annually brought from Brazil to Portugal, other such shipments to Oporto are not listed in Pinto Ferreira's study.

21. S. Sideri, *Trade and Power: Informal Colonialism in Anglo-Portuguese Relations* (Rotterdam: Rotterdam University Press, 1970), p. 35.

22. Alan K. Manchester, *British Preëminence in Brazil* (Chapel Hill: University of North

Carolina Press, 1933), p. 24. General discussion of England and the wine trade can be found in A. D. Francis, *The Wine Trade* (London: A. and C. Black, 1972).

23. This paragraph is based on information gleaned from Freire de Oliveira, *Elementos*, 6:472; 8:252–55, 532–33; 9:21–22, 35.

24. Duncan, *Atlantic Islands*, pp. 93–95.

25. Ibid., pp. 45–46.

26. In 1678, for example, the Lisbon *câmara* had collected over 27,000 cruzados from the *real d'agua* on wine. Freire de Oliveira, *Elementos*, 8:271.

27. Ibid., 8:268–69. In 1695, it was reported that Lisbon's Convento de São Vicente owed 2,408,936 reis in back taxes on wine sold to taverns from 1681 to 1694. Ibid., 9:399–400. Seven years later, contractors for the wine tax complained that various *conventos* in Lisbon, including that of São Vicente, were still selling wine to the public. ANTT, Conselho da Fazenda, *maço* 1, *consulta* of May 9, 1702.

28. Freire de Oliveira, *Elementos*, 8:304.

29. Ibid., 8:467–77, 544.

30. Silva e Andrade, *Collecção*, 10:208.

31. Ibid., 10:246.

32. *Cortes de Lisboa dos Annos de 1697 e 1698, Congresso da Nobreza* (Lisbon: Academia Real das Sciencias, 1824), pp. 100–108. Evidently, the unpopular *real d'agua* was, in part at least, replaced with a 4.5-percent levy on grants, pensions, and salaries. On May 28, 1698, the crown promulgated an *alvará* that inaugurated this latest tax. Freire de Oliveira, *Elementos*, 9:509. Also see 9:488–90.

33. For a brief discussion of beer production in Portugal, see Serrão, ed., *DHP*, 1:556.

34. Freire de Oliveira, *Elementos*, 9:141.

35. Ibid., 9:274.

36. Godinho, "Portugal and Her Empire, 1680–1720," p. 520.

37. Franz-Paul de Almeida Langhans, *Apontamentos para a História de Azeite em Portugal* (Lisbon: Tipografia Portuguesa, Lda., 1949), pp. 141–42, 146.

38. Andrade e Silva, *Collecção*, 8:189.

39. Ribeiro de Macedo, *Obras Ineditas*, pp. 118–19.

40. Serrão, ed., *DHP*, 1:717.

41. H. E. S. Fisher, *The Portugal Trade: A Study of Anglo-Portuguese Commerce 1700–1770* (London: Methuen and Company, 1971), p. 7.

42. Ibid., pp. 142–43.

43. Serrão, ed., *DHP*, 4:211.

44. Andrade e Silva, *Collecção*, 10:80, 129, 242, 325; Serrão, *DHP*, 1:547.

45. Freire de Oliveira, *Elementos*, 9:542–49.

46. Ibid., 9:256.

47. BNL, Fundo Geral, 510, fl. 214v. This price per alquiere was nearly four times the normal price. Godinho, "Portugal and Her Empire, 1680–1720," p. 527. (In Lisbon, 1 alquiere equaled 13.8 liters, and 60 alquieres equaled 1 moio.) Tentative conclusions on the demographic effects of grain shortages in Portuguese Estremadura can be found in U. M. Cowgill and H. B. Johnson, Jr., "Grain Prices and Vital Statistics in a Portuguese Rural Parish, 1671–1720," *Journal of Bio-Social Science* 3 (1971):321–29.

48. Freire de Oliveira, *Elementos*, 9:564.

49. Ibid., 10:201–2.

50. On this, see Harold A. Innis, *The Cod Fisheries* (New Haven: Yale University Press, 1940), chapters 2–5.

51. Paixão, *Monstruosidades*, 4:21–22.

52. Freire de Oliveira, *Elementos*, 8:231–32.
53. Boxer, "Vicissitudes of the Anglo-Portuguese Alliance," p. 33, n. 1.
54. V. M. Shillington and A. B. W. Chapman, *The Commercial Relations of England and Portugal* (London: Routledge and Sons, 1907[?]), p. 212.
55. BNL, Fundo Geral, 748, fls. 212v–213.
56. Fisher, *The Portugal Trade*, p. 17. Further data on the cod trade can be found in Pinto Ferreira, *Visitas de Saúde*, passim.
57. It should be noted, however, that the crown did grant a limited fishing monopoly to a contractor named Estevão Luz in 1694. In his petition for the contract, Luz, a resident of Lisbon, argued that Portugal should not be experiencing a shortage of fish when there were plenty to be had along the country's coast. On the basis of this and other arguments, Luz received an exclusive four-year contract to launch large fishing expeditions (one per year) within an area extending eight leagues from the Portuguese coast. It is not clear what became of this venture, but Portuguese fishermen were not pleased with Luz's monopoly. Freire de Oliveira, *Elementos*, 9:362–63, 366, 371–73.
58. For a discussion of the expansion of the Brazilian whaling industry, see Myriam Ellis, *A Baleia no Brasil Colonial* (São Paulo: Edições Melhoramentos, 1969).
59. Andrade e Silva, *Collecção*, 10:54, 296.
60. BNL, Pombalina, 475, fls. 197–215v.
61. Ibid., Fundo Geral, 510, fl. 214v.
62. Passenger travel was also a chancy business. Even as late as the 1760s, a foreign traveler named José Gorani could disgustedly report that it was "easier to find a ship going to Goa or Brazil than a coach for Coimbra or Braga." Quoted in Villiers, "Portuguese Society," p. 206.
63. Serrão, ed., *DHP*, 4:211–12.
64. Bluteau, *Instruccam sobre a Cultura*, pp. 45–46.

Chapter IX

1. In fact, it has been estimated that the number of ablebodied Portuguese men in the Far East never exceeded 10,000. C. R. Boxer, *The Portuguese Seaborne Empire: 1415–1825* (New York: Alfred A. Knopf, 1969), p. 53. At the end of the sixteenth century, the total number of Portuguese in the Far East was estimated at 16,000. Sérgio, *Antológia*, p. 134.
2. Wallerstein, *The Modern World-System*, pp. 328–39. Portuguese west Africa may indeed be viewed as a sort of "semiexternal" area during this period. Though this category was not part of Wallerstein's analysis, it represents a possible addition to a model in which the distinction between world economy and external areas seems too sharply drawn.
3. Fernando Novais, *Estrutura e dinâmica do sistema colonial (séculos XVI–XVII)* (Lisbon: Livros Horizontes, 1975), pp. 9–10.
4. C. R. Boxer, "The Portuguese in the East, 1500–1800," in H. R. Livermore, ed., *Portugal and Brazil* (Oxford: Clarendon Press, 1953), p. 231.
5. For a discussion of England's abandonment of Tangier in 1684, which offended the Portuguese since they were not given the chance to regain control over the Moroccan stronghold, see Edgar Prestage, *O Conde de Castelmelhor e a Retrocessão de Tanger a Portugal* (Coimbra: Imprensa da Universidade, 1917). Portugal's lengthy tenure in North Africa is discussed in Robert Ricard, *Études sur l'Histoire de Portugais au Maroc* (Coimbra: Imprensa da Universidade, 1955).
6. Manuel Godinho, S.J., *Relação do Novo Caminho Que Fez por Terra e Mar Vindo da*

NOTES TO CHAPTER IX

India para Portugal no Anno de 1663 (Lisbon: Imprensa Nacional—Casa da Moeda, 1974), p. 17.

7. Boxer, "The Portuguese in the East," pp. 235–36.

8. Eric Axelson, *Portuguese in South-East Africa 1600–1700* (Johannesburg: Witwatersrand University Press, 1964), p. 144.

9. Ibid., p. 154.

10. Alexandre Lobato, *Relações Luso-Maratos, 1658–1737* (Lisbon: Centro de Estudos Históricos Ultramarinos, 1965), pp. 28–34. Additional information on Goa in the 1680s can be found in ANTT, Convento da Graça, Misc. Manuscritos, *caixa* 6, *tomo* 3.

11. C. R. Boxer, *Fidalgos in the Far East, 1550–1770* (London: Oxford University Press reprint, 1968), pp. 170–72.

12. Abbé Carré, *The Travels of Abbé Carré in India and the Near East, 1672 to 1674*, 3 vols., Lady Fawcett, trans., Sir Charles Fawcett, ed., with the assistance of Sir Richard Burn (London: Hakluyt Society, series 2, vols. 95–97, 1947–1948), 97:715.

13. Andrade e Silva, *Collecção*, 10:24.

14. Axelson, *Portuguese in South-East Africa*, pp. 180–81.

15. Ibid., p. 182.

16. Tito Augusto de Carvalho, *As Companhias Portuguesas de Colonização* (Lisbon: Imprensa Nacional, 1902), p. 39. Six years later, D. Pedro II also began urging wealthy Bahians to finance a proposed Junta do Comércio da India. J. R. Amaral Lapa, *A Bahia e a Carreira da India* (São Paulo: Companhia Editora Nacional, 1968), pp. 265–68.

17. Quoted in Axelson, *Portuguese in South-East Africa*, p. 184. Additional discussion of Portugal's unruly subjects can be found in Allen F. Isaacman, *Mozambique: The Africanization of a European Institution, the Zambesi Prazos, 1550–1902* (Madison: University of Wisconsin Press, 1972), passim; and M. D. D. Newitt, "The Portuguese in the Zambesi: An Historical Interpretation of the Prazo System," *Journal of African History* 10 (1)(1969):67–85.

18. Details of the heroic defense of Mombasa can be found in C. R. Boxer and Carlos de Azevedo, *Fort Jesus and the Portuguese in Mombasa, 1593–1729* (London: Hollis and Carter, 1960), pp. 58–73. A manifest of men and material aboard a relief ship prepared by the viceroy of India is in BNL, Pombalina, 439, fls. 261–68. Also see Amaral Lapa, *A Bahia*, pp. 205–6.

19. Carvalho, *As Companhias Portuguesas*, pp. 46–47.

20. Godinho, "Portugal and Her Empire, 1680–1720," p. 517. Evidence of this commercial upswing is clearly seen in the growth of tobacco revenues collected by the local monopoly (*estanco*) in Goa. In 1681, 26,666 xerafins were collected, and by 1704 revenues had soared to 101,500 xerafins. ANTT, Junta do Tabaco, Consultas, *maço* 4, December 18, 1681; ibid., Cartas do Brasil e India, *maço* 96, December 18, 1704.

21. Godinho, *L'Economie de l'Empire Portugais*, p. 672.

22. Paixão, *Monstruosidades*, 3:41. For data showing the decline in shipping, see Mauro and Parker, "Portugal," p. 73; and Boxer, *The Portuguese Seaborne Empire*, pp. 381–82.

23. Virginia Rau, et al., "Les Escales de la Carreira da India (XVIᵉ–XVIIᵉ Siècles)," in Recueils de la Société Jean Bodin, *Les Grandes Escales* vol. 33 (Brussels: Ediciones de la Librairie Encyclopédique, 1972), pp. 17–18. Information on some of the ships stopping in Bahia during the seventeenth and eighteenth centuries can be found in Alexander Marchant, "Colonial Brazil as a Way Station for the Portuguese India Fleets," *The Geographical Review* 31 (July 1941):454–65.

24. C. R. Boxer, "The Carreira da India, 1650–1750," *Mariner's Mirror* 46 (February 1960):42–43.

25. Amaral Lapa, *A Bahia*, pp. 21–22, 255.
26. Vieira, *Cartas*, 3:630, 647.
27. Victorino Magalhães Godinho, "Portugal, as Frotas," p. 82. In 1660, it was reported that between five and six thousand men were employed in the annual voyages of the Brazil fleet. Freire de Oliveira, *Elementos*, 7:cvi. During the eighteenth century, the number of ships (and probably men) sailing in the annual voyage of the *frota* to Portugal remained roughly the same, though a hundred merchant ships, including two from India, reached the mother country in 1759. During this century, approximately one-tenth of the vessels in the *frota* proceeded to Oporto. Eulalia Maria Lahmeyer Lobo, "As Frotas do Brasil," *Jahrbuch für Geschichte von Staat, Wirstschaft und Gesellschaft Lateinamerikas* 4 (1967):472–73. During D. Pedro II's reign, at least ten to twelve English vessels took part in the annual voyages of the *frota*. Boxer, "Vicissitudes of the Anglo-Portuguese Alliance," p. 28.
28. Mauro, *Le Portugal et L'Atlantique*, pp. 238–39.
29. AHU, Bahia, Papeis Avulsos, 1st uncatalogued series, *caixa* 10, manifests of June 23–27, 1668.
30. Freitas, *A Companhia Geral*, p. 110.
31. Paixão, *Monstruosidades*, 4:44.
32. Freitas, *A Companhia Geral*, p. 320.
33. The best study on the founding of the Brazil Company is C. R. Boxer, "Padre António Vieira, S.J., and the Institution of the Brazil Company in 1649," *HAHR* 29 (1949):474–97.
34. Quoted in ibid., p. 490.
35. Further discussion of complaints against the Brazil Company can be found in Freitas, *A Companhia Geral*, pp. 98–102.
36. Ibid., pp. 107–10.
37. The *regimento* was printed in Andrade e Silva, *Collecção*, 8:207–20.
38. A brief but useful discussion of the forces that led to the decline of Brazilian sugar's predominance on the world market can be found in Matthew Edel, "The Brazilian Sugar Cycle of the Seventeenth Century and the Rise of West Indian Competition," *Caribbean Studies* 9 (April 1969):24–44. Even though prices dropped after 1650, Brazilian sugar production and the number of *engenhos* in operation actually increased between 1650 and 1690. See Mauro and Parker, "Portugal," p. 710.
39. Alfândega de Lisboa, Museu Histórico, *Reflexos Aduaneiros dos Descobrimentos e Conquistas* (Second Exposição Temporária) (Lisbon, 1960), p. 42.
40. Godinho, "Portugal, as Frotas," p. 74. Also see Schwartz, "Free Labor in a Slave Economy," pp. 191–95.
41. Caribbean planters, however, also bemoaned the heavy tax burden laid on their sugar. See E. Littleton, *The Groans of the Plantations, or a True Account of Their Grievous and Extreme Sufferings by the Heavy Impositions upon Sugar* (London: M. Clark, 1689).
42. The pastel (or woad) trade collapsed after 1650. Although taxes were blamed, the mortal blow was dealt by growing exports of indigo from the Americas, a product that was less expensive and more productive of *indigotin*, the common dye constituent of the two substances. See Duncan, *Atlantic Islands*, pp. 86–92.
43. Freire de Oliveira, *Elementos*, 9:130–31.
44. Quoted in Boxer, *The Portuguese Seaborne Empire*, p. 152. The complete passage is in Vieira, *Cartas*, 3:597. Two years later, Vieira wrote that matters had grown even worse! Ibid., 3:629.
45. Boxer, *The Portuguese Seaborne Empire*, p. 153.
46. Andrade e Silva, *Collecção*, 10:131–32.

NOTES TO CHAPTER IX

47. Ibid., 9:421–22.
48. Mello, *Olinda Restaurada*, pp. 279–93.
49. Andrade e Silva, *Collecção*, 10:87, 254, 268, 359–60, 403, 456. Letters written by an English businessman describing depressed conditions in Recife can be found in AHU, Pernambuco, Papeis Avulsos, *caixa* 6.
50. Virginia Rau and Maria Fernanda Gomes da Silva, *Os Manuscritos do Arquivo da Casa de Cadaval Respeitantes ao Brasil*, 2 vols. (Coimbra: Imprensa da Universidade, 1956–1958), 1:203.
51. Quoted in Russell-Wood, *Fidalgos and Philanthropists*, p. 65.
52. Vieira, *Cartas*, 3:629. The great Jesuit also reported hearing that Bahians had lost more than 500,000 cruzados as a result of the devaluation. Ibid., 3:646.
53. BA, 51-IX-30, fl. 14.
54. Vivaldo Coaracy, *O Rio de Janeiro no Século 17*, 2nd ed. (Rio de Janeiro: José Olympio, 1965), p. 216.
55. Vieira, *Cartas*, 3:654.
56. For an explanation of the probable origin of the term *bandeirante*, consult Richard M. Morse, ed., *The Bandeirantes: The Historical Role of the Brazilian Pathfinders* (New York: Alfred A. Knopf, Borzoi Books, 1965), pp. 22–23.
57. Manuel Cardozo, "A History of Mining in Colonial Brazil, 1500–1750" (unpublished Ph.D. dissertation, Stanford University, 1939), pp. 87–88. For details on Mendonça's role in the mineral quest, see Lopes Sierra, *A Governor and His Image*, passim.
58. Rau, *Os Manuscritos*, 1:206.
59. Cardozo, "A History of Mining," p. 88.
60. Ibid., pp. 91–92.
61. ANTT, Livraria, Manuscritos Brasileiros, no. 33, fl. 30. Data on deliveries of gold and silver to the Lisbon mint from 1605 to 1675 can be found in Mauro and Parker, "Portugal," p. 74.
62. Manuel Cardozo, "Dom Rodrigo de Castel-Branco and the Brazilian El Dorado, 1673–1682," *The Americas* 1 (1944):139.
63. Ibid., p. 140. Castel-Branco's personal expense account came to 400,000 reis. Those of his principal lieutenants, João Vieira de Morães and Jorge Soares de Macedo, came to 200,000 and 100,000 reis, respectively. ANTT, Livraria, Manuscritos Brasileiros, no. 33, fl. 36.
64. Francisco Varnhagen, *História geral do Brasil*, 3rd ed., 5 vols. (São Paulo: Companhia Melhoramentos, 1927[?]–1948), 4:145.
65. Cardozo, "Dom Rodrigo," pp. 140–58.
66. In 1690, for example, the crown granted the governor of Rio de Janeiro the right to grant honors and rewards to Paulistas who discovered gold or silver mines. Honors included elevation to *fidalgo* status and membership in one of the three largest military orders. Eight years later, these incentives were extended to individuals who discovered copper, tin, saltpeter, or other useful mineral deposits. Basilio de Magalhães, "Documentos relativos ao 'bandeirismo' paulista e questões connexas, no periodo 1664 a 1700," *Revista do Instituto Histórico e Geographico de São Paulo* 18 (1914):283–84, 364. For a discussion of D. Pedro II's contemporaneous encouragement of copper production in Angola, see, for example, the 1676 *regimento* of Governor Aires de Saldanha de Meneses e Sousa, BNL, Fundo Geral, 8554, fl. 12, 14–14v; and the laws of 1693 and 1694 published in Andrade e Silva, *Collecção*, 10:319, 361.
67. Quoted in Cardozo, "A History of Mining," p. 122.

NOTES TO CHAPTER IX 323

68. Rau, *Os Manuscritos*, 1:233–44. During the preceding three years Brazilian officials had urged "defensive expansion," Mario Rodríguez, "Dom Pedro of Braganza and colônia do Sacramento, 1680–1705," *HAHR* 38(1958): 190.

69. Luís Ferrand de Almeida, *A Diplomacia Portuguesa e os Limites Meridionais do Brasil (1493–1700)* (Coimbra: Imprensa da Universidade, 1957), p. 109. Exploiting the vast cattle herds found in the Rio de la Plata region also offered Portugal relief from its dependence on England and Ireland for hides. Documentation on Portugal's protectionist measures for hides and English displeasure over them was published in Freire de Oliveira, *Elementos*, 8:341–44, 473–74, 563–64, 588.

70. AHMF, Provisões do Conselho do Estado, 407 (9/48/407), *paracer* of September 12, 1680.

71. Almeida, *A Diplomacia Portuguesa*, pp. 163–80.

72. Jonathas da Costa Rego Monteiro, *A Colônia do Sacramento, 1680–1777*, 2 vols. (Pôrto Alegre: Livraria do Globo, 1937), 1:115–18.

73. Andrade e Silva, *Collecção*, 6:153.

74. AHU, Bahia, Papeis Avulsos, 1st uncatalogued series, *caixa* 11, *consulta* of February 17, 1671. At some point, tea was also introduced into Pernambuco since two small cases of prepared leaves were shipped to Lisbon in the *frota* of 1661. Alfândega de Lisboa, *Reflexos Aduaneiros*, p. 24.

75. Andrade e Silva, *Collecção*, 10:190.

76. Luís Ferrand de Almeida, "Aclimatação de plantas do Oriente no Brasil durante os séculos XVII e XVIII," *Revista Portuguesa de História* 15 (1975):380.

77. J. R. Amaral Lapa, "O Problema das Drogas Orientais," in *Economia Colonial* (São Paulo: Editora Perspectiva, 1973), p. 122.

78. Almeida, "Aclimatação de plantas," p. 380.

79. Ibid., pp. 382, 386–87.

80. Ibid., pp. 392, 394–96. Despite the concerted effort to establish cinnamon production, ginger, also a transplant, remained the principal spice of the Portuguese Atlantic. Mauro, *Le Portugal et l'Atlantique*, p. 368.

81. Amaral Lapa, "O Problema das Drogas," pp. 135–37.

82. Serafim Leite, *História da Companhia de Jesus no Brasil*, 10 vols. (Lisbon: Livraria Portugalia, 1938–1950), 5:161.

83. Ibid., 4:157.

84. Almeida, "Aclimatação de plantas," p. 416.

85. During this era, France renewed a long-standing claim to territory adjoining the mouth of the Amazon. This subject was discussed in Andrew S. Szarka, "Louis XIV and Brazil: The French Probe into Maranhão, 1697–1700," *Proceedings of the French Colonial History Society* 2 (1977):133–48.

86. Almeida, "Aclimatação de plantas," p. 373.

87. For a recent and valuable study of the enslavement and "civilizing" of Indians in Brazil, see John Hemming, *Red Gold: The Conquest of the Brazilian Indians, 1500–1760* (Cambridge: Harvard University Press, 1978).

88. Mathias C. Kieman, *The Indian Policy of Portugal in the Amazon Region, 1640–1693* (New York: Octagon reprint, 1973), pp. 138–43.

89. Ibid., pp. 148–53, 158–63.

90. Sue A. Gross, "Labor in Amazonia in the First Half of the Eighteenth Century," *The Americas* 32 (1975):221.

91. Magalhães, "Documentos relativos," p. 287.

NOTES TO CHAPTER IX

92. Boxer, *Salvador de Sá*, p. 231.

93. Philip D. Curtin, *The Atlantic Slave Trade: A Census* (Madison: University of Wisconsin Press, 1969), p. 119. For slave prices, see Schwartz, "Free Labor in a Slave Economy," p. 194.

94. The question as to how many Indians perished following European expansion into the Americas is still far from resolved. Casualties may well have been in the tens of millions. For a valuable collection of articles on the population question, see William M. Denevan, ed., *The Native Population of the Americas in 1492* (Madison: University of Wisconsin Press, 1976). The latest estimate for the Indian population of Brazil in 1500 is 2,431,000. Hemming, *Red Gold*, p. 492.

95. For a discussion of Portuguese activity on the Mina coast after 1637, see John Vogt, *Portuguese Rule on the Gold Coast, 1469–1682* (Athens: University of Georgia Press, 1979), pp. 189–204; and A. F. C. Ryder, "The Re-establishment of Portuguese Factories on the Costa da Mina to the Mid-Eighteenth Century," *Journal of the Historical Society of Nigeria* 1 (1958):157–83.

96. Pierre Verger, *Flux et Reflux de la Traite des Nègres entre le Golfe de Bénin et Bahia de Todos os Santos du XVIIe au XIXe Siècle*. (Paris: Mouton, 1968), p. 29.

97. Boxer, *Salvador de Sá*, pp. 279–82.

98. The classic contemporary account of the Angolan campaigns is António de Oliveira de Cadornega, *História Geral das Guerras Angolanas* (1680), 3 vols. (Lisbon: Agencia-Geral do Ultramar, 1972).

99. BNL, Fundo Geral, 8554, fl. 17v.

100. David Birmingham, *Trade and Conflict in Angola: The Mbundu and Their Neighbors under the Influence of the Portuguese, 1483–1790* (Oxford: Clarendon Press, 1966), p. 134.

101. Verger, *Flux et Reflux*, pp. 66–67.

102. Birmingham, *Trade and Conflict in Angola*, pp. 134–35.

103. BNL, Fundo Geral, 6825, fl. 4–4v.

104. Birmingham, *Trade and Conflict in Angola*, p. 137. Between 1710 and 1731, the average number of slaves exported from Angola was about 6,400 per annum. Ibid.

105. Walter Rodney, "Portuguese Attempts at Monopoly on the Upper Guinea Coast, 1580–1640," *Journal of African History* 6 (1965):315–16.

106. Candido da Silva Teixeira, "Companhia de Cacheu, Rios e Comércio de Guiné," *Boletim do Arquivo Histórico Colonial* 1 (Lisbon, 1950):92. (This first *Boletim* was also the last.)

107. Ibid., pp. 101–3.

108. Ibid., pp. 110–32.

109. Duncan, *Atlantic Islands*, p. 210.

110. Verger, *Flux et Reflux*, p. 66.

111. Andrade e Silva, *Collecção*, 6:159, 240.

112. Catherine Lugar, "The Portuguese Tobacco Trade and Tobacco Growers of Bahia in the Late Colonial Period," in Dauril Alden and Warren Dean, eds., *Essays Concerning the Socio-Economic History of Brazil and Portuguese India* (Gainesville: University Presses of Florida, 1977), p. 26.

113. This theme is examined in Carl A. Hanson, "Monopoly and Contraband in the Portuguese Tobacco Trade, 1624–1702," *Luso-Brazilian Review* (forthcoming in 1981).

114. Raul Esteves dos Santos, *Os Tabacos: Sua Influência na Vida da Nação*, 2 vols. (Lisbon: Seara Nova, 1974), 1:28, n. 2.

115. Ibid., 1:29.

116. ANTT, Junta do Tabaco, Decretos, *maço* 50, March 28, 1678.

117. Ibid., Consultas, *maço* 6, "Traslado de Regimento dos Superintendentes [June 28, 1678]," p. 51.
118. John Colbatch, *An Account of the Court of Portugal under the Reign of the Present King Dom Pedro II* (Lisbon: Thomas Bennet, 1700), p. 23.
119. ANTT, Junta do Tabaco, Decretos, *maço* 50, November 8, 1674.
120. Colbatch, *An Account of the Court of Portugal*, p. 17.
121. Lugar, "The Portuguese Tobacco Trade," p. 36.
122. Azevedo, *Épocas de Portugal Económico*, p. 481. Total public revenues for 1716 exceeded 3.94 billion reis. Ibid.
123. Andrade e Silva, *Collecção*, 8:203.
124. Alfândega de Lisboa, *Reflexos Aduaneiros*, p. 15.

Chapter X

1. ANTT, Junta do Tabaco, Consultas, *maço* 2, January 10, 1684; ibid., June 23, 1884. Also see ibid., Decretos, *maço* 50, July 18, 1681. Tobacco revenues for 1681 are given in chapter VI, table 3.
2. Ibid., Decretos, *maço* 51, March 26, 1697.
3. Ibid., Consultas, *maço* 2, February 14, 1682.
4. After its establishment in 1674, the junta became increasingly involved in the sale of diamonds, cloth, pepper, and saltpeter coming from India. Ibid., Decretos, *maço* 50, September 9, 1680. For a discussion of the India House, see Serrão, ed., *DHP*, 2:505–13.
5. ANTT, Junta do Tabaco, Consultas, *maço* 3, June 9, 1687; ibid., *maço* 4, March 14, 1695.
6. This amount was probably somewhat less than that normally shipped during the 1660s. Mauro, *Le Portugal et L'Atlantique*, p. 372. Mauro's actual figure is 20,000 quintais, which equaled about 5,000 arrobas. At this time, a roll of tobacco, which consisted of thick strands of cured tobacco wrapped around a staff and then encased with a hide, weighed about 4 to 5 arrobas (about 128 to 160 pounds). By the 1690s, however, Brazilian planters were shipping enormous rolls weighing 11 or 12 arrobas. To curb this method of shipping, the crown ordered in 1696 that no rolls were to exceed 8 arrobas. ANTT, Junta do Tabaco, Consultas, *maço* 4A, November 23, 1696. Rolls shipped to west Africa during this era were smaller, usually weighing around 3 arrobas.
7. AHU, Bahia, Papeis Avulsos, *caixa* 10, manifests of June 23–27, 1668.
8. ANTT, Junta do Tabaco, Consultas, *maço* 2, September 20, 1685.
9. Ibid., *maço* 3, May 2, 1687, October 30, 1686.
10. Godinho, "Portugal and Her Empire, 1680–1720," p. 519.
11. J. H. Galloway, "Northeast Brazil 1700–1750: The Agricultural Crisis Re-examined," *Journal of Historical Geography* 1 (1975):21–28. Also see Rae Flory, "Bahian Society in the Mid-Colonial Period: Sugar Planters, Tobacco Growers, Merchants, and Artisans of Salvador and the Recôncavo, 1680–1725" (unpublished Ph.D. dissertation, University of Texas, 1978), passim.
12. André João Antonil (pseudonym), *Cultura e Opulencia do Brasil por suas drogas e minas*, texte de L'edition de 1711, traduction et commentaire critique par Andrée Mansuy (Paris: Université de Paris, 1968), pp. 332–35. The Portuguese, in turn, apparently consumed small quantities of foreign tobacco in addition to domestic and Brazilian varieties. Between Michaelmas (September 29) 1696 and March 1697, for example,

NOTES TO CHAPTER X

5,528 pounds of Virginia tobacco were exported from London to Portugal. C. M. MacInnes, *The Early English Tobacco Trade* (London: Kegan Paul, Trench, Trubner and Company, 1926), p. 168.

13. Jacob M. Price, *France and the Chesapeake: A History of the French Tobacco Monopoly, 1674–1791, and of Its Relationship to the British and American Tobacco Trades*, 2 vols. (Ann Arbor, University of Michigan Press 1973), 1:173–83.

14. Verger, *Flux et Reflux*, pp. 34, 66–67.

15. ANTT, Livraria, Manuscritos Brasileiros, no. 33, fls. 108v–110v.

16. For a discussion of the negotiations leading up to Spain's signing the *asiento* agreement with the Cacheu Company, see Georges Scelle, *La Traite Négrière aux Indes de Castile*, 2 vols. (Paris: L. La Rose and Forcel, 1906), 2:20–37. The 1696 contract was printed in Andrade e Silva, *Collecção*, 10:491–506.

17. Godinho, "Portugal and Her Empire, 1680–1720," p. 515.

18. Scelle, *La Traite Négrière*, 2:66. Not all Portuguese wre displeased with loss of the contract since failure to meet the minimum delivery obligation (4,000 slaves) had been a source of concern. Ibid., 2:44–45.

19. Pierre Verger, *Bahia and the West Coast Trade (1549–1851)* (Ibadan: Ibadan University Press, 1964), p. 11.

20. For a discussion of Mafra and other baroque edifices constructed with the help of Brazilian gold, consult Serrão, ed., *DHP*, 2:884–86, and the sources cited there.

21. Boxer, *The Golden Age*, p. 35.

22. Antonil, *Cultura e Opulencia*, pp. 368–70.

23. Alfândega de Lisbon, *Relfexos Aduaneiros*, pp. 54–55.

24. Antonil, *Cultura e Opulencia*, p. 480.

25. Myriam Ellis, *A Baleia no Brasil Colonial*, pp. 38–43; Antonil, *Cultura e Opulencia*, pp. 488–89.

26. For a discussion of the scarcity of documentation on the brazilwood trade, see Mansuy's comments in Antonil, *Cultura e Opulencia*, p. 488, n. 5. The best source, though it is largely limited to the first half of the seventeenth century, is Mauro, *Le Portugal et L'Atlantique*, pp. 115–45.

27. Azevedo, *Épocas de Portugal Económico*, p. 259.

28. ANTT, Convento da Graça, Misc. Manuscritos, *caixa* 5, *tomo* 2, fl. 82.

29. Rau, *Os Manuscritos*, 1:251.

30. Mauro, *Le Portugal et L'Atlantique*, pp. 131–37. A lesser figure, 6,000 quintais per year, was given in Edgar Prestage, *Tres Consultas do Conselho da Fazenda de 1656 a 1657* (Oporto: Typographia da Empresa Literaria e Typographica, 1920), p. 11.

31. Andrade e Silva, *Collecção*, 10:400.

32. Antonil, *Cultura e Opulencia*, p. 488.

33. Rau, *Os Manuscritos*, 2:216.

34. Azevedo, *Épocas de Portugal Económico*, p. 259.

35. Galloway, "Northeast Brazil 1700–1750," pp. 26–27.

36. Ibid., p. 37.

37. For an important study of this theme that focuses on post-1710 Minas Gerais, see A. J. R. Russell-Wood, "Local Government in Portuguese America: A Study in Cultural Divergence," *Comparative Studies in Society and History* 16 (March 1974):187–231.

38. Andrade e Silva, *Collecção*, 8:141–42.

39. BNL, Fundo Geral, 8554, fl. 15v.

40. Andrade e Silva, *Collecção*, 10:481.

41. ANTT, Junta do Tabaco, Consultas, *maço* 4, September 17, 1698.

NOTES TO CHAPTER X 327

42. Paixão, *Monstruosidades*, 3:108–10.

43. Some of the ransom money was raised by clerics begging alms. During the years 1667 through 1676, Portuguese collections of this sort came to approximately 50,000 reis per annum. BNL, Fundo Geral, 427, fl. 20. In 1671, D. Pedro beseeched the impecunious Lisbon city council to donate funds for the ransom of prisoners in Algiers and thereby set an example for other *câmaras* in the realm. Freire de Oliveira, *Elementos*, 7:288–89.

44. Paixão, *Monstruosidades*, 4:21–22.

45. Godinho, "Portugal and Her Empire, 1680–1720," p. 515.

46. In 1703, for example, thirty-eight captives were gotten out of Algiers after a ransom of 10,553,116 reis was paid. BNL. Fundo Geral, 6504, fls. 117–117v.

47. Andrade e Silva, *Collecção*, 10:400.

48. Manuel Cardozo, "The Collection of the Fifth in Brazil, 1695–1709," *HAHR* 20 (1940):365–69.

49. Ibid., p. 372.

50. Boxer, *The Golden Age*, pp. 59–60.

51. Cardozo, "The Collection of the Fifth," p. 377. It was also proposed in 1709 that additional smelting houses be established, but apparently cost also stood in the way of this suggestion. Rau, *Os Manuscritos*, 2:63–64.

52. The two codes were compared in Affonso de Escragnolle Taunay, *História Geral das Bandeiras Paulistas*, 11 vols. (São Paulo: Typografia Ideal, H. L. Canton, 1924–1950), 9:244–54.

53. Andrée Mansuy, "Memoire Inédit D'Ambrose Jouffret sur le Brésil a l'Epoque de la Découverte de Mines D'Or (1704)," in *Actas* of the Fifth Coloquio Internacional de Estudos Luso-Brasileiros, 5 vols. (Coimbra: Imprensa de Universidade, 1965–1968), 2:425; Boxer, *The Golden Age*, p. 58.

54. Cardozo, "A History of Mining," p. 220.

55. Antonil, *Cultura e Opulencia*, p. 464.

56. Governor Albuquerque's actions during the conflict are described in Boxer, *The Golden Age*, pp. 75–83.

57. Ibid., p. 56.

58. ANTT, Junta do Tabaco, Decretos, *maço* 50, January 30, 1683; ibid., Consultas, *maço* 2, March 9, 1684.

59. Ibid., Decretos, *maço* 50, November 28, 1684. This document, like numerous others in *maço* 50, is a *consulta* that has become mistakenly mixed in with the bundle of decrees.

60. Ibid., Consultas, *maço* 1, April 29, 1676; ibid., September 23, 1676.

61. Ibid., *maço* 5, March 20, 1700; ibid., January 30, 1700.

62. Ibid., Decretos, *maço* 50, April 10, 1683; ibid., Consultas, *maço* 2, August 31, 1683.

63. Ibid., Consultas, *maço* 4A, November 14, 1695; ibid., Cartas do Brasil e India, *maço* 96A, January 20, 1701; ibid., *maço* 96, April 15, 1702.

64. The reform program probably took on increased urgency when it was discovered in 1699 that tobacco revenues would not provide the additional 600,000 cruzados. BACL, Mss. Azul 556, Mendo Fois de Pereira to D. Luís da Cunha, February 29, 1699.

65. dos Santos, *Os Tabacos*, 1:32–34.

66. ANTT, Junta de Tabaco, Cartas do Brasil e India, *maço* 96A, July 21, 1699.

67. Earlier efforts to require the marking of *caixas* are noted in Schwartz, "Free Labor in a Slave Economy," p. 185, n. 108. A great number of producer brands appear in inventories in ANTT, Junta de Tabaco, Cartas do Brasil e India, *maço* 96A.

68. Ibid., Consultas, *maço* 4A, December 28, 1698.
69. Ibid., Cartas do Brasil e India, *maço* 96A, May 23, 1698; July 30, 1698.
70. Ibid., "Copia do Regimento que o Sr. Dom João Lencastro . . . fez . . . para melhor arreccadação do Tabaco . . . [Bahia, September 8, 1699]."
71. Lugar, "The Portuguese Tobacco Trade," p. 37.
72. Verger, *Flux et Reflux*, pp. 67–68. In another effort to harness the financial power of the Bahian mercantile community, D. Pedro II decreed that the merchants could annually send three trade ships to India. Though the junta opposed this, the military's need for scarce saltpeter overrode the monopoly's objections. ANTT, Junta de Tabaco, Consultas, *maço* 5, February 15, 1701. Other contemporaneous efforts to involve Bahian merchants in royally controlled commercial activities were examined in Carvalho, *As Companhias Portuguesas*, passim; and Amaral Lapa, *A Bahia*, pp. 165–68.
73. Flory, "Bahian Society," pp. 244–46.
74. Ibid., p. 238; Verger, *Flux et Reflux*, pp. 69, 72. According to Pierre Verger, the origins of Brazilianist feelings can be traced, in part at least, to the emerging rivalry between tobacco merchants in Lisbon and Bahia. This suggestion warrants further inquiry, but it should be borne in mind that the Bahian mercantile community was constantly replenished by Portuguese immigrants. Moreover, these immigrants constituted the vast majority of that community. See Rae Flory and David Grant Smith, "Bahian Merchants and Planters in the Seventeenth and Early Eighteenth Centuries," *HAHR* 58 (1978):574–77. For the correspondence of one great Lisbon merchant of the era, Francisco Pinheiro ([?]–1749), see Luis Lisanti Filho, *Negócios Coloniais (Uma Correspondência Commercial do Século XVIII)*, 5 vols. (Brasilia and São Paulo: Ministerio da Fazenda, 1973).
75. For a brief biographical sketch of this talented administrator and brilliant military leader, see Pereira and Rodrigues, *Portugal*, 4:1113–15.
76. ANTT, Junta do Tabaco, Consultas *maço* 4A, December 4, 1698.
77. Antonil, *Cultura e Opulencia*, pp. 336–37.
78. The original contract, which was for the staggering sum of 1,536,000 cruzados, can be found in ANTT, Junta do Tabaco, Decretos, *maço* 51. After this agreement was signed a great deal of wrangling over its terms went on between the crown and Gómez, during which the Spaniard renegotiated the purchase price down to 320,000 cruzados. Ibid., Consultas, *maço* 5, July 28, 1701.
79. The *regimento* is printed in Antonil, *Cultura e Opulencia*, pp. 539–40.
80. *Regimento da Administracam do Tabaco* (Lisbon: Miguel Deslandes, 1702). For a copy see BNL, Reservados, 101^4.
81. ANTT, Junta do Tabaco, Consultas, *maço* 5, August 21, 1700.
82. Francisco Iglesias, "Minas e a Imposição do Estado no Brazil," *Revista de Historia* (São Paulo) 50 (1974):263–65. This is not to say, however, that the restiveness in Minas ended. For a valuable study of the socioeconomic bases of the famous Mineiro conspiracy of 1788, see Kenneth R. Maxwell, *Conflicts and Conspiracies: Brazil and Portugal 1750–1808* (Cambridge: Cambridge University Press, 1973).

Chapter XI

1. A. D. Francis, "John Methuen and the Anglo-Portuguese Treaties of 1703," *The Historical Journal* 3 (1960):107.
2. Ibid., pp. 110–12. Franco-Portuguese relations during this period were ably discussed in Andrew S. Szarka, "Portugal, France, and the Coming of the War of the

NOTES TO CHAPTER XI 329

Spanish Succession, 1697–1703" (unpublished Ph.D. dissertation, Ohio State University, 1976).

3. BNL, Fundo Geral, 749, fls. 33–33v. For the third estate's views on the alliance question, see Franz-Paul de Almeida Langhans, "Advertencias feitas á Casa dos Vinte e Quatro de Lisboa em 1701 sobre a política que conduziu á Guerra da Successáo de Espanha," *Revista Portuguesa de História* 4 (1949):343–59.

4. BNL, Fundo Geral, 674, fls. 243–46.

5. Virginia Rau, *D. Catarina de Brangança* (Coimbra: Coimbra Editora, 1941), p. 328.

6. Francis, *The Methuens*, p. 179; Luis de Sampayo, *Para a História do Tratado de Methuen* (Coimbra: Imprensa da Universidade, 1928), p. 19. Copies of the treaties can be found in José Ferreira Borges de Castro, *Collecção dos Tratados, Convenções, Contratos e Actos Publicos Celebrados entre a Coroa de Portugal e as Mais Potencias desde 1640 até ao Presente*, 30 vols. (Lisbon: Imprensa Nacional, 1856–1880), 2:140–87.

7. Quoted in Francis, *The Methuens*, p. 198.

8. Dias, *Os Lanifícios*, 1:59.

9. Andrade e Silva, *Collecção*, 10:64–65.

10. Ibid., 9:165.

11. "Papel sobre o Registro das Fazendas," BNL, Fundo Geral, 748, fls. 209–19v.

12. Ibid., fls. 209–10v, 213–16.

13. Andrade e Silva, *Collecção*, 10:271.

14. Cidade e Selvagem, *Cultura Portuguesa*, 10:25. for a discussion of accusations against Ericeira that may have exacerbated his condition, see BL, Additional, 20,944, fls. 261–277.

15. BNL, Fundo Geral, 510, fls. 21v–22v. A similar account can be found in Conde de Sabugosa, *Gente d'Algo*, 3rd ed. (Lisbon: Portugal-Brasil Limitada, 1923), pp. 286–88.

16. Freire de Oliveira, *Elementos*, 8:422–23.

17. Ibid., 9:561–63.

18. Dias, *Os Lanifícios*, 1:70–72.

19. Francis, *The Methuens*, p. 200.

20. Dias, *Os Lanifícios*, 1:70.

21. Luís da Cunha, *Testamento Politico* (Lisbon: Impressão Regia, 1820), p. 37. It should also be noted that in an undated *paracer* (circa 1702) da Cunha had urged adherence to the Bourbon camp, giving the unfavorable impact of English trade on the Portuguese economy as one of his reasons. BNL, Fundo Geral, 674, fls. 130v–132v.

22. This uncomplicated view is expressed in Godinho, "Portugal and Her Empire, 1680–1720," p. 523.

23. Shillington and Chapman, *The Commercial Relations of England and Portugal*, pp. 202–4. The privileged position of English merchants in Portugal was examined in H. B. Livermore, "The Privileges of an Englishman in the Kingdoms and Dominions of Portugal," *Atlante* 2 (April 1954):57–77. For a discussion of the merchant community in Lisbon, see Sir Richard Lodge, "The English Factory at Lisbon: Some Chapters in Its History," *Transactions of the Royal Historical Society*, 4th series, 16 (1933):211–47.

24. Following the Lisbon earthquake of 1755, the marquis of Pombal did impose additional duties on English merchants. Shillington and Chapman, *The Commercial Relations of England and Portugal*, p. 264.

25. Samir Amin, *Unequal Development: An Essay on the Social Formations of Peripheral Capitalism*, Brian Pearce, trans. (New York: Monthly Review Press, 1976), pp. 133–40.

26. Sideri, *Trade and Power*, pp. 4–5.

27. As Karl Marx so cogently observed, "No social order is destroyed before all the productive forces for which it is sufficient have been developed, and new superior relations of production never replace older ones before the material conditions for their existence have matured within the framework of the old society." Karl Marx, *Early Writings* (New York: Vintage Books, 1975), pp. 425–26.

28. Robert Brenner, "Agrarian Class Structure," p. 67.

29. Ibid., p. 68.

30. For a study tracing England's rise to financial supremacy over France, see Roland Mousnier, "L'Evolution des Finances Publiques en France et en Angleterre pendant les Guerres de la Ligue d'Augsbourg et de la Succession d'Espagne," *Revue Historique* 205 (1951):1–23.

31. Though definitions of dependency vary, this discussion follows that given in Theotonio dos Santos, "The Structure of Dependence," *American Economic Review* 60 (May 1970):231.

32. Most discussion of dependency has been confined to core and periphery in the nineteenth and twentieth centuries. Though relatively little attention has been paid to its origins or stages prior to 1800, it is generally presumed that dependency originated during the mercantilist era. See, for example, James D. Cockcroft, André Gunder Frank, and Dale L. Johnson, *Dependency and Underdevelopment: Latin America's Political Economy* (Garden City: Doubleday, Anchor, 1972), pp. xi, 20–25.

33. For a useful essay on Iberia's emerging dependence on northern Europe, see Stanley J. Stein and Barbara H. Stein, *The Colonial Heritage of Latin America: Essays on Economic Dependence in Perspective* (New York: Oxford University Press, 1970), pp. 4–26.

34. V. I. Lenin, *Selected Works in Three Volumes* (Moscow: Progress Publishers, 1967), 1:742–43.

35. Quoted in C. R. Boxer, "Brazilian Gold and British Traders in the First Half of the Eighteenth Century," *HAHR* 49 (1969):459.

36. Quoted in Shillington and Chapman, *The Commercial Relations of England and Portugal*, p. 222.

37. Quoted in Villiers, "Portuguese Society," pp. 182–83.

38. Ibid., pp. 188–89.

39. Adapted from quotation in Shillington and Chapman, *The Commercial Relations of England and Portugal*, pp. 260–61.

40. William H. Shaw, *Marx's Theory of History* (Stanford: Stanford University Press, 1978), p. 145.

41. Barry Hindness and Paul Q. Hirst, *Pre-Capitalist Modes of Production* (London: Routledge and Kegan Paul, 1975), p. 292.

BIBLIOGRAPHY AND INDEX

BIBLIOGRAPHY

Manuscript Sources

Arquivo Histórico do Ministerio das Finanças (AHMF)
   Provisões do Conselho do Estado, 407 (9/48/407).
Arquivo Histórico Ultramarino (AHU)
   Bahia, Papeis Avulsos, 1st uncatalogued series *caixas* 10, 11, 12.
   Pernambuco, Papeis Avulsos, *caixa* 6.
Arquivo Nacional do Torre do Tombo (ANTT)
   Conselho da Fazenda, *maço* 1.
   Conselho da Guerra, Decretos, *maços* 32, 35, 39, 40, 57. Avisos, *maço* 3.
   Convento da Graça, Miscellanea, *caixa* 5, *tomo* 2; *caixa* 6, *tomo* 3.
   Corpo Cronológico, Part 1, *maço* 120. Part 2, *maco* 373.
   Junta do Tabaco, Cartas do Brasil e India, *maços* 96, 96A. Consultas, *maços* 1, 2, 3, 4, 4A, 5, 6. Decretos, *maços* 50, 51. Receita e Despesa, *maço* 201.
   Livraria, Manuscritos Brasileiros, no. 33 (C3 E2 P7).
   Papeis dos Jesuitas, *caixa* 2.
Biblioteca da Academia das Ciências de Lisboa (BACL)
   Mss. Azul 556.
Biblioteca da Ajuda (BA)
   Cod.: 44-XIII-42, 44-XIII-43, 44-XIII-60, 44-XIV-1, 50-V-37, 51-IX-30.
British Library (BL)
   Additional, Cod.: 15,169, 20,844, 20,944, 20,958. Sloane, Cod.: 2,294.
Biblioteca Nacional de Lisboa (BNL)
   Fundo Geral, Cod.: 275, 427, 510, 589, 674, 730, 748, 749, 851, 868, 1459, 1532, 1538, 2632, 3542, 6504, 6825, 7626, 7701, 7982, 8554. Caixas 2, 14, 64. Mss. 13, no. 18.
   Pombalina, Cod.: 67, 439, 473, 475, 738.

Printed Documents, Laws, and Treaties

Alfândega de Lisboa. Museu Histórico. *Reflexos Aduaneiros dos Descobrimentos e Conquistas.* Second Exposição Temporária. Lisbon, 1960.
Andrade e Silva, José Justino de. *Collecção Chronologica da Legislação Portugueza (1603–1702).* 10 vols. Lisbon: F. X. de Souxa, 1854–1859.
Borges de Castro, Jose Ferreira. *Collecção dos Tratados, Convenções, Contratos e Actos Publicos Celebrados entre a Coroa de Portugal e as Mais Potencias desde 1640 até ao Presente.* 30 vols. Lisbon: Imprensa Nacional, 1856–1880.
Freire de Oliveira, Eduardo. *Elementos para a História do Município de Lisboa.* 17 vols. Lisbon: Tipografia Universal, 1882–1911.
Mağalhães, Basilio de. "Documentos relativos ao 'bandeirismo' paulista e questões connexas, no periodo a 1664 a 1700." *Revista do Instituto Histórico e Geographico de São Paulo* 18 (1914):274–544.
Rau, Virginia, and Silva, Maria Fernanda Gomes da. *Os Manuscritos do Arquivo da Casa de Cadaval Respeitantes ao Brasil.* 2 vols. Coimbra: Imprensa da Universidade, 1956–1958.

Letters and Contemporary Works

Amzalak, Moses B. *Uma Carta de Duarte Gomes ao Duque de Lerma.* Lisbon: Gráfica Lisbonense, 1943.

Antonil, João André (pseudonym for Giovanni Antonio Andreoni). *Cultura e Opulencia do Brasil por suas Drogas e Minas,* texte de l'edition de 1711, traduction et commentaire critique par Andrée Mansuy. Paris: Université de Paris, 1968.

Auto do Iuramento que o serenissimo Principe Dom Pedro Nosso Senhor Fez aos Tres Estados destes Reynos, de os Reger, e Governar no impedimento perpetuo d'El Rey Dom Affonso VI. Lisbon: António Craesbeeck de Mello, 1668.

Bluteau, Rafael. *Instruccam sobre a Cultura das Amoreirras e Criação dos Bichos da Seda.* Lisbon: Jodo da Costa, 1679.

———. *Prosas Portuguesas.* Lisbon: José Antonio da Silva, 1728.

———. *Vocabulario Português e Latino.* 8 vols. Coimbra: Collegio das Artes da Companhia de Jesu, 1712–1721. *Supplemento.* 2 vols. Lisbon: José Antonio da Silva, 1727.

Bonaccorsi, Florentino. "O Comércio dos portos de Lisboa, Setúbal e Porto nos fins do século XVII, conforme um documento italiano da mesma época." *Boletim da Sociedade de Geografia de Lisboa,* series 53, 9–10 (1935):337–45.

Bromley, William. *Several Years Travels through Portugal, Spain, Italy, Germany, Prussia, Sweden, Denmark and the United Provinces.* London: A. Roper, 1702.

Cadornega, António de Oliveira de. *História Geral das Guerras Angolanas* (1680). 3 vols. Lisbon: Agencia-Geral do Ultramar, 1972.

Carré, Abbé. *The Travels of Abbé Carré in India and the Near East, 1672 to 1674.* 3 vols. Translated by Lady Fawcett and edited by Sir Charles Fawcett with the assistance of Sir Richard Burn. London: Hakluyt Society, 2nd series, vols. 95–97, 1947–1948.

Chagas, António das. *Obras Espirituais do Espiritual, e Veneravel Padre Frey António das Chagas.* Lisbon: Miguel Deslandes, 1701.

Child, Sir Josiah. *Brief Observations Concerning Trade, and Interest of Money.* London: E. Calvert and H. Mortlock, 1668.

Clement, Pierre, ed. *Lettres, Instructions et Memoires de Colbert.* 10 vols. Paris: Imprimerie Impériale, 1861–1882.

Coelho, Francisco. *Thesouro da Nobreza.* Lisbon, 1675.

Colbatch, John. *An Account of the Court of Portugal under the Reign of the Present King Dom Pedro II.* London: Thomas Bennet, 1700.

Cortes de Lisboa dos Annos de 1697 e 1698. Congresso da Nobreza. Lisbon: Academia Real das Sciencias, 1824.

Dupineaut, Teófilo. "Memoire touchant la Marine de Portugal (Memoria sôbre a Marina Portuguesa no reinado de D. Pedro II—Notas de Prof. Edgar Prestage e do Comte Quirino da Fonseca)." *Arquivo Histórico da Marinha* 4 (Lisbon, 1936):267–75.

Fortrey, Samuel. *England's Interest and Improvement.* Cambridge: John Field, Printer to the University, 1663.

Geddes, Michael. "A view of the Court of the Inquisition in Portugal with a LIST of the Prisoners that came forth in an Act of the Faith Celebrated at Lisbon, in the Year 1682." In *Miscellaneous Tracts,* 3 vols., vol. 1, pp. 389–448. London: printed for A. and J. Churchill, 1702.

Godinho, Manuel, S.J. *Relação do Novo Caminho Que Fez por Terra e Mar Vindo da India para Portugal no Anno de 1663.* Lisbon: Imprensa Nacional—Casa da Moeda, 1974.

Lisanti Filho, Luis. *Negócios Coloniais (Uma Correspondência Commercial de Século XVIII).* 5 vols. Brasilia and São Paulo: Ministerio da Fazenda, 1973.

Littleton, E. *The Groans of the Plantations, or a True Account of Their Grievous and Extreme Sufferings by the Heavy Impositions on Sugar.* London: M. Clark, 1689.
Lopes Sierra, Juan. *A Governor and His Image in Baroque Brazil: The Funeral Eulogy of Afonso de Castro do Rio de Mendonça.* Edited by Stuart B. Schwartz and translated by Ruth E. Jones. Minneapolis: University of Minnesota Press, 1979.
Mansuy, Andrée. "Memoire Inédit D'Ambrose Jouffret sur le Brésil a l'Epoque de la Décourverte de Mines d'Or (1704)." In *Actas* of the Fifth Coloquio Internacional de Estudos Luso-Brasileiros, 5 vols, vol. 2, pp. 407–44. Coimbra: Imprensa de Universidade, 1965–1968.
Mascarenhas, João. *Contrato dos rendimentos dos consulados das alfandegas da cidade do Porto, Vianna, Aveyro, Buarcos, e As mais de Barlovento do Tejo pera o Norte entrando Peniche, que se fez com Simão da Sylva de Govea, e seus companheiros.* Lisbon, 1675.
Meneses, D. Luís de (count of Ericeira). *História de Portugal Restaurado.* 4 vols. Oporto: Livraria Civilização, 1946.
Paim, Roque Monteiro. *Perfidia judaica, Christus Vindex, Manus Principis Ecclesiae ab Apostatis liberata.* Madrid, 1671.
Paixão, Alexandre da. *Monstruosidades do Tempo e da Fortuna (1662–1680).* 4 vols. Barcelos: Companhia Editora do Minho, 1938–1939.
Pimentel Serrão, Luís. *Methodo Lusitanico de Desenhar as Fortificacoens das Praças Regulares e Irregulares, Fortes de Campanha, e Outras Obras Pertencentes a Architectura Militar.* Lisbon: António Craesbeeck de Mello, 1680.
Prestage, Edgar. *Memórias sobre Portugal no reinado de D. Pedro II.* Lisbon: Archivo Histórico de Portugal, 1935.
Regimento da Administracam do Tabaco. Lisbon: Miguel Deslandes, 1702.
Ribeiro, João Pinto. *Uzurpação, Retenção, Restauração, de Portugal.* Lisbon: Lourenço de Anvers, 1642.
Ribeiro de Macedo, Duarte. *Obras Ineditas.* Lisbon: Impressão Regia, 1817.
Sánchez Rivero, Angel, ed. *Viaje de Cosme de Medicis por España y Portugal (1668–1669).* Madrid: Centro de Estudios Históricos, 1933.
Serrão, Joaquim Verissimo. "Uma Relação do reino de Portugal em 1684." *Boletim da Biblioteca da Universidade* 25 (Coimbra, 1962):66–170.
Serrão, Joel, ed. *Alterações de Évora (1637).* Lisbon: Portugália Editora, 1967.
Silva, João Soares da. *Gazeta em Forma de Carta (1701–1716).* Lisbon: Biblioteca Nacional, 1933.
Solis, Duarte Gomes. *Alegación en Favor de la Compañia de la India Oriental y Comercios ultramarinos que de Nueuo se Instituyó en el Reyno de Portugal.* 2nd ed. Edited by Moses B. Amzalak. Lisbon: Editoria Império, 1955.
———. *Discursos sobre los Comercios de las Indias.* 2nd ed. Edited by Moses B. Amzalak. Lisbon: n.p., 1943.
Souza, António Caetano de. *Historia Geneologica da Casa Real Portugueza.* 12 vols. Lisbon: José Antonio da Silva, 1735–1748.
Sprat, Thomas. *L'Histoire de la Société Royal de Londres.* Geneva: Jean Herman Widerhold, 1669.
———. *Histoire de l'Institution dessein et Progrès de la Société Royal de Londres.* Paris: O. de Varennes, 1670.
Stevens, John. *The Ancient and Present State of Portugal.* London: W. Bray, 1713.
Vieira, António. *Cartas.* 2nd ed. 3 vols. Edited by João Lúcio de Azevedo. Lisbon: Imprensa Nacional, 1971.
———. *Obras Escolhidas.* 12 vols. Lisbon: Sá da Costa, 1951–1954.

———. *Obras Inéditas*. 3 vols. Lisbon: Seabra and Antunes, 1856.
Whereas the Portugal Trade is very advantageous to this Nation. London, circa 1678.

Secondary Sources

Alcochete, Nuno Daupiás de. "Negócios da Feitoria francesa de Lisboa no Final do Século XVII." In *Actas* of the Fifth Colóquio Internacional de Estudos Luso-Brasileiros, 5 vols., vol. 2, pp. 155–64. Coimbra: Imprensa da Universidade, 1965–1968.

Allan, John C. "A Mineração em Portugal na antiguidade." *Boletim de Minas* 2 (3) (Lisbon, July-September 1965):139–75.

Almeida, Fortunato de. *Historia da Igreja em Portugal*. 4 vols. in 6. Coimbra: Imprensa Academica, 1910–1922.

———. *História de Portugal*. 6 vols. Coimbra: Imprensa da Universidade, 1922–1929.

Almeida, Luís Ferrand de. "Aclimatação de plantas do Oriente no Brasil durante os séculos XVII e XVIII." *Revista Portuguesa de História* 15 (1975):339–81.

———. "As Cortes de 1679–1680 e o auxílio à Polonia para a guerra contra os Turcos." *Biblos* 27 (Coimbra, 1951):77–139.

———. "Cortes de Lisboa em 1677?" *Revista Portuguesa de História* 12 (1969):383–88.

———. *A Diplomacia Portuguesa e os Limites Meridionais do Brasil (1493–1700)*. Coimbra: Imprensa da Universidade, 1957.

Amaral Lapa, J. R. *A Bahia e a Carreira da India*. São Paulo: Companhia Editora Nacional, 1968.

———. "O Problema das Drogas Orientais." In *Economia Colonial*, pp. 111–40. São Paulo: Editora Perspectiva, 1973.

Amin, Samir. *Unequal Development: An Essay on the Social Formations of Peripheral Capitalism*. Translated by Brian Pearce. New York: Monthly Review Press, 1976.

Amzalak, Moses B. *A Economia Política em Portugal: O Diplomato Duarte Ribeiro de Macedo e os seus Discursos sobre Economia Política*. Lisbon: Academia das Sciências de Lisboa, 1928.

———. *Do Estudo de Evolução das Doutrinas Económicas em Portugal*. Lisbon: Oficina Gráfica do Museu Commercial, 1928.

Aston, Trevor, ed. *Crisis in Europe, 1560–1660*. New York: Basic Books, 1965.

Axelson, Eric. *Portuguese in South-East Africa 1600–1700*. Johannesburg: Witwatersrand University Press, 1964.

Azevedo, João Lúcio de. *Épocas de Portugal Económico*. Lisbon: Livraria Clássica, 1929.

———. *A Evolução do Sebastianismo*. 2nd ed. Lisbon: A. M. Texeira, 1947.

———. *História de António Vieira*. 2nd ed. 2 vols. Lisbon: Livraria Clássica, 1931.

———. *História dos Cristãos Novos Portugueses*. 2nd ed. Lisbon: Livraria Clássica Editora, 1975.

Azevedo, Pedro de. *Doença e Morte de Dom Pedro II*. Oporto: n.p., 1911.

Baião, António. *Episódios Dramáticos da Inquisição Portuguesa*. 2nd ed. 3 vols. Lisbon: Seara Nova, 1936–1938.

Barros, Eugénio Estanislau de. *Traçado e Construcção das Naus Portuguesas dos Séculos XVI e XVII*. Lisbon: Imprensa da Armada, 1933.

Basto, Artur de Magalhães. "A 'Nobreza' do Oficio de Ourives." *Estudos Portuenses* 2 (Oporto, 1963):209–14.

Beloff, Max. *The Age of Absolutism, 1660–1815*. New York: Harper and Row, Torchbooks, 1966.

Bernstein, Harry. *The Portuguese Juiz do Povo*. Lisbon: forthcoming.
Biblioteca Nacional de Lisboa. *Exposição Bibliográfica da Restauração*. 2 vols. Lisbon, 1940–1941.
Billacois, François. "La Crise de la Noblesse européene (1550–1650): Une Mise au Point." *Revue d'Histoire Moderne et Contemporaine* 23 (1976):258–77.
Birch, Thomas. *The History of the Royal Society of London*. 4 vols. Introduction by Rupert Hall. New York: Johnson Reprint Corporation, 1968.
Birmingham, David. *Trade and Conflict in Angola: The Mbundu and Their Neighbors under the Influence of the Portuguese, 1483–1790*. Oxford: Clarendon Press, 1966.
Borges de Macedo, Jorge. *Problemas de História da Indústria Portuguesa no Século XVIII*. Lisbon: Associação Industrial Portuguesa, 1963.
Bourne, Edward Gaylord. *Spain in America, 1450–1580*. New York: Harper and Brothers, 1904.
Boxer, C. R. "Brazilian Gold and British Traders in the First Half of the Eighteenth Century." *Hispanic American Historical Review* 49 (1969):454–72.
———. "The Carreira da India, 1650–1750." *Mariner's Mirror* 46 (February 1960):35–54.
———. *The Dutch in Brazil, 1624–1654*. Oxford: Clarendon Press, 1957.
———. *Fidalgos in the Far East, 1550–1770*. London: Oxford University Press reprint, 1968.
———. *The Golden Age of Brazil, 1695–1750*. Berkeley: University of California Press, 1969.
———. "A Great Luso-Brazilian Figure, Padre António Vieira, S.J., 1608–1697." *Diamante* 5 (1957):1–32.
———. "Marshal Schomberg in Portugal, 1660–1668." *History Today* 26 (October 1976):653–63.
———. "Padre António Vieira, S.J., and the Institution of the Brazil Company in 1649." *Hispanic American Historical Review* 29 (1949):474–97.
———. "The Portuguese in the East, 1500–1800." In *Portugal and Brazil*, edited by H. V. Livermore, pp. 185–247. Oxford: Clarendon Press, 1953.
———. *The Portuguese Seaborne Empire: 1415–1825*. New York: Alfred A. Knopf, 1969.
———. *Race Relations in the Portuguese Colonial Empire, 1415–1825*. Oxford: Oxford University Press, 1963.
———. *Salvador de Sá and the Struggle for Brazil and Angola, 1602–1686*. London: Athlone Press, 1952.
———. "Vicissitudes of the Anglo-Portuguese Alliance, 1660–1700." *Revista da Faculdade de Letras* (Lisbon), 3rd series, 2 (1958):15–46.
———. *Women in Iberian Expansion Overseas, 1415–1815*. New York: Oxford University Press, 1975.
———, and Azevedo, Carlos de. *Fort Jesus and the Portuguese in Mombasa, 1593–1729*. London: Hollis and Carter, 1960.
Braudel, Fernand. *The Mediterranean and the Mediterranean World in the Age of Philip II*. 2 vols. Translated by Siân Reynolds. New York: Harper and Row, 1972.
———, and Spooner, Frank. "Prices in Europe from 1450 to 1750." In *The Cambridge Economic History of Europe*, 8 vols., vol. 4, pp. 378–486. Cambridge: Cambridge University Press, 1966–.
Brenner, Robert. "Agrarian Class Structure and Economic Development in Pre-Industrial Europe." *Past and Present* 70 (Febraury 1976):30–75.
Buarque de Holanda, Sérgio. *Visão do Paraíso: Motivos Edênicas no Descobrimento e Colonização do Brasil*. Rio de Janeiro: José Olympio, 1956.

Caetano, Marcelo. *A História da Organização dos Mesteres da Cidade de Lisboa*. Lisbon: Câmara Municipal, 1959.
Cantel, Raymond. *Prophétisme et Messianisme dans l'Ouvre d'Antonio Vieira*. Paris: Ediciones Hispano-Americanas, 1960.
Cardozo, Manuel. "The Collection of the Fifth in Brazil, 1695–1709." *Hispanic American Historical Review* 20 (1940):359–79.
———. "Dom Rodrigo de Castel-Branco and the Brazilian El Dorado, 1673–1682." *The Americas* 1 (October 1944):131–59.
Carqueja, Bento. *O Capitalismo Moderno e as Suas Origens em Portugal*. Oporto: Livraria Chardron, 1908.
Carvalho, Tito Augusto de. *As Companhias Portuguesas de Colonização*. Lisbon: Imprensa Nacional, 1902.
Castello Branco, Theresa M. Schedel. *Vida do Marques de Sande*. Lisbon: Livraria Ferin, 1971.
Castelo-Branco, Fernando. *Lisboa Seiscentista*. 3rd ed. Lisbon: Gráfica Santelmo, 1969.
Chagas, Manuel Pinheiro. *História de Portugal*. 14 vols. Lisbon: Livraria Moderna, 1899–1909.
Chandaman, C. D. *The English Public Revenue, 1660–1688*. Oxford: Clarendon Press, 1975.
Chaves, Luís. *D. Pedro II*. Lisbon: Empresa Nacional da Publicidade, 1959.
Cidade, Hernâni, and Selvagem, Carlos. *Cultura Portuguesa*. 18 vols. Lisbon: Imprensa Nacional de Publicidade, 1967–1977.
Clough, Shepard B., and Rapp, Richard T. *European Economic History*. 3rd ed. New: McGraw-Hill, 1975.
Coaracy, Vivaldo. *O Rio de Janeiro no Século 17*. 2nd ed. Rio de Janeiro: José Olympio, 1965.
Cockcroft, James D.; Frank, André Gunder; and Johnson, Dale L. *Dependency and Underdevelopment: Latin America's Political Economy*. Garden City: Doubleday, Anchor, 1972.
Coelho, F. Adolfo. *Os Ciganos em Portugal*. Lisbon: Imprensa Nacional, 1892.
Cole, Charles W. *Colbert and a Century of French Mercantilism*. 2 vols. New York: Columbia University Press, 1939.
———. *French Mercantilist Doctrines before Colbert*. New York: Richard R. Smith, 1931.
Coleman, D. C., ed. *Revisions in Mercantilism*. London: Methuen, 1969.
Cowgill, U. M., and Johnson, H. B., Jr. "Grain Prices and Vital Statistics in a Portuguese Rural Parish, 1671–1720." *Journal of Bio-Social Science* 3 (1971):321–29.
Cruz, António. *Os Mesteres do Porto*. Vol. 1. Oporto: Sub-secreteriado de Estado das Corporações e Previdência Social, 1943.
Cumberland, Charles C. *Mexico: The Struggle for Modernity*. New York: Oxford University Press, 1968.
Cunha, Luís da. *Testamento Politico*. Lisbon: Impressão Regia, 1820.
Curtin, Philip D. *The Atlantic Slave Trade: A Census*. Madison: University of Wisconsin Press, 1969.
Davis, Ralph. *The Rise of the Atlantic Economies*. Ithaca: Cornell University Press, 1973.
Denevan, William M., ed. *The Native Population of the Americas in 1492*. Madison: University of Wisconsin Press, 1976.
de Vries, Jan. *The Economy of Europe in an Age of Crisis, 1600–1750*. Cambridge: Cambridge University Press, 1976.

Dias, Luiz Fernando de Carvalho. *Os Lanifícios na Política Económica do Conde da Ericeira.* 2 vols. Lisbon: Tipografia da Sociedade Industrial de Imprensa, 1954.
Disney, A. R. *Twilight of the Pepper Empire: Portuguese Trade in Southwest India in the Early Seventeenth Century.* Cambridge: Harvard University Press, 1978.
Dobb, Maurice. *Studies in the Development of Capitalism.* New York: International Publishers, 1947.
Domínguez Ortiz, António. "La Crisis de Castilla en 1677–1687." *Revista Portuguesa de História* 10 (1962):435–51.
———. *Las Clases Privilegiadas en la España del Antiguo Régimen.* Madrid: Ediciones ISTMO, 1973.
Dória, António Álvaro. *A Rainha D. Maria Francisca de Sabóia (1646–1683).* Oporto: Livraria Civilização, 1944.
dos Santos, Theotonio. "The Structure of Dependence." *American Economic Review* 60 (1970): 231–37.
Duffy, James. *Shipwreck and Empire, Being an Account of Portuguese Maritime Disasters in a Century of Decline.* Cambridge: Harvard University Press, 1955.
Duncan, T. Bentley. *Atlantic Islands.* Chicago: University of Chicago Press, 1972.
Dutra, Francis A. "Duarte Coelho Pereira, First Lord-Proprietor of Pernambuco: The Beginning of a Dynasty." *The Americas* 29 (1973):415–41.
———. "Membership in the Order of Christ in the Seventeenth Century: Its Rights, Privileges, and Obligations." *The Americas* 27(1970):3–25.
Edel, Matthew. "The Brazilian Sugar Cycle of the Seventeenth Century and the Rise of West Indian Competition." *Caribbean Studies* 9 (April 1969):24–44.
Elliott, J. H. *Imperial Spain, 1469–1716.* New York: New American Library, Mentor Books, 1966.
———. "Revolution and Continuity in Early Modern Europe." *Past and Present* 42 (1969):35–56.
Ellis, Myriam. *A Baleia no Brasil Colonial.* São Paulo: Edições Melhoramentos, 1969.
———. *O Monopólio do Sal no Estado do Brasil (1631–1801).* São Paulo: Universidade de São Paulo, 1955.
Fisher, H. E. S. *The Portugal Trade: A Study of Anglo-Portuguese Commerce 1700–1770.* London: Methuen, 1971.
Flory, Rae, and Smith, David Grant. "Bahian Merchants and Planters in the Seventeenth and Early Eighteenth Centuries." *Hispanic American Historical Review* 58 (1978):571–94.
França, Eduardo d'Oliveira. *O Poder Real em Portugal e as Origens do Absolutismo.* São Paulo: Universidade de São Paulo, Faculdade de Filosofia, Ciências e Letras, 1946.
———. *Portugal na Época da Restauração.* São Paulo: Universidade de São Paulo, 1951.
Francis, A. D. "John Methuen and the Anglo-Portuguese Treaties of 1703." *The Historical Journal* 3 (1960):103–24.
———. *The Methuens and Portugal, 1691–1708.* Cambridge: Cambridge University Press, 1966.
———. *The Wine Trade.* London: A. and C. Black, 1972.
Galloway, J. H. "Northeast Brazil 1700–1750: The Agricultural Crisis Re-examined." *Journal of Historical Geography* 1 (1975):21–38.
Godinho, Vitorino Magalhães. "Création et Dynamisme Économique du Monde Atlantique (1420–1670)." *Annales: ESC* 5 (January-March 1950):32–36.
———. *L'Economie de l'Empire portugais aux XVe et XVIIe Siècles.* Paris: S.E.V.P.E.N., 1969.

———. *Estrutura da Antiga Sociedade Portuguesa*. 2nd ed. Lisbon: Arcádia, 1975.
———. "Portugal and Her Empire." In *The New Cambridge Modern History*, 14 vols., vol. 5, pp. 384–97. Cambridge: Cambridge University Press, 1957–1970.
———. "Portugal and Her Empire, 1680–1720." In *The New Cambridge Modern History*, 14 vols., vol. 6, pp. 509–40. Cambridge: Cambridge University Press, 1957–1970.
———. "Portugal, as Frotas do Açucar e as Frotas do Ouro (1670–1770)." *Revista de História* (São Paulo) 7 (1953):69–88.
———. "Le Probleme du Pain dans l'Economie Portugaise. XV^c–XVI^c Siècles: Blè d'Europe et Blè des Iles." *Revista de Economia* 12 (*fasc.* 3) (September 1959):87–113.
Gonnard, René. *Les Doctrines Mercantilistes au XVIIe Siècle en Portugal*. Paris: Librairie de Sciences Economiques et Sociales, 1935.
Grande Enciclopedia Portuguesa e Brasileira. 40 vols. Lisbon: Editoria Enciclopedia, Ltda., 1936–1960.
Gross, Sue A. "Labor in Amazonia in the First Half of the Eighteenth Century." *The Americas* 32 (1975):211–21.
Guimarães, Vieira. *A Ordem de Cristo*. Lisbon: Imprensa Nacional, 1936.
Guimarães, Vitorino. *As Finanças na Guerra da Restauração (1640–1668)*. Lisbon: Tipografia da L.C.G.G., 1941.
Hamilton, Earl J. *El Florescimento del Capitalismo y Otros Ensayos*. Madrid: Revista de Occidente, 1948.
———. *War and Prices in Spain, 1651–1800*. Cambridge: Harvard University Press, 1947.
Hanson, Carl A. "Monopoly and Contraband in the Portuguese Tobacco Trade, 1624–1702." *Luso-Brazilian Review* (forthcoming in 1981).
Heckscher, Eli. *Mercantilism*. 2nd ed. 2 vols. Translated by Mendel Shapiro. New York: Macmillan, 1955.
Hemming, John. *Red Gold: The Conquest of the Brazilian Indians*, 1500–1760. Cambridge: Harvard University Press, 1978.
Herculano, Alexandre. *History of the Origin and Establishment of the Inquisition in Portugal*. Translated by John C. Branner. New York: AMS Press reprint, 1968.
Hindness, Barry, and Hirst, Paul Q. *Pre-Capitalist Modes of Production*. London: Routledge and Kegan Paul, 1975.
Hobsbawm, Eric J. "Class Consciousness in History." In *Aspects of History and Class Consciousness*, edited by István Meszaros, pp. 5–21. New York: Herder and Herder, 1972.
———. "The Crisis of the Seventeenth Century." In *Crisis in Europe, 1560–1660*, edited by Trevor Aston, pp. 5–58. New York: Basic Books, 1965.
Iglesias, Francisco. "Minas e a Imposição do Estado no Brasil." *Revista de História* (São Paulo) 50 (1974):257–73.
Imbert, Gaston. *Des Mouvements de Longue durée Kondratieff*. Aix-en-Provence: Pensée Universitaire, 1959.
Innis, Harold A. *The Cod Fisheries*. New Haven: Yale University Press, 1940.
Isaacman, Allen F. *Mozambique: The Africanization of a European Institution, the Zambesi Prazos, 1750–1902*. Madison: University of Wisconsin Press, 1972.
Jago, Charles. "The 'Crisis of the Aristocracy' in Seventeenth Century Castile." *Past and Present* 84 (1979):60–90.
———. "The Influence of Debt on the Relations between Crown and Aristocracy in Seventeenth-Century Castile." *Economic History Review*, 2nd series, 26 (1973):218–36.

Kagan, Richard L. *Students and Society in Early Modern Spain.* Baltimore: Johns Hopkins University Press, 1974.
Kamen, Henry. "The Decline of Castile: The Last Crisis." *Economic History Review,* 2nd series, 77 (1964):63–76.
———. *The Iron Century: Social Change in Europe, 1550–1660.* New York: Praeger, 1972.
———. *The Spanish Inquisition.* New York: New American Library, 1965.
Kieman, Mathias C. *The Indian Policy of Portugal in the Amazon Region, 1614–1693.* New York: Octagon reprint, 1973.
Kubler, George. *Portuguese Plain Architecture: Between Spices and Diamonds, 1521–1706.* Middletown, Connecticut: Wesleyan University Press, 1972.
Ladurie, Emmanuel LeRoy. "Climat et récoltes aux XVIIe et XVIIIe siècles." *Annales: ESC* 15 (May-June 1960):434–65.
Langhans, Franz-Paul de Almeida. "Advertencias feitas á Casa dos Vinte e Quatro de Lisboa em 1701 sobre a política que conduziu á Guerra da Sucessão de Espanha." *Revista Portuguesa de História* 4 (1949):343–59.
———. *Apontamentos para a História de Azeite em Portugal.* Lisbon: Tipografia Portuguesa, Lda., 1949.
———. *A Casa dos Vinte e Quatro de Lisboa.* Lisbon: Imprensa Nacional, 1948.
———. *As Corporações dos Ofícios Mecânicos.* 2 vols. Lisbon: Imprensa Nacional, 1943–1946.
Larcher, Jorge das Neves. *Memória Histórica sobre o Abastecimento de Água a Lisboa até ao Reinado de D. João V.* Lisbon: Centro Tipográfico Colonial, 1937.
Larraz, José. *La Epoca del Mercantilismo en Castille (1500–1700).* 2nd ed. Madrid: Atlas, 1943.
Leite, Serafim. *História da Companhia de Jesus no Brasil.* 10 vols. Lisbon: Livraria Portugalia, 1938–1950.
Lenin, V. I. *Selected Works in Three Volumes.* Moscow: Progress Publishers, 1967.
Lenski, Gerhard. *Power and Privilege: A Theory of Social Stratification.* New York: McGraw-Hill, 1966.
Leonard, Irving A. *Baroque Times in Old Mexico.* Ann Arbor: University of Michigan Press, 1959.
Letwin, William. *The Origins of Scientific Economics: English Economic Thought 1660–1776.* London: Methuen, 1963.
Limborch, Philip. *The History of the Inquisition.* London: printed for W. Simpkin and R. Marshall, 1816.
Lins, Ivan. *Aspectos do Padre Antônio Vieira.* 2nd. ed. Rio de Janeiro, 1962.
Livermore, Harold V. *A History of Portugal.* Cambridge: Cambridge University Press, 1947.
———. *A New History of Portugal.* Cambridge: Cambridge University Press, 1969.
———. "The Privileges of an Englishman in the Kingdoms and Dominions of Portugal." *Atlante* 2 (April 1954):57–77.
Lobato, Alexandre. *Relações Luso-Maratos, 1658–1737.* Lisbon: Centro de Estudos Históricos Ultramarinos, 1965.
Lobo, Eulalia Maria Lahmeyer. *Aspectos da Influencia dos Homens de Negócio na Política Comercial Ibero-Americana (Século XVII).* Rio de Janeiro: n.p., 1963.
———. "As Frotas do Brasil." *Jahrbuch für Geschichte von Staat, Wirstschaft und Gesellschaft Lateinamerikas* 4 (1967):465–88.

Lodge, Sir Richard. "The English Factory at Lisbon: Some Chapters in Its History." *Transactions of the Royal Historical Society*, 4th series, 16 (1933):211–47.

Loureiro, J. Pinto. *Casa dos Vinte e Quatro de Coimbra*. Coimbra: Edição da Biblioteca Municipal, 1947.

Lublinskaya, A. D. *French Absolutism: The Crucial Phase, 1620–1629*. Cambridge: Cambridge University Press, 1968.

Lugar, Catherine. "The Portuguese Tobacco Trade and Tobacco Growers of Bahia in the Late Colonial Period." In *Essays Concerning the Socio-Economic History of Brazil and Portuguese India*, edited by Dauril Alden and Warren Dean, pp. 26–70. Gainesville: University Presses of Florida, 1977.

McCusker, John J. *Money and Exchange in Europe and America, 1600–1775: A Handbook*. Chapel Hill: University of North Carolina Press, 1978.

Machado e Costa, Alfredo Augusto de Oliveira. "A minerologia quinhentista." In *Congresso do Mundo Portugues*, 19 vols., vol. 5, pp. 295–311. Lisbon: Bertrand, 1940.

MacInnes, C. M. *The Early English Tobacco Trade*. London: Kegan Paul, Trench, Trubner and Company, 1926.

Magalhães, Joaquim Romero. *Para o Estudo do Algarve Econōmico durante o Século XVI*. Lisbon: Edições Cosmos, 1970.

Magalhães, José Calvet de. *História do Pensamento Econômico em Portugal*. Coimbra: Imprensa da Universidade, 1967.

Manchester, Alan K. *British Preëminence in Brazil*. Chapel Hill: University of North Carolina Press, 1933.

Maravall, José Antonio. *La Cultura del Barroco: Anális de una estructura histórica*. Barcelona: Ariel, 1975.

Marchant, Alexander. "Colonial Brazil as a Way Station for the Portuguese India Fleets," *The Geographical Review* 31 (July 1941):454–65.

Marques, António H. de Oliveira. "Estratificação Económico-Social de uma Vila Portuguesa da Idade Média." In *Ensaios de História Medieval Portuguesa*, pp. 163–76. Lisbon: Portugália Editora, 1965.

———. *History of Portugal*. 2nd ed. 2 vols. in 1. New York: Columbia University Press, 1976.

Marx, Karl. *Early Writings*. New York: Vintage Books, 1975.

———. *Pre-Capitalist Economic Formations*. Edited by Eric J. Hobsbawm and translated by Jack Cohen. New York: International Publishers, 1964.

Mauro, Frédéric. *Le Bresil du XVe à la Fin du XVIIIe Siècle*. Paris: Société d'Edition d'Enseignement Supérieur, 1977.

———. *L'Expansion Europeéne (1600–1870)*. 2nd ed. Paris: Presses Universitaires de France, 1967.

———. "Mercadores e Mercadores-Banqueiros Portugueses no Século XVII." In *Nôvo História e Nôvo Mundo*, pp. 119–34. São Paulo: Editora Perspectiva, 1969.

———. *Le Portugal et l'Atlantique au XVIIe Siècle (1570–1670)*. Paris: S.E.V.P.E.N., 1960.

———, and Parker, Geoffrey. "Portugal." In *An Introduction to the Sources of European Economic History 1500–1800*. Charles Wilson and Geoffrey Parker, eds. London: Weidenfeld and Nicolson, 1977.

Maxwell, Kenneth. *Conflicts and Conspiracies: Brazil and Portugal 1750–1808*. Cambridge: Cambridge University Press, 1973.

Mello, Evaldo Cabral de. *Olinda Restaurada: Guerra e Açucar no Nordeste, 1630–1654*. Rio de Janeiro: Editora Forense-Universitaria; São Paulo: Universidade de São Paulo, 1975.

Mello de Matos, Gastão. *Notícias do Terço da Armada Real (1618–1707)*. Lisbon: Imprensa da Armada, 1932.
Monteiro, Jonathas da Costa Rego. *A Colónia do Sacramento, 1680–1777*. 2 vols. Pôrto Alegre: Livraria do Globo, 1937.
Mörner, Magnus, ed. *The Expulsion of the Jesuits from Latin America*. New York: Alfred A. Knopf, Borzoi Books, 1965.
Morse, Richard M., ed. *The Bandeirantes: The Historical Role of the Brazilian Pathfinders*. New York: Alfred Alfred A. Knopf, Borzoi Books, 1965.
Mousnier, Roland. "L'Evolution des finances publiques en France et en Angleterre pendant le Guerres de la Ligue d'Augsbourg et de la Succession d'Espagne." *Revue Historique* 205 (1951):1–23.
Neves, José Acursio das. *Noções Historicas, Economicas e Administrativas sobre a Producção e Manufactura das Sedas em Portugal*. Lisbon: Impressão Regia, 1827.
———. *Variedades sobre objectivos Relativos às Artes, Commercio e manufacturas*. 2 vols. Lisbon: Impressão Regia, 1814–1817.
Newitt, M. D. D. "The Portuguese in the Zambesi: An Historical Interpretation of the Prazo System." *Journal of African History* 10 (1969):67–85.
Novais, Fernando. *Estrutura e Dinâmica do Sistema Colonial (Séculos XVI–XVII)*. Lisbon: Livros Horizontes, 1975.
Ogg, David. *Europe in the Seventeenth Century*. New York: Collier Books, 1968.
Oliveira, António de. *A Vida Económica e Social de Coimbra de 1537 a 1640*. 2 vols. Coimbra: Imprensa da Universidade, 1971–1972.
Oliveira, Aurélio de. *A Abadia de Tibães e o Seu Domínio (1630–1680)*. Oporto: Faculdade de Letras do Porto, 1974.
Pereira, J. M. Esteves. *A Industria Portuguesa (Séculos XII–XIX)*. Lisbon: Imprensa do Occidente, 1900.
Palacios Preciado, Jorge. *La Trata de negros por Cartagena de Indias (1650–1750)*. Tunja: Universidad Pedagogica y Tecnológica de Columbia, 1973.
———, and Rodrigues, Guilherme. *Portugal: Dicionario Historico, Biografico, Bibliografico, Heraldico, Chorografico, Numismatico e Artistico*. 7 vols. Lisbon: João Romano Torres, 1904–1915.
Peres, Damião, ed. *História de Portugal*. 7 vols. in 8, with supplement and indexes. Barcelos: Portucalense Editora, 1928–1966.
Personagens Portuguesas do Século XVII. Lisbon: Academia Nacional de Belles Artes, 1942.
Pinto Ferreira, J. A. *Visitas de Saúde às Embarcações Entradas na Barra do Douro nos Séculos XVI e XVII*. Oporto: Câmara Municipal, 1977.
Prestage, Edgar. *O Conde de Castelmelhor e a Retrocessão de Tanger a Portugal*. Coimbra: Imprensa da Universidade, 1917.
———. *The Diplomatic Relations of Portugal with France, England, and Holland from 1640 to 1668*. Watford: Voss and Michael, Ltd., 1925.
———. "The Mode of Government in Portugal during the Restoration Period." In *Mélanges d'Études Portugaises Offerts à M. Georges Le Gentil*, pp. 265–70. Lisbon: Instituto para a Alta Cultura, 1949.
———. *Tres Consultas do Conselho da Fazenda de 1656 a 1657*. Oporto: Typographia da Empresa Literaria e Typographica, 1920.
Price, Jacob M. *France and the Chesapeake: A History of the French Tobacco Monopoly, 1674–1791, and of Its Relationship to the British and American Tobacco Trades*. 2 vols. Ann Arbor: University of Michigan Press, 1973.

Raposo, Hipólito. *Dona Luisa de Gusmão, Duquesa e Rainha (1613–1666)*. Lisbon: Empresa Nacional de Publicidade, 1947.

Rau, Virginia. *A Casa dos Contos*. Coimbra: Imprensa da Universidade, 1951.

———. "Cenas de vida parisiense na correspondência de Duarte Ribeiro de Macedo (1668–1676)." *Bulletin des Études Portugaises*, new series, 30 (Paris, 1969):95–117.

———. *D. Catarina de Bragança, Rainha de Inglaterra*. Coimbra: Editora Ltda., 1941.

———. *A Exploração e o Comércio do Sal de Setúbal*. Lisbon: Instituto para a Alta Cultura, 1951.

———. "Fortunas ultramarinas e a nobreza portuguesa no século XVII." *Revista Portuguesa de História* 8 (1959):1–25.

———. "Os Holandes e a exportação do sal de Setúbal nos fins do século XVII." *Revista Portuguesa de História* 4 (1950):47–106.

———. "Large Scale Agricultural Enterprise in Post-Medieval Portugal." In *Contributions to the First International Conference of Economic History* (Stockholm), pp. 425–32. Paris: Mouton and Company, 1960.

———. *Política Económica e Mercantilismo na Correspondência de Duarte Ribeiro de Macedo (1668–1676)*. Separata from *Do Tempo e da História* 20 Lisbon: n.p., 1968.

———. "Rumos e vicissitudes do comércio do sal português nos séculos XIV as XVIII." *Revista da Faculdade de Letras* (Lisbon), 3rd series, 7 (1963):5–27.

———. *Subsídios para o estudo do movimento dos portos de Faro e Lisboa durante o século XVII*. Lisbon: Academia Portuguesa de História, 1954.

———. "Um 'Trabalho divertido' do Conde da Ericeira: A História de Portugal Restaurado." *Aufsätze zur Portugiesischen Kulturgeschichte* 10 (1970):304–10.

———, et al. "Les Escales de la Carreira da India (XVe–XVIIIe Siècles." In *Recueils de la Société Jean Bodin, Les Grandes Escales* 33, pp. 1–28. Brussels: Ediciones de la Librairie Encyclopédique, 1972.

Remedios, Mendes dos. "Depois da Restauração de D. João IV." *Biblos* 4 (Coimbra, 1928):1–22, 87–121.

Révah, I. S. "Les Jésuites portugais contre l'Inquisition: La Campagne pour la fondation de la Compagnie Générale du Commerce du Brésil." *Revista do Livro* (Rio de Janeiro) 3–4 (1956):29–53.

———. "Les Marranes." *Revue de Etudes Juives*, series 3, tome 1, 118 (1959–1960):29–77.

Ricard, Robert. *Études sur l'Histoire de Portugais au Maroc*. Coimbra: Imprensa da Universidade, 1955.

———. "Prophecy and Messianism in the Works of António Vieira." *The Americas* 37 (1960):357–68.

Rodney, Walter. "Portuguese Attempts at Monopoly on the Upper Guinea Coast, 1580–1640." *Journal of African History* 6 (1965):307–22.

Rodríguez, Mario. "Dom Pedro of Braganza and Colônia do Sacramento, 1680–1705." *Hispanic American Historical Review* 38(1958):179–208.

Roth, Cecil. "The Religion of the Marranos." *Jewish Quarterly Review* 22 (1931):1–33.

Russell-Wood, A. J. R. "Black and Mulatto Brotherhoods in Colonial Brazil: A Study in Collective Behavior." *Hispanic American Historical Review* 54 (1974):567–602.

———. *Fidalgos and Philanthropists: The Santa Casa de Misericórdia of Bahia, 1550–1755*. Berkeley: University of California Press, 1968.

———. "Local Government in Portuguese America: A Study in Cultural Divergence." *Comparative Studies in Society and History* 16 (March 1974):187–231.

Ryder, A. F. C. "The Re-establishment of Portuguese Factories on the Costa da Mina to the Mid-Eighteenth Century." *Journal of the Historical Society of Nigeria* 1 (1958):157–83.
Sabugosa, Conde de. *Gente d'Algo*. 3rd ed. Lisbon: Portugal-Brasil Limitada, 1923.
Sampayo, Luis de. *Para a História do Tratado de Methuen*. Coimbra: Imprensa da Universidade, 1928.
Santarem, Visconde de. *Quadro Elementar*. 18 vols. Paris: J. P. Aillaud, 1842–1854; Lisbon: Academia Real das Sciencias, 1858–1876.
Santos, Raul Esteves dos, *Os Tabacos: Sua Influência na Vida da Nação*. 2 vols. Lisbon: Seara Nova, 1974.
Saraiva, António. *Inquisição e Cristãos-Novos*. 3rd ed. Oporto: Editorial Inova, 1969.
———. "Le Père Antonio Vieira S.J. et la question de l'esclavage de Noirs au XVIIe siècle." *Annales: ESC* 6 (1967):1289–1309.
Scelle, Georges. *La Traite Négrière aux Indes de Castile*. 2 vols. Paris: L. La Rose and Forcel, 1906.
Schaeffer, Henrique. *Historia de Portugal*. 13 vols. Lisbon: José Baptista Moranda, 1842–1847.
Schwartz, Stuart B. "Free Labor in a Slave Economy: The *Lavradores de Cana* of Colonial Bahia." In *Colonial Roots of Modern Brazil*, edited by Dauril Alden, pp. 148–98. Berkeley: University of California Press, 1973.
———. *A Governor and His Image*. (See Lopes Sierra, Juan.)
———. "Magistracy and Society in Colonial Brazil." *Hispanic American Historical Review* 50 (1970):715–30.
———. *Sovereignty and Society in Colonial Brazil*. Berkeley: University of California Press, 1973.
Sella, Domenico. "European Industries, 1500–1700." In *Fontana Economic History of Europe*, 6 vols., edited by Carlo M. Cipolla, 2:354–426. New York: Barnes and Noble, 1977.
Sérgio, António. *Antológia dos Economistas Portugueses (Século XVII)*. Lisbon: Sá da Costa, 1974.
Serrão, Joaquim Verissimo. *Uma Estimativa da População Portuguesa em 1640*. Lisbon: *separata* from *Memorias da Academia das Ciências*, vol. 16, 1975.
Serrão, Joel. "Conspecto histórico da emigração portuguesa." *Analise Social* 8 (Lisbon, 1970):597–617.
———, ed. *Dicionário de História de Portugal*. 4 vols. Lisbon: Initiativas Editorais, 1971.
———. "Em Torno da Economia madeirense de 1580 a 1640." *Das Artes e da História da Madeira* 1(1)(1950):21–23.
Shaw, William H. *Marx's Theory of History*. Stanford: Stanford University Press, 1978.
Shillington, V. M., and Chapman, A. B. W. *The Commercial Relations of England and Portugal*. London: Routledge and Sons, 1907(?).
Sideri, S. *Trade and Power: Informal Colonialism in Anglo-Portuguese Relations*. Rotterdam: Rotterdam University Press, 1970.
Silbert, Albert. *Le Portugal Méditerranéen à la Fin de l'Ancien Régime, XVIIIe—Debut du XIXe Siècle*. 2 vols. Paris: S.E.V.P.E.N., 1966.
Silva, Chandra Richard da. "The Portuguese East India Company, 1628–1633." *Luso-Brazilian Review* 2 (1974):152–205.
Simonsen, Roberto C. *História Econômica do Brasil (1500–1800)*. 6th ed. São Paulo: Companhia Editora Nacional, 1969.

Smith, David Grant. "Old Christian Merchants and the Foundation of the Brazil Company, 1649." *Hispanic American Historical Review* 54 (1974):233–59.
Smith, Robert C. *Cipriano da Cruz: Escultor de Tibães*. Oporto: Livraria Civilização, 1968.
———. *A Igreja de S. Bento da Vitória a Luz dos "Estados" de Tibães*. Oporto: Fernando Machado, n.d.
Stein, Stanley J., and Stein, Barbara H. *The Colonial Heritage of Latin America: Essays on Economic Dependence in Perspective*. New York: Oxford University Press, 1970.
Swart, Koenraad W. *Sale of Offices in the Seventeenth Century*. The Hague: Martinus Nijhoff, 1949.
Szarka, Andrew S. "Louis XIV and Brazil: The French Probe into Maranhão, 1697–1700." *Proceedings of the French Colonial History Society* 2 (1977):133–48.
Taunay, Affonso de Escragnolle. *História Geral das Bandeiras Paulistas*. 11 vols. São Paulo: Typografia Ideal, H. L. Canton, 1924–1950.
Teixeira, Candido da Silva. "Companhia de Cacheu, Rios e Comércio de Guiné." *Boletim do Arquivo Histórico Colonial* 1 (Lisbon, 1950):87–112.
Teixeira de Aragão, A. C. *Descrição Geral e Histórica das Moedas Cunhadas em Nome dos Reis, Regentes e Governadores de Portugal*. 2nd ed. 3 vols. Oporto: Livraria Fernando Machado, 1964.
Ullmann, Walter. *The Individual and Society in the Middle Ages*. Baltimore: Johns Hopkins University Press, 1966.
Varnhagen, Francisco. *História Geral do Brasil*. 3rd ed. 5 vols. São Paulo: Companhia Melhoramentos, 1927?–1948.
Verger, Pierre. *Bahia and the West Coast Trade (1549–1851)*. Ibadan: Ibadan University Press, 1964.
———. *Flux et Reflux de la Traite des Nègres entre le Golfe de Bénin et Bahia de Todos os Santos du XVIIe au XIXe Siècle*. Paris: Mouton and Company, 1968.
Verlinden, Charles, "Virginia Rau and the Economic History of Portugal." *Journal of European Economic History* 4 (1975):243–45.
Vicens Vives, Jaime. *Historia Social y Económica de España*. 4 vols. in 5. Barcelona: Editorial Teide, 1957–1959.
Viner, Jacob. "Power versus Plenty as Objectives of Foreign Policy in the Seventeenth and Eighteenth Centuries." In *Revisions in Mercantilism*, edited by D. C. Coleman, pp. 61–91. London: Methuen, 1969.
Viterbo, Sousa. *A Armaria em Portugal*. Lisbon: Academia Real das Sciencias, 1907.
Vogt, John. *Portuguese Rule on the Gold Coast, 1469–1682*. Athens: University of Georgia Press, 1979.
Wallerstein, Immanuel. *The Modern World-System: Capitalist Agriculture and the Origins of the European World-Economy in the Sixteenth Century*. New York: Academic Press, 1974.
———. "Underdevelopment and Phase-B: Effect of the Seventeenth-Century Stagnation on Core and Periphery of the European World Economy." In *The World-System of Capitalism: Past and Present*, edited by Walter L. Goldfrank, pp. 73–83. London: Sage Publications, 1979.
Wiarda, Howard J. *Corporatism and Development: The Portuguese Experience*. Amherst: University of Massachusetts Press, 1977.
Wilson, Charles. "Cloth Production and International Competition in the Seventeenth Century." *Economic History Review*, 2nd series, 13 (December 1960):209–21.
Winius, George Davison. *The Fatal History of Portuguese Ceylon*. Cambridge: Harvard University Press, 1971.

Zuquete, Afonso Eduardo Martins. *Nobreza de Portugal.* 3 vols. Lisbon: Editorial Enciclopédia, 1960.

Unpublished Doctoral Dissertations

Bardwell, Ross L. "The Governors of Portugal's South Atlantic Empire in the Seventeenth Century: Social Background, Qualifications, Selection and Reward." University of California, Santa Barbara, 1974.
Boyajian, James C. "The Portuguese Bankers and the International Payments Mechanism, 1626–1647." University of California, Berkeley, 1978.
Cardozo, Manuel. "A History of Mining in Colonial Brazil, 1500–1750." Stanford University, 1939.
Flory, Rae. "Bahian Society in the Mid-Colonial Period: The Sugar Planters, Tobacco Growers, Merchants, and Artisans of Salvador and the Recôncavo, 1680–1725." University of Texas, 1978.
Neto, Maria Lourdes Akola da Cunha Meira do Carmo Silva. "A Freguesia de Sta Catarina de Lisboa no I.º Quartel do Século XVIII." University of Lisbon, 1956.
Sánchez, Mario L. "The Attempts at Reform in the Spain of Charles II: A Revisionist View of the Decline of Castile, 1665–1700." University of Notre Dame, 1976.
Smith, David Grant. "The Mercantile Class of Portugal in the Seventeenth Century: A Socio-Economic Study of the Merchants of Lisbon and Bahia, 1620–1690." University of Texas, 1975.
Soeiro, Susan. "A Baroque Nunnery: The Economic and Social Role of a Colonial Convent: Santa Clara do Destêrro, Salvador, Bahia, 1677–1800." New York University, 1974.
Szarka, Andrew S. "Portugal, France, and the Coming of the War of the Spanish Succession, 1697–1703." Ohio State University, 1976.
Villiers, John. "Portuguese Society in the Reigns of D. Pedro II and D. João V 1680–1750." Cambridge University, 1962.

INDEX

Afonso V, 167
Afonso VI, 6, 7, 12, 13, 14, 15, 17, 53, 87, 98, 100, 126, 162
Afonso Henriques, 23
Africa, 7, 110, 144, 186, 207, 209, 211, 213
Agricultural transplantation, 135, 227, 228, 229
Alegación (Solis), 114
Almeida, Pedro de, 228
Andreoni, Giovanni Antonio, 245, 253
Angola, 115, 231, 232
Anglo-Portuguese Treaty, 6, 270. *See also* Treaties
Anti-Semitism, 72, 73, 74, 75, 100. *See also* Jews
Antonil, 247
Argentina, 225
Armaments, 177, 178, 179
Artisans, 51–55
Assunção, João da, 228
Augustinians, 31, 32–34
Autos-da-fé, 79, 81, 82, 83, 86, 91, 97, 103, 165
Azores, 4, 197

Babylonian Captivity, 5, 77
Bahia, 49, 215, 216, 220, 224, 232, 240, 258. *See also* Ports
Bandarra, Gonçalo, 87
Bayle, John, 181
Beggars, 62, 63
Benedictines, 29, 32, 33, 34, 38
Black market, 249, 254, 255
Bluteau, Rafael, 137, 138, 164, 167, 168, 169, 206
Borba Gato, Manuel de, 244
Botero, Giovanni, 116
Bourgeoisie, 40, 41, 55
Boxer, C. R., 65, 209, 219
Bragança, Catarina de, 263, 264

Bragança, Pedro de, 12
Bragança dynasty, 5, 6, 7, 15, 24
Braudel, Fernand, 69
Bravo, António Correa, 93, 94
Brazil, 25, 29, 134, 135, 139, 144, 176, 185, 192, 208, 222, 225, 239, 259, 261, 275; gold, production of, 9, 188, 193, 197, 244; sugar, production of, 7, 134, 197, 215–22
Brazil Company, 8, 45, 47, 49, 50, 77, 86, 90, 118, 122, 160, 215, 217, 218, 234
Brazilwood, 131, 144, 175, 190, 247, 251. *See also* Exports
Brenner, Robert, 272
Brotherhood of Nobles, 73
Bullionism, 108, 112, 122, 125, 129

Cabral, 110
Cacheu, 233
Cacheu Company, 234, 242, 243, 244
Cadaval (duke of), 13, 14, 23, 24, 30, 89, 162, 221, 225, 230, 258, 263
Caldas, Pedro Álvares, 94
Cardona, Felipe, 174, 175
Caribbean, 188, 197
Carlos, Francisco, 47, 48, 49, 79, 92, 93
Carlos II, 14, 180, 262
Carré, Abbé, 210, 211
Carthusians, 30
Carvalho, António de Albuquerque Coelho de, 253
Casa dos Vinte e Quatro. *See* Houses of the Twenty-four
Castel-Branco, Manuel, 244
Castel-Branco, Ródrigo de, 223, 224, 225
Castelo Melhor (count of), 6, 263, 264
Castro, Francisco de, 77
Cavide, António, 98
Cellorigo, González, 112
Cervantes, 11

Chagas, António das, 102
Charles II, 98, 264
Child, Josiah, 133
China, 186, 208
Clement X, 96, 100
Clergy, 10, 18, 19, 21, 27–38, 40, 153; secular, 30, 36, 37
Coimbra tribunal, 76, 85, 88. *See also* Inquisition
Colbatch, John, 236
Colbert, Jean Baptiste, 116, 123, 124, 125, 126, 127, 128, 129, 136, 161, 182, 211, 265, 266. *See also* Colbertism
Colbertism, 266, 112–22, 129, 139, 165, 265–70. *See also* Colbert, Jean Baptiste
Colónia do Sacramento, 222, 225, 226, 227, 229, 246
Colonization, 111, 134, 185, 186, 187, 207, 208
Commoners, 10, 28, 36, 39, 57, 68
Cortes, 8, 13, 42, 89, 94, 98, 99, 101, 149, 236, 292n; and manufacturing, 169; and monetary reform, 152, 153, 157; and taxation, 143–52, 235, 255
Council of War, 162
Courneaut, Pierre, 177
Coutinho, Fernão de Sousa, 233
Cromwell, Oliver, 6
Cunha, António Álvares da, 309n

da Costa, Balthasar, 90, 93
da Cunha, Luís, 140, 269, 275
da Gama, Vasco, 3, 110
Defensive Triple Treaty, 264. *See also* Treaties
DeVries, Jan, 142
Dialogos do Sitio de Lisboa (Mendes de Vasconcelos), 112
Dias, Luiís, 266
Discurso sobre a introdução das artes no Reino (Ribeiro de Macedo), 129, 131, 132, 133, 134, 135, 136, 139, 150, 166, 265
Discursos (Solis), 113, 117
Dominicans, 36
Don Quixote (Cervantes), 11
Donatários, 293n
Duclos, Roland, 138, 139, 167, 168, 175

Dupineaut, Theophile, 181
East India Company, 106, 152, 160, 162, 209
Edict of Nantes, 125
Elliott, J. H., 112
Emigration, 291n
Engels, Friedrich, 67
England, 14, 15, 169, 186, 194, 195, 200, 201, 203, 204, 226, 259, 262, 263, 264, 267; Portugal's dependence on, 270–76
England's Treasure by Foreign Trade (Mun), 133
Ericeira (count of), 89, 131, 137, 156, 158, 160–84, 190, 201, 205, 265, 266, 268, 269, 271, 275
Esperanças de Portugal, Quinto Imperio do Mundo (Vieira), 87
Estanco do Maranhão e Pará, 230
Évora tribunal, 76, 78, 80, 85, 96. *See also* Inquisition
Exports, 130, 200, 267; agricultural, 135; of brazilwood, 131, 144; of sugar, 5, 7, 131, 144; of tobacco, 9, 131,144; of wine, 9, 49, 131, 193, 195

Far East, 209, 210, 228
Faria, Giuseppe de, 309n
Faro, 188. *See also* Ports
Ferdinand, 46, 75
Fernandes, Manual, 88, 93, 96, 103
Ferreira, António, 90, 92
Figueiró dos Vinhos, 179, 180
Fleets, 214–16
Foios de Pereira, Mendo, 43
Fontoura, Diogo Carneiro, 223
Fortrey, Samuel, 133
France, 186, 194, 201, 203, 263, 264, 267; and mercantilism, 122–26
Franciscans, 30, 36, 228, 230
Franco, Francisco Lopes, 167
Freitas, Gaspar de Abreu de, 99
Frois, Jorge, 170, 175
Fronde, 123
Fronteira (marquis of), 164, 169, 183, 310n

Geddes, Michael, 82, 103
General Crisis, 142, 143, 188, 260

Goa, 49, 134, 212, 213, 214, 215. *See also* Ports
Godinho, V. M., 20, 25, 28
Gold, 157, 158, 176, 190, 225, 238, 239, 246, 248, 251, 252; Brazilian, 9, 188, 193, 197, 244, 245; mining, 224
Gómez, Pedro, 258, 259
Gorani, José, 319n
Grain, 202, 203, 205, 273
Grand Alliance, 264. *See also* Treaties
Gresham's law, 114
Guinea, 233, 238, 242
Guinea Coast Company, 234, 261
Gusmão, Luisa de (Guzmán), 6, 7
Guzmán, Marín de, 243
Gypsies, 66

Hapsburg government, 5, 6, 15, 23, 32, 114, 157
Heckscher, Eli, 109, 110
Henriques, Gregório Gomes, 304n
Hides, 239, 246, 248
Hobsbawm, E. J., 104, 105, 142, 143
Holland, 5, 6, 7, 125, 169, 186, 201, 209, 262, 263, 264, 267
Houses of the Twenty-four, 51, 52, 53, 54, 56, 57, 172

Imbert, Gaston, 141
Imports, 129, 130, 131, 151, 156, 175, 176, 200, 201–5, 267, 268; of textiles, 132. *See also* Wool
India, 112, 186, 207, 208, 211, 214, 254; trade with, 94, 167, 239, 241
India Company, 96, 100
India House, 32, 239
Indian Commercial Company, 212, 213
Industrialization, 272, 273
Innocent XI, 100, 101
Inquisition, 26, 30, 36, 47, 48, 69, 70, 71, 85, 86, 89, 95, 101, 117; Holy Office of, 48, 75–85, 87, 89, 91, 96, 97, 99, 100, 106, 119, 269, 274; Lisbon, 78, 80, 85; Portuguese, 76, 78, 80, 88, 89, 100
Isabela, 46, 75

Jamaica, 197
Japan, 208

Jesuits, 28, 29, 36, 37, 83, 85, 100, 105, 106, 225, 228, 229, 230
Jesús, Manuel de, 102
Jews, 11, 17, 46, 71, 76, 79, 83, 87, 91, 96, 103, 104, 114, 119, 230, 136. *See also* Anti-Semitism
João IV, 5, 6, 12, 24, 52, 66, 77, 78, 85, 86, 87, 88, 90, 115, 150, 161, 176, 215, 217, 227, 235
João V, 29, 36, 259
José I, 275
Junta da Administração do Tabaco, 235. *See also* Junta do Tabaco
Junta do Comércio, 90, 93, 149, 218, 247, 251
Junta do Tabaco, 59, 145, 160, 222, 236, 239, 241, 249, 254, 256, 258, 259
Justinian Code, 43

Kamen, Henry, 39, 40

La Ragione di Stato (Botero), 116
Lacerda, Francisco Correia de, 136
Lawyers, 42
Lemos, Pero Gomes de, 80
Lencastre, João de, 256, 258
Lenin, V. I., 273
Leonard, Irving, 9
Letrados, 42
Lisbon, 3, 23, 40, 51, 53, 54, 63, 64, 65, 157, 158; description of, 113, 127, 128, 180, 181; foodstuff shortages in, 35, 199, 203; Inquisition, 76, 78, 80, 85, 91; port of, 188, 192, 216; and taxation, 144, 145, 148, 154; and tobacco trade, 239, 240, 241. *See also* Ports
Lopes de Leão, Miguel, 304n
Louis XIV, 14, 15, 90, 123, 124, 125, 126, 153, 194, 226, 243, 262, 264
Loyola, 85
Luanda, 49, 115, 233. *See also* Ports
Luso-Atlantic economy, 7, 187, 188, 193, 218, 221, 227, 238, 246, 247, 249, 261, 267, 269, 271, 273, 274
Luso-Dutch Treaty, 190. *See also* Treaties
Luz, Estevão, 319n

Macedo, Jorge Soares de, 226
Madeira, 4, 193, 197

352 INDEX

Magalotti, 24
Magellan, 3, 4
Malheiro, Francisco, 48
Manuel I, 75, 135
Manufacturing, 182–84, 187, 208, 261
Marques, Diogo Rodrigues, 304n
Marranism, 76, 84, 93, 104
Martins, Manuel da Costa, 146
Marx, Karl, 67
Mascarenhas, João de. *See* Fronteira (marquis of)
Mathews, John, 178
Mathews, Simon, 178
Mauro, Frédéric, 49, 141
Mazarin (Cardinal), 123
Melo, Francisco, 24, 25, 169, 171, 172, 294n
Melo, Nuno Álvares Pereira de. *See* Cadaval (duke of)
Mendes de Vasconcelos, Luís, 112, 113, 116
Mendonça, Afonso Furtado de Castro do Rio de, 223
Mendonça, Francisco Furtado de, 98
Meneses, António Luís de, 14
Meneses, Luís de. *See* Ericeira (count of)
Meneses, Rodrigo, 99
Meneses e Sousa, Aires de Saldanha, 232
Mercantilism, 108–40
Merchants, 44–50. *See also* New Christian merchants; Old Christian merchants
Methuen, John, 263, 264
Methuen Treaty, 8, 264, 265, 268, 269, 270, 271, 274. *See also* Treaties
Military orders, 19, 23, 294n
Mina coast, 232, 238, 242, 261
Minas Gerais, 197, 244, 245, 246, 247, 251, 252, 253, 257, 259
Mining, 176–82, 222, 225, 232, 238, 244, 245
Mining Code, 176
Miranda, António de, 181
Moncada, Sancho de, 112, 133
Monetary reform, 152–59
Montes Claros, 15
Moors, 166, 190
Moriscos, 91
Mozambique, 209, 210, 214, 237

Mulberry trees, 138, 167, 168, *See also* Agricultural transplantation
Mun, Thomas, 133
Muslims, 167, 210, 250

Neuborg, Mariana de, 27
New Christian merchants, 26, 45, 46, 47, 60, 67, 69, 70–107, 119, 144, 161, 165, 166, 212, 217, 218, 260, 265
Newfoundland, 203
Nobility, 10, 11, 12, 17, 18, 19, 21–27, 28, 41, 293n
Noticias de Portugal (Severim de Faria), 116
Nunes, Andre, 170
Nuns, 37, 254

Observações sobre a transplantação dos fructos da India ao Brazil (Ribeiro de Macedo), 134, 135, 139, 200
Offensive Quadrangle Treaty, 264. *See also* Treaties
Old Christian merchants, 46, 47, 74, 105
Old Regime, 36, 37, 39, 57, 60, 68, 70, 106, 275, 276
Olivares (duke of), 5
Olive oil, 190, 199, 200, 271
Oliveira, Antonio, 60
Oliveira, Aurélio de, 32, 34, 35, 63
Orange trees, 134, 138, 206, 249. *See also* Agricultural transplantation
Oratorians, 36
Overseas Council, 144, 212, 225, 227, 234

Pádua, Manuel da Gama de, 90, 94, 96, 102, 136
Paim, Roque Monteiro, 74, 156, 157, 158
Paulistas, 222, 224, 225, 231, 244, 253
Peace of the Pyrenees, 123, 126
Pedro I, 110
Pedro II, 7, 29, 42, 43, 53, 56, 58, 59, 156, 202, 203, 237, 270; absolutist regime of, 12, 44; attempted assassination of, 98; and baroque era, 8, 9; characteristics of, 12–17, 151; and clergy, 30, 31, 35, 36, 37, 253; and economic recovery, 208, 211, 212, 213, 215, 218, 219, 220, 222,

223, 227, 232, 235, 237, 239, 249, 256, 266, 267; marriage of, 27; and mining, 222, 223; and New Christian merchants, 70, 73, 79, 89, 91, 93, 95, 97, 99, 100, 101, 103, 139, 140; and slave trade, 65, 242; and taxation, 106, 143, 145, 146, 148, 154, 199; and trade, 192, 193, 194, 198, 206; treaties of, 262, 263
Penso, Fernão Rodrigues, 80, 92, 304n
Pernambuco, 5, 121, 217
Peru, 208, 222
Philip III, 5, 177
Philip IV. See Philip III
Philip V, 244, 262, 264
Physicians, 43
Pirates, 250, 251, 257
Pombal (marquis of), 36, 77, 103, 140, 260, 275, 276
Ports, 50; Bahia, 49, 215, 216, 220; Faro, 188; Goa, 49, 215; Luanda, 49; Recife, 49, 215, 216, 218, 220; Rio de Janeiro, 215, 216; Setúbal, 188
Portugal, Salvador Taborda, 310n
Portuguese East Indian Company, 114, 119
Potosí, 232, 236
Protestantism, 11

Rau, Virginia, 48
Rebellions, 60, 61, 68, 90, 102, 230
Rebelo, Vicente Gonçalves, 178
Recife, 5, 49, 192, 215, 216, 218, 220, 251. See also Ports
Relatório (Vilas Boas), 170, 171
Resende, João Duarte de, 48, 49
Restoration era, 5, 8, 23, 24, 25, 47, 57, 62, 68, 86, 116, 121, 162, 163, 178, 199, 227; of 1640, 12, 51, 77, 85, 118, 222, 232
Ribeiro, João Pinto, 5
Ribeiro de Macedo, Duarte, 126, 127, 128, 129, 130, 131, 132, 133, 134, 135, 136, 137, 138, 139, 140, 50, 162, 164, 165, 166, 168, 169, 170, 200, 206, 208, 227, 231, 246, 261, 265, 304n
Richards, John, 269
Richelieu (Cardinal), 122, 123

Rio de Janeiro, 215, 216, 238, 246. See also Ports
Rio de la Plata, 115, 222, 224, 225, 250
Roman Catholic Church, 11, 12, 27, 28, 29, 37, 64, 100, 110

Sá, Salvador Correia de, 26, 232
Sabóia, Maria Francisca de, 6
Salt, 190, 191, 192, 193, 198, 200
Sampaio, Antonio das Villas Boas, 44
Santas Casas de Misericórdia, 62
São Paulo, 225
Saraiva, António, 71, 78
Schomberg (count), 144
Sebastião, 5
Serrão, Joel, 57
Setúbal, 188, 192. See also Ports
Severim de Faria, Manuel, 116, 117, 118, 121, 132, 133, 206
Seville, 3
Shaw, William, 275
Silk, 138, 166, 167, 168, 169, 173, 174, 182, 268
Silva, Luís Lobo da, 233
Silveira, Bento Coelho da, 8
Silver, 114, 115, 131, 156, 157, 158, 176, 188, 208, 223, 225, 309n; mining, 224; Peruvian, 208, 222
Sinel, Luis Romão, 170
Slaves, 39, 57, 66, 120, 194, 208, 301n; black, 7, 47, 64, 65, 67, 222, 226, 230, 231, 232, 233, 234, 241, 242; Indian, 64, 229, 230, 231, 208n; trade in, 115, 121, 196, 232, 233, 234, 236, 238, 239, 242, 255, 257
Smith, David Grant, 46, 47, 71, 72, 84
Smuggling, 64, 146, 156, 198, 202, 249, 253, 254, 256, 259
Soares, João, 167
Soares, Manuel Mendes, 304n
Solis, Duarte Gomes, 113, 114, 115, 116, 118, 121, 133
Sotomaior, Francisco de, 12
Sousa, António Luís de, 258
Sousa, Gaspar Meres de, 309n
Sousa, João de, 29
Southwell, Robert, 309n
Spain, 14, 24, 146, 186, 194, 226, 262, 263, 264

Spices, 32, 227, 228, 229, 231, 236, 239
Stevens, John, 79
Suárez, Francisco, 24
Sugar, 5, 7, 29, 131, 144, 188, 190, 222, 236, 247; Brazilian, 134, 154, 197, 215–22, 232, 235. *See also* Exports
Suthmann, Peter, 307n

Tagus River, 181, 198, 204, 263
Taxation, 5, 18, 39, 52, 143–48, 153, 198, 199, 220, 251, 252, 253, 261, 267, 270
Teles da Silva, António, 26
Teles da Silva, Manuel, 264
Textiles, 35, 124, 132, 163–76. *See also* Silk; Wool
Tinoco, João Nunes, 8
Tobacco, 9, 131, 144, 145, 154, 185, 188, 190, 199, 216, 219, 235, 236, 239, 240, 241, 246, 248, 254, 255, 256, 257, 258, 271; sales of in India, 320n. *See also* Exports
Tobacco Council. *See* Junta do Tabaco
Tomar, 179, 180
Torre do Tombo, 13
Trade, 201–5; with India, 94, 167, 239, 241; in slaves, 115, 121, 194, 196, 233, 234, 236, 238, 239, 242, 255, 257. *See also* Slaves
Treasury Council, 149, 191, 193, 239, 314n
Treaties, 262, 263; Anglo-Portuguese, 6, 270; Defensive Triple Treaty, 264; Grand Alliance, 264; Luso-Dutch Treaty, 190; Methuen Treaty, 8, 264, 268, 269, 270, 271, 274; Offensive Quadrangle Treaty, 264; Treaty of Nijmwegen, 310n

Treaty of Nijmwegen, 310n. *See also* Treaties

Ullmann, Walter, 67
Universities, 36, 42, 43
Uruguay, 225, 226

Vasconcelos e Sousa, Luís. *See* Castelo Melhor (count of)
Vieira, António (Father), 8, 47, 85–89, 90, 96, 97, 99, 102, 103, 107, 116, 208, 215, 217, 219, 221, 227, 228, 230, 261, 271, 305n; and mercantilism, 118, 119, 120, 121, 122, 135, 136, 137, 162
Vilas Boas, Gonçalo de Cunha, 170, 171, 173, 174, 175
Viner, Jacob, 110

Wallerstein, Immanuel, 186, 187
War of the Emboabas, 253
War of the League of Augsburg, 194
War of the Restoration, 6, 15
War of the Spanish Succession, 36, 194, 226, 252, 264
Westphalia, 123, 143
Whaling, 246
Wine, 9, 49, 131, 185, 190, 193, 194, 195, 196, 197, 198, 200, 271. *See also* Exports
Women vendors, 58, 59, 60, 65, 204, 299, 84n
Wool, 166, 168, 169, 170, 172, 173, 174, 175, 182, 190, 268

Xavier, Saint Francis, 3